HANDBOOK OF
GERMAN ADMINISTRATION
AND SUPPLY

1944

The Naval & Military Press Ltd

Prepared under the direction of the Chief of the Imperial General Staff

THE WAR OFFICE,
April, 1944

Published by

The Naval & Military Press Ltd
Unit 5 Riverside, Brambleside
Bellbrook Industrial Estate
Uckfield, East Sussex
TN22 1QQ England

Tel: +44 (0)1825 749494

www.naval-military-press.com
www.nmarchive.com

CONTENTS

HANDBOOK OF GERMAN ADMINISTRATION AND SUPPLY

INTRODUCTION

1. In July, 1943, " New Notes on the German Army No. 4—the Supply and Administrative Services " was published. It sets out the theory upon which the Germans base their system of supply as it is laid down in German official publications. It is, in effect, a text-book of German Supply Administration, and is still almost wholly up to date, but it has of late become increasingly evident that it lacks the practical aspect which would make it of direct operational value to " Q " and " I " personnel at formations.

2. Consideration of the whole question of German supply administration has, therefore, been undertaken in two parts. These are, firstly, the system as it operates within Germany itself, and secondly, as it operates in theatres of mobile operations such as Italy, Russia, etc.

3. The first part attempts to describe in broad outline the administrative services and their functions within Germany itself illustrated by typical examples of the various administrative installations which are to be found throughout Greater Germany. It will be seen that certain sub-sections of the Handbook deal in brief with communications and ports which, though not strictly within the military administrative sphere, must be understood and appreciated since the whole administrative machine is inextricably bound up with the existing system of communications whether by road, rail or water. It is realized that these sub-sections are brief, but owing to the limited space available, and also to the fact that more detailed works are in course of preparation on these subjects, only the more important details of interest from the military point of view have been mentioned.

4. The second part, dealing with the German " Q " under active conditions, has been produced with the idea of incorporating modifications and practical details which are not included in " New Notes 4 ", but which have come to light in the last few months. The special circumstances pertaining to mobile operations in Italy and in Russia have modified the basic system of administration and have yielded certain detailed information on the actual mechanics of supply. Consequently, for the " Q " and " I " personnel of higher formations, who are in operational need of practical details and concrete examples of the working of the German Supply System, and whose work will at times necessitate the making of an appreciation of the supply situation from the enemy's point of view, the study of " New Notes No. 4 " should be supplemented by reference to this Handbook.

PART I

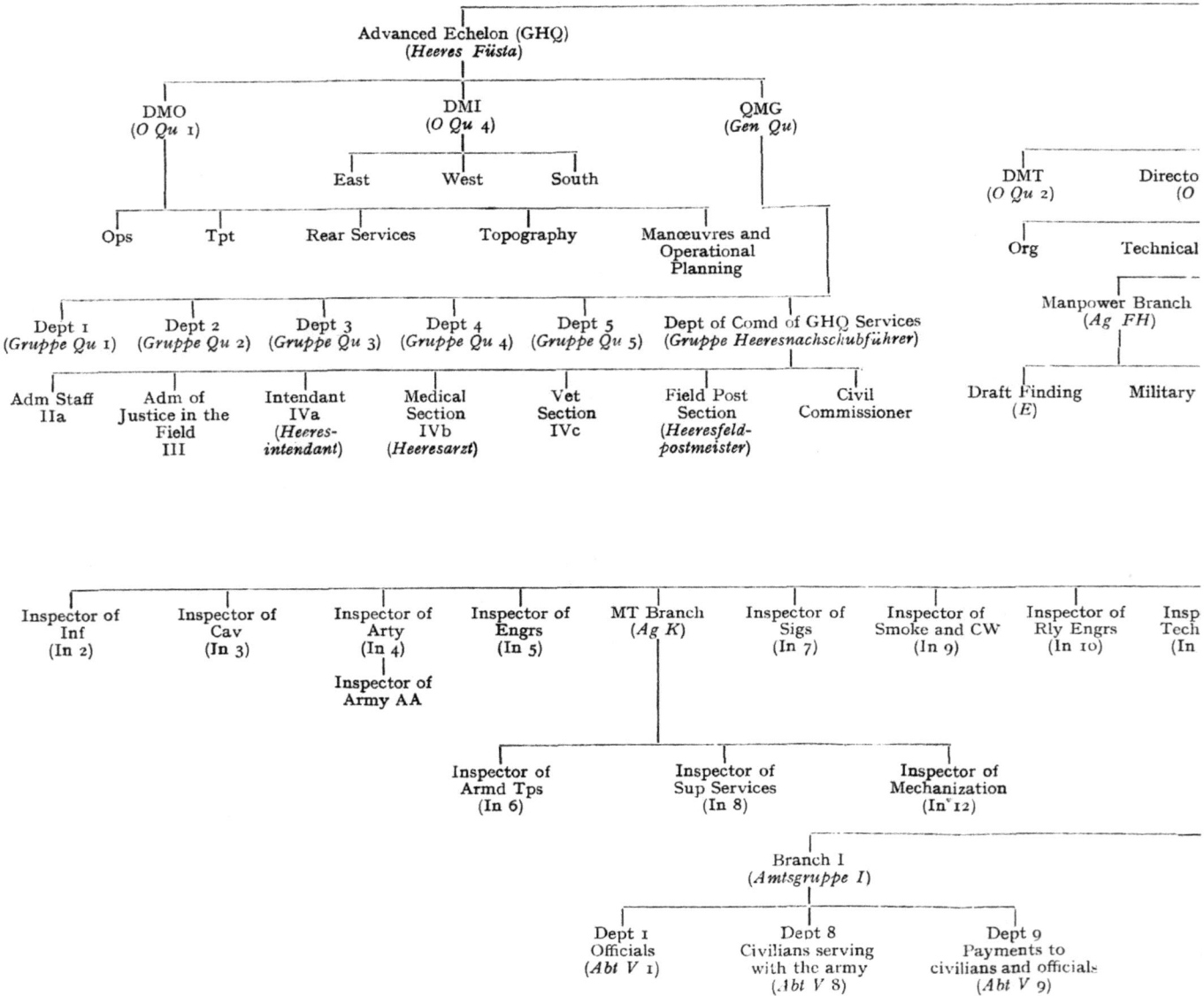

Advanced Echelon (GHQ)
(*Heeres Füsta*)

DMO
(*O Qu* 1)

DMI
(*O Qu* 4)

QMG
(*Gen Qu*)

DMT
(*O Qu* 2)

Directo
(*O*

East   West   South

Ops   Tpt   Rear Services   Topography   Manœuvres and Operational Planning

Org   Technical

Manpower Branch
(*Ag FH*)

Dept 1
(*Gruppe Qu* 1)

Dept 2
(*Gruppe Qu* 2)

Dept 3
(*Gruppe Qu* 3)

Dept 4
(*Gruppe Qu* 4)

Dept 5
(*Gruppe Qu* 5)

Dept of Comd of GHQ Services
(*Gruppe Heeresnachschubführer*)

Adm Staff
IIa

Adm of Justice in the Field
III

Intendant
IVa
(*Heeres-intendant*)

Medical Section
IVb
(*Heeresarzt*)

Vet Section
IVc

Field Post Section
(*Heeresfeld-postmeister*)

Civil Commissioner

Draft Finding
(*E*)

Military

Inspector of Inf
(*In* 2)

Inspector of Cav
(*In* 3)

Inspector of Arty
(*In* 4)

Inspector of Engrs
(*In* 5)

MT Branch
(*Ag K*)

Inspector of Sigs
(*In* 7)

Inspector of Smoke and CW
(*In* 9)

Inspector of Rly Engrs
(*In* 10)

Insp Tech
(*In*

Inspector of Army AA

Inspector of Armd Tps
(*In* 6)

Inspector of Sup Services
(*In* 8)

Inspector of Mechanization
(*In* 12)

Branch I
(*Amtsgruppe I*)

Dept 1
Officials
(*Abt V* 1)

Dept 8
Civilians serving with the army
(*Abt V* 8)

Dept 9
Payments to civilians and officials
(*Abt V* 9)

NOTES

1. The title *Oberquartiermeister* is not capable of a literal translation; for instance, it will be seen above that *O Qu* 4 is equivalent to

2. It will be seen that the QMG controls a department known as the Dept Commander of GHQ Services. Though this is part of the role is discussed in Part I, section 1 of the text.

3. It is now clear that the Inspectorates, shown under the Director of Training in the Training Army, are actually still *directly* su framework of the General Army Branch. The Director of Training, however, does direct the activities of the Inspectors, *i.e.*, a dis

OF THE GERMAN ARMY

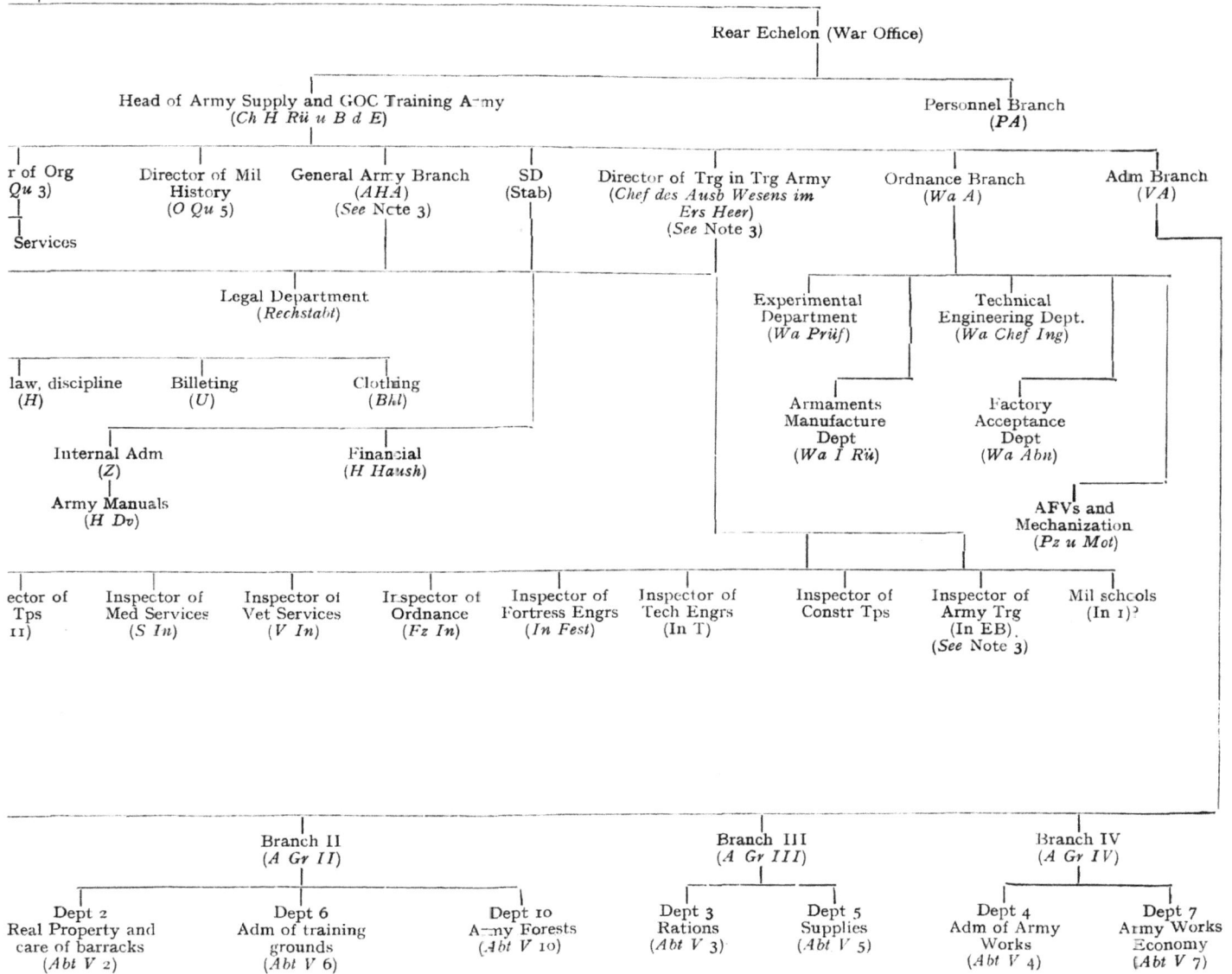

(OKH)

Rear Echelon (War Office)

Head of Army Supply and GOC Training Army
(Ch H Rü u B d E)

Personnel Branch
(PA)

r of Org
Qu 3)

Director of Mil
History
(O Qu 5)

General Army Branch
(AHA)
(See Note 3)

SD
(Stab)

Director of Trg in Trg Army
(Chef des Ausb Wesens im Ers Heer)
(See Note 3)

Ordnance Branch
(Wa A)

Adm Branch
(VA)

Services

Legal Department
(Rechstabt)

Experimental
Department
(Wa Prüf)

Technical
Engineering Dept.
(Wa Chef Ing)

law, discipline
(H)

Billeting
(U)

Clothing
(Bkl)

Armaments
Manufacture
Dept
(Wa I Rü)

Factory
Acceptance
Dept
(Wa Abn)

Internal Adm
(Z)

Financial
(H Haush)

Army Manuals
(H Dv)

AFVs and
Mechanization
(Pz u Mot)

ector of
Tps
II)

Inspector of
Med Services
(S In)

Inspector of
Vet Services
(V In)

Inspector of
Ordnance
(Fz In)

Inspector of
Fortress Engrs
(In Fest)

Inspector of
Tech Engrs
(In T)

Inspector of
Constr Tps

Inspector of
Army Trg
(In EB)
(See Note 3)

Mil schools
(In I)?

Branch II
(A Gr II)

Branch III
(A Gr III)

Branch IV
(A Gr IV)

Dept 2
Real Property and
care of barracks
(Abt V 2)

Dept 6
Adm of training
grounds
(Abt V 6)

Dept 10
Army Forests
(Abt V 10)

Dept 3
Rations
(Abt V 3)

Dept 5
Supplies
(Abt V 5)

Dept 4
Adm of Army
Works
(Abt V 4)

Dept 7
Army Works
Economy
(Abt V 7)

the British DMI but the term Deputy Chiefs of General Staff (DCGS) would appear to be the nearest British approximation.
General Staff it is not known exactly how many of these CHQ Services Commanders there are, nor their precise relationship with the QMG. Their

bordinate to the Head of Army Supply, with the one exception of the Inspectorate of Army Training, and that they are contained within the
tinction is drawn between the Inspectors and the Inspectorates.

1. General System of Supply Organization

(a) *Higher Administration in the High Command of the German Army.*

(i) Supply of the German Army is administered in the High Command of the German Army (*Oberkommando des Heeres—OKH*), save for certain broad aspects, particularly that of transportation, which are administered through the Supreme Command of the Armed Forces (*Oberkommando der Wehrmacht—OKW*). The OKW controls inter-service policy, and directs the broad conduct of the war, and the Army, GAF and Navy are regarded as branches of a single service—the Armed Forces (*Wehrmacht*). It will be found, therefore, that certain aspects of supply are considered as purely Army matters while others are considered as Armed Forces' responsibility.

(ii) The division of the High Command of the German Army in war-time into an advanced echelon or Army GHQ, and the rear echelon or War Office, is well shown in the chart showing the organization of the OKH facing this page. It will be seen that responsibility for supply in the field, that is, the " Q " part of the advanced echelon, is invested in the QMG (*Generalquartiermeister—Gen Qu*). His function is to control all questions affecting the administration and supply of the armies in the field, but not in Germany or certain of the occupied countries. He acts under the general direction of the C-in-C and the CGS. The supply of ammunition, anti-gas equipment, weapons, AFVs, POL, tyres, horses and construction materials is handled by the QMG's staff according to the indent of Army. Other supplies are indented for by Army directly on the Head of Army Supply at Rear Echelon or War Office or the relevant institutions appointed by the Head of Army Supply within Reich territory.

(iii) Under the QMG, it will be seen, are five departments (*Gruppen*). It is possible that the number of departments has been increased of late to meet demands arising from increased L of C problems, but there has been no evidence of this. For some time, however, it has been clear that the functions of the departments have been as follows :—

Dept 1. (*Gruppe Qu* 1) is divided into two sections, designated Ia and Ib. Section Ia deals with the supply situation generally of the various groups of armies, with particular regard to the organization of the supply system. It keeps situation maps; has a considerable share in the laying down of rearward lines of demarcation between operational zones, L of C areas, etc; ensures the best possible use of existing supply routes; has liaison with the Director-General of Transportation on questions of supply routes and existing transport facilities; controls the activities of GHQ supply troops; issues the necessary directives for the operation of the supply services in the field, and keeps a War Diary.

Section Ib deals with the organization of the rearward services; supply of GHQ troops; War Establishments of supply units; returns for battle-strengths and ration-strengths of all field units; traffic questions; road-construction; supervision of the field post system and acts as an information bureau on supply questions.

Dept 2. (*Gruppe Qu* 2) deals with evacuation of supplies or of civilian personnel from operational areas; handles questions to do with exploitation of operational areas; issues directives for the civil population in operational areas in conjunction with the civil commissioners at GHQ; is responsible for air protection and camouflage in the L of C areas; handles the supply of troops of occupation and of prisoners of war; is responsible for salvage and captured material; and deals with questions concerning spiritual welfare and war graves.

Dept 3. (*Gruppe Qu* 3) deals specifically with the indent and supply of certain materials and for that purpose functions in three sections. The first section deals with ammunition, weapons and anti-gas equipment and is responsible for receiving the indents from Army for these, and for arranging for their supply from depots in Reich territory by arrangement with the Head of Army Supply. It is responsible for GHQ dumps of these materials.

The second section deals similarly with POL, tyres, AFVs, repair of MT and supply of spare parts for all types of vehicles, and is responsible for GHQ dumps of these materials.

The third section deals similarly with engineer material and construction materials.

Depts 4 and 5 are responsible for occupied territories, where they are probably located.

(iv) On the Staff of the QMG it will be seen, there is also a Commander of the GHQ Services Department. The duties of the GHQ Services Commander are clearly laid down but it is not quite certain how many of these appointments there are. Three such GHQ Services Commanders are known to be operating in the rear areas of the Russian front, for example. The GHQ Services Commander is directly subordinate to the QMG and it is thought that the supply staff, which includes for example the GHQ intendant and GHQ MO among others, is subordinate in its turn to the GHQ Services Commander, which is the way in which it has been shown in the OKH table. The GHQ Services Commander is in disciplinary command of those GHQ rear services which are not already under the control of specialist commanders; this would make it appear that the GHQ supply staff mentioned above, including the GHQ intendant and GHQ MO, are not subordinate to the GHQ Services Commander, but exist independently and are directly subordinate to the QMG. It would seem most likely, however, that the GHQ Services Commander does in fact have a great measure of control over the Staff, for he is also responsible for the maintenance and supply of the GHQ Supply troops themselves. He also looks after the supply to the field army of such materials for which the QMG is answerable and for which Dept 3 (*Gruppe Qu* 3) does not already take responsibility. The Staff itself is composed of the GHQ intendant (dealing with rations, clothing and pay of GHQ troops), GHQ MO, GHQ Veterinary Officer, GHQ Field Postmaster, the GHQ Civil Commissioner (dealing with questions of civil administration in the operational area) the GHQ Judge-Advocate-General, the GHQ Adjutant Section (responsible for security measures within GHQ as well as for the organization of GHQ staff and personal records of officers in GHQ staff). There is also a registry and a commandant's section, the latter being responsible for local administration of the staff (in so far as it is not covered by other sections) and for local protection and traffic control.

GHQ indeed, is constructed on the lines of all German Staffs of field formations, with a full complement of all the classifications of sections on which the Germans base their field staffs, and the " Q " section is very fully developed, in that it is a complete staff in itself.

It will also be seen that under the DMO (*O Qu* 1) is a section dealing with " Q" matters. This section corresponds to the British " Q Ops "; that is to say, the Germans regard " Q Ops " as a " G " function rather than a " Q " function.

(v) The whole basic structure of the German War Office in BERLIN is under the command of the Head of Army Supply and GOC the Training

Army (*Chef der Heeresrüstung and Befehlshaber des Ersatzheeres—Ch HRü uBdE*) an appointment held since its inception by Col Gen FROMM, referred to throughout this Handbook as Head of Army Supply. Among his responsibilities is the provision of equipment of all kinds both for the armies in the field and for all troops stationed in the area of the Home Command, and to this extent, therefore, he has some measure of control over the activities of the QMG. The channel of indent and supply for the field is through the QMG, but the link between design and production on the one hand and storage and provision on the other exists in the person of the Head of Army Supply. A study of the chart of the OKH shows the main branches of the various directorates, concerned with supply, to which occasional reference is made in this Handbook.

(vi) The organization of the OKW is not sufficiently relevant to the study of supply to warrant inclusion here of the whole of its complex layout, but the following are the main branches:—

(1) Operational Directorate.

(2) Directorate of Intelligence and Security.

(3) Directorate of General Matters concerning the Armed Forces. (This last-named directorate includes a Supply Department of the Armed Forces (*Wehrmachtversorgungs-Abteilung-W.Vers*) which deals, in broad outline with quarters' buildings, food, currency and allowances for the armed forces.)

(4) War Economics Directorate of the Armed Forces. (This fulfils the functions both of a Ministry of Supply and of a Ministry of Economic Warfare. It includes departments for War Economics, for Armaments and for Raw Materials.)

(5) Central Department.

(6) Finance and Administration Department. (This deals with all Armed Forces' expenditure, being the channel between the High Command and the Finance Ministry.)

(7) Legal Department, Supreme Military Court of Justice and Academy of the Armed Forces.

(8) Director-General of Transportation (*Chef des Transportwesens*). (This appointment corresponds to the British Movement Control, and being of importance in the study of supply is dealt with in the following paragraph.)

(9) Inspector of Signals Communications of the Armed Forces.

(10) Equipment Office of the Armed Forces: Clothing and Equipment for the Armed Forces.

(vii) Movement Control in the OKW is vested in the appointment of Director General of Transportation (*Chef des Transportwesens*), Gen GERCKE, who formerly controlled three departments—the Planning Dept (*Planungsabt*), Field Transport Dept (*Feldtransportabt*) and Home Transport Dept (*Heimattransportabt*). In October 1943, however, the Home Transport Dept was disbanded, and its duties were taken over by the Field Transport Dept and by Armed Forces Transport Directorate " Central " (*Wehrmachttransportleitung Mitte*). To assist the Director-General of Transportation in co-ordination and correlation of problems of all aspects of transportation a complex organization of civil and military representatives has been set up. These representatives are experts on various aspects of transportation and include the following:—

Chief of Motor Transport in the Armed Forces (formerly called General of Motorization), who himself has a staff composed of transportation representatives of the Army, Navy and Air Force, and whose duties are laid down as:—

The planning of standardization and steady development of motor transport in the forces (except armoured vehicles).

Distribution of MT vehicles to the three services and to allied and friendly states.

Liaison with all Government authorities in matters relating to motor transport.

Collaboration with the Inspector-General of Motorization in the OKH (In 12—*see* chart of OKH organization).

Representatives of the Reich Ministry of Transport, Reich Railways, Reich Inland Waterways and the Inspector-General of Road Communications.

Representatives of the Transport officers in the Military Districts (*Wehrkreise*).

Transport Administrative Offices for rail, road and inland waterways (*Transport Kommandanturen für Eisenbahn, Landstrassen und Wasserstrassen*).

GAF Liaison officers. (There is probably one such officer for each theatre of operations, but the total number is known to vary from time to time. They advise on matters of air transportation.)

The Director-General of Transportation functions through the Armed Forces Transport Directorates (*Wehrmacht-transportleitungen*) of which there are thought to be four at the present time, namely East, West, South and Central (*Ost, West, Süd* and *Mitte*), which are believed to include a representative assembly (in each) of the various departments and specialists enumerated above, and which obviously work on a territorial basis and cover all means and aspects of transportation.

(viii) Armed forces transportation is intimately bound up with the civilian organization and section 10 of this Handbook sets out in some detail the relationship which the civilian organization behind the road, rail and inland waterway systems bears to the armed forces organization. Movement in the field is a matter for the QMG at GHQ. As set out in paragraph (iii) above, the relevant department in the QMG's staff is department 1 (*Gruppe Qu 1*), which has liaison with the Director-General of Transportation on questions of supply routes and transport facilities.

(ix) All movements of troops or supplies, therefore, by any means, whether within or without Reich territory, come ultimately under the control of the Director-General of Transportation. Movements of supply trains for example are arranged between the QMG (GHQ), the Head of Army Supply (OKH) and the Director-General of Transportation (OKW); again the movement of a division from South-Western France into Northern Italy is done by the Director-General of Transportation in conjunction with *O Qu 1* (German equivalent of British DMO) at GHQ; yet a further example is the supply by air of German forces which is done by the Director-General of Transportation through his GAF liaison staff in conjunction with the QMG at GHQ.

(b) *The Organization of Supply within Germany.*

There appears little doubt that the supply organization within the Army in Germany itself is largely run on text-book lines. The higher organization has been dealt with in the previous paragraph, and it establishes the principle that responsibility for supply within Germany lies with the Head of Army Supply, and that the whole complex system of supply administration under the QMG at GHQ is in no way concerned. The Supply of the various commodities to garrison, depot and training units within Germany is dealt with in detail under the various headings of Ordnance, POL, MT, etc, in Part I of this Handbook, but the following brief notes may serve to illustrate the system.

(i) *Ordnance Stores and Ammunition* (see *Section 2, Part I*).—Indent is made in the normal fashion from unit to regiment, thence to division, corps and Army. Army indents direct upon the Ordnance inspectorate (under the Head of Army Supply) which allocates the appropriate depot to undertake the supply of the material or ammunition indented for. In practice, with static units, this system can to a certain extent be short-circuited and indent made direct upon the depot. It should be noted that the system within Germany depends very much upon the Military Districts (*Wehrkreise*), and that depots normally supply only such garrison units as are stationed within the geographical limits of the Wehrkreis in which the depot is situated. However, if, for example, NÜRNBERG, in Wehrkreis XIII supplies all recruits for a unit to be trained in KÖNIGSBERG, in Wehrkreis I, it is normal for NÜRNBERG to continue to be responsible for this unit's ordnance supply and first issue of ammunition. Wehrkreis I bears no such responsibility for the unit. To carry this example further, if a depot unit, say Ersatz battalion I is stationed in NÜRNBERG, and its field unit, Infantry Regiment I is fighting in Russia, NÜRNBERG is responsible for supplying Infantry Regiment I with ordnance and ammunition. Should, however, the Ersatz battalion be moved in its entirety to KONIGSBERG in Wehrkreis I, then KÖNIGSBERG would have to assume responsibility for the field unit, Infantry Regiment I in Russia.

(ii) *POL* (see *Section 3, Part I*).—The amount of POL required by garrison units, is as a rule, comparatively small. The term includes fuel for petrol and Diesel-engined vehicles, lubricating oil, gear oil, grease and anti-freeze compounds. As with formations in the field, petrol is calculated in the consumption unit (*Verbrauchssatz*) which is the amount of fuel required to take each of the formation's vehicles 100 km. Mechanized units keep a reserve of a certain number of consumption units, and in Germany itself, most of the examples available would appear to indicate that three consumption units is the normal reserve. Most garrisons in Germany have no dump or depots to draw from, with the exception that the reserve of fuel consumption units is usually held available in the barracks or billet garages. Local garages under military control keep a fuel stock and act as filling stations for the vehicles of the units supplied. These filling stations are supplied with petrol from military reserves or sometimes direct from synthetic petrol plants or refineries on the written instructions of the supply staffs responsible for their administration and only on receipt of a corresponding number of petrol vouchers (*Tankscheine*). The filling stations issue petrol to the vehicles of allocated units, usually at specified times of the day, on receipt of valid petrol vouchers which have to be cancelled by stamp.

GAF units in the area are supplied with MT fuel by the Army filling stations, and send their vehicles each day to be refilled, in exactly the same way as do the Army vehicles. The barracks of wholly mechanized units of either GAF or Army very often have their own filling stations constructed inside the barracks.

(iii) *Rations*.—The system of rations supply within Germany is outlined in section 4 (*a*) of Part I of this Handbook. It should be mentioned that the base rations stores (*Ersatz Verpflegungs Magazine or EVM's*) do not normally serve garrison units directly. This is normally done through the nearest Army Rations Depot (*Heeresverpflegungsamt*) or Army Rations Main Depot (*Heeresverpflegungshauptamt*). As the army rations depot do not as a rule have a bakery, garrison troops get their fresh bread from civilian bakers. Fresh meat is obtained from civilian butchers, and the Intendants of garrison units are empowered to purchase locally such fresh vegetables, etc, as they can.

(iv) *M.T.*—The system of supply of motor vehicles to garrison units is included in section 5 (*b*) of Part I of this Handbook. Most of the industrial firms manufacturing MT have an MT depot attached. These depots are called *Wehrmachtlager bei Kraftfahrzeugfirma,* and they exist to facilitate the supply of vehicles from industry to the static home MT parks (*Heimat Kraftfahrparke*). These parks play a similar part in the supply of MT, to that played by the Ordnance depots in the ordnance supply system and they hold, maintain and repair all types of motor vehicles. Garrison units are supplied direct from the parks.

(c) Supply of the GAF.

(i) Responsibility for supply of the GAF lies with the Director-General of Equipment at the Air Ministry in BERLIN, in conjunction with Department 4 of the General Staff at the Air Ministry. Rations and MT fuel are normally provided by the existing Army organizations (*see* sections 3 and 4, Part I), the GAF drawing from Army stocks at levels above corps only. GAF supply can be considered as operating in two broad divisions, that of the provision of aircraft equipment, and that of the provision of ammunition, aircraft fuel, etc.

(ii) Ammunition, aircraft fuel, etc, is stored in main ammunition depots and main fuel depots in Germany and is supplied direct from plants or factories. From the depots supplies are allocated to the various *Luftgaue* (air district administration) in Germany or the *Luftgaue* in occupied territories. The office in the *Luftgau* responsible for the issue of supplies is known as the Equipment Group. In Germany, aircraft fuel and ammunition are generally delivered from the main depots direct by rail to the airfields, though some miscellaneous supplies are delivered through the air park of the equipment group. Most of the storage of fuel and ammunition in *Luftgau* areas in occupied territories is in field tank depots and field ammunition depots, whence the supplies may be transported either direct to airfields or by way of forward dumps which may be in the open. Fuel in these forward dumps is normally in the 200 litre barrels, but is occasionally seen in the 20 litre jerricans. Field depots and forward dumps are operated by specially trained squads in GAF supply companies, who may also set up ammunition points or petrol points to facilitate issue.

Transport of GAF supplies, as with the Army, is preferably by rail, but water and road transport will naturally be used. GAF MT supply columns consisting of either transport columns or POL columns are available, and the GAF has greater recourse to air transport than has the Army under circumstances warranting the use of aircraft. The diagram below shows the possible channels of supply. Supplies to units in Germany may go by routes 1 or 2; those for field units may go by routes 3, 4 or 5. Field depots and field air parks are controlled by the Equipment Group of the *Luftgau* and forward dumps are controlled by the supply stations attached to the Airfield Regional Commands.

(iii) Supply of ammunition, aircraft fuel, etc, to the GAF.

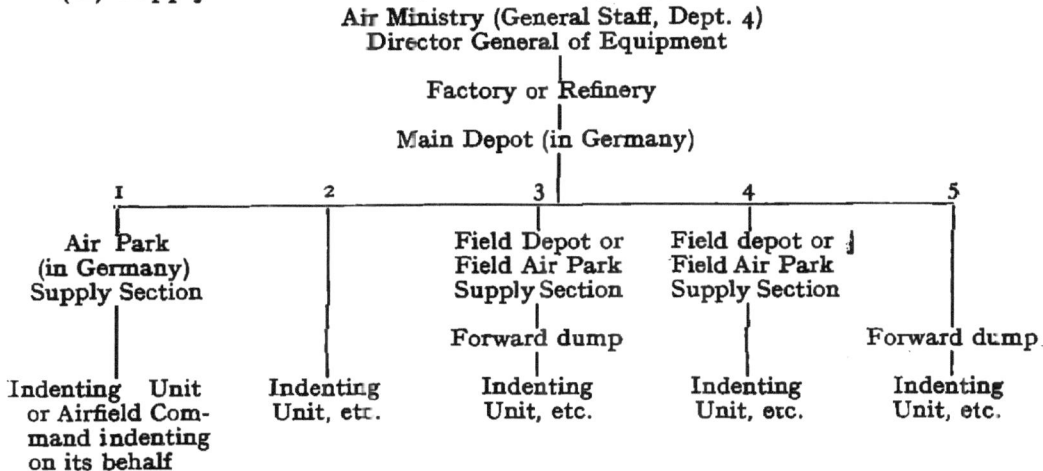

Air Ministry (General Staff, Dept. 4)
Director General of Equipment

Factory or Refinery

Main Depot (in Germany)

1	2	3	4	5
Air Park (in Germany) Supply Section		Field Depot or Field Air Park Supply Section	Field depot or Field Air Park Supply Section	
		Forward dump		Forward dump
Indenting Unit or Airfield Command indenting on its behalf	Indenting Unit, etc.	Indenting Unit, etc.	Indenting Unit, etc.	Indenting Unit, etc.

(iv) *Supply of aircraft equipment.*—The main stocks of aircraft equipment are stored in Air Ministry equipment depots in Germany, some of which specialize in particular kinds of aircraft engines or equipment. The equipment group in each *Luftgau* controls the issue of equipment within the *Luftfau*. The main *Luftgau* stocks of equipment are stored in one or more air parks, or (in occupied territories or in active operational zones) in field air parks.

In the field, a further decentralization is necessary, and equipment issuing stations are set up at or near the main airfields of airfield regional commands, or smaller and more mobile ones at or near the airfields occupied by short-range units. These smaller equipment issuing stations, dealing in equipment for particular types of aircraft, are fully mechanized and may even be air-transported. The field workshop units which maintain aircraft in the battle zones, hold small stocks of spare equipment or are near to equipment issuing stations. Equipment required urgently and not in stock in equipment stations is delivered by air from air parks or even equipment depots, and air transport may be extensively used for delivery of aircraft equipment where the transport system is inadequate. The diagram below shows the possible channels of delivery of aircraft equipment. Aircraft equipment for units in Germany may go by routes 1 or 2, and that for units in the field may go by routes 3, 4 or 5. The most normal routes are 1 and 3. The equipment issuing stations in occupied territories or in the battle zones have the double function of storage of equipment and control of its issue.

(v) *Supply of aircraft equipment to the GAF.*

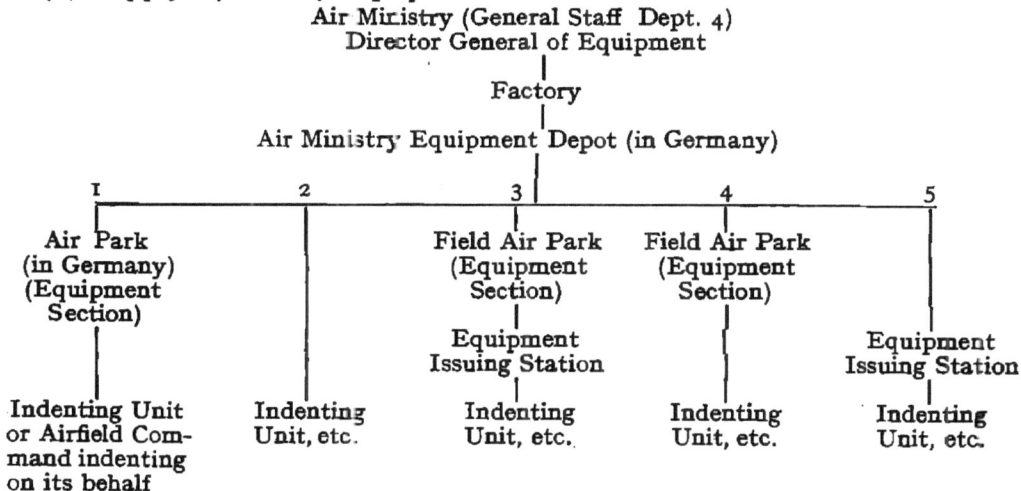

Air Ministry (General Staff Dept. 4)
Director General of Equipment

Factory

Air Ministry Equipment Depot (in Germany)

1	2	3	4	5
Air Park (in Germany) (Equipment Section)		Field Air Park (Equipment Section)	Field Air Park (Equipment Section)	
		Equipment Issuing Station		Equipment Issuing Station
Indenting Unit or Airfield Command indenting on its behalf	Indenting Unit, etc.	Indenting Unit, etc.	Indenting Unit, etc.	Indenting Unit, etc.

(vi) There are, in Germany, eight Air Ministry Equipment Depots. (*Luftzeugämter*) for holding stocks of both aircraft and aircraft equipment. These are as follows:—

ERDING	...	(Me 109)
FINOW	...	(Ju 87 and Ju 88)
KOELLEDA	...	(Hs 126, Hs 129, Do 17, and Fi 156)
LIEGNITZ	...	(Me 110, Me 210, FW 189, and FW 190)
SAGAN-KUEPPER		(He 111, He 177)
SCHWERIN	...	(ARADO-land)
TELTOW	...	(Signals equipment)
TRAVEMUENDE		(Sea-borne aircraft)

There is also an equipment depot for the Eastern fronts at WARSAW.

(vii) *The supply of GAF flak units.*—Responsibility for supply of GAF units lies entirely with the GAF except, in the case of rations and MT fuel, where the GAF system is fused on to the Army system and Army depots are drawn upon by GAF units, but this is on a high level, and the small GAF unit will receive its rations and MT fuel through a higher GAF formation. Drawing from Army rations or MT fuel stocks by the GAF normally takes place at GHQ or Army level, rarely at corps or below. In certain cases units attached to Army formations for operations in the field have been known to obtain other supplies through Army channels, but this is irregular and exceptional.

Mechanized AA batteries (*Abteilungen*) have supply columns which comprise approximately 20 vehicles and 70 personnel: Non-mechanized batteries have no supply columns of their own; requirements which cannot be met by their limited unit MT, are met by resort to flak transport troops (*Flak Transport Batterien*) which can normally carry an entire non-mechanized flak battery. All GAF flak unit supply columns are mechanized.

The same chain of supply as that shown in the diagram in paragraph (iii) applies to the supply of GAF flak units. In theatres of operations, however, exceptions may arise owing to the exigencies of the situation. Field flak issuing stations, for example, may be subordinated to airfield regional commands, and units may indent directly on GAF dumps which may even include purely GAF rations dumps, and MT fuel dumps.

In a flak division there is an I*b* officer (second general staff officer) complete with staff, exactly as in an Army division, responsible for supply. At *Flakgruppe*, which corresponds to regiment, responsibility for supply is invested in the OC, but there is a technical officer for ammunition, equipment and MT, etc, an intendant for rations and pay, and the senior MO for medical supply and administration. There is a similar organization at *Flakuntergruppe*, which corresponds to battalion.

(viii) *Supply of GAF field divisions.*—Rations, fuel and ammunition are supplied to the GAF field divisions by the Army, but, initially, equipment (guns, MT, horses and vehicles) are provided by the appropriate authorities at the German Air Ministry.

(ix) *Supply of parachute divisions.*—All equipment for parachute troops, including MT and guns, is provided by the GAF. In addition, some forms of special ammunition used by parachute troops, is provided by the GAF. Otherwise, rations, MT fuel and ammunition, together with such things as building material, are supplied by the Army.

2. Ordnance Supplies.

Ordnance material, ammunition, and, to a certain extent, AFVs, must be considered together within the framework of German supply as far as higher organization of ordnance supply is concerned, for not until administration and responsibility have been traced down to the level of Ordnance Stores HQs within Germany can the lines of supply and administration for ammunition and ordnance material divide and go their separate ways.

(a) *Higher Organization.*—(i) The Head of Army Supply (*Chef der Heeresrüstung und Befehlshaber des Ersatzheeres*), in the High Command of the German Army in BERLIN (the *OKH*) is responsible for the provision of equipment of all kinds, both for the Armies in the field and for all troops stationed in the area of the Home Command. Under him, it will be seen by reference to the Chart of the *OKH* at the beginning of this Handbook, is, among the various Inspectorates, the Inspector of Ordnance (*Feldzeuginspektion*). This Inspectorate is under the immediate direction of an Ordnance Supply Controller (*Feldzeugmeister*). The ordnance Inspectorate controls three Ordnance Groups (*Feldzeuggruppen*) of which one is in BERLIN, one in KASSEL and the third in MUNICH, obviously from a geographical consideration, each being intended to be the administrative supply centre for specific areas. Each of these three Groups is sub-divided into six or more Ordnance Stores HQs (*Feldzeugkommandos*) which, in the majority of cases, are numbered according to the Wehrkreis in which they are situated. It is at this level that the lines of supply for ammunition and for ordnance divide. The Ordnance Stores HQs each control a number of depots and branch depots. The term " depot " in English unfortunately does not convey the full sense of what is meant by the German terms. The ordnance depots are called *Heereszeugämter* and the branch ordnance depots *Heeresnebenzeugämter*, while the ammunition depots are called *Heeresmunitionsanstalten* or *Munas* and the branch ammunition depots *Heeresnebenmunitionsanstalten*. Ordnance depots, in fact, are more than mere storage installations. They can and do repair and maintain ordnance equipment as well as handling the whole administrative aspect of supply from their stocks. The Ammunition depots as well as being places where ammunition is stored, normally, also have facilities for making accessories, such as fuzes and for filling. In no event, however, does it appear that they manufacture the shell cases themselves. In any case, ordnance depots are of considerably greater proportions than the normal ammunition or ordnance dumps at army, their layout being to some extent standardized and the buildings being of a permanent nature. This standardization of the ordnance depots is well shown in the illustrations at the end of Part I of this Handbook, the depots at Ingolstadt and at Munich/Milbertshofen being particularly good examples of the " typical " buildings in " typical " layout.

(ii) The word " ordnance " is defined by the German depots as meaning the following weapons and equipment:—

Weapons—
  All guns, mortars and accessories.
  All small arms (excluding hand grenades which come under the heading of ammunition).

Instruments and Equipment—
  All equipment for horses.
  All HT vehicles and their equipment.
  Special equipment for MT vehicles and AFVs which is not an essential part of the vehicle.

Artificers' tools and equipment.

Farriers' equipment.

All instruments except signals equipment, but including optical instruments and their leather accessories.

Map-reading and computing equipment.

All anti-gas and gas-detecting equipment.

All printed regulations issued by the *OKH* and *OKW* with the exception of Paymaster regulations.

Tents and accessories, including various types of lamps.

Engineer materials, tools and implements.

Field kitchen equipment.

Coal and other fuels for field kitchens.

All camouflage material.

Generating sets, except those used by signals.

(iii) The plan of this higher organization is as follows:—

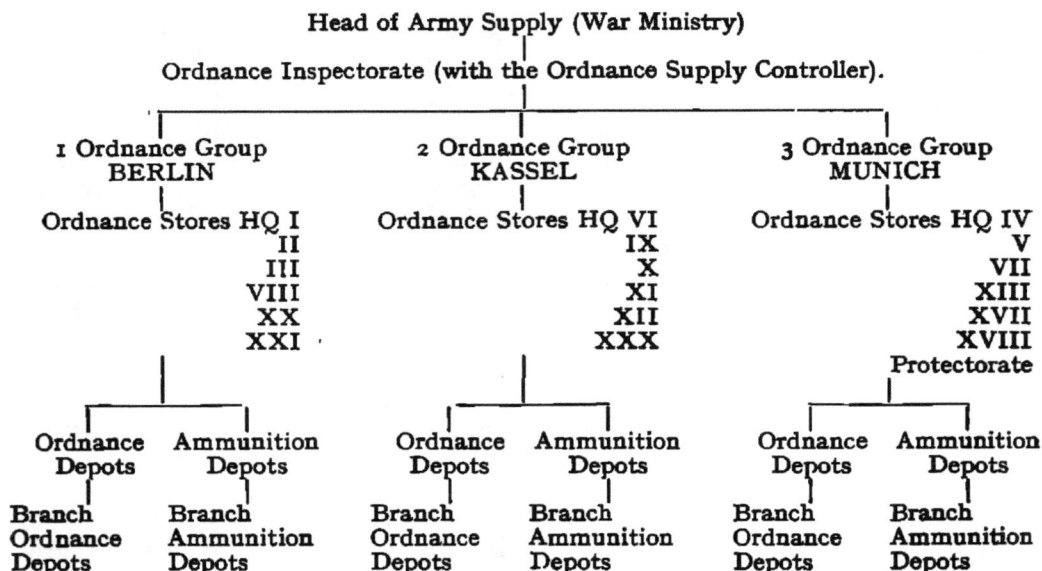

Head of Army Supply (War Ministry)

Ordnance Inspectorate (with the Ordnance Supply Controller).

1 Ordnance Group BERLIN	2 Ordnance Group KASSEL	3 Ordnance Group MUNICH
Ordnance Stores HQ I	Ordnance Stores HQ VI	Ordnance Stores HQ IV
II	IX	V
III	X	VII
VIII	XI	XIII
XX	XII	XVII
XXI	XXX	XVIII
		Protectorate
Ordnance Depots — Ammunition Depots	Ordnance Depots — Ammunition Depots	Ordnance Depots — Ammunition Depots
Branch Ordnance Depots — Branch Ammunition Depots	Branch Ordnance Depots — Branch Ammunition Depots	Branch Ordnance Depots — Branch Ammunition Depots

(iv) The organization shown above handles ordnance collectively, that is to say supply of weapons, equipment, ammunition and AFVs all pass, at this level through the same channels. At the storage stage, however, ammunition is kept in the ammunition dumps or Munas, having come direct from the factories, and all other ordnance material is kept in the Ordnance depots, which, similarly, draw directly upon the factories.

GHQ forwards indents from the field army for ammunition of all types to the Head of Army Supply and gives instructions under direction from the Head of Army Supply, as to the proportion of ammunition to be held ready in the depots, according to the policy directed on a still higher level and dictated by questions of production, design and strategical planning. Army indents on GHQ and keeps the stocks received either in Army ammunition dumps (*Armeemunitionslager or AMLs*) or less often as a mobile reserve stock in trains or in army transport columns. The line of supply thenceforward is entirely a matter of field supply and is therefore dealt with in Part II of this Handbook.

(b) *Functions of Depots.*—(i) The Ordnance depots usually specialize to some extent in particular types of equipment (*see* paragraph (ii)) and the allocation of a particular depot for a particular sector of the operational zone has to be worked out by the Ordnance Supply Controller (*Feldzeugmeister*). In the last war weapons and ammunition were manufactured almost exclusively by so-called military factories which were factories and testing-grounds and storehouses combined, but this war has seen the development of two parallel organizations. On the one hand is the armaments industry under the Ministry of Armaments and War Production (*Reichsminister für Rüstung und Kriegsproduktion*) with his armaments control centres (*Rüstungskommandos*), which are the Minister's means of controlling design and production at the factories. The armaments control centres are linked together under armaments inspectorates (*Rüstungsinspektionen*).

On the other hand is the Ordnance supply system as outlined in paragraph (a) above, designed to hold the products of the armaments industry until they are called for by the troops. More than mere storage is, however, demanded of the various depots. The ordnance depots repair German war material and ammunition; such material for example as rusted and weather-damaged ammunition and captured war material is overhauled at the ordnance depots. In the ammunition depots, ammunition is filled and assembled by civilian labour, including a very high proportion of women, and then it is stored for issue. The *Heeresmunitionsanstalt* at FEUCHT, for example, assembles complete ammunition for the following:—

> 3·7-cm Pak
> 5-cm Pak
> 7·5-cm Pak
> 7·5-cm IG
> 3·7-cm Flak
> 5-cm Flak and
> 8·8-cm Flak

It manufactures cartridges for:—

> 10·5-cm le FH
> 15-cm s FH
> 7·5-cm IG

It fills fuzes for:—

> 10·5-cm le FH
> 15-cm s FH
> 7·5-cm IG
> all A-tk guns
> all Flak ammunition

The shells for which these fuzes are designated are turned at MAN's factories or by Baumann and Co, and they are filled at SCHWABACH. These products of the *Muna* at FEUCHT are supplied to all neighbouring garrison units, to the AA units in the NÜRNBERG area and to various areas of the fronts—for example, in the spring of 1942 it sent its supplies of ammunition to KIEV.

(ii) Some of the Ordnance depots specialize to a very great extent. Signals equipment, of example, is the exclusive commodity of the depots at Wien-Strebersdorf and Berlin-Schöneberg. AFVs are handled principally at the great tank depot at Magdeburg-Königsborn, an air-photograph of which is shown among the illustrations at the end of Part I of this handbook. Magdeburg-Königsborn stocks spare parts of AFVVs as well as complete tanks and all types of assault guns and armoured carriers.

It supplies Italy, the Balkans, the whole of the Russian front and used to supply North Africa. It would appear unusual that in this one matter of AFVs there has not been the same decentralization of storage that there is in the matter of other equipment; the answer may be found in that the margin of surplus of production over rate of acceptance is very small, and that supply is virtually direct from producer to the front line.

(c) *The Home Parks and their connection with the depot system.*—The ordnance depot system is supplemented by a system of home parks (*Heimatparke*) for certain types of ordnance, such as certain engineer equipment, MT equipment, etc. They take the same place in the chain of indent and supply as do the depots, that is to say, the Ordnance Inspectorate designates the appropriate depot or park according to the nature of the indent and the geographical location of the indenting formation. Army also has parks for the various types of ordnance, and although these parks are largely for repair, they are also holding units and they in their turn may forward ordnance equipment either directly or through an Army equipment collecting station (*Armee Gerätesammelstelle*). These last-named act merely as an extra forwarding print, as their primary function is that of salvage. It will thus be seen that ordnance equipment may come direct from the ordnance depot or home park (if certain engineer equipment, for example, is required) direct to Division, or it may come through Army and divisional forwarding points of various types, supplemented if need be by similar institutions in the Corps area.

(d) *Storage of ammunition in buildings.*—A certain amount of the information which follows belongs also to Part II, Section 13 of this Handbook, which deals with ammunition in the field.

Under this category is included all ammunition housed in temporary constructions such as wooden or corrugated iron huts; and permanent constructions such as brick or concrete ammunition sheds and houses; fortresses and other buildings. Where buildings are not available for housing ammunition, cover may of course take the form of dugouts or recesses cut into the ground with a supporting frame of wood or sheet iron; cavities recessed or sunk into the ground with wooden or corrugated iron walls and earth or concrete floors; marquees or demountable ammunition sheds, but this properly speaking refers to the storage of ammunition in the field and will be dealt with in Part II.

(i) Ammunition huts (*Schuppen*). Huts are often sited on the same pattern as stacks, *viz*, in fives, or in staggered formation, as at Nürnberg/Feucht for example where they are arranged in this way. (*See* illustration at the end of Part I.) In some cases mixed types of dump are found, ammunition being stored partly in huts and partly in stacks as for example at the Hagenow/Trebs dump.

A maximum superficial area of 25 square yards is recommended for huts, the walls being strengthened by sandbags in order to reduce the effects of explosion. Spacing between huts: 50 yds; huts containing charges are spaced at least 100 yards from sheds containing shells or grenades and explosives.

Huts may be roofed with corrugated iron or roofing felt and have plank walls and floors; if recessed into the ground, spaces of 3 ins and 6 ins respectively are left between wall or floor and soil.

Ammunition stored in huts is usually stacked on racks, in baskets, or in boxes, or in their absence on wooden distance pieces (2 or 3 yds long by 1 in by 1½ in) between the individual rows of shells (*see* illustrations at the end of Part I). Mortar bombs, incendiary bombs, explosives and detonators, Teller and S mines, cartridges for signal pistol flares, MG and machine carbine ammunition are always stored in their original packing cases.

(ii) Ammunition sheds and houses. The following rules apply to the layout and siting of brick or concrete ammunition sheds (*Munitionsbehälter*) and ammunition houses (*Munitionshäuser*) at ammunition depots (*Munitionsanstalten*) especially constructed for housing ammunition (*see* illustrations at end of Part I).

Ammunition sheds or houses must be at least 20 yards from entrances or exits or MT garages, 50 yards from petrol stations and 50-75 yards from guard houses.

If SAA is stored in addition to shells in sheds or houses, the artillery ammunition will be divided into two halves separated from one another by a large stack of SAA.

(iii) Layout of buildings used as ammunition depots and workshops.
The following are the German regulations regarding the housing of ammunition in buildings employed for the storage of ammunition.

In buildings of two or more floors ammunition is as a rule only stored on the lowest floor. The upper floors may be used under exceptional circumstances when of sufficient strength—if the lower floors are damp, dark or less accessible than the upper floors.

A vacant space which can be filled if required by SAA in airtight packings must be left between two rooms housing ammunition. If ammunition is stored on two floors it must be arranged in chessboard pattern so that an empty space is left between rooms on each floor which may likewise be used to store SAA in air-tight packings.

The ammunition should be stacked as in ammunition houses. If the size of the rooms permits, the stacks should be a yard from the walls. The top of the stack should be at least a foot from the ceiling. Very large rooms may be partitioned. Rooms used for the storage of ammunition should be separated from one another by massive partition walls at least one yard thick of brick or concrete ($\frac{3}{4}$-yard thick if of reinforced concrete) without windows, doors or other apertures and also separated, as stated above, by a vacant space (which may be utilized to store equipment or SAA in watertight packings). Special access to every vacant space must be provided. Two adjoining rooms with a common entrance count as one room.

Ammunition workshops may be located on the upper floors except those in which shells of over 10·5-cm calibre are filled or powder is handled. The latter may not be connected by doors (or windows) with rooms in which shells are being filled. All ammunition workshops must be separated from one another by solid walls at least 8 ins thick. They must be as far away as possible from rooms in which ammunition is stored or at least separated therefrom by a vacant space with solid walls one yard thick. Ammunition may not be stored below or above rooms used as workshops. The only heating system permitted in rooms used to store or work on ammunition is central heating or the special stove for munitions works.

(iv) *Method of stacking.*—In stacking ammunition there must be a space of at least $\frac{1}{2}$-yard from the walls, the gangways between stacks being likewise $\frac{1}{2}$-yard wide. The individual stacks in ammunition houses or sheds should be provided with stack cards (*Stapelkarten*) or boards giving the contents of the stack.

SAA.—The bottom-most layer of packages should lie on a bed of planks and half blocks or boards. To economize space double stacks may be used. Full boxes of cartridges may be stacked one above the other to a height of two yards. Stacks must be placed ¾-yard from the walls. MG ammunition in belts may be stacked eight layers high.

2-cm ammunition stored in its original packing need not be dispersed in separate stacks. Otherwise as for SAA.

Artillery and mortar ammunition is stored, unless otherwise ordered, in the original packages (standard and transport). Whether removed or not from their baskets or packages, shells must be stored on rests or in racks of planks and blocks not exceeding two yards in height.

Racks are made up of planks of standard dimensions (30 yards long 10 ins wide and 3 ins thick) and of blocks (5 ins square with length equal to the width of the stack) as distance-pieces. Racks are usually made three planks wide though the width may be increased to six planks to utilize better the space available. Half blocks are placed below the bottom-most plank for the sake of ventilation.

Distance-pieces must lie perpendicularly above one another, the end ones being sufficiently far from the extremities of the planks to allow four rows of 10·5 or 15-cm shells and five rows of 7·5-cm shells to be placed one each free end of the plank.

Racks not exceeding a width of four planks must be accessible on one longitudinal side, and on both sides in excess of this width.

Only ammunition of the same type should be stored in a stack.

(e) Description of a depot.—The ammunition depot at Hohensalza is a typical example of the standard plan combining ammunition shelters, permanent buildings and workshops. This particular depot was completed in 1942 and a plan of it is shown in the illustrations at the end of Part I of this Handbook, together with diagrams of the shelters. It was largely built by the Organization TODT, and it contains 80 to 100 ammunition shelters arranged in the form of a horseshoe, with rail and road connection to each, and workshops and permanent buildings in the middle of the horseshoe. The ammunition is stored, either empty or filled, but normally empty, in which case it is filled in the workshops in the centre before issue.

The shelters themselves are of different sizes, the average size being about 25 ft square. They are built on ground level, the walls are of 17 in concrete, not reinforced and 4 in bricks, and the roof is of 15 to 17 in concrete, reinforced with a single layer of prefabricated steel netting. This is 6 mm gauge netting (*Baustahlgewebe*), made in rolls of 15 yds by 2 yds by *Baustahlgewebe GmbH*, Düsseldorf. The roof is supported by a centre pillar and four brick arches. The concrete is insulated against damp by a layer of specially prepared cardboard. The height from floor to ceiling is 10 ft with a door 6 ft high, and there is one ventilation shaft. The whole shelter is covered with soil and camouflaged.

(f) Gas equipment.—The ammunition depots are known to keep CW ammunition, though it is thought that only selected depots do this. War gases, both in solid and liquid form are also known to be stored in the *Munas*. The chief centre of storage for war gases is undoubtedly AUGSBURG, which, it appears, handles the bulk of the stocks. Others among the principal centres of storage of war gases are THORN, GRAUDENZ, FEUCHT and CELLE. All anti-gas and gas-detecting equipment, as outlined in paragraph *(a)* (ii) above is kept in the Ordnance Depots, and most of these hold stocks of such equipment. The chief centre of storage for this type of equipment, if a chief centre can be said to exist, is probably SPANDAU. All units, for example, equipped with glass phials of war

gases for training and identification purposes are occasionally required to send certain of these phials to SPANDAU for replacement or destruction or renewal. As with other equipment, there exist parks, at army level, which hold CW equipment. These parks issue anti-gas equipment at army or corps level and there is normally one such park for each army in the field.

(g) *Lists of depots.*—(i) Following are lists of the principal ordnance, branch ordnance, ammunition and branch ammunition depots in Germany with their military districts (*Wehrkreise*). Many of these have been damaged in Allied air attacks, notably the depots at KASSEL, HAMBURG, MAGDEBURG and HANNOVER. Illustrations of some of them appear at the end of Part I of this Handbook, from which it will be seen that they are of considerable size and capacity. The lists, particularly those of the branch depots will not, of course, be complete, but there is no doubt that the vast majority of them have been located.

(ii) *Heereszeugämter* (*Ordnance Depots*).

Serial No.	Ordnance Depots								Military District (*Wehrkreis*)
1	HZa	...	...	...	SPANDAU	...	...	...	...	III
2	HZa	...	...	...	NAUMBURG	...	...	...	...	IV
3	HZa	...	...	...	ULM	...	...	...	...	V
4	HZa	...	...	...	KASSEL	...	...	...	...	IX
5	HZa	...	...	...	MAINZ...	...	...	...	...	XII
6	HZa	...	...	...	WIEN	...	...	...	...	XVII
7	HZa	...	...	...	GRAUDENZ	...	...	...	...	XX
8	HZa	...	...	...	POSEN	...	...	...	...	XXI
9	HZa	...	...	...	KÖNIGSBERG	...	...	...	I
10	HZa	...	...	...	GÜSTROW	...	...	...	...	II
11	HZa	...	...	...	UNNA	...	...	...	...	VI
12	HZa	...	...	...	MÜNCHEN	...	...	...	...	VII
13	HZa	...	...	...	FREILASSING	...	...	...	XVIII
14	HZa	...	...	...	INGOLSTADT	...	...	...	VII
15	HZa	...	...	...	BRESLAU	...	...	...	...	VIII
16	HZa	...	...	...	HAMBURG	...	...	...	...	X
17	HZa	...	...	...	GLINDE	...	...	...	...	X
18	HZa	...	...	...	MAGDEBURG	...	...	...	...	XI
19	HZa	...	...	...	HANNOVER	...	...	...	...	XI
20	HZa	...	...	...	MAINZ-KASTEL	...	...	...	XII

(iii) *Heeresnebenzeugämter* (*Branch Ordnance Depots*).

1	HNZa...	...	...	HEILBRONN	...	...	...	V
2	HNZa...	...	...	STEINEN-IN-BADEN	...	...	XVII
3	HNZa...	...	...	KASSEL	...	...	...	IX
4	HNZa...	...	...	GIESSEN	...	...	...	IX
5	HNZa...	...	...	TRIER	...	...	...	XII
6	HNZa...	...	...	BROMBERG	...	...	...	XX
7	HNZa...	...	...	THORN	...	...	...	XX
8	HNZa...	...	...	POSEN	...	...	...	XXI
9	HNZa...	...	...	LÖTZEN	...	...	...	I
10	HNZa...	...	...	ALLENSTEIN	...	...	...	I
11	HNZa...	...	...	GUMBINNEN	...	...	...	I
12	HNZa...	...	...	ARYS	...	...	...	...	I
13	HNZa...	...	...	BARTENSTEIN	...	...	...	I
14	HNZa...	...	...	KÖSLIN	...	...	...	II
15	HNZa...	...	...	SCHWERIN	...	...	...	II
16	HNZa...	...	...	STARGARD	...	...	...	II
17	HNZa...	...	...	JÜTERBOG	...	...	...	III
18	HNZa...	...	...	BERLIN-TEMPELHOF	...	...	III
19	HNZa...	...	...	KÜSTRIN	...	...	...	III
20	HNZa...	...	...	COTTBUS	...	...	...	III

Serial No.	Ordnance Depots			Military District (*Wehrkreis*)
21	HNZa	POTSDAM	... ...	III
22	HNZa	LEIPZIG	... ...	IV
23	HNZa	RIESA		IV
24	HNZa	PLAUEN	... ...	IV
25	HNZa	RAVENSBURG-WEINGARTEN ...		V
26	HNZa	DÜSSELDORF	... ...	VI
27	HNZa	BITBURG	... ...	XII
28	HNZa	DÜREN	... ...	VI
29	HNZa	MÜLHEIM	... ...	VI
30	HNZa	BIELEFELD ...	... ...	VI
31	HNZa	OSNABRÜCK...	... ...	VI
32	HNZa	AUGSBURG ...	... ...	VII
33	HNZa	ROSENHEIM	... ...	VII
34	HNZa	KEMPTEN	... ...	VII
35	HNZa	HRABIN	... ...	VIII
36	HNZa	GLOGAU	... ...	VIII
37	HNZa	OPPELN	... ...	VIII
38	HNZa	ERFURT	... ...	IX
39	HNZa	FULDA	... ...	IX
40	HNZa	ALTONA	... ...	X
41	HNZa	BREMEN	... ...	X
42	HNZa	BRAUNSCHWEIG/RAUTHEIM ...		XI
43	HNZa	SCHNEVERDINGEN	... ...	XI
44	HNZa	STENDAL ...	... ...	XI
45	HNZa	NORTHEIM ...	... ...	XI
46	HNZa	WIESBADEN	... ...	XII
47	HNZa	DARMSTADT...	... ...	XII
48	HNZa	FRANKFORT/O	... ...	III
49	HNZa	ST WENDEL	... ...	XII
50	HNZa	KAISERSLAUTERN	... ...	XII
51	HNZa	HEIDELBERG	... ...	XII
52	HNZa	BAYREUTH ...	... ...	XIII
53	HNZa	REGENSBURG	... ...	XIII
54	HNZa	FÜRTH	... ...	XIII
55	HNZa	AMBERG	... ...	XIII
56	HNZa	ANSBACH	... ...	XIII
57	HNZa	WIEN ...	... ...	XVII
58	HNZa	LINZ ...	... ...	XVII
59	HNZa	HALL ...	... ...	XVII
60	HNZa	GRAZ ...	... ...	XVIII
61	HNZa	MARIENBURG	... ...	XX
62	HNZa	STREBERSDORF	... ...	XVII
63	HNZa	HOHENSALZA	... ...	XXI
64	HNZa	KALISCH ...	... ...	XXI
65	HNZa	LISSA	... ...	XXI
66	HNZa	LITZMANNSTADT ...	... ...	XXI
67	HNZa	SONDERHAUSEN ...	... ...	IX
68	HNZa	LIEGNITZ ...	... ...	VIII
69	HNZa	DORTMUND ...	... ...	V
70	HNZa	AALEN ...	... ...	V
71	HNZa	TÜBINGEN ...	... ...	V
72	HNZa	BRANDENBURG	... ...	III

(iv) *Specialist Ordnance Depots.*

1	HNachrZa (Signals) ...	WIEN-STREBERSDORF ...	...	XVII
2	HNachrZa (Signals) ...	BERLIN-SCHÖNEBERG ...	...	III
3	HPanzerZa (Tanks) ...	MAGDEBURG-KÖNIGSBORN ...		XI
4	HPanzerNZa (Tanks, branch depot).	OPPELN ...	... ...	VIII
5	HPanzerNZa (Tanks, branch depot).	OLMÜTZ ...	... ...	Protectorate

(v) *Heeresmunitionsanstalten (Ammunition Depots)*.

Serial No.				Ordnance Depots						Military District (*Wehrkreis*)
1	HMa	...	...	...	DEMMIN	...	...	...	...	II
2	HMa	...	...	...	GÜLZOW	...	...	...	...	II
3	HMa	...	...	...	KRUGAU	...	...	...	...	III
4	HMa	...	...	..	PINNOW	...	...	...	...	III
5	HMa	...	...	..	SONNENBURG	...	...	...	III
6	HMa	...	...	..	ALTENHAIN	...	...	...	IV
7	HMa	...	...	..	KÖNIGSWARTHA	...	...	...	IV
8	HMa	...	...	..	STRASS	...	...	...	...	VII
9	HMa	...	...	...	URLAU	...	...	...	...	V
10	HMa	...	...	...	WULFEN	...	...	...	...	VI
11	HMa	...	...	...	LÜBBECKE	...	...	...	...	VI
12	HMa	...	...	...	St GEORGEN	...	...	...	VII
13	HMa	...	...	...	KOTZENAU	...	...	...	VIII
14	HMa	...	...	...	LANDESHUT	...	...	...	VIII
15	HMa	...	...	...	REHDEN	...	...	...	...	X
16	HMa	...	...	...	ZEVEN	...	...	...	...	X
17	HMa	...	...	...	WALSRODE	...	...	...	XXI
18	HMa	...	...	...	BODENTEICH	...	...	...	XI
19	HMa	...	...	...	SIEGELSBACH	...	...	...	XII
20	HMa	...	...	...	LUNDENBURG	...	...	...	XVII
21	HMa	...	...	...	GRAUDENZ	...	...	...	XX
22	HMa	...	...	...	THORN	...	...	...	...	XX
23	HMa	...	...	...	POSEN	...	...	...	...	XXI
24	HMa	...	...	...	GALKOWEK	...	...	...	XXI
25	HMa	...	...	...	DIEKHOLZEN	...	...	...	XI
26	HMa	...	...	...	SONDERSHAUSEN	...	...	XXX
27	HMa	...	...	...	POWAYEN	...	...	...	I
28	HMa	...	...	...	LUDWIGSORT	...	...	...	I
29	HMa	...	...	...	STABLACK	...	...	...	I
30	HMa	...	...	...	KÖNIGSBERG	...	...	...	I
31	HMa	...	...	...	BARTENSTEIN	...	...	...	I
32	HMa	...	...	...	LOCKNITZ	...	...	...	II
33	HMa	...	...	...	GÜSTROW	...	...	...	...	II
34	HMa	...	...	...	GODENAU	...	...	...	...	III
35	HMa	...	..	...	JÜTERBOG	...	...	...	...	III
36	HMa	...	. .	...	TÖPCHIN	...	...	...	...	III
37	HMa	...	..	...	NEURUPPIN	...	...	...	IV
38	HMa	...	..	...	ZEITHAIN	...	...	...	...	IV
39	HMa	...	...	...	TORGAU	...	...	...	...	IV
40	HMa	...	...	...	DINGELSTEDT	...	...	...	IV
41	HMa	...	...	...	ASCHERSLEBEN	...	...	IV
42	HMa	...	...	...	SENNE	...	...	...	...	VI
43	HMa	...	...	...	MÜNSTER	...	...	...	...	VI
44	HMa	...	...	...	INGOLSTADT	...	...	...	VII
45	HMa	...	...	...	DESCHING	...	...	...	...	VII
46	HMa	...	...	...	HOHENBRUNN	...	...	...	VII
47	HMa	...	...	...	SIEGERTSBRUNN	...	...	VII
48	HMa	...	...	...	NICKLASDORF	...	...	...	VIII
49	HMa	...	...	...	PRIEBUS	...	...	...	...	VIII
50	HMa	...	...	...	WILDFLECKEN	...	...	...	IX
51	HMa	...	...	...	OBERGEBRA	...	...	...	IX
52	HMa	...	...	...	KASSEL	...	...	...	...	IX
53	HMa	...	..	...	BERNTERODE	...	...	...	IX
54	HMa	...	..	...	WOLFRAMSHAUSEN	...	...	IX
55	HMa	...	...	...	HERFA	...	...	...	...	IX
56	HMa	...	...	...	BERKA	...	...	...	...	IX
57	HMa	...	...	...	MUNSTERLAGER	...	...	X
58	HMa	...	...	...	LOCKSTEDTER LAGER	...	...	X
59	HMa	...	...	...	MÖLLN	...	...	...	...	X
60	HMa	...	...	...	HÄNIGSEN	...	...	...	...	X

Serial No.	Ordnance Depots							Military District (*Wehrkreis*)
61	HMa	...	...	...	LEHRE	...	...	...	...	XI
62	HMa	...	...	...	CELLE	...	...	...	...	XI
63	HMa	...	...	...	SEHNDE	...	...	...	...	XI
64	HMa	...	...	...	DESSAU	...	...	...	...	XI
65	HMa	...	...	...	ALTENGRABOW	...	...	...	XI
66	HMa	...	...	...	GRASLEBEN	...	...	...	XI
67	HMa	...	...	...	GODENAU	...	...	...	...	XI
68	HMa	...	...	...	AHRBERGEN	...	...	...	XI
69	HMa	...	...	...	SONNENBURG	...	...	...	XII
70	HMa	...	...	...	DARMSTADT	...	...	...	XII
71	HMa	...	...	...	BAMBERG	...	...	...	...	XIII
72	HMa	...	...	...	FEUCHT	...	...	...	...	XIII
73	HMa	...	...	...	GROSSMITTEL	...	...	...	XVII
74	HMa	...	...	...	AUGSBURG	...	...	...	VII
75	HMa	...	...	...	HOHENSALZA	...	...	...	XXI

(vi) *Heeresnebenmunitionsanstalten* (*Branch Ammunition Depots*).

1	HNMa	...	...	KUPFER	...	...	...	...	V
2	HNMa	...	...	ULM	...	...	...	...	...	V
3	HNMa	...	...	LÜTZEL	...	...	...	...	VI
4	HNMa	...	...	WILHELMSDORF	...	...	...	VI (?)
5	HNMa	...	...	NECKARZIMMERN	...	...	...	V
6	HNMa	...	...	DÖLLERSHEIM	...	...	...	XVII
7	HNMa	...	...	GRAUDENZ	...	...	...	...	XX
8	HNMa	...	...	POTSDAM	...	...	...	...	III
9	HNMa	...	...	KÖLN	...	...	...	...	VI
10	HNMa	...	...	NEUHAMMER	...	...	...	VIII
11	HNMa	...	...	OPPELN	...	...	...	...	VIII
12	HNMa	...	...	OLINDE	...	...	...	...	X
13	HNMa	...	...	KAROLINENHOF	...	...	...	X
14	HNMa	...	...	SCHNEVERLINGEN	...	...	...	XI
15	HNMa	...	...	LITZMANNSTADT	...	...	...	XXI
16	HNMa	...	...	HOCHWALDE	...	...	...	XI (?)
17	HNMa	...	...	STASZFURT	...	...	...	XI (?)

3. POL.

(*a*) *Civilian Supply and Storage System.*—(i) Germany's organization for the supply and storage of oils includes the administration of natural oil centres, petroleum refineries and the production of synthetic oil.

The German Ministry of Economics (*Reichswirtschaftsministerium*) has a department which concerned itself until the end of 1942 with the supply and storage of oil fuel. It is called the *Reichsstelle für Mineralöl* (department for mineral oil) and is directed by the Commissioner for Mineral Oil (*Reichsbeauftragter für Mineralöl*), an appointment at present held by Dr. E. R. Fischer. About the end of 1942 the direction was put on a broader basis by the setting up of a " *Lenkungsbereich* " which is a generic term describing the authorities responsible for industrial organization, and includes the various *Reichsstellen* and the trade associations. The *Lenkungsbereich* can now ensure that Fischer's orders are directed without delay to the trade associations. The *Reichsstelle für Mineralöl* is the channel through which decrees affecting the civilian use of oil are issued and is probably responsible for the rationing system which is to some extent put into execution by local authorities.

In September, 1943, the entire control of industrial production in Germany was put into the hands of Speer; consequently all the *Reichsstellen* for various commodities, including the one for oil, take their orders, as far as production is concerned, from the Ministry of Armaments and War Production. Allocations of all war materials are made by the various *Lenkungsbereiche*, apparently acting on principles laid down at a higher level.

(ii) *Natural Oil.*—Production of natural oil is centred in North-West GERMANY at:—

NIENHAGEN—production about 300,000 tons per year.
REITBROOK—production about 300,000 tons per year.
HEIDE—production about 50,000 tons per year.

Total production of natural crude oil in GERMANY for 1942 is estimated at 800,000 tons.

(iii) *Petroleum Refineries.*—Total refining capacity in 1938 was 3,000,000 tons a year. It was centred in the HAMBURG area and in the HANOVER area.

A secondary concentration was on the RHINE and RUHR, chiefly at:—

EMERICH

DORTMUND

DÜSSELDORF

Imports were refined at REGENSBURG.

(iv) *Synthetic Oil* (GERMANY'S main source of oil supply).—Principal synthetic oil plants:—

Location	Name of Plant	Estimated annual capacity (1,000 tons p.a.)
Bergius Hydrogenation Plants—		
Leuna-Merseburg	Ammoniawerke Merseburg GmbH ...	400
Pölitz-Stettin	Hydrierwerke AG	400
Scholven-Buer/Ruhr ...	Hydrierwerke Scholven Hibernia AG	350
Gelsenkirchen/Ruhr ...	Gelsenkirchen-Benzin AG	325
Troglitz-Zeitz	Braunkohle-Benzin AG	320
Magdeburg...	Braunkohle-Benzin AG	300
Wesseling	Union Rheinische Braunkohlen Kraftstoff AG	250
Böhlen-Rotha	Braunkohle-Benzin AG	200
Lutzendorf Mücheln ...	Wintershall AG	125
Welheim Bottrop-Ruhr ...	Buhröl GmbH	100
Blechhammer/Silesia—		
(*a*) North	IG Farbenindustrie	750
(*b*) South	IG Farbenindustrie	750
Fischer Tropsch Plants—		
Ruhland-Schwarzheide ...	Braunkohle-Benzin AG	400
Lutzendorf-Mücheln ...	Wintershall AG	200
Rauxel/Ruhr	Klockner-Wintershall AG	200
Homberg/Ruhr	Treibstoffabrik Rheinpreussen ...	200
Holten/Ruhr	Ruhrbenzin AG	130
Nanne-Eickel/Ruhr ...	Krupp Treibstoffwerke	130
Dortmund/Ruhr	Hoesch-Benzin GmbH	130
Deschowitz...	Schaffgotsch'sche Benzin GmbH ...	110
Kamen Dortmund/Ruhr ...	Chemischewerke Essener Steinkohle AG	50

Oil Storage.—The following list indicates the storage capacity available at the principal oil storage centres. In each of the town areas it is distributed over a number of individual plants, but in no case is it possible to give even an estimate of the actual quantities which are likely to be in storage.

Place								*Capacity in tons*
Berlin ...	...	...	...	...	...	...	...	68,900
Bremen	...	...	...	...	...	...	...	748,800
Bremerhaven ...	...	...	...	...	...	...	...	459,700
Danzig	...	...	...	...	...	...	...	5,800
Duisburg	...	...	...	...	...	...	...	66,500
Düsseldorf	...	...	...	...	...	...	...	31,800
Emden	...	...	...	...	...	...	...	43,500
Frankfurt/Main	...	...	...	...	...	...	...	141,200
Hamburg	...	...	...	...	...	...	...	1,361,200
Hanover	...	...	...	...	...	...	...	287,300
Kiel ...	...	...	...	...	...	...	...	737,300
Köln ...	...	...	...	...	...	...	...	14,000
Münich	...	...	...	...	...	...	...	69,000
Rostock	...	...	...	...	...	...	...	11,000
Stettin	...	...	...	...	...	...	...	187,000
Stuttgart	...	...	...	...	...	...	...	17,500
Wilhelmshaven	...	...	...	...	...	...	...	221,000

The following underground army oil storage depots are definitely known to be in use:—

Place				*Capacity in tons*
Hitzacker (Lüneburger Heide) ...	...	...	...	2,400,000
This depot consists of 114 " holes " or " departments ", each of which contains five storage tanks.				
Farge (14 miles NW of Bremen) ...	...	...	...	340,000
Nienburg (Lüneburger Heide) ...	...	...	...	193,200
Loccum (Lüneburger Heide) ...	...	...	...	15,600

These figures are by no means complete but they represent the locations of the principal depots. Few details of air damage are available.

(b) *Military supplies of POL in Germany.*—(i) It is not yet clear to what extent the civilian system of POL distribution and storage in Germany is bound up with the military supply system. Production, as outlined in the previous section, is now directly subordinate to the Ministry of Armaments and War Production.

(ii) The Army MT parks, and, to an even greater extent the home MT parks provide MT companies and supply staffs among whose principal duties are the setting up and administration of filling stations. The petrol depots and dumps at GHQ level are normally underground installations—the Lüneburger Heide is known to have many such depots. Other depots are located at those centres enumerated in paragraph (a) above. Administration for military purposes at these depots falls broadly into two divisions. The first is the despatch by rail (under the administration of the *Lenkungsbereiche* and the Army supply staffs combined), of consignments of POL to the field. The second is the distribution of POL to filling stations for the purpose of supply to garrison units. The supply staffs provide written instructions for this latter purpose and a system of petrol vouchers (*Tankscheine*) is maintained, whereby units draw petrol each day from the filling stations. As already outlined in section 1 (b) (ii), most units depend upon the filling stations for their reserves of POL. All vehicles' tanks are filled up each night, and each unit keeps a reserve of so many consumption units (*Verbrauchssätze*), a consumption unit being the amount of fuel requried to take each and all of the formation's vehicles 100 km (60 miles).

(iii) Military supply of POL from Germany to the field is based both on direct export by rail from Germany to a forward line of tank installations, and on indirect supply, mostly by rail and heavy lorries through main GHQ reserves which are served by water and by rail and which may amount to some 3,000,000 gallons each. Under GHQ, fuel supplies are kept in tanks or as mobile reserves on tanker trains. The latter system is almost certainly a little used resource, for it is scarcely credible that considerable numbers of valuable tanker wagons should be tied up in this way. It would appear to give way normally to stocks of the 200 litre (44 gallons) containers. Army reserves take the form mainly of dumps of 200 litre (44 gallons) containers, though, in rare cases, mobile reserves on trains appear to be under Army as well as under GHQ. Divisional dumps are served by rail and road from Army dumps and from forward GHQ tankage, and advanced petrol points by road (containers of 200 litres (44 gallons), 50 litres (11 gallons) and 20 litres (4½ gallons)). The majority of important petrol depots are sited along the best roads.

(iv) The consumption of motor fuels by the Armed Forces (*Wehrmacht and Waffen SS*) is not subject to the restrictions applying to motor fuel consumption in the Reich in general.

Liquid fuels may be supplied only against order forms which must be signed by Military District or Naval Station HQ (*Wehrkreiskommando* or *Marinestationkommando*) or against *Wehrmacht* vouchers.

(v) Liquid gas fuel is issued against gas control vouchers bearing the stamp " W ".

(vi) *Wehrmacht* vouchers are only issued by the following offices :—

Central Office for Mineral Oil Ltd, Berlin (*Zentralbüro für Mineralöl GmbH*).

Mineral Oil Distribution Warthe District Ltd, Posen (*Mineralölvertrieb Warthegau GmbH*).

Mineral Oil Distribution Vistula District Ltd, Danzig (*Mineralölvertrieb Weichselgau GmbH*).

Central Agency of the accredited distributing firms in the protectorate of Bohemia and Moravia. (*Blockaktion der zugelassenen Verteiler firmen im Protektorat Böhmen und Mähren*).

(vii) Deliveries of motor fuels against *Wehrmacht* vouchers can only be made if, at the same time, the following certificates are being produced :—

The usual travel permit issued for the various formations and units of the *Wehrmacht*.

The travel permit book for " motor vehicles temporarily used by the *Wehrmacht* ".

The travel permit of the *Waffen SS* accompanying the requisitioning papers for motor vehicles issued by Defence Reserve Inspectors (*Wehrersatzinspektionen*) marked on the top right corner with an italic " K " or " KK ".

(c) *Substitute fuels.*—(i) It is known that substitute fuels are used to a considerable extent in Germany. The various substitute fuels are as follows :—

Producer gas from wood, coal, coke, peat-coke, charcoal, etc.

Permanent gases, including natural gas (geological methane), sewage gas (biological methane) and town gas (from gas works or coke plants).

Liquid gases such as propane and butane.

Acetylene (not in common use in Europe).

(ii) According to a decree published in Germany in September, 1943, all restrictions previously placed on the conversion of vehicles to producer gas were " cancelled ". It now appears that this referred to the types of vehicles permitted to be converted or excluded from the general conversion order, and not to the unrestricted manufacture of producer-gas units, which presumably remains strictly controlled. In brief, all civilian and a proportion of military vehicles are to be converted to operate on substitute fuels. The statement has recently appeared in the German Press, for example, that all civilian motor traffic, as well as a large number of *Wehrmacht* vehicles, are to be run exclusively on solid fuels or gas. The article continues that the conversion that has so far taken place has saved Germany many hundreds of thousands of tons of liquid fuel, although it has applied so far only to the heavier vehicles. Now, however, passenger cars, taxis, ambulances, hearses, vans, lorries of all kinds, tractors and buses are to be converted; in addition, subsidies are to be granted for the conversion of machines used in constructional work such as compressors, surface-levelling machines, and traction units operating on rails. Petrol allowances will be available mainly for vehicles owned by municipalities, presumably such as fire engines and certain vehicles engaged in ARP work. The Reich Minister of Transport has issued detailed instructions regarding conversions to be carried out, including the type of fuel and generator to be used on the various vehicles. Generally speaking, the lighter type of vehicle, particularly cars and light delivery vans, will use high-pressure gas or producer gas from charcoal; cars of over 2 litres capacity will use producer gas, excluding that made from charcoal; buses will generally operate on town gas, both high and low pressure; the remaining types of vehicles will be converted to producer gas, excluding that made from charcoal, which is reserved for cars and vans.

(iii) This new drive to convert vehicles to operate on substitute fuels has undoubtedly required a great deal of organizing, and has greatly increased the demand for wood. Much publicity has lately been given in the German Press to the urgent need to increase the collection of wood and to economize in the use of firewood, which is now referred to as ranking in importance with petrol, coal and iron; particular stress is laid on its importance as a generator fuel.

Generators are to be fuelled with wood either in the form of raw blocks or as charcoal. In addition, as wood supplies are insufficient, other solid fuels, such as brown coal, anthracite, and low-temperature coke must be used. Charcoal and peat coke will be available only in limited areas.

Considerable details regarding the processing of wood fuel have recently been published. The preparation of wood is carried out by private enterprise, the wood blocks being sold to the *Generatorkraft AG*. This company owns a development plant which is responsible for the development of a technique suitable to the preparation of wood fuel for vehicles. Charcoal fulfils the dual role of being a fuel for use on cars and vans, and as an auxiliary to wood fuel; in the latter case the charcoal is referred to as a reducing fuel. It is placed in the bottom of the generator, filling about half the space below the tuyeres. Wood blocks are then placed on top to fill the remaining space in the hopper. The charcoal bed, reaching a high temperature in less time than the wood, enables a more efficient conversion of the carbon dioxide gas to carbon monoxide to take place. The charcoal bed would also be beneficial in abstracting the liquid fractions given off by the wood, thus simplifying the duty of the filtration system. Whilst there had been previous evidence of the use of charcoal in the base of the

Imbert generator, particularly in the occupied territories, it had not previously been realized that its use was general in Germany. It is believed that this is a development of recent origin in the latter country, and is closely associated with the endeavour to obtain easier starting and cleaner gas whilst having to use inferior wood fuel. The use of charcoal does not necessitate any modification of the Imbert generator.

(iv) It has been stated that charcoal was chosen as the fuel for cars and vans because it offers the least difficulties to the driver, and it is hoped that the opposition hitherto existing among car drivers accustomed to the use of liquid fuel will be overcome. The conversion of these vehicles to operate on charcoal has necessitated the design of a light-weight generator unit. In collaboration with the NSKK the Generator Board was reported in October, 1943, to have completed the testing of 30 generators submitted for cars; the one type selected by the committee of experts for large-scale production was to be announced later. It is evident that the conversion of cars had not been started at that time, although it had been authorized; it is stated that the date on which conversion is to begin will be announced when the preliminary organization and testing have been completed. A list of filling stations is also to be published; it is expected that solid fuel supply stations, under the control of the *Generatorkraft AG* will be located at distances of 50-60 km. throughout Greater Germany. There are two types of station: the main supply station deals in large quantities and supplies regular customers; and the so-called tanking station, dealing in small quantities, supplies passing traffic. Regional distribution of fuel will also be organized in order to reduce transport; for example, wood or charcoal will be supplied in forest areas, mineral fuels in the mining areas.

(v) *Alterations to engine, etc.*—It is likely that alterations will be of the simplest possible nature (which often involves a loss in efficiency). It appears also that re-conversion to petrol has always been a carefully considered feature in design.

Petrol engines.—Operation on producer gas is similar to that on petrol. The carburettor must be by-passed with the gas pipe and the ignition advanced to allow for slower burning of the gas. The accelerator is disconnected from the carburettor and connected up to the gas line. The gap on the sparking plugs should be increased/decreased. There are also various pipe connections. These are the necessary alterations. Others not likely to be encountered are alterations to cylinder and fitting of new pistons, both to boost efficiency.

Diesel engines.—Self-ignition cannot be achieved with a gaseous fuel. The Germans appear to have adopted a partial conversion known as the " gas diesel ". This involves reducing the volume of liquid fuel injected to about one-third the normal requirement, producer gas being drawn in in place of air. (If this were not done, it would be necessary to have distributor, sparking plugs, etc).

Permanent gases.—It is not considered necessary to make any changes when converting a petrol vehicle except the introduction of new pipes, and the cutting off of petrol supply and changing accelerator control.

Liquid gases—as in permanent gases.

Acetylene—as in permanent gases.

(vi) *Efficiency of Substitute Fuels* (compared with petrol).

Producer gas.—Converted petrol engine. Efficiency is reduced for hill climbing purposes; power and average running speeds are lower. This has been referred to in England as " Running one gear less on producer gas ".

If increased running time of 15 per cent per day is available, no serious loss in ten-miles per day is likely to be experienced. The tractive power is not sufficient for very rough ground. 60 per cent efficiency of petrol may be expected.

If the generator is carried on the vehicle, there will be a loss of 10-25 per cent in the maximum load due to the floor space occupied. There is, of course no loss if the generator is on a trailer.

The gas normally is not pure even after passing through the filtration stages in the generator. Small particles and acids not held in the filter cause an increased wear on the moving parts of the engine, particularly piston rings, valves, etc. This also means that maintenance becomes increasingly important. It is estimated that a half-hour per day is needed for the generator and its accessories, and an additional three hours per week for cleaning filters and servicing.

Converted diesel engines: the loss due to the smaller amount of liquid fuel being used is almost entirely offset by the use of producer gas instead of air. Power output is about 90 per cent of that achieved with normal fuel.

A certain amount of training is necessary for drivers. They must be taught how to tend to the generator, light it, and obtain maximum efficiency from it. Also controls must be explained. Diagrams of the generator and controls are available for the German Imbert and other types, and of the generator for all of the French types. The Imbert is the standard type in the German Army.

In general, generator fuels are not interchangeable. This is due chiefly to the fact that the filters are designed for particular purposes, *e.g.*, to remove the tar content from wood produced gas. Trouble from the filter and trouble in starting, etc, may result, therefore, from using the wrong fuel.

Permanent gases.—There is little or no loss of efficiency on converting petrol engines to use with pure Methane. Town gas involves a loss of 10 per cent. If steel bottles are used, the increased weight causes loss of carrying capacity. Range for steel bottles is 60/40 miles. Gas bag storage reduces this range considerably. Engine running is flexible with easy starting from cold; no increase in running time need be allowed. Use of permanent gas effects 30 per cent economy in oil consumption, lengthening the life of the engine, maintenance being normal.

Liquid gases.—Performance is equal to that on petrol. Power at lower speeds is greater than that on petrol. The weight of the bottles lowers carrying capacity, but this is offset by increased range and lower consumption of fuel.

Acetylene performance is 5 per cent less than that of petrol. When a generator is used 15 lbs carbide are equivalent to 1 gallon of petrol (*i.e.*, same range). Greater range with increased power can be obtained with solvent acetylene in bottles; chief disadvantage is increased lubricating requirements and engine wear.

(vii) *Reconversion from producer gas to petrol.*—It is almost certain that all vehicles manufactured since 1941 will be capable of rapid re-conversion to petrol fuel. This is the result of German control, a policy dictated by military considerations, *i.e.*, requisition of civilian vehicles by the *Wehrmacht* in operations. In the German Imbert type generator, as used by the *Wehrmacht,* it is possible to return to petrol fuel by simply turning a cock at the carburettor, or in the case of diesel conversions to pure diesel fuel, by means of a relatively small alteration. It is believed that for nearly all other types, the re-conversion is achieved by some such simple means. This applies also to civilian vehicles in France, Belgium, Holland and Germany.

(viii) *Use of substitute fuels in German army vehicles.*—Wood or charcoal are the fuels used by the German Army, and to a lesser extent peat or coke, depending upon the area in which the vehicles are working.

The first reference to the use of producer gas in military vehicles was early in 1942. At the end of 1942 there was a definite conversion programme in hand. This affected the conversion of vehicles in the Occupied Territories of France, Belgium and Holland. Conversion to *producer gas only* was considered, and the *Imbert type was standard;* the conversion was done locally.

There is no direct evidence to indicate the number of vehicles likely to be converted. Re-conversion to petrol is rapid and simple.

A German Army technical publication of October, 1943, mentions that the conversion of a considerable number of *Wehrmacht* vehicles to a generator system has been ordered. This is to save fuel for operational purposes. It is known that the extent to which the conversion is being effected has recently increased considerably. Much of the transport of lower grade formations in the West has now been converted. The Todt Organization use locally requisitioned vehicles to a considerable extent, and are not allowed to use petrol fuel.

Nearly all German lorries in Holland, *both diesel and petrol* have been fitted with German built Imbert wood burning gas plants. During the first year of the war, many Dutch users had Imbert wood burning plants, but they cannot use them as the Germans need all the wood supplies. The Dutch now have plants working on peat coke or coal. The Germans have requisitioned the largest petrol pump stations generally with repair garages. They have one or two such stations in each large town. They can refuel there with wood or petrol.

Fuel consumption, brown coal, coke 100 lbs = 100 miles.

Wood	130 lbs = 100 miles.
Charcoal	70 lbs = 100 miles.
Anthracite	70 lbs = 100 miles.

4. *Rations.*

(a) *System for the Armed Forces.*—(i) The German Army has always possessed a static supply organization which forms a basis for the more extensive system required in wartime. In the OKH there is an Army Administration Department (*Heeresverwaltungsamt*) which is responsible, *inter alia,* under the direction of the Head of Army Supply, for the general survey and organization of the supply of rations. This department directs the flow of rations supply from the manufacturers and other sources of production to the base rations stores (*Ersatz Verpflegungs Magazine* or EVM). The GAF still does not possess a parallel higher organization and consequently the Army has taken over all food supply for the whole of the GAF. Thus the EVMs serve both Army and GAF units. These EVMs were formed on the outbreak of war from the Army Rations Main Depots (*Heeresverpflegungshauptämter*) which already existed in peace-time and many of which still remain. The EVMs have an average capacity of one month's rations for 300,000 men. They are distributed throughout Reich territory and at present there are about 40 of them. The main ones are given in the list at the end of this section. They control a certain number of Army Rations depots which are of two main types, the HVA and HV Haupt A, that is to say Army Rations Depot (*Heeresverpflegungsamt*) and the Army Rations Main Depot (*Heeresverpflegungshauptamt*). This decentralization of stocks of food has the advantage that the best use can be made of supply firms and that food stocks in bulk do not have to be moved considerable distances at short notice. The principal differences between the EVMs and the Army Depots is that the former are not merely larger but that they normally have a large bakery attached and are invariably rail-served, whereas the Army depots, the HVAs and the HV Haupt As have no bakery and may not always be rail-served. Decentralization may be carried even further and an HVA may have branch depots (*Nebenstellen*). The *Heeresverpflegungshauptamt* at INNSBRUCK, for example looks after all the garrison troops of the TIROL-VORARLBERG of Wehrkreis XVIII, all newly set up or assembled units in the area, travelling-rations and iron-rations of departing units and rations for escort personnel for supply trains, in addition to supplying certain field formations when called upon to do so. The Red Cross canteen in the main station at INNSBRUCK also gets its allocation of rations from this depot. In no case, however, does the depot supply fresh bread or fresh meat, which units must obtain from civilian bakers and butchers. The depot has a number of branch depots (*Nebenstellen*), the number varying from time to time according to need, and it keeps these branch depots supplied with two months' rations for the specific number of units served by each branch depot. The permanent staff of the *Heeresverpflegungshauptamt* at INNSBRUCK as about 50 men.

The next stage in the chain of rations supply is the Army Rations Dump (*Armee Verpflegungslager* or AVL). These appear, naturally, in operational zones, and the whole aspect of rations supply under active operations is treated in Part II of this book under the heading "Rations supply in theatres of active operations" (qv). For basic military rations scales, *see* paragraph (*c*) (i), below.

(*b*) *Civilian system.*—(i) Food rationing in Germany is under the control of the Reich Minister of Food and Agriculture who issues all decrees in connection therewith. Under his direction operate Provincial (*or State*) Food Offices which in turn supervise the activities of the local Food Offices (*Ernährungsämter*).

The latter are divided into two sections. Section A deals with the control of supplies, *i.e.*, production and marketing, most economic use of local products, efficiency of firms and provision of seeds, fertilizers and plant. Section B deals with consumption and rationing, estimates requirements, distributes ration cards and fixes shopping hours. It is staffed by officials of the ordinary local government service.

Practically every article of food is rationed, either on a national basis or by a system of local distribution. The foods nationally rationed are bread, flour, *Nährmittel* (cereal products, alimentary pastes, potato flour, sago, etc.), meat, fats, cheese, sugar, jam, coffee substitute, eggs, cocoa, artificial honey and whole milk. Cocoa and artificial honey are reserved for children and whole milk for children, expectant, lying-in and nursing mothers and workers in certain unhealthy occupations. Locally rationed foods include potatoes, vegetables, fruit, fish, poultry, sweets and skimmed milk.

(ii) The rationing or distribution period is 28 days. All ration quantities are quoted for this period (except milk which is a daily ration) and the weekly ration is simply one-fourth. Separate cards (actually sheets of paper) of distinctive colours are issued to normal consumers for bread (and flour), "*Nährmittel*", meat, fats (including cheese), sugar and jam, eggs and milk. Coupons for cocoa and artificial honey are on the children's fats card and coupons for coffee substitute are on the " *Nährmittel* " card. Separate cards are issued for children and supplementary cards for night workers, heavy and very heavy workers. Thus the German housewife handles a large number of cards. A family consisting of man (heavy worker), wife (expectant) and two children aged 10 and 5, gets 43 separate cards, besides any local cards for the distribution of unrationed foods.

Each card has a main portion (" *Stammabschnitt* ") on which is printed the number of the distribution period, period of validity, title of card, the Nazi Eagle and in the case of a city, the city's coat of arms, the name of the Food Office, serial number and directions regarding the use of the card. Space is provided for insertion of holder's name and address. The rest of the card consists of coupons on which are printed the name of the foodstuffs, the quantity purchaseable and the validity of the coupon. Certain cards also have order vouchers (*Bestellscheine*) for the use of the retailer in obtaining his immediate requirements. Order vouchers are confined to the fats, sugar and jam, egg and milk cards. When the retailer detaches this voucher from the card he merely cancels the customer's coupons. Coupons of cards without order vouchers are detached. When there is an order voucher on the card, the customer is tied to his retailer for the distribution period. Otherwise he can purchase where he chooses.

One method of distribution of cards is for the " *Blockwärt* " (party official responsible for A.R.P. and other services of a block of flats or dwelling area) to collect old cards, notify the Food Office of any changes in his area and distribute the new cards. When this is not practicable, announcements are made through the press when and where new cards may be collected by consumers themselves.

Coupons and order vouchers surrendered to retailers and coupons given up to restaurant keepers are exchanged at the Food Office for buying permits with which to make purchases from wholesalers. Wholesalers, in turn, receive in exchange for these buying vouchers, other buying permits for purchases from manufacturers. Butchers are allotted quotas in accordance with their current sales and records are kept at the Food Office of quantities of meat and fat supplied and quantities accounted for by surrendered coupons.

(iii) Travel and restaurant stamps (*Reisemarken*) are issued mainly for the convenience of foreign visitors, but may also be used by travellers in Germany. They are printed in sheets of 100 like postage stamps. The visitor is given a supply at the frontier, sufficient for a few days and renews his stock through the hotel proprietor or by direct application to the Food Office. Travellers are given a supply sufficient for the duration of their journey.

These stamps are for small quantities of bread, meat, butter and margarine, " *Nährmittel* " and cheese. No stamps are issued for jam, sugar, eggs or substitute coffee as certain quantities of these foodstuffs are supplied to hotels and restaurants. Stamps called " *Lebensmittelmarken* " are also issued to certain consumers like persons without a permanent residence and to persons entitled to special rations such as sick people, expectant and nursing mothers, blood donors, vegetarians, etc.

Restaurants, as already mentioned, received limited quantities of sugar, jam, eggs and substitute coffee. For all other rationed foods served food coupons must be surrendered. Every restaurant must provide daily at least one coupon-free dish at a prescribed maximum price according to the class of restaurant. This dish may be prepared from a range of unrationed foods like vegetables, fish, poultry, rabbit, etc. Any cuttings of meat and fat from the kitchen may be used in the preparation of these dishes.

(16779)   B

(iv) Consumers are divided into the following classes:—
Normal consumers,
Light workers,
Night and long hour workers,
Heavy workers,
Very heavy workers,
Children under 3, Children 3 to 6,
Children 6 to 10,
Children and Adolescents 10 to 20.

Separate scales of rations are given to each of these classes. Special rations are also given to expectant, lying-in and nursing mothers, sick persons, blood donors, vegetarians, diabetics, human milk donors, harvest workers, etc. Miners get extra supplies of locally rationed potatoes and workers in certain chemical industries get a ration of whole milk. Whole milk is otherwise exclusively reserved for children, expectant, lying-in and nursing mothers. Special rations are also granted for family celebrations, cooking classes, etc.

(v) Apart from the national rationing plan, systems of local distribution of unrationed foods are in force in all the large towns. A potato card is issued for a total period covering six four-weeks rationing periods and the amounts purchaseable are announced from time to time. Rations in bulk are obtainable in advance for storing when sufficient supplies are available. Skimmed milk is distributed in communes of over 10,000 inhabitants to consumers over six years of age by means of buying permits which also cover six rationing periods. Local cards are issued for the purchase of fruit and vegetables. Large cities like Berlin and Hamburg have a comprehensive system of local rationing by means of buying permits called *Bezugsausweise*. Practically every kind of unrationed food can be distributed with these cards and announcements regarding distributions are published in the local Press.

(vi) Collective Feeding is provided by canteens, factory kitchens and communal restaurants for the benefit of the large numbers of workers who are away from home for long periods to enable them to have at least one hot meal during the daytime.

Canteens in public offices and works are organized and conducted by the superior officials or the management may be allocated to a lessee. When this is not practicable a contract may be made with an independent restaurant under proper supervision. Free water, fuel, gas and electricity may be granted by the local authorities for the preparation of hot food and drinks provided that the saving effected is applied to lowering the prices charged for meals. In the cases of small offices and works where the provision of a canteen is not possible, the canteen of another office or works may be used.

Fixed prices are charged for meals and these prices may be reduced by the grant of rebate coupons, the difference in cost being borne out of the finances of the office or works. Coupons must be given up for rationed food served.

Factory kitchens are given special distributions of rationed and unrationed foods such as flour, " *Nährmittel* ", sugar, coffee substitute, eggs, skimmed milk, pulses, etc. Additional allowances are made to factories engaged on war work and special distributions are granted in the case of undertakings engaged in the manufacture of explosives. These kitchens are mainly used by heavy workers who are in possession of supplementary ration cards intended, in fact, for use in obtaining meals in such establishments. Communal Restaurants are provided for these workers and officials who have no facilities for using factory kitchens or canteens. The arrangement is for the restaurant to place itself entirely or partially at the disposal of a local war work firm and provide hot meals on similar lines to those provided in factory canteens. The firm collects from its employees food coupons and cash which are handed over to the restaurant in exchange for meal cards.

No attempt has been made to introduce communal feeding generally, but the result of air raids have forced the authorities to encourage the expansion of all existing forms of communal feeding in the bombed areas. Air raid victims are cared for and fed by a special branch of the N-S party in co-operation with the Welfare Organization.

In addition to the above forms of communal feeding, there are welfare kitchens for old people, workers camps for the use of workers drawn from all parts of the Reich and foreign workers, day nurseries and Hitler Youth camps.

(vii) Producers of rationed foods, as self-suppliers, are entitled to retain for their own consumption and that of their family and regular workers special scales of rations as follows:—

> Grain producers get special rations of bread grain. Livestock slaughterers receive a combined meat and fats ration (exclusive of butter, of which they get the normal ration). Milk producers receive from the creameries to whom they deliver their milk special rations of butter. They may also retain certain quantities of milk. Poultry keepers retain the produce of 1½ hens for the consumption of each member of their household. Sugar beet growers draw from the factory to which they deliver their beet a special annual ration of sugar. They are also entitled to extra sugar by way of premium according to the quantity of beet delivered. Oilseed growers receive a yearly ration of oil, provided they renounce their margarine, fat and edible oil coupons and deliver the prescribed quantity of seed required by the regulations.

All classes of self-suppliers get normal consumers' rations of any rationed foodstuffs which they do not produce.

(*c*) *Ration Scales.*—(i) *Military Ration Scales.* (Basic only.)—Scales of rations have varied somewhat from time to time during the war but the following scale for soldiers, in ounces per week, was current during the greater part of 1943 and represented a fairly stable basis for calculation.

Commodity	Front Line Tps	Garrison Tps
	ozs per week	ozs per week
Bread	147	142½
Meat	47¼	26
Fats (butter, margarine, lard)	8¾	6½
Sugar	10	10
Jam	10½	14
Coffee substitute	7	7
Cheese	4⅛	4⅛
Rice...	3½	3½
Pulses	4½	Nil
Potatoes	282	317
Fresh vegetables	50	29
Bratling (a kind of savoury)	5½	10¾
Shell fish	3½	3½

Soldiers up to 21 years old receive an additional 23½ ozs. of bread and 6 of meat a week.

(ii) *Civilian Ration Scales.*—Civilians' scales of rations have varied much more widely than military ration scales and they are based on the classification of consumers given in para. 6, sub-para. (iv) above. The following is the most recent scale and represents a fair average of the ration scales for the last twelve or eighteen months. Note that:—

NC   = Normal consumer.
LW   = Light worker
HW   = Heavy worker.
VHW = Very heavy worker.
NW   = Night and long hours worker.
Ch   = Children.
Ad   = Adolescents.

Classification of Consumer	Bread	Meat	Sugar	Fats	Milk	Skimmed milk
	ozs per week	ozs per week	ozs per week	ozs per week	pts per week	pts per week
NC	85	9	8	8	...	...
NW	109	16	8	8¼	...	...
HW	134	21	8	11½	...	...
VHW ...	169	30	8	21	...	...
Ch under 3 ...	44	3½	8	4½	9	...
Ch 3—6	48	3½	8	7	6	...
Ch 6—10	70	10½	8	10	...	...
Ch and Ad 10—20	97	10½	8	10	...	...
Expectant mothers	...	...	...	...	6	...
Nursing mothers...	...	...	...	...	6	...
Men in unhealthy occupations	...	...	...	...	6	...
Ch 6—14	...	...	...	...	3	...
NC and others ...	...	...	...	...	...	2

It will be seen that heavy civilian workers receive approximately the same rations as soldiers on garrison duty

Other rationed foodstuffs are flour, cakes and pastries, cheese (1¾ oz per wk), curds (1½ oz per wk), jam (6 oz per wk), *Nährmittel* (5 oz per wk), artificial honey (1½ oz per wk), eggs (2 per month), coffee substitute (2 oz per wk). There is local rationing of potatoes, fruit, vegetables, fish and sweets.

LUXEMBOURG and ALSACE have the same rations as the REICH.

(d) *Principal armed forces rations depots in Greater Germany.*—

Wkr I ...	HVA		PREUSSISCH-EYLAU.
Wkr IV ...	EVM		DRESDEN controls HVA BAUTZEN and HVA CHEMNITZ.
	EVM		LEIPZIG.
	HV Haupt A ...		DRESDEN.
	HV Haupt A ...		PLAUEN.
Wkr V ...	EVM		ULM.
	EVM		AALEN.
Wkr VI ...	HV Haupt A ...		MÜNSTER.
	EVM		MÜNSTER.
Wkr VII ...	EVM		MUNCHEN.
	HV Haupt A ...		AUGSBURG.

Wkr VIII	EVM	... ...	BRESLAU controls HV Haupt A OPPELN.
	EVM	... ...	LIEGNITZ controls HV Haupt A SCHWEIDNITZ and HVA BUNZLAU.
	HV Haupt A	...	GLOGAU.
	HV Haupt A	...	LIEGNITZ.
Wkr IX ...	EVM	... ...	FRANKFURT (MAIN) controls HVA ASCHAFFENBURG and HV Haupt A HANAU.
	HV Haupt A	...	FRANKFURT (LAHN).
Wkr X ...	HV Haupt A	...	LÜBECK.
	HV Haupt A	...	BREMEN.
	EVM	... ...	HAMBURG.
	EVM	... ...	BREMEN.
Wkr XI ...	HVA	... ...	RATHENOW.
	HV Haupt A	...	HILDESHEIM.
	HVA	... ...	FRIEDRICHSBRUNN.
Wkr XII ...	EVM	... ...	MAINZ controls HV Haupt A DARMSTADT and HV Haupt A KAISERSLAUTERN.
	EVM	... ...	METZ (Lorraine) controls HV Haupt A TRIER and HVA BAUMHOLDER.
	HV Haupt A	...	KOBLENZ.
	HV Haupt A	...	MAINZ.
	HV Haupt A	...	MANNHEIM.
	HV Haupt A	...	METZ.
	HVA	... ...	LANDAU.
Wkr XIII	EVM	... ...	BAMBERG.
	HVA	... ...	GRAFENWÖHR.
Wkr XVII	HVA	... ...	LINZ.
Wkr XVIII	EVM	... ...	GRAZ.
	HV Haupt A	...	INNSBRUCK.
Wkr XX ...	EVM	... ...	DANZIG controls HV Haupt A ELBING and HV Haupt A BROMBERG.
	HVA	... ...	THORN.
	HVA	... ...	KONITZ.
	HVA	... ...	DEUTSCH-EYLAU.
	HVA	... ...	MARIENBURG.
Wkr XXI	EVM	... ...	POSEN controls HV Haupt A LITZMANNSTADT and HVA KALISCH.

Protectorate (Bohemia and Moravia)—

	EVM	... ...	PRAG (operates in Bohemia) controls HVA PARDUBITZ.
	EVM	... ...	OLMÜTZ (operates in Moravia) controls HVA BRÜNN.

Alsace-Lorraine—

	HV Haupt A	...	STRASBURG.
	HV Haupt A	...	METZ. } *see* under Wehrkreis
	EVM	... ...	METZ. } XII.

5. *Motor Transport.*

(*a*) *Civilian Position.*—(i) At the outbreak of war Germany did not compare favourably with several of the other countries so far as the density of her motor traffic was concerned. The beginning of the motorization of Germany coincided with the advent of Hitler and prior to that date the use and technical development of motor vehicles was in a backward state compared with conditions in other leading motor vehicle-producing countries. In spite of the production of motor vehicles being expanded annually, the vehicle density in 1939 did not equal that of other industrialized countries.

(ii) The German lorry output capacity is taken to be 200,000 units per annum although there is no *direct* evidence to support this. It is known that the maximum lorry output for civilian requirements in peace-time was approximately 65,000 units per annum. Military holdings of lorries were negligible at the beginning of 1935 and probably amounted to about 470,000 units by the end of 1939. This increase gives an average annual lorry output of 94,000 units or a total output of 159,000 units per annum. In view of the fact that lorry production for military requirements would be a minimum in 1935 and probably a maximum by 1939, it would appear most probable that the German industry has a production capacity of about 200,000 per annum.

(iii) The estimated total number of vehicles in operation in Germany in 1942 was 1,533,000 including approximately 38 per cent cars and 62 per cent lorries. The civilian vehicles referred to here include all vehicles in operation outside the fighting services, namely vehicles used in the transportation of goods for domestic consumption, or of goods and materials used in connection with the German war effort, including industrial requirements for armaments, and the vehicle holdings of semi-military organizations such as the NSKK and Todt organizations.

(iv) In the campaign in Russia in 1942 and '43, Germany sustained very heavy losses in motor vehicles. The holdings of civilian lorries have been reduced, partly because of the stringent economies practised in the use of liquid fuel and the apparent inability of German industry to manufacture sufficient producer gas units to maintain the industrial transport system at the level of previous years. The rate of loss of military lorries arising from accident and depreciation increased rapidly throughout the year whilst there was heavy loss due to war damage on the Eastern Front. There remained a useful number of lorries in the pool of civilian vehicles at the beginning of the period and some new production was available, at least in the occupied countries. It is possible that by December, 1942, or early in 1943, when the 1942 losses had been replaced that this result was achieved by practically exhausting the pool of useful vehicles. Since then the collapse of Italy materially increased the numbers of vehicles available to Germany.

It is difficult in the absence of any direct evidence to make an accurate estimate of the value of the pool of vehicles to Germany. The fact remains that the pool has been of extreme usefulness to Germany and it is known that some of the occupied countries have been denuded of their vehicles to a marked degree. Holland, for example, has been reported to have lost 70 per cent of her lorries as the result of German requisitioning. In other words, Germany will have continued to add to her industrial fleet of vehicles to maintain its efficiency, whilst the vehicles in the occupied countries will have been steadily decreased in number due to German requisitioning, the effects of the fuel, oil and rubber shortage, and sheer inability to obtain new vehicles in serviceable condition. Many of the less popular civilian makes of vehicle will have been put out of action because spares will not be available. Damaged vehicles are a source of supply for the repair of other vehicles. Bearing all these factors in mind it will be realized that an accurate estimate of the total numbers of vehicles in operation in Europe is not possible.

(v) Requisitioning of civilian transport is arranged through the HQs of the Military Districts (the *Wehrkreise*), or through military staffs (*Kommandanturen*) set up for the purpose in the larger cities. All available commercial vehicles and probably most of the large American private cars. which existed in large numbers in Belgium and Holland have been requisitioned. At the present time many are useless owing to lack of spare parts for it is known that the spare part situation is more serious than the MT situation. Civilian transport on the road is limited to essential purposes. such as for doctors, transport of workers and for industrial purposes. All makes and types of vehicles are still available, including American and some British and Russian cars and lorries. No general requisitioning has been done, and the German intention up to the present is more one of control. The *Kommandanturen,* in most of the larger towns, are known to have made arrangements for lorries to be collected at certain strategic points in the event of Allied invasion.

(vi) The mechanical condition of transport as a whole in Germany and the Occupied Territories is not good and is deteriorating steadily. This is partly due to the general lack of spare parts, to the excessive wear and tear of wartime conditions, and to the fact that the great scarcity of low friction metal has made the repair and overhaul of engines very unsatisfactory.

(b) *Military organization for supply of MT and AFVs.*—(i) Distribution of MT vehicles to the three services is in the hands of the Chief of Motor Transport in the Armed Forces (formerly called General of Motorization, *see* section 1, para. (*a*) (vii)). When, in September, 1943, the entire control of industrial production in Germany was put into the hands of Speer, a MT commission was set up, of which Speer was head. Already, there existed in the Reichsministry for Armaments and War Production a department dealing with " Mechanization " (*Motorisierung*). The War Ministry also contained a similar department. This is part of the Ordnance Branch of the War Office under the Head of Army Supply (*see* chart of the OKH at the beginning of the Handbook) and is called the department for AFVs. and Mechanization (*Abteilung Panzer und Motorisierung*). One man, Col. Holzhäuer, at the present time holds both of the appointments of Head of the Department for AFVs and Mechanization in the War Office and the Head of the Department for Mechanization in the Reichsministry for Armaments and War Production. He is also chairman of the MT commission under Speer.

This apparent duplication of effort as well as of responsibility, is at first very confusing, but in practice it works out as follows. On the one hand is the civil organization of trade design and production harnessed to the German war effort under Speer. A link between production and military requirements had to be established, and that link is Col. Holzhäuer, On the other hand the distribution and storage of vehicles, as well as their utilization within the armed forces, is dealt with by the Chief of Motor Transport in the Armed Forces who has liaison with the Inspector General of Mechanization in the War Office as well as with Col. Holzhäuer.

As in all other matters, the Head of Army Supply has nominal control of supply of MT and AFVs within Reich territory proper and certain of the occupied territories, and the QMG has control of the supply in the field.

(ii) The Ordnance depots hold only certain MT equipment, that which is not essentially part of a vehicle, but certain depots which are normally termed ordnance depots hold MT only. AFVs are held at Magdeburg-Königsborn which is the principal tank depot or at one of the branch depots given in the list in section 2 (*g*) (iv) above. The huge MT depot at Oranienburg, north of Berlin, of which an air photograph is shown among the illustrations at the end of Part I of the Handbook is probably the largest of its kind. As Oranienburg is the principal supply base of the *Waffen SS,* it is possible that this MT depot serves both the Army and the *Waffen SS*, or possibly the depot itself functions in two broad divisions—one part for the Army, the other for the *Waffen SS*.

(iii) The system of MT parks is the basis of the whole MT supply and maintenance organization. Some facts about these parks are given in Part II, section 16 (*b*) of the Handbook. There are three types of MT park. The first is the home MT Park (*Heimat Kraftfahrpark*), the second is the GHQ MT Park (*Heeres Kraftfahrpark*), and the third is the Army MT Park (*Armee Kraftfahrpark-AKP*). As GHQ and Army MT parks belong, properly speaking, to supply in the field, they are dealt with in Part II, section 16, but it is as well to speak here concerning the abbreviations which the Germans use for these parks. For a long time confusion was caused by the fact that the Germans used the abbreviation HKP for both home and GHQ parks. Some sources still use this abbreviation for both, but it would now appear fairly general that the GHQ Park is abbreviated HeKP (*Heeres Kraftfahrpark*) and the Home Park is abbreviated HKP or HaKP (*Heimat Kraftfahrpark*). The home MT parks operate in Germany within their own Wehrkreise and are under the direct control of the Head of Army Supply. Most of the larger firms manufacturing motor vehicles have a MT depot attached to the factory, such depots being called Armed Forces depots with MT Firms (*Wehrmachtlager bei Kraftfahrzeugfirma*) and these depots facilitate transfer of vehicles from factory to park. The GHQ and Army MT Parks are directly under the QMG at GHQ and are similar in constitution and function to the home MT parks. For further details of GHQ and Army MT parks *see* Part II, section 16.

(iv) The diagram of the organization of the home MT Park at Bremen is included because it is typical. It will be seen that the park itself has four main departments and that it has branch departments in neighbouring towns. In the case of HKP, Bremen, the following are the detailed functions of the various departments:—

Dept I The registry, internal administration office, typists, paymaster's office, clothing and arms office, command post and kitchens are all under the direct supervision of Dept I. Some 40 men are employed.

Dept II has three sections, each with 20 men. There are 15 skilled hands in addition who work in any of the three sections at need. Section A handles distribution of commercial and military vehicles, controls the output of reconditioned vehicles and receives government-ordered vehicles. Section B receives vehicles of other categories than government-ordered types, handles all spare parts, and is the section chiefly concerned with repair and maintenance. Section C controls tyres, both new and reconditioned, and is responsible for receiving and reconditioning worn-out tyres.

Dept III has four sections and the total strength of the department is 60 men. Section A procures all spare parts for Dept II and stores them until needed. It also keeps snow-chains, generators, canvas, etc, and has a large card-index file of its stocks. Section B distributes spare parts and Section C keeps the accounts, and checks receipt and issue of spare parts. Section D is responsible for the scrapping of old motor vehicles and the storing of serviceable spare parts.

Dept IV has two sections with a total strength of 50 men. Section A receives motor vehicles from the field and hands out new and reconditioned vehicles, which it stores, pending distribution. Section B is a registry for equipment designated for the field, and is also responsible for the storage of fuel, wood, etc.

The various branch departments are complete in themselves in that they exercise most of the functions of the four departments in Bremen, but they are largely administrative and do not store vehicles, spare parts and equipment, all of which they get from the main park at Bremen. In this particular case, the branch departments are also concerned with MT requirements of the German Navy. Oldenburg has eight personnel, Wilhelmshaven 6, Aurich 5, and Bremerhaven 5.

(v) The park itself is essentially a clearing depot and the work consists mainly of keeping records of incoming and outgoing vehicles and of storage. The main functions of the park are to examine the damaged vehicles passed back from the field and to decide whether they should be repaired or scrapped; and to receive and distribute new vehicles. The majority of badly damaged vehicles do not remain in the park for repair for long periods. Most of such vehicles are passed out to approved workshops. At Bremen, for example, the principal shop to which work is passed out is the road vehicle repair shop associated with the railway wagon repair shops. The controlling factor in deciding whether vehicles should be repaired or scrapped is the availability of spare parts. The parks handle commercial vehicles in addition to purely military vehicles. Bremen park, in 1942, received about 1,500 damaged vehicles, mainly from the Eastern Front, with about 500 engines in addition. Of these vehicles less than half were repaired, the rest being scrapped and " cannibalized ". Of the damaged vehicles brought in rather less than 50 per cent were German and about 35 per cent were Russian. The rest were of a variety of makes, including American lorries.

(c) *Organization of typical Home MT Park.*

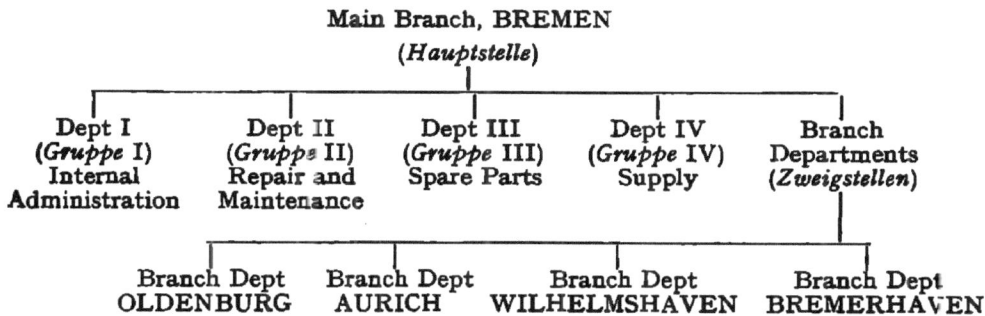

Main Branch, BREMEN
(*Hauptstelle*)

Dept I (*Gruppe* I) Internal Administration	Dept II (*Gruppe* II) Repair and Maintenance	Dept III (*Gruppe* III) Spare Parts	Dept IV (*Gruppe* IV) Supply	Branch Departments (*Zweigstellen*)

| | Branch Dept OLDENBURG | Branch Dept AURICH | Branch Dept WILHELMSHAVEN | Branch Dept BREMERHAVEN |

6. *The Medical system in Germany.*

(a) *Public Health Organization.*—The public health organization in the German Reich is controlled by the State Health Bureau in the Ministry of the Interior. Subsidiary to this are various organizations, the principal of which are the Reich Committee for Public Health, the Reich Health Bureau, and the Red Cross. Under the Ministry of Labour are the departments for Reich Health Insurance and for Reich Land Insurance. In Germany, where universal health insurance is compulsory for all persons, these latter offices have considerable influence in promoting public health measures. These various departments combine to oversee public health activities in the following fields: Infant and school hygiene, industrial hygiene, sanitary measures regarding the distribution and treatment of water and sewage, prevention of epidemics, instruction of public health field officials, inspection of hospitals, and the development of synthetic foods, drugs, and vitamins. Local health measures are activated by officers chosen from the region (*Kreis*). Statutes exist for the legal control of these activities. These

Regional medical officers (*Kreisärzte*) work with the magistrate, the Bürger-meister and the Commissioners of Police. Their duties include:—

(i) Confidential medical duties connected with legal procedure and the sanitation police.

(ii) Provision of health certificates for officials applying for appointments or pensions.

(iii) Supervision and inspection of public institutions including health in schools and prisons.

(iv) Supervision and inspection of bathing pools, spas, food supply, housing plans, water supply and health of women and juveniles in industry.

In 1936 there were, in the Reich, 744 local public health bureaux: of this number, 424 were in Prussia, 139 in Bavaria, and the remainder were distributed, more or less evenly through the other German provinces. The personnel of 22,265 officials and employees included 48 per cent who received full-time employment. On the staff were 7,218 doctors, of whom 15·6 per cent served full-time as public health officials; 3,981 nurses; 326 specialists; 196 deputies; and 444 technical assistants.

(i) *Sanitation.*—The shortage of food or its lowering in calorific value has led to many cases of rickets and other vitamin-deficiency diseases, and probably has been a factor in reducing the increase in the number of cases of tuberculosis reported recently. The lack of raw materials has curtailed the development of new water and sewerage systems, and has rendered it difficult to keep the existing systems in repair. The number of doctors is inadequate for civilian care, and severe local outbreaks of many of the communicable diseases, including scarlet fever, influenza, dysentery, and probably typhus fever, have appeared during the winters of 1942 and '43. The scarcity of soap and the lack of sufficient clothes to allow for clean changes, has resulted in a lowering in the level of personal cleanliness. Troops returning from fronts in Russia and in the African desert have imported cases of diseases not commonly seen in Germany, and have established *foci* for the spread of such diseases through a relatively unprotected population. The shortage of labour has led to the impressing of thousands of persons with open tuberculosis into factories, and school children are required to work a number of hours each week on farms or in industrial plants. Overcrowding is common in the large cities, and to ameliorate this condition many small houses have been built which the State has admitted to be dark, ill-ventilated, and inadequately equipped with sanitary facilities. Bomb damage in the principal cities has undoubtedly had a most serious effect on sanitation systems, and has contributed to the problem of overcrowding.

(ii) *Water.*—In 1937, 70 per cent of the population, including almost all urban dwellers, were served by central-piped water distribution systems. Most of the water was obtained through deep-driven wells; a less commonly utilized source was groundwater. Large cities, such as Hamburg, were the only communities to use water taken from rivers and streams. Adequate facilities for the treatment of the water were to be found in connection with the majority of the distribution systems. Chlorination and filtration are the most commonly utilized purificatory measures. Plumbing in Germany is not so well developed as in this country, and the old fashioned pitcher and bowl will still be found in many modern homes. In many large and medium-sized cities, hot water was piped to the homes by the city or by utility companies, and the use of this commodity is now strictly rationed. Bombing has affected the water supply of towns and less precautions are now taken than formerly to ensure purity of water for domestic purposes.

In rural regions, wells, pumps and cisterns are the principal sources of water. There has also been a marked increase in the number of private wells dug in the towns since the onset of the war, since these serve as emergency sources in the event of the disruption of the main distribution systems during bombings. So great has been the increase in the number of wells that the State organized a well-diggers' school. In most rural communities, wells and cisterns are inspected for nearness to outhouses and human dwellings, for faulty construction, and for the possibility of contamination by surface flow or seepage.

On the whole it may be said that, prior to the war, the piped water supplies in Germany could be used without further treatment; however, conditions have been altered by the war, and the general inability to carry out sanitary purification and distribution methods completely, and the disruption, with consequent contamination, of distribution systems by bombings would make it necessary to examine all water supplies before use.

(iii) *Sewage.*—Methods for the treatment of sewerage disposal in urban communities were, prior to the outbreak of war, said to be further advanced in Germany than in any European country. Forty-nine per cent of the population (representing the great majority of city dwellers) were provided with closed water-borne sewage disposal systems. The plants for the treatment of sewage were well equipped and efficiently organized. Screening of the gross material, sedimentation, filtration, activation and chemical treatment were the principal methods employed. Dispersion over large areas and dilution in rivers were also utilized, and partially purified material in some instances was further treated by disposal in large fish ponds. Rain-water canals in most cities were separate from the sewage systems. Street cleaning and rubbish removal were also controlled by the State and severe penalties were imposed on those responsible for public nuisances. In many of the towns of southern Germany and especially in the Schwarzwald, streams are diverted into channels which course through the middle of the streets and facilitate removal of dust, manure, etc. Recent reports of the use of wooden sewage pipes indicates lack of material for future development of sewerage and further upkeep of existing equipment.

While the removal of sewage is controlled by the State in the cities, responsibility in the rural regions is placed directly on the inhabitants. As a result sanitary conditions are less satisfactory. A moderate number of properly constructed and adequately maintained pit privies will be found, and concrete storage cisterns emptied into closed removal tanks are not uncommon; but, in many of the back districts, outhouses will be found which are filthy, and without screens, constituting sources of constant contamination for the surrounding soil and nearby water sources. In such regions, it is common for night soil to be utilized as fertilizer; a practice which may facilitate the spread of the enteric diseases.

(b) *Epidemiology—appreciation of disease situation in Europe.*—(i) *Venereal Diseases.*—" Venereal diseases continue to remain a wartime danger and the subject of worry ", stated Dr. Leonardo Conti the Reich Minister of Health early in 1942. The pre-war trend was downward, and the following are German published figures up to 1940:—

	1927	1934	1940
New cases of gonorrhœa (thousands)	273	175	161
New cases of syphilis (thousands)	75	73	34
Ratio of syphilis to gonorrhœa (cases)	1 : 3·6	1 : 4·1	1 : 4·7
New infections with venereal disease per 10,000 persons—			
Men	66·4	*...	23·1
Women	23·1	...	12·9

* Not available

Regional studies indicate primarily an increase in syphilis during wartime; the sulfonamide treatment of gonorrhœa is said to have brought about amazing improvements.

Measures designed to prevent the spread of venereal diseases have been further intensified during the war. In the autumn of 1940 it was provided that anyone with venereal disease in the infectious stage who is unable to pay for treatment should receive free treatment at public expense.

In 1942 the regulations were tightened further by the provision that physicians must in every case of infection make investigations as to its source. In the past they had simply been required to file a report with the health department if the patient was liable to endanger others or refused treatment.

At the present time, news from German-dominated Europe is more alarming than the reports concerning conditions in Germany. A Paris authority is reported to have stated in March, 1943, that infections had trebled over the previous three years. Legislation was introduced in France which aims at preventing the spread of the diseases in accordance with the regulations prevailing in Germany. In Norway, which before the war used to have only a few cases of gonorrhœa and no syphilis at all, these diseases have now become more widespread owing to the growth of prostitution and other factors. During the first six months of 1942, more cases of syphilis were reported in Oslo than in each of the entire preceding years.

(ii) *Typhoid and Paratyphoid Fever.*—There has been a large increase in typhoid and paratyphoid fever in Germany, and a less pronounced increase in Italy. The rise was especially striking in Germany in 1942. The following table indicates conditions in the expanding territory of Germany with respect to typhoid fever from 1936 to 1942:—

Year	No. of cases	No. of deaths	Cases per 10,000 inhabitants	Deaths per 100 cases
1936	2,953	333	·44	11
1937	3,081	321	·45	10
1938	2,957	360	·43	12
1939	2,733	353	·39	13
1940	9,163	971	1·0	11
1941	7,723	805	·86	10
1942	16,291	1,622	1·8	10

Typhoid fever incidence per ten thousand inhabitants has thus risen four-fold even though allowance is made for the increase in population and territory. The case-fatality rate has remained stationary. The cases in 1940 included 3,030 in the Old Reich, 1,452 in the Alpine and Danube Gaue and the Sudetenland, 1,462 in the districts of Ciechanov and Katovice, and 2,595 in Danzig-Westpreussen and Wartheland.

The situation with respect to paratyphoid fever is similar. The following table presents figures for this disease in the expanding territory of Germany from 1936 to 1942:—

Year	No. of cases	No. of deaths	Cases per 10,000 inhabitants	Deaths per 100 cases
1936	3,136	110	·47	4
1937	3,558	107	·52	3
1938	3,296	205	·48	6
1939	3,072	112	·44	4
1940	4,197	183	·47	4
1941	4,883	156	·54	3
1942	6,076	187	·68	3

The paratyphoid fever incidence per ten thousand inhabitants has thus increased by nearly one-half. Of the 4,883 cases in 1941, 4,047 occurred in the Old Reich and 836 in the newly acquired eastern provinces. The increase in the incidence of both diseases is thus in no way exclusively indicative of conditions in the new areas.

Germans expecting to travel in the occupied sections of Eastern Europe, the Government-General, and foreign countries were advised in the spring of 1942 to obtain protective vaccinations against typhoid and paratyphoid fever before leaving. Vaccines are supplied from the Robert Koch Institute in Berlin or the Behring Works in Marburg. Early in 1943 all residents of the Government-General between the ages of 8 and 55 were made subject to an annual anti-typhoid vaccination.

In this as in other cases of contagious diseases, contact with the population of Eastern Europe has contributed much to the spread in Germany. Over 800,000 Germans from Eastern Europe were resettled elsewhere after 1939. It must be considered that the degree of immunization is higher among these people than it is in Germany proper, and that migratory movements of the magnitude which have occurred in Europe cannot but affect the less immune inhabitants. Among the migrants themselves, the change in environment may have contributed to the outbreak of the disease. In general the strain of the work, of war conditions, and of malnutrition have lessened the powers of resistance to infection.

The severity of the war has been brought fully home to the Italian people only in recent time; it may be that the figures for Italy are not sufficiently recent to reflect the seriousness of the situation. Cases of typhoid and paratyphoid fever increased as follows:—

Year								Number of Cases
1937	...	...	...	...	...	...	...	36,713
1938	...	...	...	...	...	...	...	41,824
1939	...	...	...	...	...	...	...	30,023
1940	...	...	...	...	...	...	...	30,328
1941	...	...	...	...	...	...	...	43,011
1941 Jan to October	...	...	...	...	...	...	30,782
1942 Jan to October	...	...	...	...	...	...	45,116

In Greece, 289 cases of typhoid were reported to the Ministry of Hygiene in January 1943, and 170 in February. The main cause is probably the bad water-supply.

The spread of typhoid in Northern Italy is evidenced by a report in a Swiss newspaper indicating that all the communes in the Canton Ticina along the Swiss-Italian frontier adopted strict precautionary measures against the dangers arising from the typhoid epidemic on the Italian side of the frontier.

In Hungary, the inhabitants of Budapest were ordered to have themselves inoculated against typhoid in November 1942; there were, however, 27 cases of typhoid in Budapest in April 1943, and 11 cases of endemic typhoid fever were brought from the country to the Budapest hospitals during that month. Altogether there were 12,412 cases in 1942.

In Bulgaria, the Plovdiv municipal health service appealed to all citizens, particularly those living in the outskirts of the town, to be inoculated against typhoid. Owing to the use of water from uncontrolled sources, the possibility of a typhoid epidemic was said to exist in July, 1943.

In Yugoslavian communities orders were given in December, 1942, for a re-inoculation of the population. General Mihailovich's Chief of Medical Services states that 21,000 cases of typhoid occurred in 1942.

The increased damage to which the territory of Germany proper has been exposed by air raids has led to a deterioration of drinking water and to local scarcities. In Hamburg, the population was urged to boil water before use. There were also free anti-typhoid inoculations. Similar reports have arrived from Berlin.

It is stated that air raids have resulted in scarcity of drinking water and a breakdown in the sanitary system. As a result, many Berliners are said to have become ill from drinking liquids other than tap water.

Dysentery.—Cases of dysentery have increased considerably in Germany, as has the fatality rate of this disease. There has been no increase in Italy.

The following table indicates conditions with respect to dysentery in the expanding territory of Germany from 1936 to 1942:—

Year	No. of cases	No. of deaths	Cases per 10,000 inhabitants	Deaths per 100 cases
1936	4,816	152	·75	3
1937	7,545	177	1·7	2
1938	5,265	174	·79	3
1939	6,190	227	·91	4
1940	24,458 (12,790)(a)	1,497	2·7	6
1941	10,330 (8,641)(a)	672	1·1	7
1942	15,148	1,872	1·7	12

(a) Figures in parenthesis refer to the old territory of the Reich.

As conditions deteriorate, a further increase in the incidence of this disease may be anticipated. It is to be remembered that there were no less than 69,000 cases of dysentery in Germany in 1917. As the war has progressed, the disease has become more severe. The fatality rate, which used to be between 2 and 3 per 100 cases, is now 12 per 100 cases.

Cases in Italy were as follows:—

Year	Number of Cases
1937	2,004
1938	1,997
1939	1,327
1940	1,725
1941	1,768
1942, Jan-May	363
1943, Jan-May	885

As the figures for the early part of 1943 indicate, there was a considerable increase during that year.

Dysentery is undoubtedly on the increase in other countries in Europe.

Diseases of the Stomach.—In German medical literature of the last few years much space is devoted to the description and discussion of wartime conditions and their impact upon the diseases of the stomach. As the various writers invariably point out, there has been a universal increase in stomach and duodenal ulcers.

A considerable increase in perforations of ulcers is reported. During 44 months before the outbreak of the war (1 January, 1936 to 1 September, 1939) the number of perforations was 64 and they amounted to 1·35 per cent of all operations; for 16 months after the outbreak of the war the corresponding figures are 44 and 2·69 per cent, respectively.

The German medical authorities draw the following conclusions from these trends:—

In wartime, a larger proportion of perforations of ulcers befalls cases who have had no previous complaints.

These and similar disturbances are not so much caused by nutritional deficiencies as by the overwork, nervousness, changes in the pattern of living, and tension which war entails. Also important are irregular food habits and long periods during which the stomach is empty.

The increase in morbidity observed during the years preceding the war must be attributed in part to the growing burden of work.

The reduction of such foods as eggs, milk, and fats seems to have caused the relapse of patients who have suffered from duodenal ulcers before.

The decrease of duodenal ulcers relative to stomach ulcers may be due to the reduction of foods stimulating acidity of the stomach, such as coffee, spirits, certain spices, meat, and meat-concentrates.

The food situation has caused an increase in ulcers not so much because of the change from fats and animal albumen to carbohydrates as main suppliers of calories, but possibly because of the consumption of dark bread, certain types of cabbage, and certain types of fats. This is especially true of participants in community feeding.

Since the treatment required for these patients is approximately one month, it is pointed out that the considerable increase in " the army of people having a sick stomach " deserved attention not only for general hygienic and medical reasons but because of its impact upon production. It is also said that a large number of patients was in very poor condition and that in many cases the routine and quiet of hospitalization apparently contributed much to their recovery.

It is interesting to note that none of the primary types of diet customarily prescribed in stomach-ulcer therapy in Germany is fully available at present; eggs and butter, olive oil, and cream are all scarce. Owing to the difficulties of a permanent diet, doctors, it is pointed out, will be inclined to operate more frequently in case of obstinate ulcers than before.

Additional food rations for the sick are preferably granted to those useful in the war effort.

Stomach disorders are also increasing in Italy, as indicated by the following figures. They refer to non-specified " diseases of the digestive tract " and are indicative of a considerable increase in morbidity. The figures are as follows:—

Year	No. of deaths	Deaths per 100,000 inhabitants
1939	10,778	24·24
1940	12,951	28·86
1941	14,053	30·98

(iii) *Insect-borne Diseases.—Malaria.*—Germany is not a malarial country and such increase in morbidity as has occurred may be ascribed largely to the newly acquired Eastern areas. The following table indicates conditions with respect to malaria in the expanding territory of Germany:—

Year	No. of cases	No. of deaths	Cases per 10,000 inhabitants	Death per 100 cases
1939	282	4	·041	1·4
1940	422	3	·047	·71
1941	1,613	3	·18	·19
1942	716	3	·079	·42

In 1941, morbidity increased four-fold, but there was a considerable decline in the severity of the disease. In 1942, morbidity declined by 50 per cent.

The principal malarial countries of Europe are Italy, the Balkans, Russia and Poland.

So far as Italy is concerned, experience indicates that malaria is prevalent along the entire South coast of Calabria, through Bianca Novo, Bianca Leone and Catanzaro, up to Taranto, on a narrow shelf of flat land extending over an area from about 100 yards in width to a mile or so at the deeper deltas of rivers. Right behind the shore are dry, semi-arid hills. Cultivation is carried out in the highly malarious river bottoms. Two insect vectors of malaria breed on the coastal shelf in slightly brackish delta waters. A third mosquito is a stream breeder which prevails throughout the Near East in semi-arid country. It breeds in the gravel edge of running water for some distance up streams and rivers.

In Greece it is estimated that there are at present some 1,500,000 malarial persons. Another source estimates the number as between 2,000,000 and 2,500,000. Reports indicate that malaria is rampant in Arcadia and that in certain villages all the inhabitants are suffering from the disease. It is suggested that in places where only 25 per cent of the population was suffering from malaria in 1942, the proportion may well be 75 to 100 per cent in 1943, and 100 per cent in 1944. Disease statistics are said to be available only for certain groups of the population, for example, school children in certain districts who undergo examinations. Malaria has increased enormously during the last few years. Especially the tropical form, the most dangerous one, has spread rapidly. Macedonia and Epirus were previously particularly bad malaria districts but now the disease has spread to areas where hitherto only a few or no cases at all occurred.

In March, 1942, reports from Yugoslavia indicated the outbreak of malaria in the district of Posavina (Bosnia). There were reported to be 150,000 cases.

The Stockholm Press reported the following cases in Poland in 1943:—

| 1940 ... | 1,949 |
| 1941 ... | 17,800 |

In general, the main danger rests with the possibility of having a new strain of the malaria parasite introduced in regions of countries which are already infected by another strain. The population may have acquired immunity against the local strain, but is extremely receptive to any imported parasite.

Typhus.—The following table, giving the number of cases of typhus fever in various European countries for recent years, indicates the spread of this disease.

Typhus is carried by lice and the spread of the disease is promoted by overcrowding in sleeping places, lack of clean linen and changes of clothing, lack of soap and other facilities for bodily cleanliness. In regions of standing endemic typhus, hunger, excessive hardship, or other debilitating conditions may produce epidemics as well as a greater severity of the disease.

Number of Reported Cases of Typhus Fever in Europe, by Countries,
1939-1943

Country	1939	1940	1941	1942	1943
Germany(a)	2	556	1,969	2,043	800(b)
Bulgaria	108	155	284	709	1,250(d)
Yugoslavia	404	282	(c)	(c)	117(e)
Greece	45	43	(c)	(c)	(c)
Turkey	471	533	704	427	2,593(d)
Slovakia	(c)	(c)	(c)	(c)	325(f)
Rumania	942	1,403	1,827	3,992	5,585(d)
Hungary	57	97	652	827	658(f)
France	0	1	2	230(g)	2
Portugal	27	(c)	50	1	5(d)
Spain	62	14	9,560	4,144	404(d)
Lithuania	153	115	(c)	(c)	(c)

(a) Deaths from typhus fever in Germany in the indicated years were : 1938, 0 ;
1939, 0 ; 1940, 95 ; 1941, 326.
   (b) The figure is for the first seven weeks of the year only.
   (c) Not available.
   (d) The figure is for January to May only.
   (e) The figure is for January to March only.
   (f) The figure is for January to June only.
   (g) All cases except one occurred in the unoccupied zone.

As in 1914-18 and immediately thereafter conditions in Poland were favourable to the spread of the disease as early as 1939. The number of cases reported from December, 1939, to June, 1940, reached 3,976 in the district of Warsaw, of which 1,746 were in the town proper. During the corresponding half-year of 1939, the number of cases had not exceeded 33 (with a single death).

In the part of Poland now known as the Government General cases of typhus rose as follows (according to a German medical writer):—

Year							Number of Cases
1936 ...	...	...	...	...	...	...	740
1937 ...	...	...	...	...	...	...	680
1938 ...	...	...	...	...	...	...	700
1939 ...	...	...	...	...	...	...	?
1940 ...	...	...	...	...	...	...	7,900

As this writer points out, the figure for 1940 should be doubled or trebled to take account of the cases which escaped notification.

In the western part of Poland, now called Wartheland, typhus was extremely rare, and only some 40 cases were reported in 1938. This figure rose to 486 in 1940 and to 1,241 in 1941.

In the northern part of the Warsaw Voivodie, which is now annexed to Eastern Prussia to form, with part of the Bialystok Voivodie, the district of Zichenau (Ciechanow), some dozens of cases were reported annually before the war. There were 8 in 1940 and 550 in 1941. There are no later reliable figures available and for the rest of Poland, no figures are available at all.

Events in eastern Europe have led to an increase in typhus in those regions, where the disease occurs in normal years sporadically in Bulgaria, Greece, and Yugoslavia.

In Greece it is reported that there were 422 cases in Athens-Piræus during the winter of 1942. Since the disease is greatly feared, it is believed that the cases have been reported relatively completely. One hundred and sixteen cases were reported in Salonica and vicinity during the winter of 1943. Otherwise there have been only isolated cases. The two epidemics mentioned were relatively mild, with few deaths.

In Yugoslavia the disease is said to be spread by the partisan troops. It is reported that the occupation authorities may be using the typhus scare to control population movements and combat partisan activities. It is interesting to note that this has also been reported with respect to the occupation authorities in Poland. There they repeatedly made use of the typhus scare in order to segregate the Jews and control population movements as a means of preventing the leakage of military information.

In Rumania, typhus was extremely rare in Transylvania; it was endemic in Bessarabia and Bukovina, and sporadic in the other provinces. In Transylvania, both in the part occupied by the Rumanians and in that occupied by the Hungarians, typhus spread extensively in 1941.

In 1942 and 1943 the disease increased rapidly.

Figures for Bulgaria are likewise presented in the table. As is evidenced in the table, the situation has deteriorated in recent months. Reports indicate that the campaign against the disease has been intensified and people are urged to greater cleanliness. If the exhortations are not effective, the authorities will have recourse to forcible de-lousing. In 1943, the incidence of typhus was reported to be double that of 1942.

In 1941, and to a greater degree early in 1942, typhus appeared not only in Transylvania and in Sub-Carpathian Ruthenia, where typhus used to be endemo-sporadic, but in sporadic form in several parts of Hungary which had hitherto been free from the disease.

The disease was reported to be rampant in the spring of 1943.

A similar spread of the disease also occurred in Germany during the later months of 1941. Outside those territories taken from Poland where the spread of typhus was particularly marked in 1940-41, no civilian cases of typhus were recorded in Germany in 1939 and only six cases were reported in 1940. In 1941 there occurred no less than 395, nearly all of them during the months of November and December. During these two months, typhus occurred in no less than 44 administrative divisions out of the 74 of Greater Germany. The incidence of cases was considerably greater in the east than in the central, western and southern parts of the country. During the first two quarters of 1942, when 459 and 1,273 cases respectively were reported, the distribution was more uniform, foci occurring even in the north-western part of the country.

The cases reported relate exclusively to civilians. In view of the traditional cleanliness of the German civilian population, the widespread and rapid distribution of typhus can be explained only by the existence of active foci of infection, either within the country among the military population, for which figures are not published (German and foreign troops, and in particular, Russian prisoners), or outside in Poland or in the theatres of operation in the USSR.

During active military operations involving the movements and relief of many divisions and the transportation of hundreds of thousands of wounded, prisoners, and civilian workers, it must obviously be difficult to prevent the entry into Germany or Hungary of carriers of lice (and even carriers of the Rickettsia itself) coming from the zone of operations where typhus is endemic.

Reports from Germany emphasize the following factors as responsible for the spread of the disease in Germany and in the East: deterioration and insufficiency of food which lessen the power of resistance; insufficient supply of clothing, which is not conducive to cleanliness and causes individual pieces of clothing to be worn for a long stretch of time; homelessness owing to the destruction of lodgings; greater density of inhabitants per lodging owing to the same cause; lack of soap and disinfectants.

The extent of the disease among prisoners of war can be judged from the fact that the number of doctors required for its treatment and prevention made it necessary to recall Jewish physicians, who were no longer allowed to practice their profession, and to send them to the prisoner of war camps to practice.

The distribution of the cases in Germany is reported to show high incidence in industrial areas, a phenomenon which would be indicative of the movement of foreign industrial labour from Eastern Europe to German industrial centres. Ninety-seven per cent of the 1942 cases (first nine months) are said to concern " *nicht Volksdeutsche* " (racially not Germans). In 1939 and 1940 nine cases occurred among the Germans who had been removed from the East. The mortality of the disease is said to be higher among Germans than among Poles, who have acquired a certain degree of immunization. Among the latter, the mortality is reported with only 5 to 6 per cent in 1938-40.

Typhus is endemic not only in Eastern Poland and Bessarabia, the bases from which operations were directed against the USSR, but also in the territories of the Soviet Union itself. Figures for years after 1937 are lacking for that country. Those available for the previous fifty years, however, leave no doubt about the existence of typhus endemicity there. Moreover, the mass exodus of civilians during the Russian retreat, their precarious settlement away from their homes, extensive military movements, and the hardships of the winter campaigns of 1941-42 and 1942-43 are powerful factors tending to aggravate the pre-existing typhus endemic. In areas where active operations take place, the systematic or accidental destruction of houses also plays its part, as it entails the crowding together of the remaining civilians and of the invading armies in the few habitable buildings. The possibilities of the spread of typhus among Germans and Russians in Russia differ greatly. It is, of course, practically impossible to keep either German or Russian troops at the front absolutely free from lice, especially in winter. However, while the chances of the Rickettsia being brought to the Russian troops are doubtless greater, the German troops are practically all receptive to it, whereas some Russian troops may be resistant on account of the immunity acquired in past years.

In western Europe, the epidemic which, as indicated in the table, raged in Spain in 1941 and in the beginning of 1942 has now receded. It does not seem to have been due to the importation of the virus from the outside but to a revival of endemo-sporadic typhus which had almost disappeared in the years preceding 1939. This revival must in part be ascribed to the destitution engendered by the Civil War and the severe economic disturbances to which it gave rise.

The appearance of typhus in France is clearly due to this increase above the endemic rate. France had for many years been quite free from typhus. The cases reported in recent time occurred in the central and southern part of that country, not only among individuals arriving from North Africa but also among natives from those countries working in France. Apart from special cases, the disease did not spread to the surrounding French population, since most of them were free from lice. The only secondary foci recorded occurred in the prisons of Marseilles, where obviously lice infestation was rife. The number of cases there far exceeded one hundred.

There are sufficient indications of the apprehension with which the spread of typhus in Europe was regarded by the German authorities. In September, 1939, the Minister of the Interior issued a circular largely dealing with disinfestation and measures to be taken by doctors for their personal security. No allusion was then made to any sort of prophylaxis by means of vaccination. Early in 1942 Dr. Leonardo Conti, the Reich Health

Leader, made a statement to the effect that typhus had been brought into the Reich from the east. The disease had been suppressed at once but the highest degree of attention was still necessary. Germany then ceased publishing statistics on typhus and did not resume until early in 1943. In the meantime considerable effort had been made at preventing the spread of the disease. A centralized integration of all anti-typhus activities was established at Hitler's headquarters under Dr. Karl Brandt, Hitler's representative in matters of public health. New typhus institutes were established in Berlin (Director: Professor Hofmann), Riga (German Hygienic Institute for the Ostland), Kiev, Kherson, Cracow (Typhus Research Institute of the German High Command), and elsewhere. The establishment of a typhus hospital was reported from Leipzig. According to Conti, a sanitary demarkation line was drawn in the Baltic States, over which no one might pass without having been deloused three times. The number of delousing facilities in the East was increased greatly and the population was exhorted to make use of mobile hot-air chambers. Leaflets, illustrated advertisements, and exhibitions constantly draw the attention of the population in the east to the dangers of typhus and the methods of meeting it. While the people are continually reminded about cleanliness, there is little soap, and hardly any of the special de-lousing ointments which used to be available before. In the summer of 1943, the production of louse-proof underwear was reported from Germany. This is supposed to kill lice and prevent them from penetrating.

Protective vaccinations against typhus seem thus far to have been limited to special groups. These are said to include French prisoners in German camps, the medical personnel attending to typhus hospitals and other facilities, the population of Athens, of French towns, of " about 80 per cent of the population of Warsaw ", " all persons between 2 and 80 years in Presov (near Bratislav) ", and " 16,000 persons in Poland ". Medical science has produced a considerable number of anti-typhus vaccines but thus far most of them cannot be made available on a mass production basis which would facilitate the vaccination of large populations. Weigl's vaccine is produced from artificially inoculated lice; one injection (three seem to be required) contains the intestinal contents of 90 to 175 lice. It goes without saying that the production of this vaccine in large numbers is, for all practical purposes, impossible. The Cracow-Lemberg army institute, which seems to be the only German agency producing this vaccine, is said to employ approximately 500 persons, and its output is reportedly sufficient for the treatment of 500 persons each month. It is reported that 160,000 persons in Poland were thus vaccinated; they are said to be immune for one to two years. There is also an institute called " Working Union of the German Serum Institutes Ukraine ". but it is not known what types of vaccine they produce.

Cox's method, which is widely used in the United States, requires relatively large amounts of egg-yolks. 60,000 fertile eggs would theoretically be required to provide vaccine for the treatment of 1,000,000 persons. Cox's method was introduced in Germany by Otto, Wohlrab, Gildemeister and Haagen and productive facilities have been established in Lemberg under the auspices of the I.G. Farben (Behring Works, Marburg-Lahn) and in Frankfurt-Main by the State Institute for Experimental Therapeutics. It seems that this vaccine was first used primarily for the vaccination of medical and sanitary personnel. Approximately 1,000 of such persons are reported to have been vaccinated in 1939-40 and 30,000 in 1941-42. Only 44 cases of typhus fever are said to have occurred among these people. In more recent times the use of this vaccine seems to have become more comprehensive. Official regulations provide for three inoculations of ·5cc, ·5cc, and 1·0cc of the vaccine which are to take place in periods of five days. If the environment is such that the danger of infection continues, the vaccination has to be repeated after one year. The amounts which are then given are ·5cc and 1·0cc. If necessary, a third vaccination takes place in the following year. It consists of 1·0cc only. The same regulation indicates that vaccine for medical personnel is held in readiness at the Robert Koch Institute in Berlin, and lists as other suppliers the Behring Works of Marburg and the Serum Institute of Anhalt in Dessau. Mention is also made of new producers which had supplies available in the second quarter of 1943. These new producers are the Serum Works of Saxony in Dresden, the Schering AG of Berlin, and the Serum Works of Hamburg. This information seems to indicate a shift from the previously preferred Weigl vaccine to that prepared after Cox's method. It seems that the output of Weigl's vaccine has been even more disappointing than was anticipated. Moreover, the output of the Cracow-Lemberg army institute has in no way been reserved for the East, but has been used for the inoculation of German troops elsewhere. The German units in the African theatre of war used anti-typhus vaccines of various kinds, including those prepared by the Pasteur Institutes of Paris and Tunis, Weigl's vaccine prepared in Cracow-Lemberg, and vaccine supplied by the Institute for Experimental Therapeutics of Frankfurt. This is an innovation since the General Army Regulations on 23 April, 1942, contain references only to Weigl's vaccine. There were indications of strained supplies of anti-typhus vaccine for the German armed forces in North Africa. Most use seems to have been made of vaccines from the Cracow-Lemberg Institute and from the Pasteur Institute of Tunis.

The vaccine preparations which have been mentioned so far do not consist of Rickettsia. One source reports that Germany continues exclusively to use killed vaccines while another indicates that canned live bacteria are used by the Cracow Institute. In view of the traditional aversion to the use of live bacteria not much credence should be given this information.

Killed vaccine of the Durand-Giroud type is produced from mice lungs. White mice, particularly the so-called Swiss mice, are especially useful in the manufacture of this vaccine. Germany bought huge quantities of these mice from Switzerland in the early part of 1940 and paid for them in Swiss francs, an indication of the importance which Germany attributed to this transaction. Whether the mice were actually used for the production of vaccine of the Durand-Giroud type is not certain.

Elsewhere in Europe the stocks of available vaccines are being used up locally. The institutions producing them are few. Bucharest prepares a vaccine of the Durand-Giroud type for the army. The Pasteur Institute of Paris makes vaccine from rabbits' lungs, probably according to Giroud's latest methods. In September, 1942, Germany requested 40 to 80 litres of lung emulsion from the Institute, an amount which would suffice for 12-24,000 vaccinations. One litre of this vaccine, an amount sufficient for 300 vaccinations, can be obtained from a 4-lb rabbit. This process of production is subject to the same drawback as others, that is, lack of material for mass production.

Spain makes live vaccine of the Laigret type which is produced from rat brain coated in egg-yolk or from mouse brain. Vaccine of Cox's type is also produced by the Institute for Military Hygiene, Madrid. There have been reports in 1942 that Spain had pressing need for an anti-typhus "serum" and that preparations did not meet the requirements.

The serum mentioned in the report from Spain is not used for the purpose of immunization, but designed for the treatment of existing cases of typhus. Up to the present time medical science has not been successful in developing a serum which may be injected into patients already affected with typhus.

The extent to which typhus will become a threat to a larger proportion of the population of Western Europe and Germany proper depends largely upon the course which military events take. If infestation with lice is aggravated by such factors as hunger, disorganization of administrative powers, badly organized troop movements, conditions of extreme crowding in lodgings, homelessness and the like, a spread of the disease may be anticipated. A disorganized retreat of the German armies from the east would have a similar effect.

(iv) *Infectious Diseases.—Common Cold, Influenza, Pneumonia.*—There are no specific figures to show an increase of these diseases in Europe.

In Italy a moderate increase in mortality caused by influenza and pneumonia has been observed in recent years. The figures are as follows:—

Year	Number of deaths per 100,000 inhabitants	
	Influenza	Pneumonia
1939	18·68	174·60
1940	18·00	176·38
1941	19·71	176·04

There have thus far been no indications of an influenza epidemic as serious as that after the First World War. Authorities are inclined to regard such an epidemic as the greatest possible threat.

In Norway, the average number of cases per year during the ten-year period from 1930 through 1939 was 6,657 for broncho-pneumonia and 5,025 for pneumonia crouposa. The figures were about the same in 1940, but in 1941 a marked upward trend became evident, with 9,722 and 8,500 cases, respectively, reported. During the first ten months of 1942 the figures continued to rise and pneumonia crouposa in particular seems to have taken the lead, with 10,341 cases reported for the period. The month of October was especially serious.

Whooping Cough.—A temporary increase in whooping cough occurred in Germany in 1940 and 1941. After the incidence of the disease had returned almost to its previous level, there was a new increase in 1943. Figures for the expanding territory of the Reich are as follows:—

Year	Cases		Deaths	Cases per 10,000 inhabitants	Deaths per 100 cases
1939	82,068	(78,941)(b)	925	11·8	1·1
1940	133,479	(126,994)(b)	1,373	14·8	1·0
1941	107,543	(93,694)(b)	1,335	11·9	1·2
1942	87,960	—	1,028	9·8	1·2
1942(a)	32,010	—	(c)	(c)	(c)
1943(a)	73,319	—	(c)	(c)	(c)

(a) First six months.
(b) Figures in parenthesis refer to the old territory of the Reich.
(c) Not available.

Diphtheria.—There was a striking increase in cases of diphtheria in Germany after the outbreak of the war and a further considerable increase in 1942. The figures for the expanding territory of the Reich are as follows:—

Year	Cases		Deaths	Cases per 10,000 inhabitants	Deaths per 100 cases
1936	149,973	—	6,284	22·0	4
1937	146,733	—	5,665	21·7	4
1938	149,627	—	5,557	21·8	4
1939	143,585	—.	6,355	20·6	4
1940	174,052	(142,058)(*b*)	8,500	19·3	5
1941	204,918	(173,052)(*b*)	9,607	22·8	5
1942	289,863	—	14,764	31·2	5
1942(*a*)	121,602	—	(*c*)	(*c*)	(*c*)
1943(*a*) ...	124,007	—	(*c*)	(*c*)	(*c*)

(*a*) First six months.
(*b*) Figures in parenthesis refer to the old territory of the Reich.
(*c*) Not available.

The disease has undoubtedly spread over the whole Reich and is the cause of particular anxiety everywhere. It is not limited to children. Schools have had to be closed and hospitals have been overcrowded. Diphtheria, together with dysentery, has been referred to as the worst menace on the Russian front, where the wounded were infected through open wounds. However, the principal causes of the spread of the disease in the Reich are decreased powers of resistance, population shifts and overcrowding.

In March, 1940, the German Minister of the Interior recommended vaccination against diphtheria in areas where a spread of the disease was feared. He arranged for the exclusive employment of vaccines controlled by the State and charged the Robert Koch Institute in Berlin with the collection and assessment of the results of the vaccinations.

Vaccination has not been applied universally in Germany. Early in 1942 it was reiterated by the Reich Health Leader that the voluntary character of anti-diphtheria vaccinations would not be changed. In March, 1943, it was stated that production of 1,000-fold serum was possible only in limited amounts, while less concentrated serum, for example, 500-fold, was available in sufficient quantities.

The increase in diphtheria is also noticeable in the Protectorate Bohemia-Moravia, Denmark, Netherlands, Portugal, Sweden, Switzerland, Norway and elsewhere.

In the Protectorate, figures for Bohemia increased from 15·7 per 10,000 in the first quarter of 1941 to 28·9 in the corresponding quarter of 1942; the increase was less rapid in Moravia (from 17·5 to 22·7). This compares with an increase in morbidity for the Reich from 18·8 to 27·7.

Diphtheria has also made much headway in the Netherlands. An epidemic started in the autumn of 1942 and was still spreading in the spring of 1943. In 1942, the number of cases was about ten times higher than in 1937-39. Figures are as follows:—

Year							*No. of Cases*
1937	...	...	...	...	...	...	1,068
1939	...	...	...	...	...	...	1,273
1940	...	...	...	...	...	...	1,733
1941	...	...	...	...	...	...	5,434
1942	...	...	...	...	...	...	12,225

The increase was the smallest in those provinces where diphtheria has been prevailing for some time and the disease was most severe in older people. Vaccination has been applied on an increasing scale. In 1942, 394 of the 1,034 municipalities had children under 14 years vaccinated. The serum is supplied by the Rijksseruminstituut.

In Sweden, it was planned to vaccinate 1,500,000 children in 1943. Cases of diphtheria numbered 100 in 1939 and 1,000 in 1942. Switzerland reports lack of success of protective vaccinations in some districts.

Reports from Norway indicate that the situation has deteriorated greatly under German occupation. Before the war, medical science had fought diphtheria practically to a standstill (without the use of prophylactic immunization), and the number of cases reported until some months after the German occupation rarely averaged more than 10 cases a month for the entire country. During the period from July, 1940 to June, 1941, an average of 40 cases per month were reported. In July, 1941, came the second rise, and for the whole year of 1941 a total of 2,609 cases was reported. During the first 10 months of 1942, 5,054 cases were reported. In normal times, about 70 per cent of the cases occur in rural districts and 30 per cent in urban. For diphtheria, a gradual process of reversion has taken place during the occupation. The percentage of cases of diphtheria occurring in urban districts rose from 34·9 per cent in 1939 to 39·9 per cent in 1940 and 56·8 per cent in 1941. If the normal distribution of the population is taken into account, with 29 per cent living in urban and the rest in rural districts, this analysis indicates that the morbidity of diphtheria is about three times as high in the urban as in the rural districts. In 1942, the diphtheria epidemic spread to the following districts in Norway:—

Aakra	Faaberg	Horten	Skien
Aamot	Gjerpen	Hell	Stavanger
Arendal	Gjovik	Karmoy	Trondheim
Bamble	Grue	Krageroy	Ostre Toten
Bergen	Gvarv	Lillehammer	
Brandbu	Haugesund	Mangor	
Brevik	Heroya	Notodden	

A number of cases also occurred in other districts in the provinces (*fylker*) of Ostfold, Akershus, Hedmark, Hordaland and Rogaland. The city of Stavanger had a very high incidence.

Meningitis.—Meningitis, an epidemic inflammation of the brain, has considerably increased in Germany and Italy. It is also said to prevail in eastern Slovakia, the adjacent Hungarian districts, and the Carpatho-Ukrainian area occupied by Hungary. Cases for Italy and Germany are as follows:—

Year	Italy	Germany			
	Cases	Cases	Deaths	Cases per 10,000 inhabitants	Deaths per 100 cases
1937	1,037	1,595	831	·24	52
1938	1,276	1,790	861	·26	48
1939	1,330	5,120	1,980	·74	39
1940	2,783	7,211	2,089	·80	29
1941	3,836	4,767	1,367	·53	29
1942	(a)	2,754	947	·31	34

(a) Not available.

The decline which occurred in Germany in 1942 can also be observed in Italy, where the number of cases reported for the period from January to May was 1,780 as compared with 2,850 for the corresponding period of 1941.

The severity of the disease has declined in Germany as is indicated in the fatality figures.

Reports from Norway indicate the following increase in the number of reported cases:—

Year								No. of Cases
1939	...	...	...	...	...	...	...	28
1940	...	...	...	...	...	...	...	88
1941	...	...	...	...	...	...	...	490

The rise started in the beginning of 1941 and culminated in the spring. The situation has later improved considerably, but the average number of cases reported is still much bigger than before the war.

Scarlet Fever.—No disease has become more widespread in Germany in recent years than has scarlet fever. Figures for the expanding territory of the Reich are as follows:—

Year	Cases		Deaths	Cases per 10,000 inhabitants	Deaths per 100 cases
1936	124,570	—	993	18·5	1
1937	117,544	—	829	17·2	1
1938	114,243	—	807	16·6	1
1939	129,495	—	1,032	18·5	1
1940	159,597	(138,759)(*b*)	1,700	17·7	1
1941	279,117	(247,744)(*b*)	3,233	31·0	1
1942	401,011	—	4,454	44·6	1
1942(*a*)	219,676	—	(*c*)	(*c*)	(*c*)
1943(*a*)	185,920	—	(*c*)	(*c*)	(*c*)

(*a*) First six months.
(*b*) Figures in parenthesis refer to the old territory of the Reich.
(*c*) Not available.

Of the 160,000 cases in 1940, 128,000 were children under 15 years. It seems that the disease has been most severe in adults.

Denmark had 9,186 cases of scarlet fever in 1941 and 14,302 in 1942. Hospitals are badly crowded. Cases are often followed by complications. A marked increase in the occurrence of the disease is reported from Norway, and it is stated that in 1942 there occurred the most severe scarlet fever epidemic in 50 years. There are also numerous reports of the disease in Sweden. In Italy, no increase has been observed.

Jaundice.—Though much is made of jaundice in reports from Germany, Switzerland and France, exact over-all figures are not available. An increase in the number of cases is also reported from Norway. In the German Press it is stated that " jaundice has occasionally been more frequently observed in recent times ". Jaundice was, next to diphtheria and scarlet fever, the most widespread disease in Germany in 1942 and early 1943. It appears to have occurred in epidemic form and is reported from all regions of Germany.

Trachoma.—This disease, which is endemic in some eastern parts of Europe, has increased greatly in Germany and the increase is not limited to the newly acquired' territories. Figures for the expanding territory of the Reich are presented in the following table:—

Year	Cases	Deaths	Cases per 10,000 inhabitants	Deaths per 100 cases
1936	625	—	—	·084	—
1937	697	—	—	·10	—
1938	533	—	—	·074	—
1939	652	—	—	·092	—
1940	5,586 (2,979)(a)	—	—	·62	—
1941	6,196 (2,770)(a)	—	—	1·0	—
1942	8,564	—	—	·95	—

(a) Figures in parenthesis refer to the old territory of the Reich.

East Prussia is the principal focus of the infection, which has been spread by returning Germans from Wolhynia, Galicia, Bessarabia and Lithuania. It is also found among Polish and Italian labourers.

Smallpox.—In Germany, an order of 22 January, 1940, fortified the law of anti-smallpox vaccination, which dates from 1874, and applied it to the whole territory of the Reich. As long as vaccines are produced, a spread of smallpox in central Europe seems improbable. France, which before the war used to have a few cases per year, had 57 cases in 1942, of which 44 were in the Seine department and 13 in the unoccupied zone. There were only two cases in the first half of 1943.

Tuberculosis.—Statements of German medical authorities indicate awareness of the impact of war conditions on the incidence of tuberculosis. The Reich Health Leader refers to tuberculosis as the object of his greatest worry. New methods such as the intracutaneous test for detecting tuberculosis among small children and progress in the field of X-ray diagnosis have made much headway. Of special importance is the need for good housing facilities.

The following figures are for the territory of Germany as it expanded after 1939.

	1939	1940	1941	1942	1942(b)	1943(b)
Tuberculosis of the lungs and larynx :—						
Cases	69,482	98,062	117,558	126,965	68,500	71,515
Deaths	31,114	42,989	49,653	53,999	(a)	(a)
Cases per ten thousand inhabitants	10	11	13	14	(a)	(a)
Tuberculosis of the skin :—						
Cases	1,714	1,667	1,909	1,837	(a)	(a)
Cases per ten thousand inhabitants	·25	·19	·21	·20	(a)	(a)
Tuberculosis of other organs :—						
Cases	6,366	9,779	15,512	16,996	(a)	(a)
Deaths	3,349	4,867	5,636	6,101	(a)	(a)
Cases per ten thousand inhabitants	·92	1·1	1·7	1·9	(a)	(a)
Deaths per hundred cases ...	(a)	50	36	36	(a)	(a)

(a) Not available.
(b) First six months.

There was thus a severe increase in cases of tuberculosis of the lungs and larynx, no increase in tuberculosis of the skin and a serious increase in tuberculosis of other organs. The case fatality figures indicate that the new cases are not so frequently fatal as was the smaller number of cases in the past.

The increase in tuberculosis of lungs and larynx (respiratory tuberculosis) is by no means a statistical consequence of the acquisition of new territories. Cases for the old territory are as follows:—

Year	Annual Total	First Quarter	Second Quarter	Third Quarter	Fourth Quarter
1935	80,376	15,649	16,200	18,186	10,341
1936	60,727	15,835	16,095	18,218	10,579
1937	63,570	16,881	17,787	15,034	13,868
1938	60,420	16,052	16,441	14,233	13,694
1939	67,890	19,431	18,448	15,816	14,195
1940	73,267	17,096	21,778	17,514	16,879
1941	82,043	20,660	24,155	20,266	16,962

In 1941, there was thus a 34 per cent increase for the Old Reich in new cases of respiratory tuberculosis over the average of cases in 1935-38.

In the large cities of Greater Germany, deaths from all forms of tuberculosis per 10,000 people were as follows:—

1939	1940	1941	1942
6·6	7·3	7·6	8·1

Progress in the detection of tuberculosis is due to the extensive use of mass radiography, a serial diagnosis by means of miniature X-ray photographs by the Abren process. In certain areas it is proposed to establish a " tuberculosis register " by radiophotography of the whole population, but these pre-war plans are not being carried out so extensively as was intended. In 1939 more than 500,000 persons had already been examined in Mecklenberg. In addition, this method of diagnosis has been applied to various political and youth organizations, to school children, officials, workers in certain industries and to PW camps, etc. By this method, however, only preliminary surveys are possible; it is necessary further to investigate suspected cases fluoroscopically and radiographically.

The tuberculosis situation is more serious among the various foreign elements of the German labour force than it is among the Germans themselves.

The organized placement of tubercular persons in institutions, sanatoria, and special settlements seems to have been much disturbed owing to war conditions. It is objected that measures like this are now " very unpopular ", and that newly detected cases must wait three to four months instead of two to three weeks until they are admitted to an institution. Much is also made of the poor housing conditions of people suffering from open tuberculosis, a situation which is bound to deteriorate under the impact of recent air raids. It is estimated that 25,000 persons affected with open tuberculosis live together with 61,600 healthy persons in overcrowded lodgings. No systematic effort has as yet been made in the direction of removing the danger of such lodgings. There are complaints about the lack of initiative and co-operation among the various authorities.

In view of the growing shortage of labour much attention is being paid to the problem of utilizing the productive powers of tubercular people. Altogether there are 1,600,000 tubercular persons in Germany; of these, 4-500,000 suffer from open tuberculosis. Of the latter, only 100,000 receive treatment and 200,000 are not known as sick persons.

Figures published in April, 1942, indicate that about 60 per cent. of all persons with open pulmonary tuberculosis and 80-90 per cent of those with stationary tuberculosis were then employed, some in very unsuitable positions.

In other parts of Europe complaints about a deterioration of the situation are frequent.

(v) *Diseases affecting man and animal.—Tularæmia.—*Tularæmia has been observed in Poland and Austria. It is conveyed by rodents and especially by hares.

*Trichinosis.—*Reported cases of trichinosis have increased from none in Germany in 1936 to one in 1937, 20 in 1938, and 30 in 1939. It is now reported from Warthegau as well as from Austria and Poland. Its sporadic appearance seems to be due to the consumption of bad pork as well as of badgers and foxes. It is likely that there are many more cases of trichinosis than are reported to the health authorities.

(vi) *Miscellaneous diseases.—Vitamin deficiencies.—*An order by Hitler of 15 August, 1941, established a Reich Institute for Vitamin Research and Testing (*Reichsanstalt für Vitaminprüfung und Vitaminforschung*). For the time being this Institute is still located in temporary quarters in Leipzig.

Germany seems to be well stocked with all vitamins except Vitamin A (commonest commercial source is fish liver oil). This vitamin affects growth, skin and the mucous membrane; lack of it causes night blindness and the tendency of wounds to suppurate. Since early in 1941, oleomargarine is enriched in Germany by a Vitamin A concentrate from liver oil of the blue whale, halibut and cod-fish. The concentrates are diluted with peanut oil and used in the following standardized form: 10 Kg. concentrate per 1,000 Kg. fat (=1,250 Kg. margarine).

Germany's optimum requirements of Vitamin A and D concentrates are estimated at 6,000,000,000,000 international units of which 4,200,000,000,000 are supplied from Norway in the form of cod liver oil.

With respect to Vitamin B, much is made in Germany of the whole grain bread (*Vollkornbrot*). The germ and other components of the grain which are contained in this bread has a content of Vitamin B-1, but it has been pointed out that the baking process may destroy the latter to some extent.

Vitamin C is anti-scorbutic. Since this vitamin is contained in potatoes, the large consumption of potatoes in Germany necessarily makes some vitamin available to the population.

During the past two and a half years, the German labour front has also arranged for the distribution of vitamin preparations combining A, B, C and D vitamins among heavy workers. The distribution takes place in spring. The preparation is called *Vitamultin.* It consists of grain germs, thiamin, ascorbic acid, calcium biphosphate, sugar, and lemon. Ninety tablets are issued per head.

Lack of Vitamin D causes rickets, decalcification of teeth and bones, and sometimes even spontaneous fractures. Vitamin D can be produced by irradiating relatively small amounts of fish oil. Early in 1943 it was reported that two German chemists, Dimroth and Stockstrom, had succeeded in producing a synthetic Vitamin D. It is not known whether synthetic production is practicable, however.

Vitamin E is contained in the whole grain bread produced in Germany which retains the germs and other components of the grain. Lack of this vitamin brings about miscarriage and premature births, the number of which is increasing rapidly in parts of Europe.

Calorific Deficiencies.—Estimates of the 1942-43 nutritive value of average diets in various countries are as follows (in calories):—

Germany	...	...	2,784	Netherlands	...	2,461
Italy	...	...	2,619	France	... ...	2,431
Denmark	...	...	3,283	Norway	... ...	1,980
Bulgaria	...	...	3,120	Belgium	... ...	1,713
Yugoslavia		...	2,620	Albania	... ...	1,420

For rations, *see* Part I, Section 4.

(c) *Numbers and Quality of Personnel.*—(i) *Declining Number of Doctors.*—The following table compares the population of various areas of Germany and Axis Europe with the number of doctors theoretically available early in 1942:—

Territory	Population (thousands)	Number of doctors
Germany, including Austria, Sudeten territory, Memel, Danzig, incorporated Polish territories, Eupen-Malmedy ...	95,162	76,983
Alsace-Lorraine	1,906	717
Luxemburg	301	180
Protectorate Bohemia-Moravia	7,700	567
Total	105,069	78,447

This table indicates the number of doctors who would be available in peace-time. With the exception of 1,400 young doctors who were called to military service immediately upon the termination of their education, the table gives no indication of the number of doctors who have been absorbed by the armed forces. On the other hand, it includes approximately 7,700 doctors who because of age or for other reasons were not practicing when the census were taken. Thus, 70,747 doctors were available for the medical care of a population of 105,000,000 as well as for medical service with the armed forces.

Prior to the onset of the present war, the German medical schools were graduating large numbers of well-trained and competent physicians. The need of doctors for the military has been great, however, and it is reported that the course of study has been reduced from five to three years, that a year's interneship following graduation is no longer required, and that the majority of students, upon graduation, are inducted into Army service. It is of interest to note that medical students, upon completion of their three year's course of study, are required to serve as orderlies and nurses for some months. Official apologies for the inadequate number of physicians to perform strenuous service, indicates that only those practitioners unfit for military service, either by virtue of age or infirmity, remain to care for civilian needs. In 1939, 12,407 " *Heilpraktikers* " or irregular practitioners were licensed by the State as capable of practicing medicine. In 1938, there were in Germany 49,907 licensed physicians, 14,833 dentists, 8,000 pharmacists, 128,000 nurses, 24,500 midwives, and 14,300 unqualified dental assistants. In 1939 there were about 76,000 doctors of whom 9,250 were women. About one third of available doctors have been called up for military service, and the civilian shortage is acute. It is believed that there are now about 3 to 5 doctors per 10,000 of the population but an isolated report gives the figure of 1 doctor to 10,000 population.

(ii) *Conditions of Medical Practice.*—The shortage of medical personnel finds expression in a greater preponderance of women doctors, whose number is 40 per cent higher than in 1929, and in the undue proportion of doctors who practice notwithstanding their age. Reports indicate that there are about 300 doctors aged 80 and over and 3,000 aged 70 and over in practice in Germany.

In view of the growing scarcity of medical personnel, the authorities have made efforts to relieve physicians from certain routine jobs. The inspection of the state and communal health offices, which normally took place every three years, has been postponed until after the war. Officials are urged to be economical in their requests for medical examinations of the public. Women desirous of marrying a member of the armed forces no longer need a special medical certificate; that certifying to their general physical fitness for marriage suffices. The same rule applies to applicants for marriage loans.

(iii) *Collectivization of Medical Services.*—These measures of rationalization are supplemented by the growing collectivization of medical services. Most important in this respect is the increase in the provision of medical care in factories. The increase since the outbreak of the war has been 261 full-time and 3,080 part-time work doctors. Part-time work doctors care for about 1,200 workers, while one full-time work doctor is in charge of factories employing from 2,000 to 6,000 workers. Such doctors are especially useful in view of the strain under which the call for increased output places all workers and in the face of increasing employment of women workers and partly disabled persons. The quality of the medical care provided by the work doctors is, however, a poor substitute for that provided by the family physician or, for that matter, the physician of the sick-funds, to which the overwhelming majority of German workers used to have recourse for medical attention.

Further evidence of the collectivization of medical care and the resulting economy is the large number of doctors employed by numerous public and party organizations. The Nazi state is said to have established 1,100 health offices with 12,600 doctors. Another 1,100 doctors are reported as working for the various labour authorities; another 670 are employed by the German Labour Front. 3,000 doctors attend to the Hitler Youth. Venereal disease and tuberculosis are fought in 1,300 special offices, and the " Mother and Child " organizations have 63,000 advisory agencies.

(iv) *Shortage of Nurses.*—Among non-professional personnel there exists a severe shortage of nurses. According to an order of the Minister of the Interior of 8 July, 1942, nurses and technical assistants and sub-assistants are now allocated centrally by the health organization of the Reich to the various institutions and places of employment. The training period has been shortened.

The supply of doctors in other parts of Europe has shrunk to a similar extent, largely due to the claim which Germany has made upon foreign medical personnel and facilities.

(v) *Decline in the Quality of Medical Personnel.*—To the deterioration of medical care resulting from the decline in the number of doctors must be added the deterioration of the quality of the medical personnel. Factors responsible for this deterioration can be conveniently summarized under the following headings: elimination of qualified physicions and admission of unqualified physicians. The elimination of some 10,000 Jewish doctors has deprived the German medical profession of some of its best talent, while, on the other hand, the educational and ethical standards of the profession have been gradually lowered. To consider only war measures proper: after the outbreak of hostilities in 1939 no less than 5,837 medical students, a number equal to 10 per cent of the doctors then available, were prematurely admitted to practice without having to serve their year of hospital interneship. At about the same time the medical curriculum was reduced from eleven to ten terms, the time required for taking the state examinations was drastically curtailed, and the year of hospital interneship, which previously had to be served immediately after the state examination, was incorporated into the undergraduate schedule. The total reduction of the medical curriculum brought about by these measures has been estimated at two years.

(vi) *Medical Services in the Civil Defence Organization.*—All doctors holding official positions such as medical officers of health, were obliged, even before the war, to take a course of training at a Reich Air Protection School, and the organization of first aid posts has long been well advanced. The medical services take orders only from the air protection police, and all casualties must, in the first instance, report or be taken to a first aid post and not proceed direct to a hospital.

First aid service.—First aid posts were provided on a substantial scale before the war, about 200 such posts being established in Berlin, that is, one to each police sub-section. All casualties are dealt with first at the first aid post. Originally all German first aid posts were to have had an emergency operating theatre with a view to preventing congestion at the hospitals. Shortage of qualified personnel would appear to have modified this scheme however. In Hamburg most of these posts are situated in the cellars of school buildings. Hospitals are also supposed to provide an emergency patrol service of ambulances each with a doctor and staff to travel through the streets during and after an air attack.

Hospitals.—It would appear that hospital accommodation in Germany is not merely strained but quite inadequate. Information of November, 1943, relates to the building of a standardized type of hospital in large numbers outside the towns. At first wooden structures were used, but now the buildings are of concrete, one storey high and each building being at a distance of from 30 to 35 yards from its neighbour. Some of the buildings are as much as 100 yards long and 13 yards wide.

In April, 1943, it was decreed that only walking cases and those which can easily be moved may be housed on the upper floors of hospitals, and when a warning sounds they must go to the staff shelter. Serious cases must be accommodated in splinter-proof wards where they remain throughout raids.

Ambulances.—In a decree of 30 Nov, 1943, the ambulance service throughout the Reich was brought under control of the German Red Cross organization. Previously no less than 947 different organizations. local authorities, fire brigades, hospitals and private undertakings conducted ambulance services.

A new type of standardized ambulance was described in June, 1943, as a " three decker ", with accommodation for 6 stretcher cases and 29 sitting cases.

(d) *Quantity and Quality of Facilities.*—(i) *Hospitals.*—For many decades, the hospitals in Germany probably represented some of the most completely-equipped and efficiently-run organizations in the world. New hospitals were being built in accordance with the plans of the Central Bureau for Health Control in the Reich at the time of the outbreak of the war. How far such plans were carried out is not fully known, but it is probable that few civilian establishments have been constructed since 1939, and that the systematic bombings to which many of the large cities have been subjected have resulted in damage to some of the existing medical centres. It is known that there is a lack of essential medical supplies such as iodine, bandage material, and drugs. The return of large numbers of casualties from combat areas has overcrowded the hospitals to such an extent that, unless absolutely necessary, civilians are being refused admission. In 1936, there was a total of 6,552 hospitals in Germany, with 661,500 beds. Of this number, 3,196 with 316,000 beds were general hospitals; 463, with 32,000 beds were tuberculosis sanatoria; and 301 with 165,000 beds were insane asylums. The remainder was composed of maternity centres, pediatric and isolation hospitals, and homes for the aged or infirm.

At the end of 1939 there were 4,861 hospitals in Germany (including Memel territory and Ostmark; excluding Saar, Sudeten territory and incorporated former Polish territories). Of these, 2,267 were public, 1,519 free charitable, and 1,075 private hospitals. The number of beds was 662,996, compared with 686,459 at the end of 1938. This decline was due to the taking over of some hospitals by the armed forces. Of these, 65 per cent were in public, 29 per cent in free charitable, and 6 per cent in private hospitals.

With the outbreak of the war conditions grew much worse. Though new facilities in schools, etc, were made available, the access of civilians to hospital facilities was necessarily curtailed and standards of hospital care had to be lowered. As in the field of public health in general, measures of rationalization and collectivization which are designed to economize the available facilities were undertaken.

Complaints about the deterioration of hospital care are numerous. There are said to be premature discharges, patients in excess of hospital beds, and inclination to resort to amputations, lack of sufficient medical and nursing personnel, and poor food. Furthermore, the lack of equipment has caused a deterioration of hygienic standards and medical care. Linen is short and bed sheets are not changed so often as before; there is lack of gauze for bandages and surgical laundry is sharply economized.

There is much evidence that hospital conditions, in absolute terms, are in a state of even greater deterioration in the German-dominated countries.

(e) *Drugs and Medical Equipment.*—(i) *The General Situation.*—Shortages of drugs in various European countries are due to the cessation of imports of various materials and to economies in manpower and other resources required by the war.

Excessive hoarding of medicaments has occurred everywhere and prices have gone up substantially. There has been much standardization of drugs and the introduction of new preparations has been stopped. Advertising has been severely restricted. Many drugs are sold only by prescription. If a prescription cannot be supplied, the druggist may, within certain limitations, substitute another preparation for it. Containers must generally be returned.

(ii) *Medical Equipment.*—There are numerous complaints about the decline in the quality of surgical instruments and the tight supply situation. It is reported to be difficult even to have surgical instruments sharpened. In order to economize in steel, only the blades of surgical instruments are now said to be made of that metal the remainder being made from aluminium.

In view of the general shortage, in June, 1943, the production of medical instruments in Germany was ordered to be maintained. Industries engaged in this branch of manufacture are forbidden to lower their output by accepting orders outside their field.

Concerning electrical medical equipment, Swiss importers complain about the quality of small electrical bulbs for surgical instruments and of X-ray tubes. They are obtainable only with great difficulty in Germany and do not last nearly so long as before the war. In 1942 enterprises producing electrical medical equipment were instructed by the authorities concerning priorities in the use of their capacity. Repair and maintenance hold the first rank and are followed by replacements. New installations are to be made only if they do not exclusively serve a regular peacetime need but are capable of being fully utilized in wartime also. In 1943, all doctors, dental surgeons, dentists and healers using X-ray equipment were required to register it with the authorities of the Reich Defence Commissary. Manufacturers and dealers were exempted from this order. Subsequent changes in the possession of the equipment also had to be reported. This measure is indicative of a growing shortage of such equipment and shows that the authorities were preparing themselves for the allocation of available installations according to the most urgent need. The order expressly pointed out that equipment and X-ray tubes which were not in current use were also to be reported.

The supply of optical implements seems to have been curtailed, though some supplies of optical goods are still available for export. It was reported in April, 1943, that Bulgaria is to receive optical instruments and apparatus to the total value of 22 million levas for the observatory at the Sofia University. No air-raid damage seems to have been inflicted on the Zeiss Works in Wetzlar as yet.

There has been much standardization in the field of medical glass articles and more bottles are recovered now than in the past. Many articles of tubular and flat glass are no longer produced. The size of the paper labels on bottles has been reduced to save paper.

Germany uses gloves made from synthetic rubber. These gloves are inferior in that they cannot be exposed to paraffin, fat, or alcohol; they tend to stick and are not uniformly elastic. They are, however, more resistant to benzine than rubber gloves.

Paper bandages of low quality are widely used. In view of the shortage of adhesive plaster, bandages are occasionally fastened directly to the skin by glue. Army surgeons are requested to economize in adhesive tape, using if possible only half of the normal width by cutting the tape into two parts. Cotton wool and gauze are very scarce and bandages have to be washed and reused. Paper bedsheets have replaced linen in military hospitals. Sheets can thus be changed more often.

(iii) *Medicaments.*—The following is a list of medicaments known to be in short supply:—

Glycerine, gumtragacanth, cocoa butter, lanolin, vaseline, lard, borates, chlorides and chlorates, cresol, iodine and iodides, bismuth, arsenic, agar-agar, insulin, quinine, camphor, caffeine, radium, liver extracts, surgical sutures, opium and opiates, soap, sera of most types, anti-mosquito nets, alkaloids, non-synthetic vitamins, sulphur drugs, cardiazol, barbiturates, lysol, phosphates of all kinds, theobromine, theophylline, atropin, codein, emetine, santonin, and most glandular products.

These are articles of which the Germans are known to be in need, and very detailed reports are available. It is likely therefore that supplies of these commodities would be very hard to procure in the course of operations in Germany and occupied Europe.

(f) *Summary of evidence of medical situation as a whole.*—The main conclusions which can be drawn from the above evidence are as follows:—

    (i) the German medical services have been subjected to a very severe strain on the Russian front, leading to certain serious shortages of medicaments, equipment (particularly high grade surgical instruments), and of qualified personnel; as well as of skilled labour in the industry;

    (ii) there is a growing shortage of essential raw materials for the manufacture of certain medical products in Germany itself;

    (iii) reserves of captured medical material in the occupied territories have now been exploited to the limit;

    (iv) reserves of bed-accommodation in Germany and the occupied territories have been virtually exhausted due primarily

        to the great influx of wounded from the Eastern front and

        to the effect of intensive bombing of Western Germany;

    (v) transport difficulties have affected the system of distribution of supplies of medical stores.

(g) *The Higher Military Medical Organization.*—(i) In the OKH, is the Inspector of Medical Services (*see* chart of OKH at the beginning of Part I of this Handbook). He has an Army Medical Inspectorate (*Heeres Sanitätsinspektion*) through which the whole of the higher organization of the military medical services is administered. He is primarily responsible, however, only for the organization as it is set up in Germany, and for that purpose he has close liaison with the civilian organization, principally with the State Health Bureau in the Ministry of the Interior. Medical organization in the field is in the hands of the GHQ MO (*Heeresarzt*) who is to be found in the department of the commander of GHQ services under the QMG.

The successive stages of responsibility under the GHQ MO are those of Army MO (*Armeearzt*), Corps MO (*Korpsarzt*), Divisional MO (*Divisionarzt*) and the unit MO (*Truppenarzt*).

(ii) The hospitals in Germany, mainly " *Reservelazarette* ", (base hospitals) comprise the majority of civilian hospitals. It is probable that most of them have retained their civilian staffs. Before the war there was a number of static military hospitals in the garrison areas. These were classified as *Standortlazarette, Lagerlazarette* and *Kurlazarette* (static hospitals, camp hospitals and sanatoria). These still exist but the organization, as it now exists in wartime, is dwarfed by the enormous expansion of the military medical organization. To what extent civil and military hospital staffs work side by side is not clear, but it would appear that civilian specialists, as well as ordinary general practitioners are being put into uniform and called military MO's with little or no training in the military aspects of their work. Long lists of these reserve hospitals are available, from which it would appear that the larger towns usually have three, four or more *Reservelazarette* which are numbered with Roman numerals, thus *Reservelazarett* I, Hamburg *Reservelazarett* II, Hamburg, and so on.

(iii) The categorization of the various wards of the *Reservelazarette* is laid down as follows:—

    I for medical cases
    II for surgical cases
    III for skin disease and VD cases

IV for ophthalmic cases

V for ear, nose and throat cases

VI for neurotic and psychopathic cases.

(iv) Medical equipment and drugs have already been dealt with in the preceding paragraphs, but it should be mentioned that most military medical equipment destined chiefly for the field is kept in the medical parks (*Sanitätsparke*). There are not many of these, and they would appear to be mobile, for the location of the same park has frequently been noticed to change.

7. *Postal system.*

(*a*) The field postal system, though part of the German Army, is also the system for all three services, with special provision for naval units. Postal communication to members of the armed forces, whether in the field or in depot units, is free. Soldiers on leave within the Reich, and soldiers of depot units or of units without a field post number, use the civilian postal service (*Deutsche Reichspost—DRP*), while all other members of the forces have to give a field post number and post their communications at their unit. In matters of military discipline and administration, units of the field postal service are subject to the formation to which they are allocated, but in technical matters they are subject to the control of the State Ministry of Postal Services (*Reichspostministerium*).

(*b*) The head of the field postal service is the Army Postmaster-General (*Heeresfeldpostmeister—HPM*). It will be seen in the chart at the beginning of Part I of this Handbook that the HPM is part of the QMG's staff, and probably subordinate to the GHQ Services Commander. Under the instructions of the QMG, and subject in technical matters to the State Ministry of Postal Services, the HPM controls the organization and personnel of the field postal service.

(*c*) Liaison between the civilian postal system (DRP) and the field postal system (FP) is very close. In principle the FP takes over from the DRP, in wartime, the entire postal service of the Armed Forces outside the Reich. The FP is essentially an extension outside the Reich of the DRP, military control beginning at the frontiers of the Reich. In each military district (*Wehrkreis*) there is a postal collecting office (*Postsammelstelle*) of the civilian postal service. This postal collecting office sends its mail through its despatch points (*Postleitpunkte*) to the field post despatch office (*Feldpostleitstelle*) which forwards it, either direct or through the army postal station (*Armee Briefstelle*). This link between the DRP and the FP works for either outgoing or in-coming mail. Thus, in MUNICH, for example, the FP has its field post despatch office and the DRP has its despatch point. Mail for the greater part of Southern Europe is transferred between the field post despatch office and the despatch point. Incoming mail is sent direct by the despatch point to civilian post offices for delivery in the Reich, while outgoing mail addressed, for example, to a corporal, giving his field post number, will go from the postal collecting office in the Wehrkreis in which it was posted, to the despatch point where it is transferred to the field post despatch office and thence into the field.

(*d*) Briefly, the system of post for naval units is that naval units at sea but based on ports in the Reich collect their mail from the port in the Reich on which they are based. The central Naval post office in BERLIN (*Marinepostbüro*) sends mail to the civilian post office of the port concerned. For all other naval units, the Field Post Register (*Feldpostübersicht*) kept by the *Heeresfeldpostmeister* directs mail through the Wehrkreise where it is sorted and sent in the manner outlined in the previous paragraph, outside the Reich—in this case to a field post office most conveniently situated near the base port of the naval unit concerned. From this field post office each unit would fetch its mail.

(e) GAF units obtain their mail by similar channels, that is via the Wehrkreise, etc, as outlined in the two preceding paragraphs, and they also collect their mail from the nearest field post office, to which their mail would have been directed by the field post despatch office.

8. *System of billeting and German barracks system.*

(a) The Army Billeting Administration (*Heeres Unterkunftverwaltung—HUV*) attends to all arrangements for accommodation of troops and sees to the maintenance of billets. In occupied countries, ORs are not billeted with families, but buildings are requisitioned entirely by the Army, the aim being to prevent troops having too close a contact with civilians of an occupied country; officers are usually billeted in hotels, or in private furnished apartments. In Germany, however, troops are frequently billeted with families. Accommodation, therefore, whether in barracks, barrack-huts, commandeered houses, hotels, private furnished apartments or with civilian families is entirely a matter for the HUV.

(b) In the War Ministry the relevant branches concerned with billeting are firstly the billeting department of the Manpower Branch, which is part of the General Army Branch under the Head of Army Supply. It is shown in the chart of the OKH at the beginning of Part I of this Handbook. Secondly, in Branch II of the Administrative Branch, also under the Head of Army Supply, is Department 2, concerned with real property and care of barracks. It is this department which issues the notices about care of barracks which are to be seen on the walls of German billets of all types.

(c) Numbers of large new barracks were built in the few years preceding the war, and some since its outbreak, as many of the old barracks were found to have become unsuitable from the point of view of accommodation and location.

Most (though not all) of the barracks built since the beginning of the war (especially those hastily erected in occupied countries) have been little more than hutted camps (*see* para. (f) below).

Generally speaking the barracks are built with little regard for initial economy, but with the aim of saving labour in maintenance, and reducing as much as possible the menial tasks which the soldier has to perform. The most usual type of modern barracks consists of a number of blocks of buildings, so that, for example, if a battalion is to be housed there, one block is used for battalion HQ, one for each company, and one for the messing and recreation building (*Wirtschaftsgebäude*). Each company barrack block is, usually, a three-storeyed building consisting on the ground floor of offices for the company commander, the orderly officer, the CSM and specialist NCOs. and the serjeant-major's and a subaltern officer's quarters. Before the war, the latter's quarters used to consist of bedroom, sitting-room, bathroom, kitchenette and boxroom, but it is not known whether this still applies—in any case, this accommodation was normally reserved for very junior officers only, the others being required to find their own quarters in the town if it were possible.

It was the National Socialist policy before the war to do everything possible to make the Wehrmacht popular with the people. In particular every effort was made to ensure that men from working-class homes should during their conscript service, be better fed and more comfortably housed, than they could hope to be in civil life.

(d) The first and second floors consist of barrack rooms and lecture rooms, the former predominating.

Barrack rooms, which have accommodation for five or six men, under the charge of a NCO are used both for sleeping and also for eating (except in the case of the midday dinner).

The system of two-tiered bunks is now believed to be abandoned, and soldiers have single beds with straw mattresses, NCOs have spring beds. Two blankets are usually issued to each man, and this, in view of the normally good heating arrangements, is adequate. The two-tiered bunks, however, are still used in barrack-huts.

The " *Stubenältester* " (senior soldier of the room) of each barrack room is nominated by the company commander for the duration of the company's stay. He acts as a representative for the other members of the room, when complaints have to be made, and is responsible for seeing that the room is kept in order, by delegating the tasks of the day to the various members of the room in turn each day. Instructions are issued to the man on duty with regard to the cleaning and airing of the room, and provision of drinking and washing water for the occupants, and he is responsible for seeing that the room is locked when empty. During his period of duty he is not allowed to leave the barracks.

An additional cupboard is provided in each room to hold all the materials for cleaning.

Very detailed instructions concerning the tasks of the senior member of the room, and of the room-orderly are issued by the War Ministry in pamphlet form—one to each room—together with a set of rules concerning barrack life, almost all dealing with the preservation of cleanliness and order.

Of the lecture-rooms (usually on the 2nd floor of each block) one at least has to be large enough for a whole company, and all are fitted with wireless sets; the large lecture-room has a sound film cinematograph in addition. The basements are fitted with laundries and drying-rooms, and have space for bicycles, motor-cycles, sports gear, etc.

The battalion HQ block contains offices for the battalion commander, the battalion adjutant, the orderly-room clerks and the battalion specialists, medical inspection rooms, and accommodation for the battalion tailor, shoe-maker, etc, and the battalion band, as well as detention cells, unless there should happen to be a centralized detention block. The rest of the block corresponds fairly closely to the other blocks.

The messing and recreation block (*Wirtschaftgebäude*) contains the kitchens, messrooms, canteens and main recreation-rooms. The kitchens are usually large and well planned.

Ancillary buildings, such as stables, riding-schools, garages and workshops vary greatly according to the size of the barracks.

(*e*) New German barracks are normally brick-built and are cement-washed. The standard type of block is about 85 yards long, 20 yards broad and four storeys high, including a storey in the roof with dormer windows but not including the basement. As will be seen by the photograph of the old and new barracks at Wiesbaden, at the end of Part I, the layout of the barracks has not altered much, for old and new are laid out on the same principle. Such barracks are normally easily identifiable from the air with the parade grounds and four-storey buildings with approximately 20 windows in the length to each floor. Behind the main buildings there is normally a range and a number of smaller buildings including garages.

(*f*) Barrack huts, of which there are a very great number being produced in Germany, are of a more or less standard design. They are normally 80 to 100 yards long by 10 yards wide and 15 feet high. Down the centre of the hut runs a three-yard wide corridor with a double swing door at either end, an outer door, and wooden steps.

In the centre of the hut on one side are the washhouse and lavatories, and opening off the corridor on either side are a varying number of rooms, normally 28 to 32 in all. These rooms are of different lengths and have from two to five windows in each. The smallest rooms hold four or five NCOs. The other rooms will accommodate from 15 to 65 men. In each room there is a NCO who is responsible for the conduct of the men in it, and who usually has a bed to himself. All the other beds are arranged in two tiers, and in groups of two together. In emergency extra bed fittings and mattresses can be screwed on the top of these double-tier units. Space for undressing is extremely cramped, but in this way each barrack hut can accommodate 400 to 600 men. The depot of a training regiment of about 10,000 men can be accommodated in 18 such huts.

(g) A report of the end of January, 1944, stated that the plywood hut had stood the test of the winter in the east outstandingly well. This type of hut is shaped like a tent and accommodates 20 people.

Plywood planks, 12 of which form the wall when arranged in a rectangular position, and 12 wedge-shaped planks which form the roof are the principal building material. By appropriate treatment during the processing, the planks become so waterproof that they can be exposed to all weathers and covered with snow or earth without further protection. The Finns were the first to consider the use of plywood planks in building huts.

The plywood hut is well known in many sectors of the front and is particularly popular because it is easily transportable. While a train of 19 wagons is needed if 500 men are to be accommodated in wooden barracks, plywood huts for a similar number of people can be transported in one single wagon. Ten people can set up a hut in 55 minutes. The internal installations are fixed when the outer structure is completed. Hooks, supplied with the huts, are screwed in so that clothes and equipment can be hung up. An iron stove is erected on a base of stones in the centre of the hut. Finally, the flue with a chimney-cowl, which provides ventilation is fixed. A glass panelled door admits light to the hut. Other windows can easily be installed. While the internal installations are being seen to, the hut is camouflaged and surrounded with snow.

The hut, which may now be manufactured in an angular shape, is supplied by factories of the Occupied Eastern Territories. Specially adapted plywood huts are manufactured to accommodate horses.

THE SUPPLY AND ADMINISTRATION OF THE SS

9. (*a*) *Introductory Notes.*—(i) The *SS* maintains its own service of supply and administration. This service is separate and distinct from that of the German Armed Forces and is not subject to control or supervision by the latter. It forms part of the general organization of the *SS* under HIMMLER who is responsible directly to HITLER.

(ii) The various organizations and branches of the *SS* which the *SS* supply and administrative system is designed to serve fall under the following headings:—

The General *SS* (*Allgemeine*).
The Armed *SS* (*Waffen*).
Joint *SS* and Police Administration.
Special *SS* activities.

(iii) The same supply and administrative system is responsible for all the organizations grouped under these four headings. Thus, although the supply needs of the *Waffen SS* are greater than those of any other *SS* organization, it has no special supply system of its own. Particular depots or services are specifically styled *Waffen SS*, but on the other hand, for greater convenience in occupied territory and operational areas, certain services are held in common by *Waffen SS* and Police. This intermingling of the various branches of the *SS* renders impossible a clear cut distinction between *SS* supply at home and *SS* supply in the field.

(iv) In practice the *SS* supply system is not completely adequate to all the demands made upon it. This is particularly evident in the *Waffen SS* which, in certain circumstances and for certain types of equipment, is obliged to rely on the greater depth and range of the supply services of the German Armed Forces. These exceptions to the general self-sufficiency of the *SS* fall into one of two categories.

Supply of certain types of heavy equipment, particularly tanks.
Routine supply of rations, ammunition, petrol, etc, for the *Waffen SS* formations in the field.

(v) With respect to the supply of certain types of heavy equipment, the *Waffen SS* enjoy a high priority in the allotment of heavy equipment by the High Command. In part this may be due to political reasons. It should be remembered, however, that the majority of *SS* divisions are heavily armed assault divisions that would in any case receive priority. There is no reason to suppose that all *Waffen SS* formations irrespective of fighting value or operational employment obtain particular favouritism.

(vi) With respect to routine supply in the field it may be observed as a generalization that the *Waffen SS*, which in the field are regarded by the military authorities as temporarily incorporated into the German Armed Forces, may always be found to make use of the supply services of the Army when under Army command, though this does not debar them from making simultaneous use of the *SS* supply service. But it must be borne in mind that a substantial part of the *Waffen SS* and Police forces are not incorporated in the German Armed Forces and cannot, therefore, normally rely on the latter's supply services.

(vii) It will be noticed that there is a marked tendency for *SS* depots and administrative services to be grouped round concentration camps, notably

SS Central Directorate (*Reichsführung S.S.*)

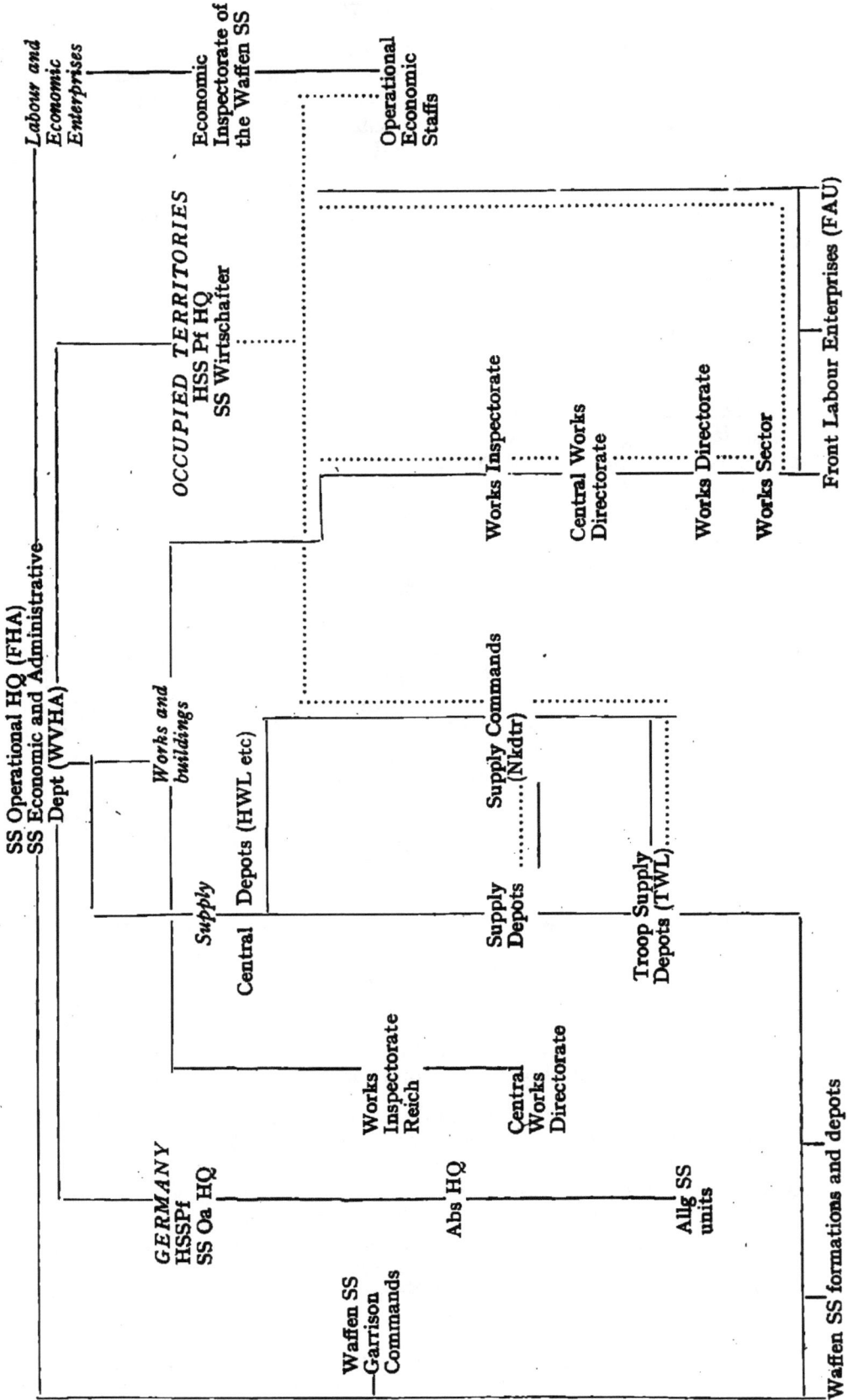

SS Operational HQ (FHA)
SS Economic and Administrative Dept (WVHA)

Labour and Economic Enterprises

Economic Inspectorate of the Waffen SS

Operational Economic Staffs

OCCUPIED TERRITORIES
HSS Pf HQ
SS Wirtschafter

Works and buildings

Supply

Central Depots (HWL etc)

Supply Commands (Nkdtr)

Supply Depots

Troop Supply Depots (TWL)

Works Inspectorate

Central Works Directorate

Works Directorate

Works Sector

Front Labour Enterprises (FAU)

GERMANY
HSSPf
SS Oa HQ

Works Inspectorate Reich

Central Works Directorate

Abs HQ

Allg SS units

Waffen SS Garrison Commands

Waffen SS formations and depots

ORANIENBURG (NW of BERLIN) and DACHAU (near MUNICH). There are several reasons for this:

The same *SS* department controls both camps and depots.

Barracks and dwelling houses of *SS* guards and administrative personnel formed a nucleus before the war for the expansion which followed.

The inmates of the camp provided a cheap source of labour.

(viii) It may be added that the *SS* economic system includes not only the salient features of a normal military supply system but also the productive exploitation of certain types of labour and raw materials both in GERMANY and the occupied territories.

(b) General Organization of the SS.

(i) It will be convenient to preface the account of the supply system of the *SS* with a brief description of the general machinery of *SS* administration.

(ii) *Central organization.*—The central directorate of the *SS* (*Reichsführung SS*) consists of Chief of the *SS* (*Reichsführer SS*—abbreviated *RfSS*) *i.e.*, HIMMLER, assisted by Personal Staff *RfSS* (*Persönlicher Stab RfSS*). This staff is primarily an advisory and co-ordinating body but it includes a number of officials with special duties, together with the heads of the

SS Main Departments (*SS Hauptämter*).

All *SS* activities are directed either by the Personal Staff *RfSS* or by the Main Departments.

(iii) *Regional Organization—GERMANY.*—For purposes of *SS* administration GERMANY is divided into districts (*Oberabschnitte*—abbreviated *Oa*) each corresponding almost exactly with a military district (*Wehrkreis*). Each *Oa* is administered by a Senior *SS* and Police Commander (*Höherer SS und Polizeiführer*—abbreviated *HSSPf*) who is HIMMLER'S immediate representative in the area concerned and has his own HQ and Staff. Each *SS Oa* is in turn divided into sub-districts (*Abschnitt*—abbreviated *Abs*) each again with its commander (*Abschnittsführer*) and staff.

(iv) *Regional Organization—Occupied Territories.*—The same general pattern of administration is found in occupied territories. Where *SS* and Police interests make it expedient, an *HSSPf* with Staff is appointed for a specific area. His status is that of an *HSSPf* of an *Oa* in GERMANY although his area is usually much bigger, *e.g.*, occupied RUSSIA was divided (1943) into three areas—Baltic, Centre and South (*Ostland, Mitte, Süd*) each with its *HSSPf*. In two cases, both immediately on the borders of the Reich, the area of an external *HSSPf* has been formally established as *Oa*. These are HOLLAND (*Oa NORD-WEST*) and NORWAY (*Oa NORD*). As a rule, however, the area of an external *HSSPf* is not called an *Oa* but is simply given a descriptive territorial title. Within this area the *HSSPf* controls all *SS* and Police activities and though co-operating closely with the local military authorities is directly responsible to the *SS* headquarters in BERLIN.

(v) *Regional Organization—Waffen SS.*—Normally all *Waffen SS* units and depots are immediately subordinate to the *SS* headquarters. Where a measure of decentralization seems advisable, a local Commander of the *Waffen SS* (*Befehlshaber der Waffen SS*) is appointed, *e.g.*, HOLLAND, BOHEMIA-MORAVIA. In addition, where *SS* troops and depots are permanently stationed in a district, *SS* Garrison Commands (*SS Standorte*) are set up with commanders and staffs.

(c) *The Organization of Supply.*—(i) *Central Organization of Supply.*—In the *Reichsführung SS* two *Hauptämter* are primarily concerned in the administration and organization of supply. Both are located in BERLIN.

SS Operational HQ (*SS Führungshauptamt* abbreviated *FHA*).—This is the chief executive department of the *SS*. It contains the executive HQs of the *Allgemeine SS* and of the *Waffen SS* (*Kommandoamt der Allgemeinen SS, Kommandoamt der Waffen SS*). Its main task has become the administration of the *Waffen SS* including both the field formations and the depot and training units which serve them.

SS Economic and Administrative Department (*SS Wirtschafts und Verwaltungshauptamt* abbreviated *WVHA*).—This department is responsible for the organization of supply and financial administration of the *SS*. It administers depots, stores and parks, work and buildings, industrial and agricultural undertakings, and also the concentration camps.

(ii) *Regional Organization of Supply—GERMANY.*—At the Staff of the *Oa* HQ there is an administrative department (*Verwaltung*) which deals direct with WVHA on matters of supply and finance. Similarly at *Abs* HQ there is an administrative service (*Verwaltungsdienst*) with the same functions.

As *Oa* and *Abs* HQ are concerned primarily with the administration of the *Allgemeine SS* which is for the most part an unpaid, part-time, paramilitary formation, the administration of finance and supply does not need very complicated machinery. Small stocks of uniforms and equipment are, however, held at *Abs HQ* and possibly also at *Oa* HQ.

(iii) *Regional Organization of Supply—Occupied Territory.*—On the staff of the *HSSPf* in occupied territory there is an economic section controlled by an official, usually with the rank of brigadier, known as an *SS Wirtschafter*. As subordinate officials at lower levels are also known by the same title, it is customary to add the HQ to which the *Wirtschafter* is attached, e.g., *SS Wirtschafter beim HSSPf NORD*.

(iv) The *SS Wirtschafter* with the *HSSPf* is responsible for the administration of all *SS* economic activity within his area, *i.e.*, depots, stores, works and buildings, industrial and agricultural undertakings, and all financial questions arising out of them. He also liaises with the competent *SS* authorities on matters of transport. The exact organization of the staff at his disposal probably varies with the area concerned but a typical division on the Eastern Front is into groups (*Gruppen*).
e.g.—

Supply Group (*Gruppe Wirtschaft*).
Works and Building (*Gruppe Bauwesen*).
Industry (*Gruppe Industrie*).
Mining (*Gruppe Bergbau*).

(v) *Regional Organization of Supply—Waffen SS.*—At the HQ of the *SS* Garrison Commands there is an administrative department (*SS Standortsverwaltung*) dealing with supply and finance. Limited stocks of clothing and equipment are held.

Where field formations of the *Waffen SS* are likely to operate in a particular area for a considerable period special *ad hoc* supply bases (*Stützpunkte*) are usually established at convenient points. These are small and temporary in character.

(d) *Chain of Supply.*—(i) The normal process for the supply by *WVHA* of units controlled by *FHA* is as follows. The unit concerned indents on *FHA* for its specific requirements. If approved, *FHA* instructs *WVHA* to make the necessary issue. *WVHA* will then either dispatch the material direct to the unit from one of the central depots or from the factory or arrange for it to be made available for the unit at the nearest convenient sub-depot.

(ii) The main stocks of supply are held in central *SS* depots. These are of two kinds.

Main Supply Depots (*Hauptwirtschaftslager* abbreviated *HWL*). Five of these have been identified:—

AUSCHWITZ (OSWIECIM Poland).
BADEN-BADEN (*Wkr* V).
BERLIN (*Wkr* III).
DANZIG (*Wkr* XX).
KASSEL-BREITENBACH (*Wkr* IX).

Special Depots.

Central Distribution Centre (*SS Zentralzulassungstelle*). ORANIENBURG (*Wkr.* III).
Central Ordnance Depot (*SS Hauptzeugamt*). ORANIENBURG (*Wkr* III).
Ordnance Depot (*SS Zeugamt*). DACHAU (*Wkr* VII).

MT Depots (*SS Kraftfahrzeug Depot*)—
ORANIENBURG (*Wkr* III).
BERLIN—LICHTERFELDE (*Wkr* III).
PRAGUE (Protectorate).
SCHROTTERSBURG (*Wkr* I).

MT Park (*SS Kraftfahrzeuglager*) PRAGUE (Protectorate).
Signals Equipment Depot (*SS Nachrichtenzeugamt*) ORANIENBURG *Wkr* III).
Chief Medical Equipment Depot (*SS Hauptsanitätslager*) BERLIN—LICHTERFELDE (*Wkr* III).
Branch Medical Equipment Depot (*SS Sanitätszweiglager*) PRAGUE (Protectorate).
Clothing Depots (*SS Bekleidungslager*)—
BERGEN—BELSEN (*Wkr* XI).
PRETTIN/ELBE (*Wkr* IV).
RIGA (Latvia).
SPREMBERG (*Wkr* III).
SCHLACKENWERTH (*Wkr* XIII).
WARSAW (General Government).

Repair and Maintenance of Clothing Depots (*SS Kleiderkasse*)—
BERLIN (*Wkr* I).
PRAGUE (Protectorate).

(iii) From these central depots are fed the chain of outlying sub-depots. These are of two kinds—

Supply Depots (*SS Nachschubslager*).

These are found both in GERMANY and in occupied territory. Only two have been so far identified inside GERMANY, *viz*—

BUCHENWALD (*Wkr* IX).
RAVENSBRUECK/Mecklenburg (*Wkr* II).

There are concentration camps at both these places and it is probable that other important concentration camps in GERMANY also have Supply Depots.

Troop Supply Depots (SS *Truppenwirtschaftslager* abbreviated *TWL*).
A large number of these exist both in GERMANY and in occupied terri-
tory. They hold stocks of clothing, light equipment, fuel and canteen goods.
The following TWL have been identified in GERMANY and Western Europe.

BERLIN (*Wkr* III).
BRUNSWICK (*Wkr* XI).
DANZIG/LANGFOHR (*Wkr* XX).
LUNEBURG (*Wkr* X).
PARIS/VILLETTE (France).
THORN (*Wkr* XX).
WEHLAU (*Wkr* I).

(iv) On the Eastern Front, which so far has absorbed most of the effort
of the *SS* Supply service, *SS* Supply Commands (*SS Nachschubskommandan-
turen* abbreviated *Nkdtr*) have been established. Five of these exist
(1943), viz:—

Nkdtr Finnland	...	...	...	HQ OULU.
Nkdtr Russland Nord	...	...		HQ RIGA.
Nkdtr Russland Mitte	...	...		HQ BOBRUISK.*
Nkdtr Russland Süd	...	...		HQ DJNEPROPETROVSK.*

* Now evacuated to Poland.

(v) Each *Nkdtr* is in itself an important group of depots and administrative offices. It is normally commanded by an *SS* officer of the rank of senior
colonel. Although subordinated for administrative purposes to the *SS Wirtschafter* with the local *HSSPf*, it is the primary link between the *SS* headquarters and main depots in GERMANY, and the *SS* units and sub-depots
in its own areas. It serves both as a distributing centre and a supply base
and in its depots are held arms, ammunition, MT, equipment, captured
material, clothing, POL, coal, wood, building material and canteen goods.
It is also empowered, subject to the approval of the *SS Wirtschafter* with
HSSPf, to make contracts or purchases with private firms in its area.

(e) *Works and Buildings.*—(i) The central authority for Works and
Buildings are two sections—
(a) Works (*Amt Bauten*)
(b) Buildings (*Amt Haushalt*)
in *WVHA*.

(ii) The regional administration of works and buildings is organized in
the following chain of command.

Works Inspectorate (Bauinspektion).
Germany proper is divided into four Works Inspectorates:—

Bauinspektion Reich Nord ...		HQ BERLIN-ZEHLENDORF (Wkr III).
,,	,, *Ost* ...	HQ POSEN (Wkr XXI).
,,	,, *Süd* ...	HQ DACHAU (Wkr VII).
,,	,, *West* ...	HQ WIESBADEN (Wkr XII).

In occupied territory each Inspectorate appears to correspond
with the area of an *HSSPf*. The title " of the *Waffen SS* and
Police " is usually affixed to the various works HQs and sectors
in its area.

Central Works Directorate. (Zentralbauleitung).
Works Directorate. (Bauleitung.)
Works Sector. (Oberbauabschnitt.)
Works Sub-Sector. (Bauabschnitt.)

(f) *Labour and Economic Enterprises.*—(i) One important aspect of the economic administration of the SS is the exploitation of occupied territory and prison labour.

In Germany prisoners in concentration camps work in quarries and gravel-pits or in light industries attached to the camp, *e.g.* :—

the SS clothing factory (SS *Bekleidungswerke*) DACHAU.

(ii) In occupied territory, particularly RUSSIA and POLAND, the SS have engaged in quarrying, mining, farming and stock-breeding, lumbering and road making, either with hired local labour or prison labour or by contract with private firms. These activities are mainly carried on by the *Waffen SS* under the direction of the Central Economic Directorate of the *Waffen SS* (*Hauptwirtschaftsleitung der Waffen SS*) in BERLIN. The regional direction is under the supervision of Economic Inspectorates (*Wirtschaftsinspektion der Waffen SS*) who probably collaborate closely with the department of the SS *Wirtschafter* with *HSSPf.*

(iii) For supervision of special economic undertakings in RUSSIA Operational Economic Staffs (SS *Wirtschaftskommandos*) were also formed. These were probably temporary *ad hoc* bodies.

(iv) To facilitate the execution of these enterprises and also to supply skilled labour and direction for ordinary SS works and undertakings in occupied territory special SS Front Labour Units (SS *Frontarbeiterunternehmen* abbreviated *FAU*) are formed. The hiring and allocation of labour other than that secured locally is co-ordinated by the SS Front Labour Control Office (SS *Frontarbeiterleitstelle*) attached to *WVHA*. Where necessary special transit camps (SS *Frontarbeiterdurchgangslager*) are set up for these front workers.

(v) In addition SS Works Battalions and Brigades (SS *Baubataillon, Baubrigade*), have been identified. These probably use concentration camp labour.

(g) *Transport.*—The transport of SS supplies is co-ordinated by the Transport Officer (*Transportoffizier* abbreviated *TO*) at *FHA*.

Other SS *TO* functions at the *Nkdtr* on the Eastern Front and at principal railway stations in GERMANY and in occupied territory.

At railway junctions particularly important for SS transport, reloading stations (SS *Umschlagstelle*) are established.

(h) *Petrol, Oil and Fuel.*—Units and depots indent on *FHA* for petrol and oil and are either supplied direct from central depots or draw from the nearest Supply Depot or *TWL*. Empty fuel containers are returned *via* the normal SS supply route.

In RUSSIA wood and peat are usually obtained locally. Coal is supplied through the ordinary SS supply channels and stocks for issue are held down to *TWL* level. To facilitate the supply of coal at the source, an SS coal liaison officer (SS *Kohlenverbindungstelle*) is set up at KATTOWITZ/Silesia.

(i) *Post and Communications.*—There is a Field Post Section (*Abteilung Feldpostwesen*) at *FHA* which is responsible for the administration of the SS Field Post service. In collaboration with the appropriate Wehrmacht authorities it allots SS Field Post numbers.

An SS air courier service is maintained with stations (*Kurierstellen*) at important SS depots and in operational areas where SS formations are engaged.

The whole long distance communication system of the SS is supervised by the Chief of Communications (*Chef des Fernmeldewesens*) on the Staff of *RFSS*.

(j) *Medical Services.*—(i) General supervision over the medical services of the *SS* is exercised by two officers:

Chief *SS* and Police Medical Officer who is attached to the Staff of *RFSS*.

Head of the *SS* Medical Corps who acts as general inspector of *SS* Medical Services.

(ii) Actual administration is carried out by the Medical Department (*Amtsgruppe D, Sanitätswesen*) in *FHA* which controls *SS* hospitals and medical services in GERMANY and in occupied territories as well as the medical units attached to *SS* formations in the field.

(iii) Within GERMANY there are the following *SS* medical institutions.

Hygiene Institute of the *Waffen SS* (*Hygieneinstitut der Waffen SS*).

BERLIN (*Wkr* III)

Medical Disabilities Examination Clinic of the *Waffen SS* (*Gesundheitsverzehrungsprüfstelle de Waffen SS* abbreviated *GV Prüfstelle*).

DACHAU (*Wkr* VII).

Neurological—Psychiatrical Observation Clinic of the *Waffen SS* (*Neurologisch—psychiatrisch Beobachtungstation der Waffen SS*).

GIESSEN/LAHN (*Wkr* IX).

SS Hospitals (*SS Lazarett*).

BAD NAUHEIM (*Wkr* IX).
BERLIN (*Wkr* III).
DACHAU (*Wkr* VII).
GIESSEN/LAHN (*Wkr* IX).
HOHENLYCHEN/BRANDENBURG (*Wkr* III).
NÜRNBERG (*Wkr* XIII).
SELLIN-RÜGEN (*Wkr* II).
VIENNA (*Wkr* XVII).

SS Convalescent Homes (*SS Genesungsheime*).

BAD HOMBURG (*Wkr* XII).
KARLSBAD (*Wkr* XIII).

SS Maternity Home (*SS Entbindungsheim*).

BERLIN-LICHTERFELDE (*Wkr* III).

(iv) In the field, besides the medical companies and field ambulances attached to *SS* formations, forward hospitals are set up. In addition mobile units of

SS X-ray Detachment (*SS Röntgen Sturmbann*)

SS Bacteriological Field Laboratory (*SS Bakteriologisches Feldlaboratorium*)

are stationed in operational areas.

(v) It does not, however, automatically follow that all *SS* casualties are evacuated through *SS* medical channels. Local circumstances may make it difficult or inexpedient to use *SS* medical facilities and it frequently happens that *SS* wounded are evacuated as far as base hospitals in GERMANY entirely through army medical channels.

(k) *Veterinary Service of the Waffen SS.*—(i) At *division* there is a Veterinary company. At *corps* there is a Veterinary Depot (*Pferdepark*).

(ii) On the Eastern Front evacuation of sick horses and supply of remounts normally pass through the following channels.

Veterinary Evacuating and Remount Station (*SS Pferdesammel und Ersatzlager*).

    ZAMOSC (Poland).

Veterinary Hospital (*SS Pferdelazarett*).

    RADOM (Poland).

Base Veterinary Hospital (*Heimatpferdelazarett der Waffen SS*).

    KIELCE (Poland).

Veterinary Depots.

    (i) The Central Veterinary Depot (*Hauptveterinärpark der Waffen SS*) WARSAW (Poland).

    (ii) Subsidiary Depots (*SS Veterinärpark*) in forward areas.

Remount Depots (*SS Remonteamt*).

    REJOWICE (Poland).
    PELTERS near METZ (*Wkr* XII).

(l) *Repair and Maintenance of Vehicles and Equipment.*—(i) In forward areas, besides the repair and recovery sections at divisions, independent sections may operate at Supply Depots or at Supply Commands (*Nkdtr*).

(ii) In GERMANY facilities for repair exist at—

(a) The appropriate SS central depots.

(b) SS Ordnance Testing Workshop (*SS Waffenamt Prüfungswerkstätte*).
    DACHAU (*Wkr* VII).
    SS Ordnance Works (*Ausrüstungswerke der Waffen SS*).
    DACHAU (*Wkr* VII).

Extensive use is also made of army repair facilities.

10. *Communications in Germany.*

(a) *Railways.*—(i) *System of working of Reichsbahn.*—*Relationship of State.*—Under the Reichsbahn re-organization of Jan, 1937, the Reichsbahn became a state-owned undertaking, with considerable financial, administrative and operating autonomy; it is regarded as a public service which should be as self-supporting as possible.

Internal Organization.—The headquarters organization of the Reichsbahn is combined with the Railway Department of the Ministry of Transport, and the posts of Minister of Transport and General Manager of the Reichsbahn are combined in one person. The headquarters organization is responsible for all matters of policy on which a common line of action is required, but it is not concerned with routine control and day to day operations which are effected by the Divisional Managements (*Reichsbahndirektionen*) of which at the beginning of 1938 there were 26. On certain matters of policy the Minister has the advice of a special Advisory Council (*Beirat*) formed of prominent representatives of industry, trade and public life.

Under the Ministry there are also two technical offices (*Reichsbahn Zentralämter*), in BERLIN and MUNICH, in charge of mechanical and civil engineering, workshops, research and other technical matters on which a common policy is required for the whole system; there are also certain other offices with special technical functions, but in every case their function is technical rather than administrative.

The operation and day to day management of the system, including the workshops, is entirely in the hands of the *Reichsbahndirektionen*, and in order to ensure the necessary co-ordination between them, there are three Area Operating Offices (*Generalbetriebsleitungen*) in BERLIN (East), ESSEN (West) and MUNICH (South) responsible for co-ordinating traffic and train working in the *Reichsbahndirektionen* under their respective control. The *Generalbetriebsleitungen* are concerned only with traffic and train working, and have no administrative control over the *Reichsbahndirektionen* which are all responsible direct to Berlin.

The various *Reichsbahndirektionen* are also allocated various special functions, for which the local district offices are responsible. Under each *Reichsbahndirektion* are the local district offices including *Verkehrsämter* (Commercial), *Bau-und Betriebsämter* (Civil Engineering and Operating) and *Maschinenämter* (Locomotives and Rolling Stock), responsible for their particular functions in their own districts.

(ii) *War-Time Changes in Organization.*—The system has expanded to cope with increased traffic at home, and to provide controlling headquarters for the railways in the occupied territories, but fundamentally the organization of the *Reichsbahn* is unchanged.

The most important organizational development was the formation, in the autumn of 1940, of a special organization for the co-ordination of all forms of transport in Germany itself. The very heavy demands on the *Reichsbahn* were necessitating not only the mobilization of its own resources but those of the entire transport machine to ensure that each form of transport played to the full that part for which it was most suited. The scheme provided for the setting up of : —

    A Central Traffic Office (*Hauptverkehrsleitung*) under the Presidency of the Ministry of Transport, and composed of the heads of the departments of the Ministry.

    Three Area Traffic Offices (*Gebietsverkehrsleitungen*) in ESSEN (West), BERLIN (East) and MUNICH (South) corresponding to the three Area Operating Offices (*Generalbetriebsleitungen*) of the *Reichsbahn* in these cities, and composed of representatives of each form of transport in the Areas;

    Divisional Traffic Offices (*Bezirksverkehrsleitungen*) corresponding to each Divisional Management (*Reichsbahndirektion*) of the *Reichsbahn*, and composed of representatives of each form of transport in the Divisions.

(iii) *Military Organization.*—*General.*—The closest co-operation is maintained between the civil and the military authorities affecting service transport. The basic structure of the railway organization, therefore, remains the same; the difference is that in war, there is a parallel military organization acting alongside, but not superior to, the civil organization. These remarks are true of Germany and the occupied countries.

Responsibility of OKW.—The German railway system, together with the railways of occupied territories, are supervised in so far as they are used by the armed forces by the *Oberkommando der Wehrmacht* (*OKW*). The *OKW* has a special department, *Abteilung V* (Department V) to deal with matters of transport. The head of the department is Gen Lt GEHRKE, a member of the General Staff, with the title of " Director-General of Transportation " (*Chef des Transportwesens*). He controls all military traffic on railways, waterways and the road system, including the *Reichsautobahn* network. Every plan of movement has to be submitted to the Head of Transportation to ensure its smooth functioning. The full details of this department are given under Section 1 of Part I.

(iv) *Organization in Germany and Occupied Europe.*—Germany and Occupied Europe are further sub-divided into five railway sub-departments (*Eisenbahn Transport Abteilungen*), one each for West, Centre, East, S-West and Paris. Each of these departments is under the control of an Armed Forces Movement Control (*Wehrmachtverkehrsdirektion*).

There are two further transport officers who act apparently independently of the " Director-General of Transportation ". They are the Supreme Transport Commander FINLAND (*Transport Bevollmächtigter FINLAND*) and the Supreme Transport Commander ROME (*Transport Bevollmächtigter ROM*). In cases of necessity a Supreme Transport Commander may be attached to an Army Group or Army.

Liaison between these offices and military units is effected by the area movement HQs (*Transportkommandanturen*), acting in collaboration with civilian officials called *Bahnbevollmächtigter*. Together they deliberate upon the transport requirements of the military and work out the best and smoothest method of meeting these requirements within their particular theatre of operation.

RTO's (*Bahnhofsoffiziere*) lately re-named *Bahnhofskommandantur II*, are appointed by the OKW in concurrence with the German Ministry of Transport. They are responsible for the police supervision of the stations to which they are attached and they establish liaison between military units and the local station authorities with particular regard to the prevention of unauthorized military interference in the working of the station. They do not command civilian railway personnel. Similarly, if they consider military interests to be jeopardized by the conduct of the civilian station authorities they can report the circumstances to the *Transport Kommandanturen*. The RTO's with their staff wear white armlets (bearing an official stamp), on the left arm.

If there is need, station HQs (*Bahnhofskommandanturen*) lately renamed *Bahnhofskommandantur I* are set up to fulfil the functions of the RTO where the larger size of the station and the importance of the traffic warrant a larger staff. Like the RTO's their function is to ensure smooth working at the stations, dealing with the flow of military supplies, maintaining order and discipline and establishing liaison between the military and civil authorities.

Whenever service personnel are passengers or escorts, the officer or NCO i/c party (*Transport Führer*) is appointed by the responsible military authority. He is responsible for discipline during the journey. If several drafts are on the train, the senior officer or NCO i/c party assumes command.

(v) *Rolling Stock and Locomotives available with Reserves.*—Steam *Locomotives.*—During the 10 years before the war, the number of locomotives owned by the Reichsbahn fell by 2,500; but during this period the number under and awaiting repair fell by 37 per cent, and the number available for service was therefore only down by 4 per cent.

In spite of the increasing average age of locomotives (22·18 years in 1937, against a life of 30-40 years) the improvements in the new building and the increased efficiency in repairs and maintenance made possible a steady increase in annual mileage.

During the war, the situation grew steadily more difficult until the severe winter 1941-42, when locomotive casualties in Russia caused a crisis. Locomotive construction was then given priority, and the situation was at least no worse, probably somewhat improved, by December, 1943. Orderly withdrawal in Russia eased matters still further.

Estimated locomotive position December, 1943.—The latest detailed information on the locomotive position in the " Old Reich " area is the state as known at the end of 1937, that is before the incorporation of the Austrian Federal Railways into the *Reichsbahn*. These figures are included below as they give a working basis for calculation of present figures. Prior to the war, the locomotive stock of the German railways was adequate to deal with the traffic normally handled and to cover additional traffic commitments at peak periods. After the outbreak of war, however, there developed a definite shortage of locomotives in Germany and German-occupied Europe generally, and this came about as the result of two major factors—firstly, the great increase in traffic, both in terms of tonnage handled and length of haul, which took place on the German railways, and secondly, the necessity for dispersing a considerable proportion of the German locomotive stock over vast areas of occupied Russia.

To alleviate the effects of this shortage in the Reich itself, locomotives were drawn into Germany from other occupied territories such as France and Belgium, a process which caused serious operating problems in those countries. At the same time Germany stimulated the production of new locomotives throughout occupied Europe, but actual output still appears to be lagging considerably behind the production programme envisaged, and only fairly recently have the Germans begun to feel the benefits of the rationalisation measures which they introduced into the locomotive industry early in the war. These measures included the concentration of production firstly on a simplified version of the series " 50 " 2-10-0 goods locomotive known as the " transition locomotive " (*Übergangslokomotive*), and latterly on the series " 52 " 2-10-0 goods locomotive known as the " war locomotive " (*Kriegslokomotive*). The latter type is designed to make the most economical use of available materials and to accelerate output and it is claimed to effect a great saving in production man-hours.

Since July, 1943, the Germans are estimated to have lost an aggregate of about 12,000 miles of railway line in Russia and Italy, while, at the same time withdrawing the majority of the locomotives previously used on those lines, estimated at about 4,000. This means, in effect, that the Germans found themselves with 4,000 extra locomotives to work a system reduced by about 12,000 route miles. Coupled with Germany's increasing locomotive production, this implies a somewhat easier locomotive position throughout German-occupied Europe. This does not mean that the German locomotive position is no longer difficult, but rather that it is now out of the " critical " stage, and the altered balance is indicated by a recent report that the temporary priority of production which locomotives enjoyed over tanks has now been withdrawn.

The following table gives the locomotive stock of the whole *Reichsbahn* system excluding Austria, as it was in 1937. It is included merely because it is the only detailed basis for calculation available.

	Number
Steam locomotives with tenders—	
With 2 coupled axles	8
,, 3 ,, ,, ...	4,513
,, 4 ,, ,, ...	4,186
,, 5 ,, ,, ...	3,518
,, 6 ,, ,, ...	44
Total	12,269
Tank locomotives—	
With 2 coupled axles	184
,, 3 ,, ,, ...	3,742
,, 4 ,, ,, ...	2,316
,, 5 ,, ,, ...	1,622
,, 6 ,, ,, ...	11
,, 8 ,, ,, ...	22
Total	7,897
Total, Steam Locomotives	20,166
Locomotives of special types	2
Electric locomotives—	
With 2 or 3 driving axles	97
,, 4 ,, ,, ...	361
,, 6 ,, ,, ...	85
Total	543
Total, all Locomotives	20,711*
Railcars—	
Steam	18
Electric	1,193
Oil and other types	808
Total	2,019

(* Of this number, only about 1 per cent (less than 250) are narrow-gauge locomotives.)

The steam locomotive stock of the *Reichsbahn* may be broadly classified under two heads—firstly, locomotives of former constituent systems of the *Reichsbahn* (Prussian State Railways, Bavarian State Railways, etc.), and secondly, locomotives of standard types (" *Einheitslokomotiven* ") built since the formation of the *Reichsbahn*. The second class includes the special wartime locomotive types (" *Kriegslokomotiven* ") designed to accelerate locomotive production and make the most economical use of available materials.

The following table shows the classification of the *Reichsbahn* steam locomotive stock under the above-mentioned heads, and also according to main types and series:—

Main Type	Classification	Series	Remarks
S	Express train locomotives with tenders	01	*Einheitslokomotive*
		01^{10}	,,
		02	,,
		02^{1}	,,
		03	,,
		03^{10}	,,
		05	,,
		06	,,
		17^{2}	Former Prussian S10² class
		17 10–12	,, ,, S10¹ ,,
		18	,, Bavarian S3/6 class
		18°	,, Saxon XVIII H class
		18^{1}	,, Wurtem C class
		18^{3}	,, Baden IV h¹⁻³ class
		19°	,, Saxon XX H V class
P	Passenger train locomotives with tenders	24	*Einheitslokomotive*
		37 0–1	Former Prussian P6 class
		38 2–3	,, Saxon XII H2 class
		38^{4}	,, Bavarian P3/5 H class
		38 10–40	,, Prussian P8 class
		39 0–2	,, ,, P10 ,,
G	Goods train locomotives with tenders	41	*Einheitslokomotive*
		43	,,
		44	,,
		45	,,
		50	,,
		52	*Kriegslokomotive*
		55 25–56	Former Prussian G8¹ class
		57 10–40	,, ,, G10 ,,
		58 2–3	,, Baden G12 class
		58^{4}	,, Saxon XIII H class
		58^{5}	,, Wurtem G12 class
		58 10–22	,, Prussian G12 ,,
		59°	,, Wurtem K class
St	Express train tank locomotives	61	*Einheitslokomotive*
Pt	Passenger train tank locomotives	62	*Einheitslokomotive*
		64	,,
		71°	,,
		74 4–13	Former Prussian T12 class
		75°	,, Wurtem T5
		75 5, 1^{0-11}	,, Baden VIc⁴⁻⁹ class
		75^{5}	,, Saxon XIV HT class
		77^{1}	,, Bavarian Pt 3/6 class
		78 0–10	,, Prussian T18 class
Gt	Goods train tank locomotives	80	*Einheitslokomotive*
		81	,,
		84	,,
		85	,,
		86	,,
		87	,,
		89	,,

Main Type	Classification	Series	Remarks
Gt— *contd.*	Goods train tank locomotives— *contd.*	93 5–20 94[1] 94 5–18 94 20–21 95[0] 96[0]	Former Prussian T14[1] class „ Wurtem Tn class „ Prussian T16[1] class „ Saxon XI HT class „ Prussian T20 class „ Bavarian Gt2×4,4 class
Z	Rack locomotives	97[1] 95[5]	Former Bavarian PtzL3/4 class „ Wurtem E+1Z class
L	Light railway locomotives ...	98[5]	Former Bavarian PtL3/4 class
K	Narrow-gauge locomotives ...	99[22] 99[32] 99[73]	*Einheitslokomotive* (1m gauge) *Einheitslokomotive* (900mm gauge) *Einheitslokomotive* (750mm gauge)

The series index numbers shown in the above table are followed by a set of three or four figures indicating the number of an individual locomotive in its particular series. Thus an engine numbered 03 124 is an express train locomotive with tender, is of the 03 " Einheitslokomotive " series, and is locomotive number 124 of that series.

There is a further method used to classify the *Reichsbahn* steam locomotives for operating purposes, and known as the " *Betriebsgattung* ". In this classification, the main type letter (as given in the above table) is used, followed by the number of coupled axles, the total number of axles, and the average axle-load in tons. Thus a locomotive of series 18 (a locomotive of the former Bavarian S 3/6 Class) has the " Betriebsgattung " rating S.36.17, *i.e.*, it is an express train tender locomotive with three coupled axles, a total of six locomotive axles, and an average axle load of 17 tons.

Electric Locomotives.—Out of a total route length of some 34,000 miles of the German State Railways in the " Old Reich " (*i.e.*, excluding Austria, etc), about 1,400 miles are electrified. Details are as follows:—

Country, Railway and Lines Electrified	Electric Mileage		Voltage	System of Electrification	Conductor	Year Electrified
	Route	All Track				
GERMANY— State Railway—						
Breslau, Gorlitz, etc. ...	217	520	15,000	1/16 2/3	o H	1914–28
Leipzig, Magdeburg, Halle	178	630	15,000	1/16 2/3	o H	1922–34
Bavaria & Württemberg ...	728	1,655	15,000	1/16 2/3	o H	1912–38
Basle-Zell, Sackingen ...	30	63	15,000	1/15	o H	1913
Höllental, Dreiseen ...	35	86	15,000	1/50	o H	1936
Saxony, near Plauen ...	3	4	650	DC	o H	1916
Hamburg Harbour... ...	1	56	3,000	1/25	o H	1911
Hamburg Suburban ...	20	...	6,000	1/25	o H	1903–24
Berlin Suburban (E) ...	158	380	800	DC	3 R	1903–33
Munich Local	38	50	750	DC	o H	...
Isar Valley	11	...	1,000	DC	o H	1903–9

As regards the numbers of electric locomotives available the total in 1937 was 543. It is thought that this figure has remained virtually the same. There exist in addition about 2,000 railcars, divided up as follows:—

Steam	18
Electric	1,193
Oil and other types	808
	2,019

Diesel railcars have been widely used on the *Reichsbahn* for two different kinds of services, *i.e.*,

Firstly for very fast long distance services between the principal cities. These services have, however, been withdrawn since the outbreak of war. The train normally consisted of two cars powered by two Maybach 410 hp diesel engines with electrical transmission.

Secondly, for semi through services, local services and express light goods trains. The railcars used for these services are of numerous types, typical being the Maybach engined 820 hp twin car sets used for accelerated inter-urban passenger traffic in the Ruhr area.

Goods Wagons.—Facts and estimates are available for additions to stock, but little is available to indicate the extent of losses by obsolescence, export, allied action or sabotage.

The average age of wagons in 1937 was 22·18 years (against a 40-year life). This was high, and required a fast building programme to compete with obsolescence alone.

There has been an acute shortage of wagons throughout the war. In January, 1940, to ease the situation, an overload of 1 ton per wagon was ordered; this was raised to 2 tons in July, 1942; during 1943 the order was cancelled, but during the autumnal traffic peak in 1943 an overload of 1 ton was re-imposed, and this has since been increased to 2 tons again. This hard use must have had an adverse effect on the condition of stock, and is symptomatic of the general wagon situation.

Pre-war figures for 1938 include the following types:—

Covered wagons	213,000
Open or Flat	399,000
Railway service	20,000

Almost all were four-wheeled, except 12,000 bogie flat wagons.
War: Estimated new building—

1940	40,000
1941	70,000
1942	100,000

Priority was at first given to oil tank wagons, then to 27-ton open trucks, and later to flats and special bogie flats for tanks. It is reported that a census of wagons in May, 1943, showed a total of 559,000 wagons.

Passenger coaches and vans.—*Peace.*—In 1938 the *Reichsbahn* owned (including Austrian) 73,543 passenger coaches, seating 3,547,000 passengers. Of these 25,727 were four-wheeled, 31,094 six-wheeled and 16,522 bogie. Vans: 22,042. This stock was adequate in quantity.

War.—For war conditions the stock was ample, and much passenger stock has been converted to hospital trains, winter accommodation for troops on the Eastern Front, and other special purposes. Some of these were " hired " from and converted by the French and Belgian railways.

(vi) *Bomb Damage.*—The amount of railway damage *beyond repair* during the present war caused by the bombing of Germany is extremely small. It is impossible to relate the extent of such totally irreparable damage to German railway facilities as a whole, as obviously no satisfactory index may be evolved for this purpose. It must, however, be borne in mind that the temporary effects of bomb damage to German railways have often been severe.

(vii) *State of repair of railways.*—All the main lines (*Hauptbahnen*) are capable of taking 18 or 20 ton axle loads, and on secondary lines (*Neben-bahnen*) the normal axle load is 15 or 16 tons.

Between the wars the *Reichsbahn* carried out a heavy programme of track renewal; and on the main lines these renewals included the latest improvements. Germany's high-speed running from 1933 onwards set the world a new standard, and its success proves the excellent quality of the track. Little-used track, points and crossings have been combed out to help in re-laying the Russian railways on the German gauge. But, in spite of all statements to the contrary, the *Reichsbahn* was in excellent condition at the outbreak of war; the meagre information available suggests that it has been well-maintained during the war, and there is no indication of any serious weakness in the German permanent way position.

(viii) *Personnel, Morale, Staff.*—*Pre-war Staff.*—Well educated and trained, technically efficient, and adequate for the traffic at that date. The higher grades especially were over-staffed. In the years before the war, Nazi Party members infiltrated less into the Reichsbahn than into other spheres of activity, and appointments were normally made on technical ability.

Wartime changes in staff.—The very heavy increase in traffic in Germany itself and the need to provide staff for the various supervisory offices established in the occupied territories, has made a heavy demand for staff, particularly in the administrative and supervisory grades.

In addition to the above demand, it has been necessary to appoint German Liaison Officers at the various railway centres and in the various railway workshops throughout the occupied territories, while in Russia a very large proportion of the operating staffs have also had to be supplied by the *Reichsbahn*, although, even in Russia, many of the lower grades were recruited from local labour; thus, in one *Reichsverkehrsdirektion* in the East (believed to be Dniepropetrovsk) there were understood to be about 5,000 Germans and 20,000 Russians.

Also, a large number of staff was required for service in the Railway Troops, and so many of the younger men were called up for service in the Armed Forces. Thus, at a time when the demand for staff in Germany itself was heaviest, an appreciable number of men had to be withdrawn from active employment in the Reich, and, in spite of the somewhat high number of administrative staff in the years before the war, the staff position in these and other grades became exceedingly difficult.

The shortage has been eased in a number of ways, including the working of considerable overtime; the suspension of normal standards of recruitment and training and the employment of any available labour; the recall of retired staff; the employment of women, said, early in 1943, to number 100,000 compared with 16,000 before the war, in the following capacities: ticket collectors, porters, guards, signal-box work, permanent way labourers, booking workers; foreign labour which is said to number well over 100,000, consisting mainly of French, Belgians, Poles and Czechs, though numerous other nationalities, such as Italians and even Spaniards are included. Prisoners of war have also been employed.

(ix) *Workshops.*—Repair shops (*Reichsbahnausbesserungswerke*) are not normally large and concentrated establishments, but are small and scattered. The usual staff is about 1,000 employees.

The larger running sheds and depots (*Betriebswerke*) also undertake repairs to locomotives and rolling stock, including fairly heavy repairs. The *Reichsbahn* does not do its own locomotive building.

Workshops have been intensely busy during the war. Large numbers of foreigners, including Russians, have been drafted in, sometimes with the specific object of working two shifts, which had not been possible before owing to labour shortage.

(x) *Marshalling yards of the German Railways.*

Railway Divisions	Yards	Maximum Capacity in wagon numbers per 24 hours
1 AUGSBURG	Augsburg	2,300
2 BERLIN	Wustermark	5,000
	Nieder-Schöneweide	3,500
	Tempelhof	2,900
	Lichtenberg-Friedf	2,700
	Pankow	2,700
	Rummelsburg	2,700
	Seddin	2,400
3 BRESLAU	Brockau	5,000
	Schlauroth	2,400
	Kohlfurt	2,200
	Dittersbach	2,000
4 DRESDEN	Leipzig Wahren	4,500
	Dresden-Friedrichstadt	4,000
	Engelsdorf	3,700
	Chemnitz-Hilbersdorf	3,500
5 ERFURT	Erfurt	2,600
	Zeitz	2,600
	Weissenfels	2,400
	Gerstungen	2,000
	Gera	2,000
6 ESSEN (Ruhr)	Hamm	10,000
	Wedau	7,200
	Osterfeld-Süd	6,800
	Essen-Frintrop	5,400
	Wanne-Eickel	5,200
	Langendreer	5,000
	Ruhrort-Hafen neu	5,000
	Dortmund Verschbhf	4,800
	Dahlhausen	3,600
	Duisburg Hbf	3,600
	Oberhausen West	3,100
	Dortmunderfeld	3,000
	Mülheim-Ruhr-Speldorf	3,000
	Kupferdreh	2,600
	Essen Verschbhf	2,600
	Herne	2,400
	Dortmund Süd	2,400
	Gelsenkirchen-Schalke	2,200
	Bochum-Riemke	2,200
	Dortmund-Eving	2,000
	Gelsenkirchen Hbf	2,000
	Sinsen	2,000

Railway Divisions	Yards	Maximum Capacity in wagon numbers per 24 hours
7 FRANKFURT (MAIN) ...	Frankfurt/Main GB... ...	2,700
	Frankfurt/Main BB... ...	...
8 HALLE (SAALE) ...	Halle	4,500
	Senftenberg	4,000
	Falkenberg 1...	3,500
	Falkenberg 2...	2,500
	Rosslau	2,250
	Bitterfeld	2,000
	Cottbus	2,000
	Merseburg	2,000
9 HAMBURG (ALTONA) ...	Wilhelmsburg	4,800
	Eidelstedt	4,000
	Rothenburgsort	3,300
10 HANOVER	Seelze	5,000
	Stendal	4,500
	Bremen R.	4,100
	Lehrte	4,000
	Magdeburg-Buchau	3,800
	Madgeburg-Rothensee ...	3,000
	Hainholz	2,100
	Halberstadt	2,200
11 KARLSRUHE	Mannheim	7,000
	Karlsruhe	3,300
	Offenburg	3,200
	Basel Rbhf	2,400
12 KASSEL	Soest	4,000
	Gottingen	2,600
	Kassal	2,300
	Nordhausen	2,000
13 COLOGNE	Hohenbudberg	6,700
	Köln-Eifeltor	6,000
	Gremburg	6,000
	Köln-Kalk-Nord	4,500
	Köln-Nippes	3,500
	Aachen-West	3,000
	Koblenz	2,600
	Rheydt	2,500
	Köln-Gereon	2,000
	Krefeld	2,000
	Neuss	2,200
	Stolberg	2,000
14 KÖNIGSBERG (PR) ...	Königsberg	2,200
15 MAINZ	Bischofsheim...	3,200
	Ludwigshafen	2,200
	Bingerbrück	2,000
	Oberlahnstein	2,000
16 MUNICH	München-Laim	2,900
	München-Ost	2,000
17 MÜNSTER (WESTF) ...	Kirchweihe	5,000
	Osnabrück	2,100
	Oldenburg	2,000
	Rheine	2,000

Railway Divisions	Yards	Maximum Capacity in wagon numbers per 24 hours
18 NÜRNBERG	Nürnberg	2,900
	Aschaffenburg	3,000
	Wurzburg	2,000
19 OPPELN	Gleiwitz	6,800
	Peiskretscham	5,000
20 OSTEN IN FRANKFURT	Frankfurt/Oder	2,700
	Schneidemühl	2,500
21 REGENSBURG	Regensburg	2,000
22 SAARBRÜCKEN	Ehrang	4,000
	Einsiedlerhof	3,500
	Saarbrücken	...
23 STETTIN	Stettin	2,500
24 STUTTGART	Kornwestheim	4,000
	Ulm	2,400
	Stuttgart-Untertürkheim	2,200
	Heilbronn	2,000
25 WUPPERTAL	Vorhalle	3,800
	Geisecke-Ruhr	3,000
	Vohwinkel	2,800
	Holzwickede	2,400
	Hengstey (Hagen)	2,350
	Schwerte	2,200
	Düsseldorf-Derendorf	2,100

(b) *Roads.*—(i) A long-term scheme for the reconstruction and elaboration—under the direction of Dr. Todt—of the German road system has been an integral part of National Socialist economic and military policy. The new road system, consisting of a complex of *Reichsautobahnen* supplementing a reorganized network of National Highways (*Reichsstrassen*) and Alpine Roads, has been co-ordinated with the other communication systems. Since 1934 the German road system has consisted of *Reichsautobahnen, Reichsstrassen,* and *Landstrassen* 1st and 2nd class. The *Autobahnen* are described in paragraph (ii) below; the *Reichsstrassen* are main roads with route numbers, metalled and about 18 ft wide. The *Landstrassen* are of two types, both metalled, the one being about 16 ft wide, the other about 12 ft wide. The 1st class might be termed main or good roads, the 2nd class as secondary roads.

The total length of road to be constructed was laid down as about 4,400 miles; the completion of the programme was officially announced for 1941-2, though it has been reported that the work would possibly be finished in 1940. By 1939 the greater part of the programme had been completed. The map of the *Autobahnen* at the end of this Handbook shows the relative stages of completion.

(ii) The *Reichsautobahnen* normally have an outside width of 72-79 ft, and are divided into two one-way tracks, each 24½ ft wide and separated from each other by a strip of turf 11½-16½ ft wide. On the outer side of either track is a bank 6½ ft wide, of which the half nearer the roadway is only slightly raised and can be driven along in emergency. The chief surface materials in use are concrete and stone sets, but tar and asphalt are occasionally used. A hedge between the track serves to prevent dazzle from headlamps and also to some extent to mask the highways as seen from the air. An average speed of 60 mph is easy to maintain and the surfaces are tested with the heaviest AFVs.

(iii) Important Autobahn connections are:—

West—East—

(a) Bremen—Lübeck (linking North Sea and Baltic);
(b) Cologne—Hanover—Magdeburg—Berlin—Breslau—Gleiwitz (linking, economically, the industrial areas of the Ruhr, Central Germany and Silesia; militarily, France and Southern Poland, and thence, south-eastern Europe);
(c) Hamburg—Berlin—Stettin—Danzig—Königsberg (thence to run to Leningrad and Helsinki);
(d) Hamm—Kassel—Dresden—Breslau;
(e) Koblenz—Erfurt—Dresden—Breslau;
(f) Karlsruhe—Munich—Salzburg (thence by National Highway via Linz and Vienna to Bratislava);
(g) A National Highroad, running West—East via Prague (to be completed in 1945), was planned by the Czecho-Slovakian Government.

North—South—

(a) Hamburg—Hanover—Cologne (loopway to embrace the Ruhr area) —Frankfurt a/M—Karlsruhe;
(b) Hanover—Kassel—Frankfurt a/M;
(c) Stettin—Berlin—Leipzig—Nürnberg—Munich;
(d) Berlin—Dresden—Nürnberg;
(e) Czecho-Slovak road (from Dresden *via* Prague to Linz or Vienna).

The road system in Southern Germany is designed to give approach to the great passes leading to Northern Italy. In the Rhineland the system is laid out to facilitate military movements westward; on the Eastern frontier, to facilitate movements to the Baltic States, Poland, and the Danube Basin.

(iv) The Germans have a system of " through " routes (*Durchgangs-trassen*) which, for the most part follow the national highways (*Reichsstrassen*). These " through " routes have been specially selected, marked and improved by the German High Command in order to facilitate movements both inside Germany and in operational zones. Where necessary, it is laid down, they will be carried on into enemy territory. It is also laid down that the sign posting of " through " routes must not be obscured by local traffic signs of units, etc, and when large formations are on the move all civilian traffic on " through " routes and the *Autobahnen* must be diverted to minor roads.

There is no doubt but that the Germans are constantly improving their " through "-route system with a view to removing bottle-necks, detours, level-crossings, etc. The HQ of the Military Districts (*Wehrkreise*) attend to all the details of maintenance, including the marking of diversions and approach roads, and the regulation of lighting at night in consultation with local authorities.

(c) *Inland Waterways.*—(i) *Administration.*—In 1921 the State assumed control of inland waterways. Since then, particularly during the period of National Socialist Government, increasing efforts have been made to improve and augment the system and large sums have been spent on the work. The general aim is to provide a cheap means of transport, which will compensate for the geographical disadvantages of a comparatively short and unfavourable seaboard and a deep hinterland, by linking up the three great river systems, *viz*: the Rhine, Ems and Weser; the Elbe, Oder and (since the occupation of Polish territory) Vistula; and the Main, Neckar and Danube. The special objects have been:—

> to relieve the railways and roads of heavy traffic, especially in ores, coal and grain;
>
> to make the Rhineland and Westphalia independent, if necessary, of the ports of Rotterdam and Antwerp for water-borne traffic, by providing direct communication with the North Sea ports of Emden, Bremen and Hamburg, as well as with the Baltic ports of Lübeck, Stettin and Danzig;
>
> to provide West and East links between the main river systems, for the encouragement and development of industry and trade in central Germany, and to connect the Silesian industry by water with its German and export market, and the eastern grain-producing districts with the industrial west.

Administration is in the hands of the Reich Minister of Transport. Technical matters, that is to say the maintenance or extension of the waterways themselves, are handled by the Speer Organization. Traffic and all other questions are controlled by the Reich Transport Group for Inland Shipping (*Reichsverband Binnenschifffahrt or " RVB "*). This body is organized on a corporative basis according to trades and occupations engaged in the running of the system. There are four main groups, the last of which is sub-divided into seven sub-groups. These groups are as follows:—

Shipowners.
Small Shipowners.
Port and Transhipment traffic.
Special Occupations:—

> Port Shipping.
> Ferry Services.
> Pilots and Skippers.
> Rafters and Loggers.
> Charterers and Brokers.
> Shipping Experts (*e.g.,* Average Adjusters, etc).
> Shipping Agencies.

This organization is divided again on a geographical basis into seven districts:—

The Rhine Region.
West German Canals and the Weser.
The Elbe Region.
Central German Waterways between the Elbe and the Oder.
The Oder Region.
East German Waterways.
Danube Region.

The Administrative Council of the " RVB " consists of a Chairman appointed by the Reich Minister of Transport. The Chairman appoints the Directors of each trade group, and these in turn appoint the head of each Trade Sub-Group, or District Group. The Chairman has two deputies, and each head of a Trade Group, Sub-Group or District Group is allowed one deputy.

The Business Administration Committee of the " RVB " consists of one managing director and one business manager and his staff resident in Berlin. District offices are situated at Duisburg, Dortmund, Hamburg, Berlin and Breslau. There are sub-offices at Königsberg and Regensburg.

(ii) *Labour and Traffic.*—The German Inland Waterways, excluding Austria are estimated to absorb about 130,000 workers, of whom about 95,000 are employed as personnel on river craft. To ensure a constant supply of skilled labour trained on Nazi lines, a three-years apprenticeship system was compulsorily introduced in 1938. In 1939 this was given the title of the " Reich Working Combine for training in Inland Shipping " and was composed jointly of representatives of the " RVB " and the Reich Labour Front. The Working Combine carries out the training scheme and is responsible for the selection of suitable training centres.

The increasing demands on German manpower led to a shortage of labour on the inland waterways. This has been partly met by the recalling of bargees employed in other industries, the diversion of men from deep sea shipping, and latterly dilution with a limited amount of female labour, largely drawn from the wives of bargees serving in the armed forces.

It is impossible to say to what extent Germany has recruited foreign labour for the inland waterways. It is, however, known that foreign semi-skilled workers both civilian and prisoners of war, have, after receiving further training, been drafted into employment, not only as ships' crews, but as dock labourers.

In pre-war days the German inland waterways carried approximately 20 per cent of freight traffic of the country, but mostly bulky and non-perishable goods. A review of inland water traffic reveals that 1941 equalled busiest pre-war years and was 20 per cent greater than in 1940, and it is claimed that in spite of exceptional ice difficulties in the early part of 1942, traffic in 1942 was 20 per cent greater than in 1941. It is estimated that traffic has risen from 133 million tons in 1937 to 160 million tons in 1942 and may have reached 180 million tons in 1943.

(iii) *The German Inland Shipping Fleet.*—In 1939 the German inland waterway fleet consisted of the following craft:—

Self-propelled Craft	Number	Deadweight Capacity	H.P.
Passenger vessels	772	40,252	112,738
Passenger and cargo vessels	318	9,127	17,190
Cargo vessels	2,104	513,580	214,968
Tankers	93	27,474	15,457
Tugs	2,387	90,815	522,701
Vessels for special purposes	18	1,532	4,462
Total of self-propelled craft...	5,692	682,780	887,516
Dumb barges	12,065*	5,785,788*	...
Total	17,757	6,468,568	...

* Including 167 tank vessels aggregating 113,696 d.w.c.

Of the self-propelled vessels 3,413 totalling 334,762 hp were diesel-driven, whilst the remainder, aggregating 552,754 hp were steam-propelled.

It is not possible to say accurately what changes have occurred in the strength of the fleet since the outbreak of war, but it is believed that new construction has balanced losses. A large number of vessels with internal combustion engines have, however, been converted to producer gas.

New construction is compulsorily confined to standard types, the Mittelland canal type, Grossplauer barge (freight and tanker) and motor tankers.

(iv) *The Rhine.*—Navigable for 2,500-ton barges up to Strasburg. No locks.

The Rhine-Rhone canal between Strasburg and Basle was completely restored and re-opened to traffic in March, 1941. All locks which were severely damaged in 1940 have been greatly reinforced. Great importance is attached to this canal; the Rhine boats use far less fuel than on the open river.

(v) *West-East Connections in the North.*—The Rhine-Herne canal, completed in 1914, runs from Ruhrort into the Dortmund-Ems canal (*see* below). It can accommodate barges of 1,350 tons and has seven locks with a total lift of 110 ft.

The Lippe canal, running from Wesel to Datteln, is an alternative to the Rhine-Herne canal. It can accommodate 1,350-ton barges and has six locks with a total lift of 119 ft. The Hünxe lock is stated to be one of the largest steel locks in the world.

The Mittelland canal leaves the Dortmund-Ems canal at Bevergern and continues, without locks, to beyond Misburg, crossing the Weser near Minden. Along this stretch the canals are kept level by numerous cuttings 60 ft deep, and embankments of about the same height have been raised. Short side canals branch off to Linden and Osnabrück.

East of Misburg at Anderten the double Hindenburg locks lift vessels 45 ft. These locks mark the beginning of the eastern stretch of the canal 25 miles beyond, to the west of Brunswick, a branch canal to Bleckenstedt-Hallendorf is under construction which will lead to the Hermann Göring works. The double locks at Allerbüttel-Sulfeld lower this canal 27 ft. Thence the level remains constant until the Rothensee ship-lift is reached. This single elevator, weighing 5,400 tons, with a length of 258 ft, a width of 36 ft, and a water-depth of $7\frac{1}{2}$ ft forms part of a series of works which include an aqueduct 2,700 ft long over the Elbe to be finished in 1942, and a double ship-lift at Hohenwarthe. The Rothensee ship-lift is intended ultimately only for use of vessels proceeding *up* the Elbe: vessels bound for Hamburg, *down* the Elbe, will use the lift at Hohenwarthe, coming out of the Ihle canal at the Niegripp lock into the Elbe.

The Mittelland canal takes barges up to 1.500 tons in the western sections, and up to 1,000 tons in the eastern.

The Ihle and Plauer canals provide alternative connections for smaller barges between the Elbe and Berlin. The former is entered by the lock at Niegripp; the latter by a lock at Parey. The Ihle joins the Plauer canal at Zerbeh, where a lock lowers vessels 15 ft from the former to the latter. The lock at Gross Wusterwitz lowers the level 12 ft.

Thence the Havel river, and the Teltow and Oder-Spree canal run southeast to join the Oder near Fürstenberg. At seven places along this stretch there are locks: at Klein Machnow there is a double lock, a third being prepared; at Fürstenberg there are three locks.

The Hohenzollern canal provides an alternative north-easterly approach to the Oder. Near Eberswalde the canal crosses the railway in a concrete aqueduct. The Niederfinow ship-lift lowers 1,000-ton vessels to the old

Oder, lying 108 ft below the canal, in five minutes; the canal bridge joining the lift with the Hohenzollern canal is 473 ft long and 85 ft wide with a water-depth of 8½ ft.

The Oder is navigable up to Cosel (and for smaller vessels to the Czechoslovakian frontier). A report of January, 1940, stated that storage basins for increasing the capacity of the Oder were completed or under construction at Ottmachau, Turawa, Klodnitz and Berghof, and that others were expected to be built at Mora Kreuzberg and Sponau. The Adolf Hitler canal, opened in December, 1939, runs from Cosel to Gleiwitz in the Silesian Coal region. This waterway is intended to accommodate 1,000-ton barges. The Adolf Hitler canal has six locks, 216 ft long and 36 ft broad; the breadth of the canal is 112 ft, the depth 10½ ft. It is planned to connect the Adolf Hitler canal by an extension to Katowitz and eventually to Crakow.

(vi) *West-East Connections in the South.*—The Rhine-Main-Danube waterway is being connected to accommodate 1,500-ton barges. The stretch from Aschaffenburg to Würzburg is complete; the remaining stretch to Kelheim, modernizing portions of the old Ludwigs canal which has 88 locks and can only take vessels up to 125 tons, is under construction. The work was to have been completed by 1945, but speeding-up is expected. In the Spring to 1940, two new power stations were added, in the Gmünden-Würzburg stretch, to the four which were opened in 1939; the electricity generated in these plants is being distributed in Bavaria. It is reported that this canal will not be open for traffic for some years.

A Rhine-Lake Constance connection is projected.

The Danube is navigable up to Ulm. Along the stretch between Ulm and Kelheim, which is being developed, only light vessels can navigate; below this point barges of at least 1,200 tons can pass, though not fully loaded (the draft of a 1,200-ton barge fully loaded is approximately 7 ft 6 in); in detail the river is navigable between Kelheim and Passau for vessels drawing up to 4 ft, from Passau to Vienna for those drawing 6 ft, though ordinary draught is 4 ft; above Vienna to Bratislava vessels drawing 5½ ft can pass at normal water levels. The river is canalised between Kelheim and Passau.

For three months—January, February and March— the river is unnavigable, while in October, November and December—when the days are short and foggy and the river much lower—traffic is restricted and vessels cannot be fully loaded. During the remaining six months, when the days are long, the nights clear and the river high, vessels can take their full load.

The chief winter harbours are at Regensburg, Deggendorf, Passau, Linz, Struden (Grein), Korneuburg, Vienna, Bratislava. A new harbour is reported as under construction at Krens. The naval dockyard at Linz is the most important in the upper Danube; a report of June, 1939, stated that 3,000 workmen were employed on the enlargement and modernization of the military port and naval yard.

The most important installation for regulating the waters of the German Danube is the Katchlet barrage 4,000 yards west of Passau. According to recent reports this dam incorporates two double-gated barge locks, a large power-station and a spillway fitted with water turbo-generators. It is stated that the power-station develops 20,000 kilowatts and supplies all Southern Bavaria with electric power and lighting. The head of water created by the dam is over 20 ft and the current is arrested for 13 miles upstream as far as Vilsofen. The dam is readily recognizable from the air, for it in no way resembles a bridge and is lengthened on the northern bank by a long construction containing the hydro-electric plant and residences of employees and officials.

There is a projected scheme for connecting the Danube with various canals to be built all over Europe, thus creating an international network of waterways reaching from Hamburg to Salonika and from Danzig to Milan. Budapest, for example, will be linked up with ports in Holland, Belgium and Northern France through the Danube-Main-Rhine canal, the greater part of which has been built. The Danube-Oder canal will lead directly to the Baltic ports, and another canal which, starting from Belgrade, will cross the Balkan Peninsula from North to South to Salonika. Lastly, a canal will be built between the Danube and the Adriatic.

The Neckar canal, under construction, will provide an alternative connection between the Rhine and Danube via Mannheim, Stuttgart, Plochingen and Ulm. The Neckar is canalized to accommodate barges of at least 1,200 tons to beyond Heilbronn. Canalization to Plochingen should be complete by 1944. A report dated August, 1942, states, however, that this canal has been open for some time and that the largest barges which can pass through are approximately 120 ft long (tonnage 500 tons). This important canal will be useful not only for the actual carriage of traffic, but because it will make possible the transfer of smaller barges between the Danube and the Rhine.

A Sarr-Palatinate-Rhine canal, connecting Metz, Saarbrücken and Mannheim is projected to take vessels of 1,200 tons; no work on it is reported.

(vii) *Connecting Waterways.*—The Dortmund-Ems canal connects the Ruhr and Rhineland on the one hand with Bremen and mediately with the Baltic ports, and on the other hand with the industrial areas of central Germany; the latter connection giving it its chief importance in war time.

It was stated in 1938 that the canal was being deepened from 8 ft to 10 ft 6 ins to accommodate vessels up to 1,500 tons in three sections; Dortmund—Bergeshovede, Bergeshovede—Gleesen, and a by-pass canal (avoiding a stretch of 60 miles having eleven locks) between Gleesen and Papenburg. The excavations in the Papenburg and Steinbild areas were seen to be flooded in July, 1941, and it would thus appear that the construction of this by-pass from its junction with the Dortmund-Ems canal is well advanced. The first section was completed in 1938. Concerning the progress of reconstruction it was reported late in 1939 that certain locks had been enlarged to take 900-ton barges where only 600-ton could be taken before. In September, 1939, there was activity on the enlargement and deepening of the canal connecting Krupp's experimental establishment at Meppen with the Ems estuary, possibly with the object of facilitating the transit of iron ore.

An old and a new aqueduct carry the canal across the Ems north of MÜNSTER.

Near the junction with the Rhine—Herne canal, at Henrichenberg, there is a ship lift, raising or lowering vessels 42 ft.

The Möhne Dam on the River Möhne, a tributary of the Ruhr, is 130 ft high; the width of its apron is 110 ft and that of its crown 22 ft. The reservoir formed is some 5·6 miles east to west. In the south a shorter arm, two miles long, extends up the flooded valley of the Heve. When the Möhne Dam was bombed by Lancaster aircraft of Bomber Command in May, 1943, air cover revealed the extensive flooding of river valleys, the destruction of bridges and other installations and the lowering of water-levels in reservoirs, resulting from the breaching of the Möhne and Eder Dams.

The Sorpe Dam was also damaged but less seriously. The Möhne Dam was breached in the centre between the valve-houses, the breach at the crown extending over approximately 230 ft, narrowing to approximately 130 ft at the base; and the main power house, which stood immediately below the centre of the dam, at the head of the compensating basin, was completely demolished. The flooding was most extensive.

The Kiel canal, 35 miles long, connects the Baltic with the North Sea thus obviating the 560 miles long, exposed route round the Skaw through the Danish Sounds and Belts. The average measurements of the canal are as follows: —

Width at mean water level	341 ft.
Depth at mean water level	37 ft.

The passage of the canal normally takes seven to eight hours, including the passage of the locks, minimum speed five knots, maximum eight knots. The canal has electric lighting along its whole length and can be used by day and night. There are nine passing places to enable large ships to pass one another.

Projected improvements include the widening of the canal to double its width, the heightening of the bridges and the construction of eight by-pass sections. The double locks at Kiel and Holtenau (NE of Kiel) are to be replaced by large single locks; work has been observed indicating the construction of underground control rooms at both ends of the canal. It was estimated, before the war, that the work would take 10 years to complete, but that the canal could be dredged to take ships of 35,000 tons in two years.

A Danube-Oder and an Elbe-Danube canal are planned. According to a report dated July, 1943, work is being carried out on the former. A lift is projected which should help to overcome the great difference in level near Weisskirchen in Moravia; *i.e.*, to reach the bed of the Danube vessels must descend 382 ft. Vessels will do so by means of 10 locks and the lift mentioned. The latter will be 33 ft higher than that at Niederfinow (at present the largest lift in Europe). The former will run from near Bratislava, via Prerow to Cosel; the latter will run from a point above Prague, via Pardubice, to join the Danube—Oder canal at Prerow. Both are to carry 1,000-ton barges.

A Danube—Lake Constance canal is also planned.

A Weser—Main canal is planned for 1,200-ton barges, using the Werra, which joins the Weser near Minden and is already canalized for some distance, and joining the Main at Bamberg.

Other connecting canals (the numbers in brackets indicate the depths of the channels as stated in 1938, though these are not subsequently confirmed):

Ems—Jade canal (6½ ft).

Küsten canal (5 ft).

Hansa canal—*Projected*.—The construction of the Bramsche—Achim stretch appears to have been postponed indefinitely.

Elbe—Lübeck canal (8 ft).—A 1938 report, not confirmed, stated that this canal was to be deepened and broadened to allow U-boats and destroyers to use this alternative route from the Baltic to the North Sea.

Elster—Saale canal.

Aachen—Rhine canal—*Projected*.

(viii) *Eastern Waterways.*—(The waterways in German-occupied Poland are administered by the Waterways Directorate at Danzig and Posen.)

According to an official German statement of early 1940, the completion of the Masurian canal in East Prussia was imminent. It is proposed to connect this canal via the Masurian lakes with the Pissa and the Narew, thus linking Warsaw directly with Königsberg.

An official German statement of early 1940 implied that the Vistula would already take vessels of 450 tons, and reported that the ultimate aim was to make the river navigable for vessels up to 1,000 tons. A radio report of August, 1940, stated that the German Government had prepared a scheme to render the Vistula again navigable, and that in the Radom sector the embankments were being repaired along a stretch of 280 kms. The Upper Vistula connects, via the San, with the Dniester.

A German agency report of November, 1940, stated that the largest barrage in Europe at Kozlow (situated east of the River Dunajec at its junction with the Vistula, east of Cracow) was nearing completion and would be in operation in the spring, 1941. The following specifications are given; capacity, 235 million cubic metres; width of wall at bottom 120 ft; length of wall 650 ft; width of wall at crown 18 ft; greatest height of wall 105 ft.

The barrage is intended to obviate floods extending far into West Prussia, and to be a source of electricity for occupied Poland.

The German report of early 1940 stated that the reconstruction of the canal system in the Wartheland and of the Bromberg canal was in hand. The Bromberg canal connects with the Dnieper via the Weichsel, Bug, Dnieper-Bug canal, and Pripet. In the Warthe district, the Warthe river is being completed for the handling of vessels of 1,000 tons, and the higher Warthe is being linked up with the Netze via Lake Goplo.

The modern Dnieper-Bug canal, improving on an old one, is designed to connect the Bug at a point near Brest Litovsk with the Pripet at a point near Pinsk, and thus to establish a direct barge-route between the Black Sea and the Baltic via the rivers Dnieper, Pripet, Bug and Vistula. The canal was declared open to traffic in September, 1940. It was previously stated that the canal was to incorporate eight locks; and it is reported that they were to be of the same dimensions as the locks on the Dnieper. It is reported that large dams, 15 miles and 25 miles west of Pinsk were built in 1939, and that in that year barges larger than 300 tons could not even theoretically be accommodated and then only during spring floods when all dams and sluices were opened. An unconfirmed report of April, 1940, stated that works, to be completed in 1941, were in hand for deepening these river systems to provide a guaranteed depth of 9 ft (in practice, $7\frac{1}{2}$ to $8\frac{1}{2}$ ft); the present average depth being 4 ft to $7\frac{1}{2}$. According to the Soviet Press of October, 1940, the Dnieper-Bug canal, which is 125 miles long, would shortly be taken over by a Government Commission.

(ix) *Damage to Inland Waterways and present state.*—Reports indicate that an unusually dry summer in 1943 caused more than the usual seasonal navigational difficulties on the German inland waterways. These reports refer to abnormally low levels on rivers as far apart as the Danube, the Meuse, the Rhine, the Elbe, and on the inter-connecting lateral canals, such as the Rhine-Herne as well as on one section of the very important Mittelland canal.

Many of them attribute the failure to maintain the minimum depth required for navigation in the Weser and in the Mittelland canal to the bursting of the Eder Dam in May. Examination of the available evidence lends more support to these reports than was at first thought reasonable. The main function of the Eder Dam was to maintain a sufficient level in the Middle Weser to permit navigation in dry seasons and to compensate for the loss of water pumped from the Weser into the Mittelland canal. For this purpose water was released from the dam at the rate of 18 cubic metres per second, and was pumped into the Mittelland canal at Minden at the rate of seven cubic metres per second. It was essential, in order to comply both with the minimum requirements of navigation and the demands of the Mittelland canal that the water level at Minden should not fall below 47 ins. Since 18 May, 1943, the level has probably dropped by 18 to 22 ins, thus making pumping impossible and also curtailing drastically the barge traffic of the Middle Weser.

It is unlikely that the Germans have been able to draw on the Harz water supplies in this emergency as pre-war suggestions that the Mittelland canal could be fed from this district were met with considerable and successful opposition from the local Harz industries, which do in fact consume all water available from local sources. It seems reasonable therefore to conclude that traffic on these very important waterways has been hampered by an exceptionally dry summer and that the effects of this have been aggravated by the loss of the Eder Dam.

Traffic on the Lower Weser has declined substantially since 1939, though its importance as an integral part of the German inland waterway system is still considerable. In 1936 nearly three million tons of cargo were carried down stream from Minden to Bremen and Bremerhaven, mostly potash and fertilizer for export. Tonnage clearing through Bremen is estimated to have declined by 90 per cent since the outbreak of war, and barge traffic down the Weser has consequently suffered a substantial decline. This has been offset to some extent by diversion of traffic from the railways and to increased traffic on the interconnecting lateral canal which utilize the Weser for short sections of its length.

Reconnaissance flown over the Rhine-Herne canal on 31 March, 1943, showed an average of 28 barges per mile, of which 20 per cent were in movement. Three months later (two weeks after the bombing of the dams) 25 barges were seen per mile, of which 24 per cent were in movement. At the end of September, when 50 miles of the canal were photographed, only 19 barges were seen per mile, of which 12 per cent were in movement. During the same periods the average number of barges seen per mile on the Rhine were 10, 29 and 8. While a certain reduction in traffic to and from the Ruhr in the summer months is explicable on the ground that industrial activity itself had been substantially reduced, there is evidence that high priority traffic normally conveyed by barge was seriously delayed at this time. For instance, it was reported recently that delivery of plates for submarines at Blohm and Voss was held up by trouble on the canals which was attributed to the blocking of the fairway by sunken barges. Moreover, it is known that by the end of July the accumulation of Swedish iron ore on the quays at Emden had reached almost unmanageable proportions, strong presumptive evidence that facilities for conveying it to the Ruhr were not available in sufficient volume.

There are many possible explanations of the difficulties which appear to have arisen and it is probable that more than one factor has been responsible. Among the possible factors are obstruction of the fairway, damage to locks, damage to embankments, etc., and shortage of water for maintenance of navigation.

There is no doubt that laden barges have been sunk from time to time and several sources have reported the sinking of the heaviest type of barge in the Rhine-Herne canal. On 12 August a direct hit on the Autobahn bridge over the Dortmund-Ems canal at Gröppenbruch caused its complete collapse and isolated Dortmund for some time. Hits have been scored on more than one of the lock gates on the Rhine-Herne canal in the course of raids on Duisburg and Essen (a direct hit on Schleuse 1 was seen in reconnaissance after the Duisburg raid of 12/13 May, 1943, while the destruction of Schleusen 3 and 4 was reported at about the same time). The lower locks also seem to have been put out of action for a time by flooding from the Rhine following the Möhne attack.

The Rhine-Herne canal proved difficult to construct owing to a tendency to subsidence; it is built for part of its length, particularly in the district north of Essen and Oberhausen, over coal workings. It has also proved difficult to maintain, and constant dredging is necessary to keep it open to navigation; 100,000 cubic metres of mud were removed when it was deepened to allow the transit of 1,300-ton barges and were used to build up the banks on the embanked sections. Large craters have been seen close to the canal bank on a number of occasions and although there is no positive evidence of breaching it is possible that the structure has been weakened. It is at any rate possible to detect some local nervousness as to, the likelihood of flooding and the German Press has announced that air raid shelters in the Emscher district (the Emscher flows immediately north and parallel to the Rhine-Herne canal) are unsafe for that reason. The water supply is obtained from the natural flow of the river Lippe via the Hamm-Datteln canal and by pumping from the Rhine via the Weser-Datteln canal. The supply should be sufficient unless a dry summer has caused the rivers to be abnormally low. There is, however, a possibility that the depletion of the Ruhr water table consequent on the Möhne Dam attack of May, 1943, has also affected the flow of the river on the northern side of the watershed, but this is a question which cannot be determined without a detailed study of the geology of the lower strata in the Ruhr area. It is, however, certain that the Germans have been extremely concerned over the loss both of the Möhne and Eder Dams, and recent reconnaissance showed that their reconstruction was being pushed forward with maximum speed (see para. vii).

Saboteurs in Belgium and France have recently turned their attention to the inland waterways and there is ample evidence that on many cases their efforts have been successful. Laden barges have been sunk in canal fairways and where those selected for sinking have been loaded with cement the subsequent removal must have taken an appreciable time.

(x) *Dimensions and Capacity of Common German River Barges*

River	Type of Construction	Length ft.	Beam ft. in.	Draught ft. in.	Capacity Tons	Remarks
Vistula	Wood and Iron ...	180	26 3	5 9	500	—
Upper and Middle Oder ...	Wood and Iron ...	131	15 1	5 ft. 3 in.—5 ft. 11 in.	210—235	—
Lower Oder and canalized stretches	Tow Barge— Wooden floor ... Iron floor ...	180 180	25 11 25 11	5 7 4 ft. 11 in —5 ft. 9 in.	500 440—540	— —
Upper Elbe	Iron, wooden floor ...	250	34 5	5 ft. 11 in.—6 ft. 3 in.	940—1000	—
Middle and Lower Elbe ...	Iron, wooden floor ...	213	26 11	6 7	680—750	—
Rhine	Iron tow barge ...	197	27 3	7 1	695	Commonest type
Lower Rhine, from Cologne down-stream.	Steel tow barge ...	220—276	27 ft. 3 in.—33 ft. 10 in.	8 ft. 2 in.—8 ft. 4 in.	1000—1520	—
Middle and Upper Rhine from Bingen to Lauterburg.	Iron tow barge ...	282 404	36 5 46 4	8 6 9 4	1700 3585	— —
Main	Steel	135	21 —	3 7	200	—
Weser	Steel	199	28 6	6 4	648	—
Aller	Steel	164	23 11	4 11	335	—
Upper Danube to Ratisbon ...	Iron tow barge ...	207	26 11	6 3	675	—
Danube	Wood	207	26 11	6 3	670	—
Lower Danube	Iron tow barge ...	236	30 2	7 6	1000	—

(xi) *Table of ice-conditions on the Inland Waterways*

Station	River	Mean No. of days with Ice	Mean No. of days with Fast Ice	Max. No. of days with Ice	Max. No. of days with Fast Ice	Mean date of First Ice	Mean date of Last Ice	Extreme limit First Ice	Extreme limit Last Ice	Extreme limit First Fast Ice	Extreme limit Last Fast Ice
						Oder					
Ratibor	Oder	28·9	14·7	65	41	21·12	25·2	11·11	24·3	23·12	2·3
Frankfurt	Oder	43·2	19·4	120	59	20·12	26·2	9·11	28·3	3·12	20·3
Schurgast	Gl. Neisse	40·2	22·4	100	60	16·12	26·2	8·11	24·3	8·12	21·3
						Elbe					
Dresden	Elbe	30·8	3·7	68	28	25·12	15·2	10·11	18·3	16·12	15·2
Magdeburg	Elbe	29·8	5·7	69	50	26·12	13·2	11·11	11·3	6·12	1·3
Hamburg	Elbe	34·9	1·0	76	15	27·12	15·2	17·11	9·3	4·2	19·2
						Weser					
Kassel	Fulda	20·2	17·8	71	68	—	—	20·11	13·3	20·11	12·3
Minden	Weser	14·8	2·7	41	13	—	—	19·11	22·2	10·12	19·2
Verden	Aller	12·7	3·6	45	26	—	—	11·11	8·3	30·12	19·2
						Ems					
Lingen	Ems	10·6	2·8	34	14	27·12	24·1	27·11	3·3	11·12	6·2
Herzlake	Hase	4·5	2·3	23	20	—	—	27·11	8·3	3·1	22·1
Mesum	Ems	17·4	10·3	37	23	—	—	20·11	26·2	21·11	26·2
						Rhein					
Konstanz	Bodensee	20·2	14·3	58	38	—	—	2·1	24·3	17·1	24·3
Mainz	Rhein	15·5	—	31	—	—	—	20·11	26·2	—	—
Koblenz	Rhein	12·8	—	35	—	—	—	7·12	28·2	—	—
Köln	Rhein	12·7	0·8	30	12	—	—	7·12	27·2	9·2	20·2
Emmerich	Rhein	10·2	1·7	28	27	—	—	8·12	26·2	20·1	15·2
Frankfurt	Main	21·9	1·4	46	15	—	—	19·11	28·2	1·1	20·2
Saarburg	Saar	6·9	—	18	—	—	—	7·12	20·2	—	—
Trier	Mosel	9·6	—	25	—	—	—	19·11	24·2	—	—
Mülheim	Ruhr	2·3	—	12	—	—	—	22·12	17·1	—	—
Hamm	Lippe	4·0	1·8	21	13	—	—	18·11	23·1	20·11	8·1

Note :—The words " Fast Ice " are given in this table as a translation of " Eissland ".

11. *Ports in Germany*.

(a) The more important ports of Germany include the following:—

HAMBURG.
BREMEN.
BREMERHAVEN and WESERMÜNDE.
CUXHAVEN.
WILHELMSHAVEN.
KIEL.
LÜBECK.
EMDEN.
STETTIN.

Brief descriptions are given below of these ports with details of the bomb damage if available.

(b) HAMBURG. (Population 1,713,000.)—(i) The largest commercial port in Germany occupying a cardinal position in the road, rail and waterway system of NW Germany; the most important German commercial and naval shipbuilding centre, particularly for U-boat construction.

When war began work was in progress on a large scale scheme for the enlargement and improvement of the port. Projected improvements included; a suspension bridge across the R ELBE at ALTONA, a new passenger quay of 1,090 yards long, a new road 120 ft wide extending 2,186 yds along the waterfront, and modernization of the existing railway system.

(ii) *Port Facilities*.—The depth of the R ELBE at HAMBURG at mean high water is 39½ ft: vessels drawing 36 ft can reach the port with the flood tide. It is stated that work for the low water regulation of the R ELBE between HAMBURG and CUXHAVEN have been satisfactorily completed.

For sea going vessels HAMBURG offers a water area of 3,876 acres. 23½ miles of mooring on dolphins and 25 miles of quayage with depths alongside of 13-40 ft. Most of the quays have ample railway connections. The port contained some 2,500 cranes and other lifting appliances, including floating cranes to lift 10-250 tons. Warehouses in the port covered nearly a million sq yds. Full details of the various quays with other facilities for unloading cargo are available, together with depths alongside.

(iii) *Shipbuilding*.—The following important establishments exist:—

Blohm and Voss.—The most important private yard in Germany, able to build the largest warships and merchant vessels, and to prepare and finish all material required for building and repairing in its own shops. These yards are at present concentrating on 500 ton U-boats. As a result of recent air attacks some 15 workshops have been destroyed and at least four hits on the slips are thought to have damaged 3 or 4 submarines under construction.

Deutsche WERFT AG.—A modern yard largely constructed on American lines. Assembly yard and building berths served by a system of 24 overhead cranes. The air attacks resulted in direct hits on the workshops and several small sheds demolished.

Deutsche Werft AG Finkenwerder.—Six large slips (reported up to 850 ft) which are at present engaged in building 740 ton U-boats. Extensive constructional progress has been carried out in this yard since July, 1941.

Howaldtwerke AG.—A further large yard having a total of twelve slips four of which were between 600-1,000 ft long. Bomb damage includes 13 miscellaneous sheds destroyed, six hits seen on the frame bending and plate furnaces and blast damage to ship building and machinery sheds.

(iv) *POL.*—HAMBURG is an important oil bunkering and storage centre. It is thought that the capacity of surface tanks is about 600,000 tons, of underground tankage also about 600,000 tons.

(v) *Transport Facilities—Waterways.*—Connected by the R ELBE with the ELBE-HAVEL canal, by the ELBE-LUBECK canal with LÜBECK and by the KIEL canal via BRUNSBÜTTEL with the BALTIC.

Rail.—HAMBURG and BREMEN are the main railway junctions of NW Germany. Main line connections with BREMEN, CUXHAVEN, TONDERN, FLENSBURG, KIEL, LUBECK, BERLIN, HANOVER. Secondary line to NEUMÜNSTER.

Road.—HAMBURG is on the BREMEN—LUBECK Autobahn and is the western terminus of a projected Autobahn to BERLIN. Main road connections exist to all the main centres in the neighbourhood of HAMBURG.

(vi) *Bomb Damage.*—The greater part of HAMBURG is now in ruins. The general destruction is on a scale never before seen in a town or city of this size. Not only has the town centre been destroyed, but the devastation extends through the dock area and widely to the East and West on both sides of the AUSSEN ALSTER (the larger of the two lakes dividing HAMBURG). There are large areas, extending for thousands of acres, especially East of the town, where every building in every street has been demolished and left roofless and gutted.

Many of the thoroughfares are seen to be blocked with débris and parts of the town have an appearance altogether deserted. It is estimated that in the fully built-up areas the destruction and damage to property amounts to over 77 per cent and is close to that figure even in the suburban districts. The storage capacity of the ports has suffered severely. Altogether nearly 500 dockside and railway warehouses have been destroyed or damaged besides many of the older type of brick warehouses, several storeys high used mainly for food storage, on the banks of the canal.

To the difficulties in the transhipment caused by the burning of so many store sheds must be added the damage to cranes and port handling gear on the quayside, and many hits on roads and railways on the river front and especially the destruction of sheds and railway tracks in the marshalling yards and goods stations serving the docks.

In the town itself the fully built-up areas have suffered most. All the big administrative as well as recreational buildings associated with a large city have been involved in the general devastation.

It must not be thought, however, that as a result of this enormous damage the port is unusable. On the contrary, ample facilities still exist for military requirements.

Full details of individual bomb damage to quays, warehouses, and administrative buildings are available.

(c) BREMEN. (Population 420,000.)—(i) Now an important U-boat building centre, Bremen is Germany's second largest commercial port situated 34 miles above Bremerhaven; the River Weser has been developed for free movement of ocean-going vessels; in ordinary tides ships drawing 28½ ft can proceed without difficulty to Bremen City.

(ii) *Port facilities.*—BREMEN City docks which are complementary to those at BREMERHAVEN comprise thirteen basins, all tidal except for one. There about 10 miles total quayage and 226 lifting appliances of all kinds up to 110 tons. All quays have ample railway connections. Quayside sheds have a total area of 260,000 sq yds.

(iii) *Shipbuilding.—Deutsche Schiff and Maschinenbau AG Werke.*— Capable of building the larger merchant vessels (ss Bremen 51,656 tons) and all types of warships. Now engaged in building 1,000 and 740-ton U-boats and destroyers.

Atlas Werke AG BREMEN.—Now building and fitting out minesweepers and could build U-boats. In addition there are good repairing and fitting out facilities.

(iv) *POL.*—Bunkering facilities at all basins. The Deutsche Vacuum Oil Company's installation which is in BREMEN is described as the largest liquid-fuel refinery store in North Germany. In addition there are many other smaller establishments.

(v) *Transport facilities.—Rail.*—BREMEN is the main railway junction for the Weser ports.

Road.—Autobahn to LÜBECK *via* HAMBURG—a large new road bridge has been built across the R WESER to the East of the railway bridge.

(*d*) BREMERHAVEN and WESERMÜNDE. (Population 100,000.)— (i) The outer port of BREMEN situated at the mouth of the R Weser, with accommodation in the extensive basins for the largest ships and having facilities for repair of all kinds. As from 1st November, 1939, the town of BREMERHAVEN was incorporated into WESERMÜNDE which was itself formed in 1924. WESERMÜNDE is the largest fishing port in Germany as well as being a Naval station. The port is now engaged in some U-boat and auxiliary warship construction and frequented by smaller naval vessels and merchant traffic.

(ii) *Port facilities.*—BREMERHAVEN comprises seven quays with a total length in excess of 63,000 feet having depths ranging from 18 feet at low water to 49 feet at high water at the COLUMBUS QUAY. There are about 70 lifting appliances ranging up to 1 crane of 125 tons. All the quays have extensive rail facilities. The total warehouse accommodation is about 104,000 sq metres floor space, mostly on the quayside. In addition there are six docks (including a graving dock) one of which will accommodate vessels up to 50,000 tons. In the case of WESERMÜNDE there are three quays with a total length of 20,000 feet with a maximum depth of 25 feet at high water.

(iii) *Shipbuilding.—Deutsche Schiff-und-Maschinenbau, AG.* This yard has three depots with a total of eight slips and at present is chiefly occupied in the construction of 740-ton U-boats. There are other minor ship-building firms which build minesweepers and other small craft.

(iv) *POL.*—As well as the normal coal bunker facilities which exist at every berth there are important storage dumps of diesel and fuel oil at BREMERHAVEN. The total capacity of these various dumps cannot accurately be stated since a certain proportion of them are underground.

(v) *Transport facilities.—Rail.*—Main double-track line to BREMEN, single-track to CUXHAVEN and HAMBURG.

Main road to BREMEN for connection with BREMEN—LÜBECK Autobahn. In addition there are main roads to CUXHAVEN and HAMBURG.

(e) CUXHAVEN. (Population 30,000.)—(i) A port of call and fuelling station for ocean-going ships and a deep-sea fishing port. Its defences command the approaches to HAMBURG and the KIEL Canal entrance. It is now used as a base for minesweepers and patrol vessels. At this point the current in the R Elbe is extremely strong and to keep the river navigable continual dredging is carried out.

(ii) *Port facilities.*—The total quayage appears to be about 14,000 feet with a minimum depth of 39 feet. The lifting appliances total seven cranes, none of them larger than 3 tons.

(iii) *Shipbuilding.*—There are two shipbuilding companies engaged primarily in repair, but R-boat building has been reported.

(iv) *POL.*—There are a number of oil tanks, many of them underground.

(v) *Transport facilities.*—*Rail.*—One main double-track to HAMBURG, single-track line to BREMEN—LÜBECK.

Roads.—Main roads to BREMEN via BREMERHAVEN and STADE, both providing connections with the BREMEN—LÜBECK Autobahn.

(f) WILHELMSHAVEN. (Population 112,760.)—(i) The sole defended Naval base permitted to Germany by the Versailles Treaty: HQ of North Sea command and North Sea Coastal Defence Commands (land and sea): the regular base for capital ships and the German North Sea U-boat flotillas: the principal naval dockyard, warships of all kinds are built, repaired and maintained.

(ii) *Port facilities.*—Vessels of any draught can enter the harbour which provides berthage from 10 to 33 ft. There are four entrances to the harbour, all leading to the naval dockyard and the other harbour basins. Although all vessels previously have had to enter the harbour by means of locks, work has been in progress to enable vessels to enter and leave WILHELMSHAVEN at any state of the tide. There are six graving docks in addition to a number of floating docks, one of which is able to lift upwards of 40,000 tons. All the latest lifting appliances are available amongst which are two floating cranes, self-propelled, to lift 250 tons and 40 tons respectively.

(iii) *Shipbuilding Yards.*—*Kriegsmarine Werft.*—This is the main naval dockyard and is capable of building the largest battleships. At present it is engaged largely in the construction of 500-ton U-boats. There is one other shipbuilding yard which has recently been re-equipped and extended as a re-fitting yard for light craft and U-boats. Large workshops exist with fitting-out basins, and in addition repairs of all kinds can be carried out.

(iv) *POL.*—The total storage capacity at WILHELMSHAVEN when last reported was 131,000 tons, but possibly this figure has since been increased. It is known that severe damage was inflicted on certain of these storage tanks in Feb, 1943.

(v) *Transport facilities.*—*Water.*—WILHELMSHAVEN is the eastern terminus of the EMS—JADE canal.

Rail.—Double-track main line via OLDENBURG to BREMEN. At VAREL a single-track line branches to RODENKIRCHEN. On the western bank of the R Weser a narrow gauge line runs to EMDEN. Recently reports indicated that considerable rail construction has taken place. From EMDEN the main line runs south to the RUHR district.

Road.—Main roads to BREMEN via VAREL and OLDENBURG. A system of secondary roads connects with the coast. A new road from RUSTRINGEN to SANDE with a branch road running in the JEVER direction approached completion March, 1941; it runs parallel to a new light railway.

(*g*) KIEL. (Population 274,000.)—(i) The chief naval base and ship-building centre in the BALTIC, and the HQ of the Fleet Command, the Northern Group Command and the Baltic Command, and the regular base of the cruiser and Baltic U-boat operational flotillas. A principal naval dockyard and the largest naval arsenal in GERMANY. Warships of all kinds are built, repaired and maintained. There are some 320 cranes which are capable of lifting up to 300 tons, amongst these are nine floating cranes, including three to lift 150 tons. There are ample graving docking facilities, the largest being capable of taking ships up to 570 ft.

(ii) *Shipbuilding.*—KIEL is one of the principal shipbuilding centres in Germany, but owing to the heavy bombing, a considerable amount of ship-building and repair has been transferred to safer areas. Amongst the most important are:—

    Deutsche Werke.—This builds and repairs all types of warships in-cluding 500-ton and broad-beamed U-boats.

    Howaldtswerke.—There are six slips, the largest of which is 590 ft long. This yard is now constructing 500-ton U-boats.

    Friedrich Krupp.—This yard builds all classes of warships. Recent construction includes the PRINZ EUGEN. The main activity since the war has been the building of all types of U-boats, up to 1,600 tons. The total personnel employed at this yard is about 12,760.

(iii) *POL.*—Again there are ample storage facilities for fuel and Diesel oil, which include large underground storage depots at MONKEBERG.

(iv) *Transport facilities.—Rail.*—Main line connections with FLENS-BURG, HAMBURG and LÜBECK.

Road.—Main road connections with same towns and the whole of the SCHLESWIG-HOLSTEIN system.

(*h*) LÜBECK and NEUSTADT. (Population 160,000.)—(i) LÜBECK, 12½ mls from the sea, is important mainly as a shipbuilding port. Smaller types of warships (particularly U-boats) and small merchant vessels are con-structed. The war has greatly enhanced the commercial importance of the port. The pre-occupation of STETTIN with rail traffic for the Eastern Front appears to have resulted in the diversion of much of the commercial traffic of the Baltic to LÜBECK, which appears to have become an important centre for the handling of Scandinavian trade.

(ii) *Port facilities.*—The depth in the channel is 24½ ft though there is a report that it has been deepened to 28 ft. There are about 20,000 ft of quayage with depths of up to 13 ft. The majority of the quays have ware-house accommodation and rail connections. The lifting appliances consist of a floating steam crane to lift 50 tons and several electric cranes lifting up to 40 tons. In addition there are three floating docks.

(iii) *Transport facilities.—Water.*—ELBE—LÜBECK Canal.

    Rail.—Main line connections BERLIN—HAMBURG, HAMBURG—STETTIN, HAMBURG—COPENHAGEN—OSLO—STOCKHOLM.

    Road.—Northern terminus LÜBECK—HAMBURG—BREMEN Auto-bahn.

(i) EMDEN. (Population 34,000.)—(i) On account of its terminal position on the German waterway system EMDEN has steadily increased in importance as a commercial port. Port facilities have been extended, principally for the handling of Swedish iron ore. The port is at present used as a base for mine-layers and mine-sweepers, and it has facilities as a ship-building and repairing port.

(ii) *Port facilities.*—EMDEN Harbour is in three parts; the outer harbour, inner harbour and the new inner harbour. The outer harbour is 28 ft deep at the outer end, 24½ ft at the inner end and has a 3,050 ft quay on the west side and 4,600 ft of berthage on the east. There is a 40-ton crane and several smaller cranes and a warehouse 150 by 160 ft. Railway connection is extensive. The inner harbour is entered by a lock which is 318 ft by 47½ ft with a depth of 22 ft on the sill, and the harbour itself has a general depth of about 17 ft. There is a quayage of about 10,000 ft. There is one 65-ton crane and over 20 much smaller ones. The DORTMUND—EMS canal and the EMS—JADE canal make a junction with the Inner Harbour. The New Inner Harbour is entered by a lock which is 853 ft by 131 ft with a maximum depth on the sill of 42½ ft. A store quay on the south side of the harbour is 3,230 ft long; the depth is 34½ ft. There are several bridge cranes as well as other types, to lift from 3 to 15 tons. There is railway connection, and the railway swing bridge leading to the Inner Harbour is 130 ft wide. There are three floating docks.

(iii) *Shipbuilding.*—NORDSEEWERKE EMDEN at present building 500 ton U-boats has three slips; Cassens Schiffswerft with eight small slips, which is possibly building E-boats; and Schulte and Bruns with nine small slips.

(iv) *POL.*—There are five gas oil tanks by the outer harbour with a total capacity of 150 tons: bunkering for small craft only, but at the Patent Fuel Works on the north side of the Inner Harbour storage facilities for several thousand tons are maintained.

(v) *Transport facilities.—Water.*—Local steamer connection with the islands, EMDEN is the terminus of the EMS-JADE and DORTMUND-EMS canals.

Rail.—Main line from EMDEN to MÜNSTER and the RUHR; single track North to NORDDEICH, single track to OLDENBURG for the WIL-HELMSHAVEN—BREMEN main line.

Road.—There is a good road connection from EMDEN to WILHELMS-HAVEN, BREMEN, NORDDEICH, MÜNSTER and LANGAKKER (for GRONINGEN in Holland).

(j) STETTIN. (Population 273,000.)—(i) The largest commercial port in the Baltic and the third largest in GERMANY, about 40 miles from the mouth of the ODER and 84 miles by rail from BERLIN. It is the eastern terminus of the inland water-way system and well situated for eastern European trade with equipment for handling coal and iron ore especially. At present it is being used as the base for the German Army in Finland.

(ii) *Port facilities.*—The least depth in the channel between SWINE-MÜNDE and STETTIN is 29½ ft while the depth alongside in at least two of the main quays is up to 29 ft. The total length of quayage available is about 20 miles. Lifting appliances include a total 96 cranes to lift 1½-40 tons in the FREIHAFEN though an unconfirmed report mentions a 100-ton crane in this dock. In the DUNZIGER KAI there are 20 travelling cranes of 1½-5-ton capacity, in the REIHERMEIDER HAFEN nine transporter bridges and in the STETTINER ODERWERKE two 60-ton floating cranes. Finally there are six floating docks, the largest with a maximum lifting capacity of 2,850 tons.

(iii) *Shipbuilding.—STETTINER ODERWERKE AG für Schiff-und Maschinenbau.* This yard has at present four slips, three of which are stated to be up to 460 ft. long; the fourth is said to be capable of taking two ships of 590 ft simultaneously. The yard now concentrates on 500-ton U-boats and minesweepers. Further important constructional work has taken place since the war.

STETTINER VULKAN WERKE.—At present there are four groups of slips engaged in the production of TLCs, 500-ton U-boats and floating docks.

In addition there are two smaller yards, one of which possibly is building E-boats.

(iv) *POL.*—In addition to good coal bunkering facilities there are probably five firms engaged in POL activities within the port. At least 15 tanks are visible and it is likely that there are others in existence underground.

(v) *Rail.*—Main double line track to STRALSUND, DANZIG, KÖNIGSBERG and POLAND, BERLIN via ANGERMÜNDE. Single track line to KÜSTRIN for FRANKFURT a/O. According to a German press report July, 1942, a double track between STETTIN and PÖLITZ has been planned.

Road.—Autobahn.—Connection south-westwards with the BERLIN by-pass eastwards (under construction) with the EAST PRUSSIAN Autobahn.

Main road connections with STRALSUND, NEUBRANDENBURG, BERLIN, FRANKFURT a/O, SWINEMÜNDE, DANZIG, BROMBERG, It is reported that the road connection with PÖLITZ has been improved.

ORANIENBURG M.T. DEPOT

Key

A. M.T.
B. Huts, probably used for storage and vehicle repair.

There are over 200 huts, most of which have access to roads. About 1900 M.T. vehicles are present, many of the very heavy lorry type.

AUGSBURG/PFERSEE RATIONS STORAGE DEPOT

This photo clearly shows the two main types of building employed in rations depots. The Bakery is characterized by its tall chimney. Barracks are in the immediate vicinity, and the whole depot is rail-served.

INGOLSTADT ORDNANCE DEPOT AND ARTILLERY PARK (Northern part)

Key

A. 2 buildings with ramps 248′ × 78′.
B. Smaller building with ramp.
C. 4 very large buildings 570′ × 145′.

Guns are present, many being parked in the area between the large buildings (C) and the modern barracks.

So large is this depot and park combined, that effective cover with reasonable definition has had to be undertaken in two photographs, those on this page and succeeding page.

Ingolstadt Ordnance Depot and Artillery Park (Southern Part)

This is the southern part of the depot, the key to which is given on the preceding page.

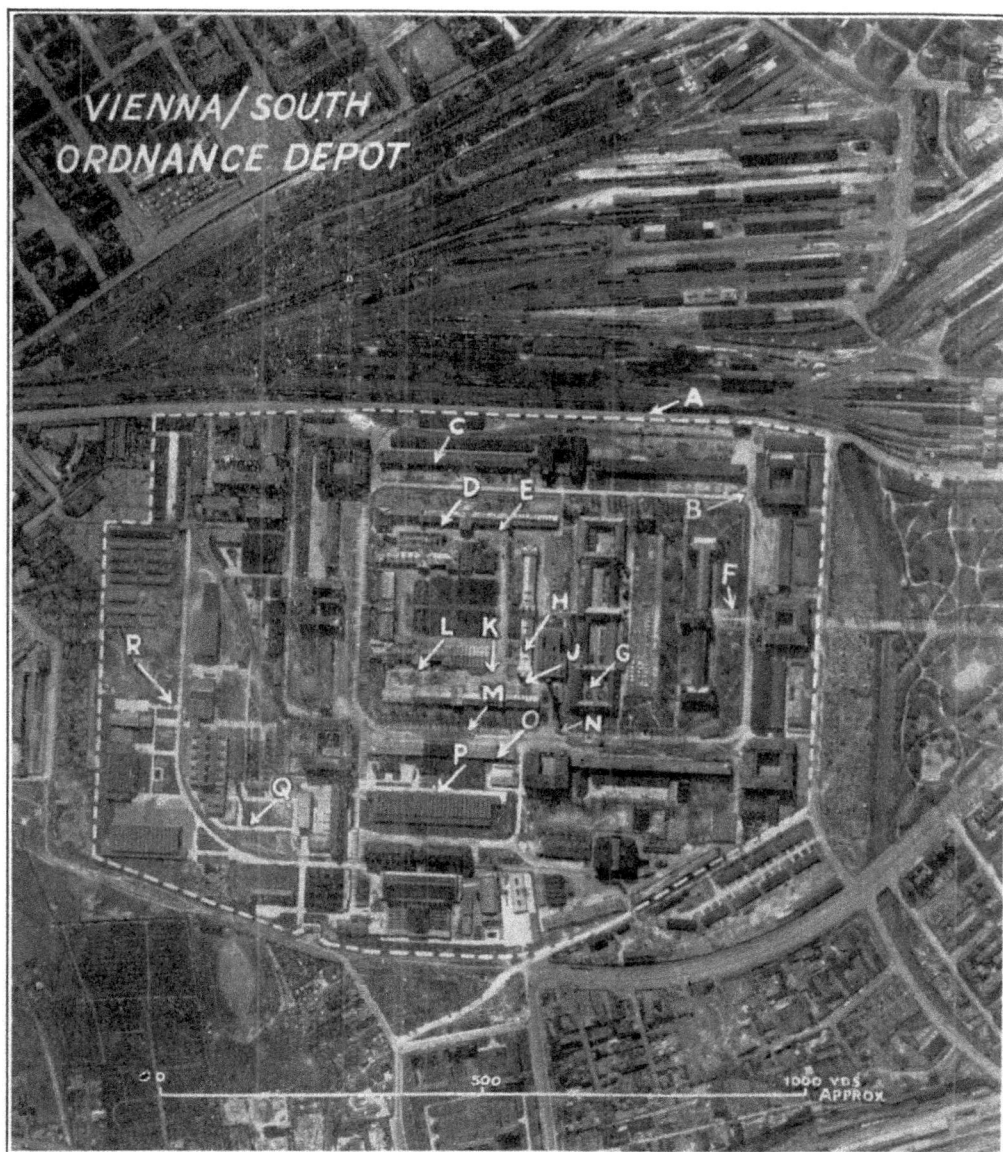

VIENNA/SOUTH ORDNANCE DEPOT

Key

A. Train containing 12 tanks on flats.
B. 2 tanks 17 ft. × 9 ft. probably lacking turrets.
C. 14 hulls 16 ft. × 7½ ft.
D. 29 hulls similar to those at C.
E. Group of vehicles including some probable tank hulls and several vehicles in motion.
F. Ten tanks, varying in size between 17 ft. × 8 ft. and 12 ft. × 6 ft. and five guns probably field and medium.
G. Small tank transporter in courtyard.
H. 5 tanks 18 ft. × 10 ft., four apparently complete and one partly dismantled.
J. 1 tank similar to those at H.
K. Large tank transporter.
L. About 50 tanks and tank chassis, some partly disintegrated.
M. 1 tank 18½ ft. × 10 ft. and 6 tanks 15½ ft. × 7½ ft.
N. Tank 17 ft. × 9 ft. being towed.
O. 10 tanks 14½ ft. and 6 ft.
P. 8 guns, probably light A.A., with carriage 12 ft long.
Q. 17 guns similar to those at P.
R. 25 guns similar to those at P.

SPANDAU/NEUSTADT GUN PARK AND ORDNANCE DEPOT

Key
A. 230 guns with trails 14 ft. (probably 15-cm. hows. or 10·5-cm. guns). Some of them have a pair of wheels on the end of the trail.
B. 80 guns with trails 10 ft. and prominent shields (probably 15-cm. infantry guns).
C. 30 small guns with trails 7 ft. (possibly 7·5-cm. infantry guns).
D. 50 medium guns (probably 15-cm. hows. or 10·5-cm. guns minus some of their component parts).
E. 150–200 miscellaneous guns, chiefly medium. Many of these are not intact.
F. 2 large gantries.
G. Large crane.
H. 11 medium guns.
J. 4 gun heavy railway A.A. battery.
K. 3 large ordnance type buildings 570 ft. × 145 ft.

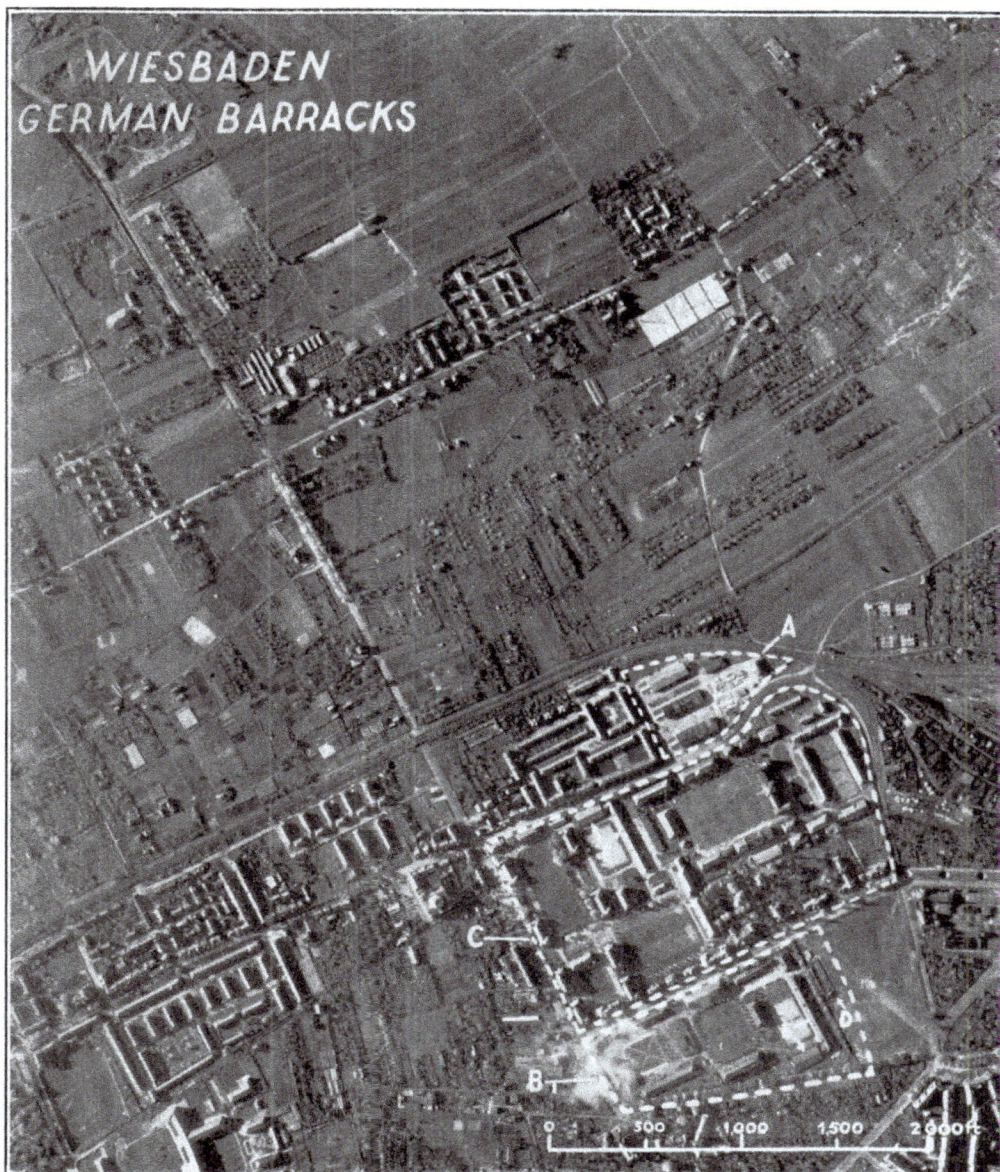

WIESBADEN BARRACKS

Barracks with small ordnance depot attached.

Key
A. Small ordnance depot with 3 buildings with ramps.
B. Small modern barracks.
C. Large old type barracks.
D. Range.
E. Stables.

MUNICH/MILBERTSHOFEN ORDNANCE DEPOT

Key
A. Gun park containing about 300 probable 10·5-cm. gun/hows., a few possible
    15-cm. infantry guns and a large number of limbers.
B. About 40 guns similar to A (probably 10·5-cm. gun/hows.).
C. About 40 guns similar to A (probably 10·5-cm. gun/hows.).
D. 15 probable 10·5-cm. gun/hows.
E. 15 possible 10·5-cm. guns or 15-cm. hows.
F. 4 guns with short stubby barrels or recuperators only.
G. About 15 scattered guns.
H. Bomb damaged buildings. Salvage work is in progress in the very badly
    damaged buildings.
L. Group of gun limbers.
M. M.T. vehicles, mostly lorries.
R. Railway trucks and trains.
T. Large tank transporters—single or in groups.

MAGDEBURG/KÖNIGSBORN ORDNANCE DEPOT

This depot contains the following examples of the three types of building common in ordnance depots (*i.e.*, very large buildings, buildings with ventilators and buildings with ramps).

Key
A.   6 very large buildings 560 ft. × 135 ft.
B.   1 building with ventilator ridge 410 ft. × 110 ft.
C.   1 building with ventilator ridge 410 ft. × 70 ft.
D.   2 buildings with ventilator ridges 320 ft. × 105 ft.
E.   6 buildings with ramps (and a similar one without ramps) 250 ft. × 77 ft.
        The ramps are 55 ft. long and 16 ft. wide.

There are numerous tanks and a few S.P. guns within the depot area.

H

HAGENOW/TREBS AMMUNITION DUMP

Key
A. Ammunition dump area containing ammunition shelters (65 ft. × 50 ft.) served by road and light railway.
B. Munition works.

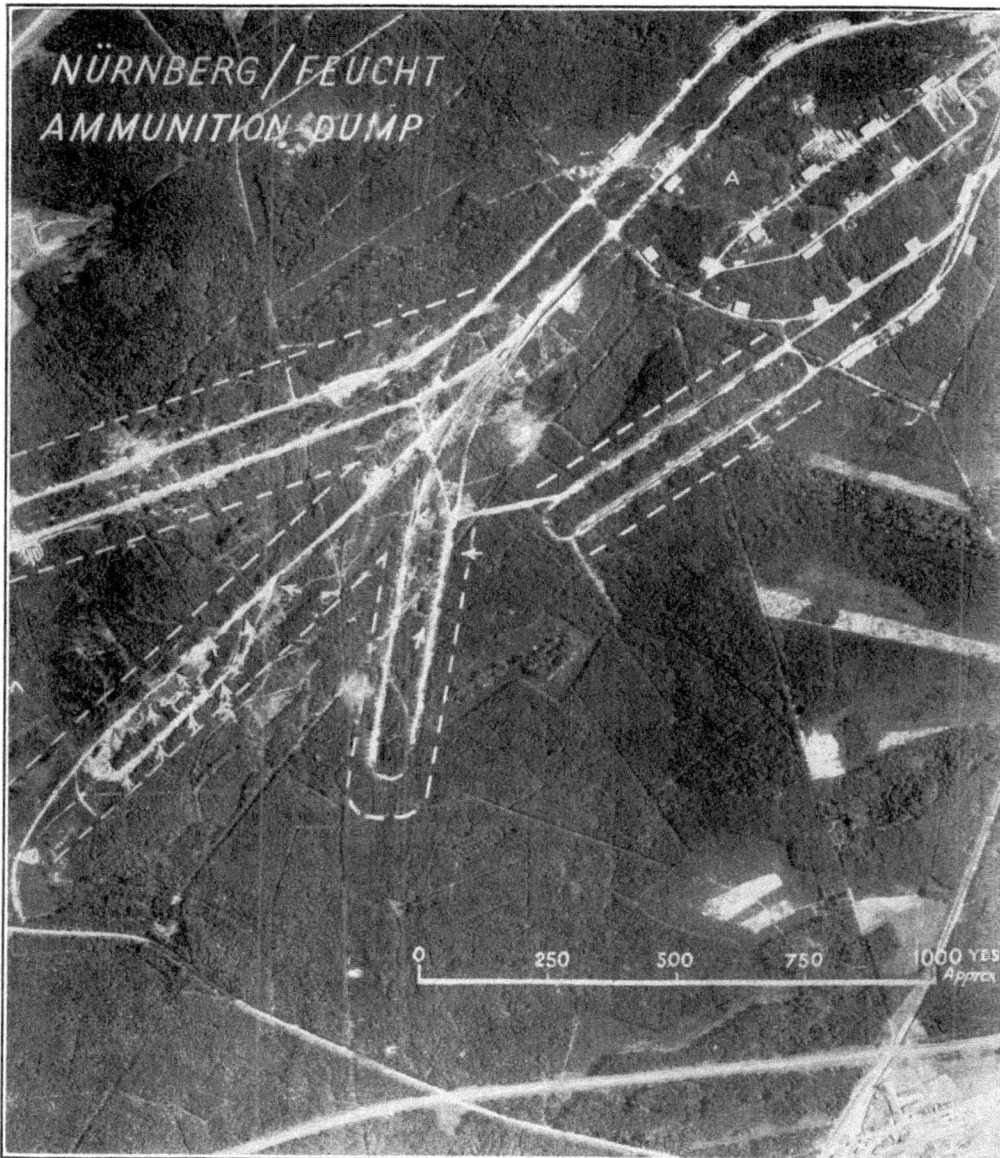

NÜRNBERG/FEUCHT AMMUNITION DUMP

A well laid-out dump in the LORENZER Forest, South East of NÜRNBERG in the area of FEUCHT. Some of the more easily visible ammunition shelters have been marked with arrows.

Key
  A.   Rail served storage sheds of various sizes.

Dotted outlines enclose areas containing rail served earth covered ammunition shelters.

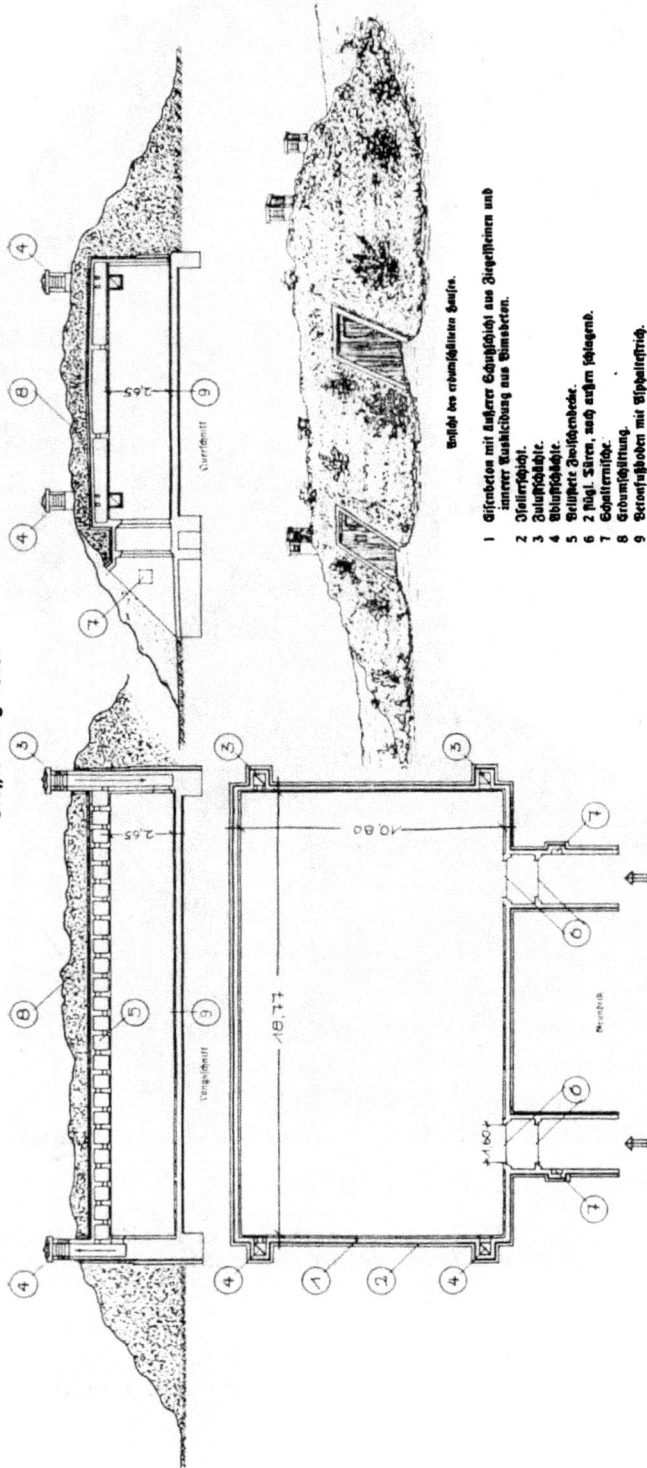

Grohes M. H. 1935.

LARGE EARTH COVERED AMMUNITION HOUSE

Längsschnitt—longitudinal cross section.
Querschnitt—cross section.

Grundriss—plan.
Ansicht des erdumschütteten Hauses—view
of houses when covered with earth.

1. Reinforced concrete with protective layer of
   bricks and internal lining of cement.
2. Layer of insulation.
3, 4. Ventilation shafts.
5. Ventilated ceiling.

6. Two folding doors opening outwards.
7. Switch panels.
8. Earth covering.
9. Concrete floor with asphalt surface.

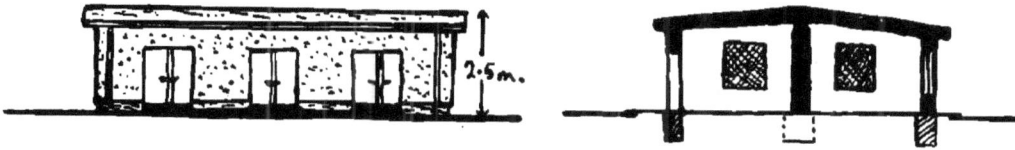

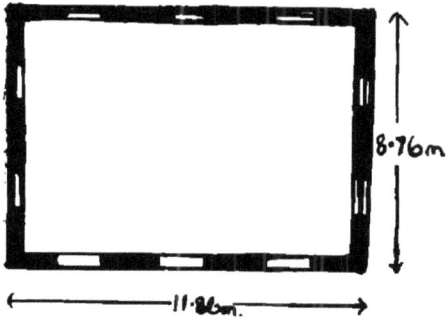

CONCRETE AMMUNITION HOUSE (*Munitionshaus*)
Holding 10 tons.
Dimensions in metres.

STACKING OF SHELLS (COMPLETE ROUNDS) ON RACKS

N.B.—Shells with base fuzes must be laid horizontally.
Dimensions in mm.

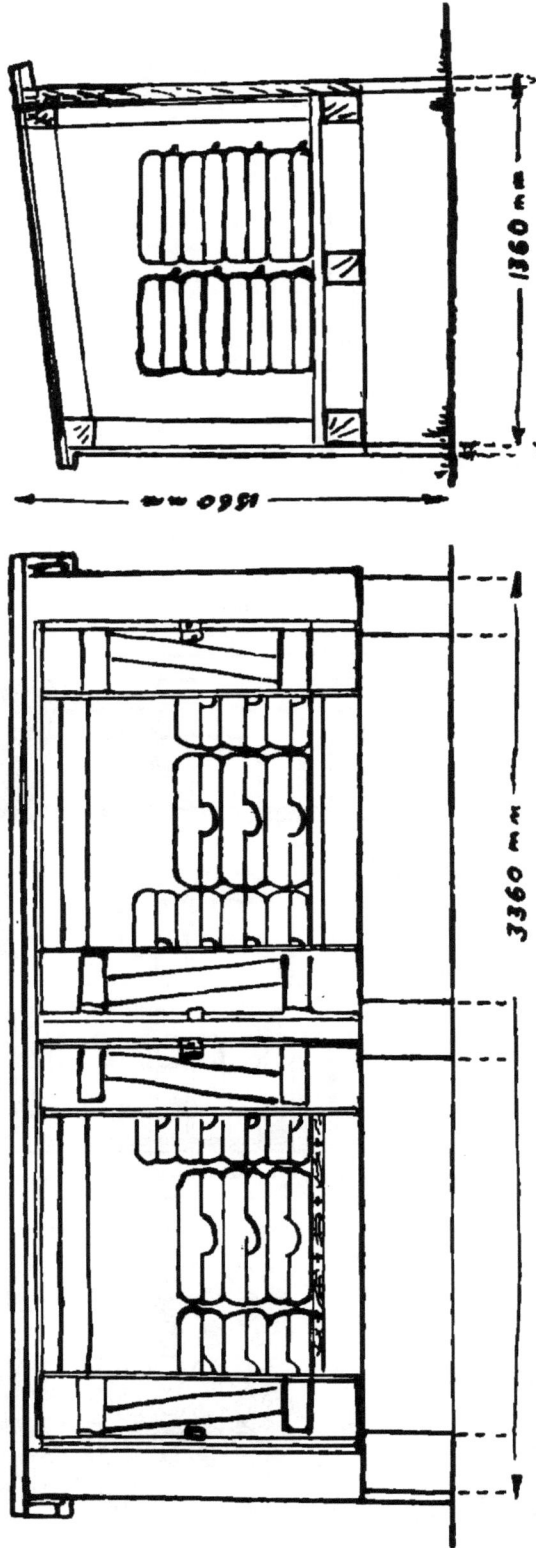

STACKING OF HAND-GRENADES IN METAL BOXES IN AN AMMUNITION SHED

Dimensions in mm.

STORAGE DEPOTS.
TYPES OF STORAGE BUILDINGS.

NOTE :- The vertical measurements are liable to error ± 10%.

TYPE A.

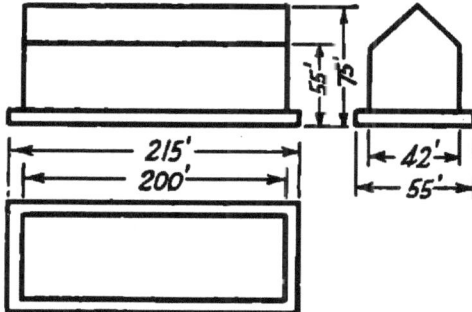

NOTE :-

1. Railway line usually runs along both sides of the building enabling direct loading or unloading from or into the building.

2. Shorter or longer buildings of this type are also found.

TYPE B.

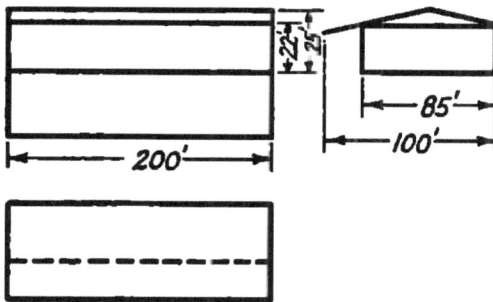

NOTE :-

1. The attendant railway line and/or road passes beneath the overhang.

2. Shorter or longer buildings of this type are also found.

TYPE C.

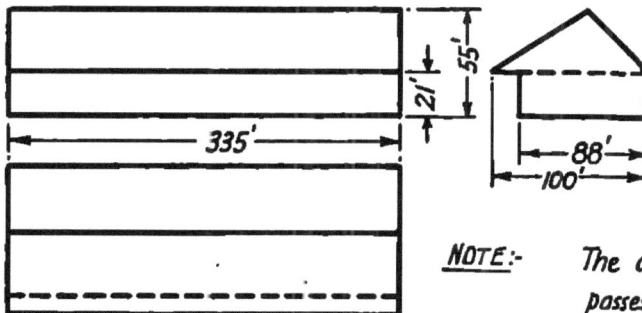

NOTE :- The attendant railway line passes beneath the overhang.

EXAMPLE OF ARMY CLOTHING STORE

Key

Building A.

Ground floor.

Room 1.—Sheets: 2,000; blankets, rugs: 3,000.
Room 2.—Blankets: 4,000; haversacks: 5,000; small cookers: 30: mess tins: 1,000.

First floor.

Room 3.—Boots: 13,000; shoes: 2,000; jackboots: 4,000; leggings: 1,000; belts: 22,000; handkerchiefs: 40,000; underpants: 37,000; trousers: 8,000; waterproofs: 13,000; sleeping bags: 2,000; crash helmets: 50; haversacks: 5,000.
Room 4.—Shoes: 15,000; socks: 2,000; shirts: 1,000; underpants: 1,000; pullovers: 1,000.
Room 7.—Offices.

Second floor.

Rooms 5 and 6.—Boots: 10,000.

Building B.

Rooms 1 and 2.—Offices.
Room 3.—Tents: 6,000; clogs: 5,000; trousers: 21,000; F.S. jackets: 10,000.

Building C.

Room 1.—Messing equipment.
Room 2 (first floor).—Mattresses: 100; pillows: 50; blankets: 500.
Room 3 (second floor).—Sets of cutlery: 40,000.

Building D.

Room 1.—Red Cross equipment, and supplies of chocolate and sugar.
Room 2 (first floor).—Clothing; and mess tins; 60,000; water bottles: 60,000; haversacks: 20,000.
Room 3 (first and second floors).—Requisitioned and confiscated weapons (shot-guns, etc.).

Example of Army Clothing Store

Fig 1.

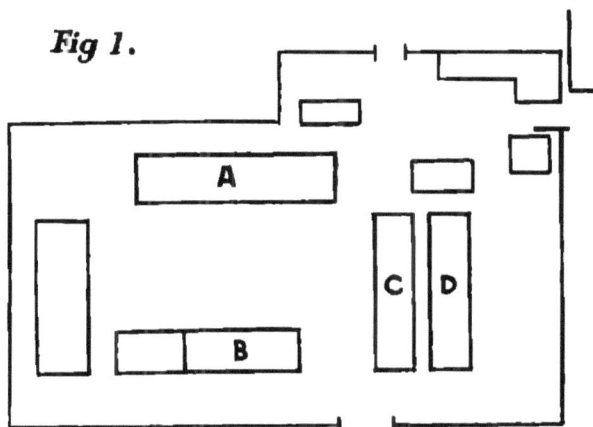

Fig 2.

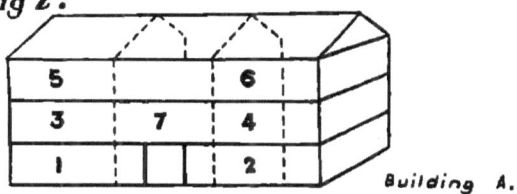

Building A.

Fig 3.

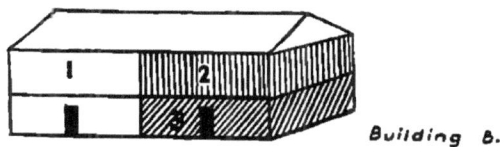

Building B.

Fig 4.

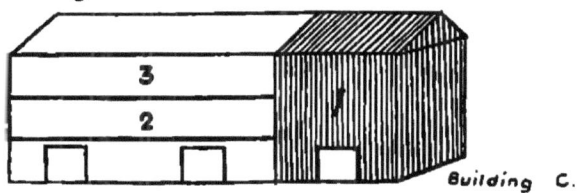

Building C.

Fig 5.

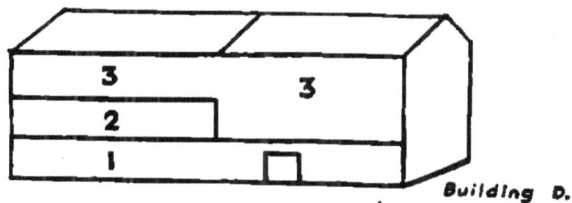

Building D.

K 2

LAYOUT OF MUNA

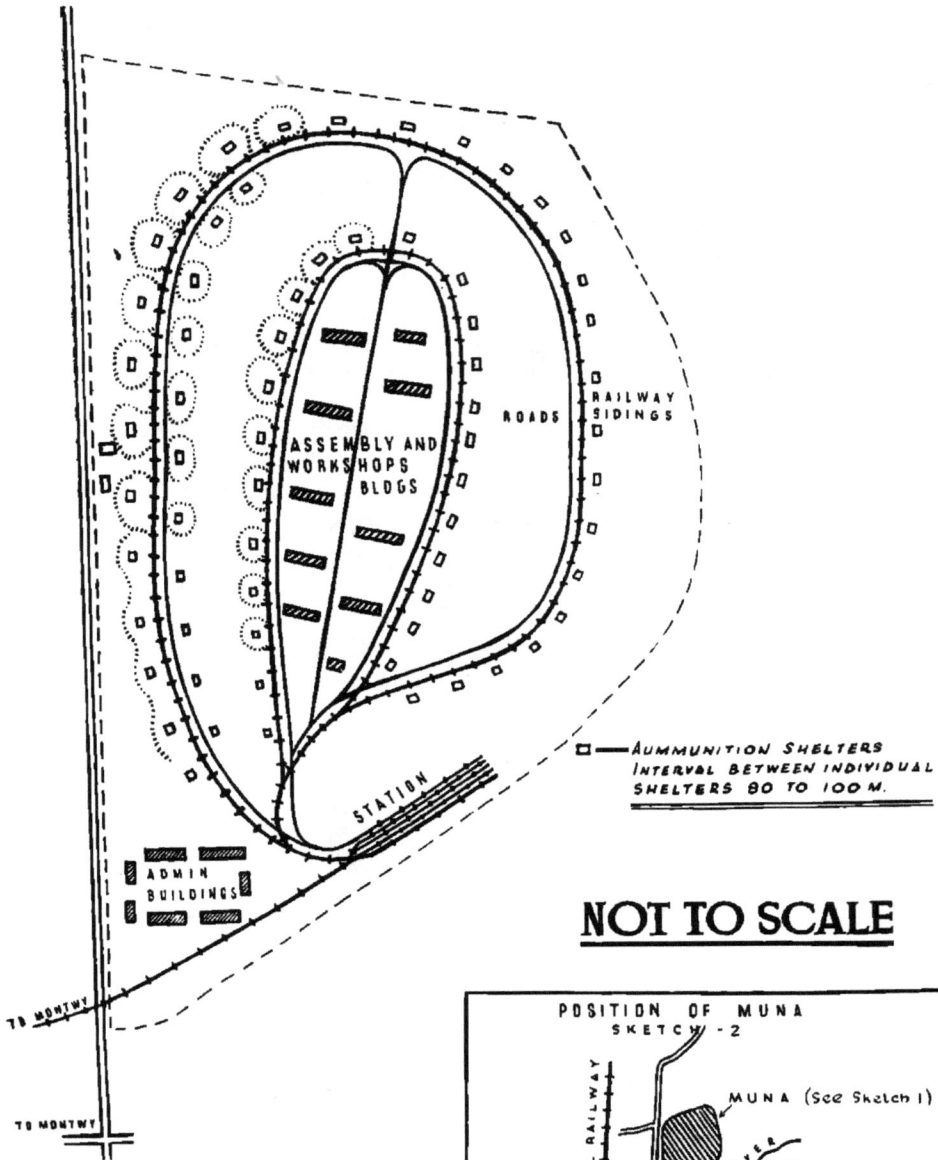

ROADS

RAILWAY SIDINGS

ASSEMBLY AND WORKSHOPS BLDGS

STATION

□— Aummunition Shelters
Interval between individual
shelters 80 to 100 m.

ADMIN BUILDINGS

TO MONTWY

TO MONTWY

NOT TO SCALE

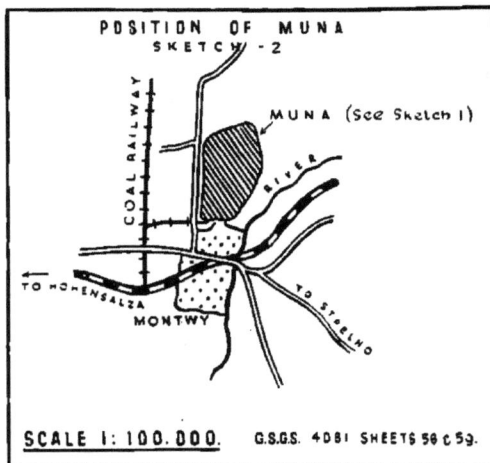

POSITION OF MUNA
SKETCH - 2

COAL RAILWAY

MUNA (See Sketch 1)

RIVER

TO HOHENSALZA

MONTWY

TO STRELNO

SCALE 1: 100.000.   G.S.GS. 4081 SHEETS 56 & 53.

AMMUNITION SHELTER

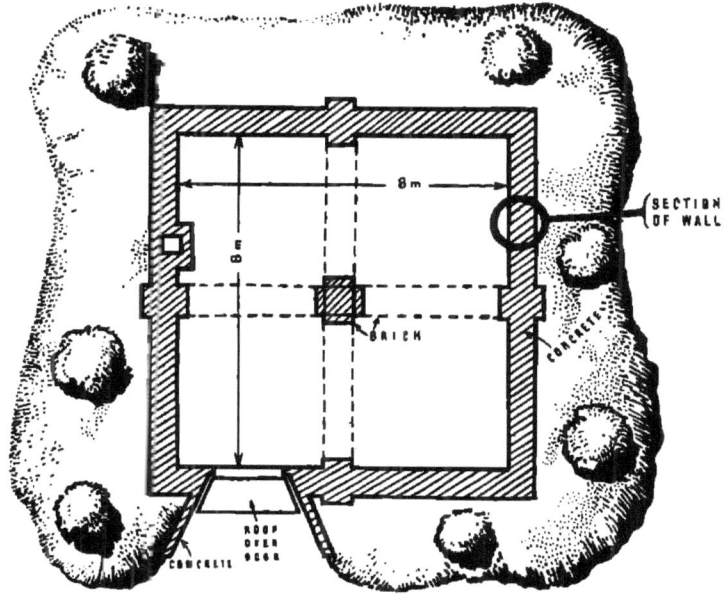

8 m

8 m

SECTION OF WALL

CONCRETE

BRICK

ROOF OVER DOOR

CONCRETE

NOT TO SCALE   PLAN

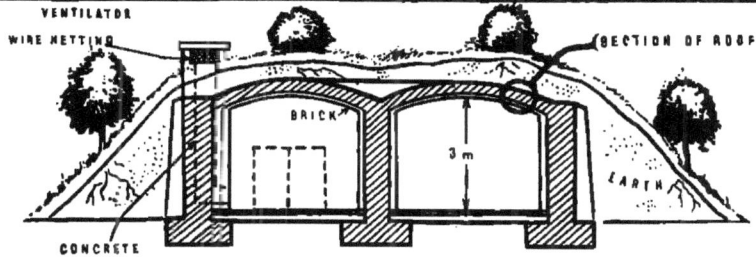

VENTILATOR

WIRE NETTING

SECTION OF ROOF

BRICK

3 m

EARTH

CONCRETE

NOT TO SCALE   SECTIONAL ELEVATION

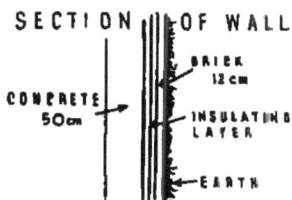

SECTION OF WALL

CONCRETE 50cm

BRICK 12 cm

INSULATING LAYER

EARTH

NOT TO SCALE

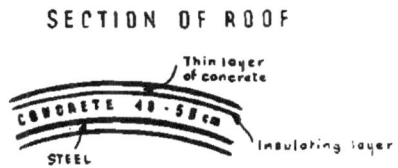

SECTION OF ROOF

Thin layer of concrete

CONCRETE 40-50 cm

STEEL

Insulating layer

PART II

12. General system of supply in the field.

(*a*) *Introductory Notes.*—(i) Detailed scrutiny of the mass of very miscellaneous information which has accumulated relating to the functions of the supply and administrative systems on the various fronts leads to the generalized conclusion that, basically, the Germans practise on almost text-book lines in their system of supply administration in the field. Such discrepancies as occur are governed by common sense application. For example, in theory, the large MT columns rely upon trailers to a very large extent to provide at least a third of their carrying capacity. It has been found that in Russia, the state of even the best roads tends to preclude the use of trailers. The " *Rollbahn* " or main route is, more often than not, good only for a few miles, then will come long stretches of improvized corduroy road (*Knüppeldamm*), followed possibly by a swampy track through forest country. Such conditions, say the German drivers, mean that a trailer will make a vehicle virtually unmanageable. Yet, though trailers are not used in such circumstances, the total carrying capacity of such a column is brought up to 60 tons by the use of all kinds of requisitioned MT, which is the text-book capacity for such a column. A supply column battalion operating between VIAZMA and RZHEV in the winter 1941/42, for example had a strength of 11 officers and 400 men which is rather below establishment, but it maintained six heavy MT columns, each of which maintained a capacity of 60 tons. The standard of the size of the columns was capacity, not number of vehicles. One column had 20 3-ton Mercedes lorries, another had a variety of Ford 2½-ton lorries and Buessing NAG 3 to 3½-tonners.

(ii) A point which has been somewhat obscure in the past has been the limits which the Germans will set on distances governing supply, *e.g.*, the distance between railhead and army dumps and thence to divisional dumps. In the field it has been found that these distances are governed less by terrain than by existing railway facilities. In Italy, as will be seen by the XIV Panzer Corps supply map at the end of this Handbook, railheads are pushed far forward, even into divisional areas. In Russia, the relative distances varied enormously. Cases occurred in Russia, for example, where supply columns had to lift supplies from railhead and carry them 60 miles to Army dumps. The average distance appeared to be about 20 or 25 miles. It was usually possible for columns to make delivery and return to their park in the same day.

As the process of changing railways from Russian to German gauge progressed, the distances covered by MT columns grew less. As soon as the railway was completed by the railway engineers (*Eisenbahnpioniere*), the supply columns were used in the immediate area of railhead, where all the various dumps were established. The illustration of the railhead dump system at SYTSCHEVKA, shown at the end of Part II of the Handbook, shows how these were laid out, and how the A.A. defences were arranged. It will be noticed that the various parks, for artillery, MT, etc, are not shown in this illustration. This is because, as a general rule, such parks were some 120 miles further back. Similarly, tank parks and spare parts parks are invariably very far back. The army MT parks, which appear, in practice, to hold some two to three hundred new vehicles (to be used as replacements) may be just as far back, thus necessitating a very long journey for damaged vehicles. Wherever possible the railway is used for these damaged vehicles, otherwise tractors and transporters are used.

(iii) All supplies are, if possible brought as far as the army area, if not further, by train. At SYTSCHEVKA, to use this example again, about three trains a day used the line for supplies. The only other trains were leave trains which departed in the evenings. The supply trains were never varied, *i.e.*, they consisted of petrol wagons or ammunition wagons only, though sometimes, at the rear of these trains were attached two mail wagons for field post. Trains carried about 450 tons—a further example of the practice of text-book theory.

(iv) More detailed information concerning the operating of the various systems in the field is given below under the heading of ordnance supply, medical systems and so on. It will be seen that circumstances have occasionally forced the Germans to practice otherwise than as they preach. The quartering or billeting of troops in the field is perhaps the best example of departure from theory. Troops in Russia have frequently been quartered in the open, and yet they undoubtedly take advantage of every conceivable form of cover if it exists. In Italy it was reliably stated that a German general order had existed for some time forbidding the quartering of troops in buildings in forward areas and there was a time when entire divisions would be found in the open. The HQ of 16 Panzer Division, for example spent most of September, 1943, in the open. The medical system in the field also is an example of how frequently improvization has to be resorted to, as will be seen by reference to section 17 below.

Following is a fairly detailed study of the supply of XIV Panzer Corps in Italy as it was functioning in December, 1943. It serves as a general illustration of the way the Germans put their supply system into practice in the field.

(*b*) Supply of XIV Panzer Corps on South Italian Front in early December, 1943. (*See* Map at the end of the Handbook.)

In early December, 1943, the following formations were identified in XIV Corps on the Southern Italian front:—

  94 Inf Div.
  15 Pz Gr Div.
  29 Pz Gr Div.

The supply system of 94 Inf Div, 15 Pz Gr Div and 29 Pz Gr Div as outlined below is probably the latest available evidence though brief and incomplete, of the working of German supply under current operational conditions.

(i) *Supply routes.*—The coast road was probably considered too vulnerable, as well as being indirect, for supplies came

  by road and rail from ROME, avoiding the coastal areas; (Route 6).
  by road and rail from AVEZZANO to join the ROME route at ARCE.

Railhead area appeared to include ARCE and CEPRANO. These two places are well forward, a circumstance which bears out the common German practice of bringing supplies by rail as far forward as possible, even into the divisional area. It would also seem as though all three divs in this sector, namely 29 Pz Gr Div, 94 Inf Div and 15 Pz Gr Div, were using this railhead, that is, a corps railhead was in effect a communal divisional railhead.

There is no doubt that the Germans attached the highest importance to this railhead area since photos showed a relatively high concentration of AA defences in this area, namely 23 heavy and 23 light guns. Similar very heavy concentrations of AA guns have been met with at railheads on the Russian front and must be expected elsewhere.

(ii) *Supply of ammunition.—In the corps and army area.*—Ammunition drawn from the army dumps which were situated well to the north of ROME came by road and rail to the railhead. An ammunition dump was reported at ANAGNI which may well have been a corps ammunition dump. Of late the Germans have tended to bring corps more and more into the chain of supply, and the probability that this dump may be a corps dump would be typical of this growing tendency.

In the divisional area.—In the neighbourhood of the railhead NW of CEPRANO and at a point two miles NW of ARCE two ammunition dumps were identified. Further dumps were indentified at ROCCASECCA and at CASTROCIELO and two in the CASSINO area. It is known that the last four named dumps were divisional dumps belonging to 29 Pz Gr Div and kept filled from the railhead by the div supply columns. It is likely, therefore, that the first two, namely at CEPRANO and ARCE were also divisional dumps since it is believed that all three divs drew ammunition from these dumps from time to time.

(iii) *Supply of rations.*—Supplies of rations travelled by the same routes as ammunition. Rations dumps were also identified in the corps area.

Corps area.—Along the main route to ROME, there was a supply dump at VEROLI. Further dumps were identified from air photos at FIUGGI and ANAGNI with another suspected dump three miles to the south. These were all almost certainly corps dumps and further illustrate the growing importance of corps in the administrative layout.

Divisional area.—The lack of confirmed locations makes any attempt to give an idea of the rations layout in the divisional area extremely difficult, for it will be remembered that most divisional rations points are located in villages, under cover. An unconfirmed report suggested that in 29 Pz Gr Div area a supply dump was located at CASTROCIELO, but no idea can be given from which Corps dump this obvious divisional dump received its supplies. A further divisional dump was identified in S GIOVANNI. This is borne out by the fact that prisoners from 129 Pz Gr Regt (15 Pz Gren Div) stated that their supplies were fetched from this dump and that a butchery unit, possibly 33 Butchery Pl of 15 Pz Gr Div, was in the area.

(iv) *Supply of POL.—In the corps area.*—Situated in the neighbourhood of the main railway line and well within the Corps area, two unconfirmed petrol dumps were reported at VALMONTONE and FROSINONE. No information is available on the type of dump, size of containers, etc.

Divisional area.—In 29 Pz Gren Div area, a petrol dump was identified at AQUINO, but again no information is available on the type or area covered. Petrol would be brought from the divisional railhead area, or from the corps dumps to the divisional dumps in tanker lorries of the POL MT coln.

(v) *Conclusion.*—It is realized that this description of the supply layout in S ITALY is extremely brief and lacking in many of the more vital details which would complete the picture. Certain interesting facts, however, emerge:—

As is borne out in RUSSIA, the Germans lay great stress on using the railway as their most important means of communication, supplementing where necessary with MT colns.

In relatively static warfare the Germans set up dumps of rations, ammunition and petrol within the divisional area and create divisional dumps, that is, they push the dump system very far forward.

Corps is emerging as an important link in the administrative layout.

(c) Supply by air.—(i) The Germans appear to have used air transport of supplies in the past mainly:—

to support air-borne operations, *e.g.*, in Crete.

to maintain forces surrounded and cut off from other sources of supply, *e.g.*, in Tunisia.

for the sake of speed when land and sea channels of supply have been unable to cope with the necessary daily replenishment of essential supplies such as rations, ammunition and POL *e.g.*, in the Kuban.

to move the equipment and ground personnel of GAF units when switched to a new operational base, *e.g.*, from France to Italy.

to supply units in difficult terrain, *e.g.*, in the mountainous areas of Yugoslavia.

(ii) *Air-landed* supplies are carried principally as follows:—

in transport aircraft (mainly Ju 52).

in gliders (DFS 230, Go 242 and Me 321).

in powered gliders (Go 244 and Me 323) for carrying bulky freight in areas not unduly exposed to enemy air attack.

(iii) *Air-dropped* supplies are categorized as follows:—

dropping of rations, petrol and other supplies in large supply bombs (*Versorgungsbombe*).

dropping of equipment in containers by parachute. The Germans have a large range of standard types of parachute-borne containers for different types of equipment. These containers are mainly used for air-borne troops.

dropping, by parachute, of heavier equipment. This is usually pushed out of the door of the Ju 52 or released from an underslung position either with or without a special container.

dropping of bulky packages without parachute from the doors of low-flying aircraft. This has frequently been done in Russia, particularly in snow-covered areas where the dispersion on the ground of the various packages is offset by the relative ease of spotting the packages in the snow.

(iv) Examples of the German ability to maintain large forces for considerable periods, exclusively or partially, by supply from the air were seen at:—

STARAYA RUSSA.—In the early stages 4 divisions, in the latter stages just over one division, were able to fight a successful defensive battle for three-and-half months, supplied almost exclusively from the air.

STALINGRAD.—For over two months the greater part of the German 6th Army was entirely cut off from land supply routes. In January, 1943, it was estimated that about 900 transport aircraft including about 400 Ju's 52 were used. Initially the bulk of the supplies was air-landed but, later, supplies had to be dropped.

KUBAN.—The supply of the Kuban forces by air was a supplementary factor, functioning chiefly when sea conditions made sea transport impossible or very difficult.

TUNISIA.—Extensive use of Ju's 52 and powered gliders was made, though very costly, to achieve speedy supply of essential equipment, ammunition and POL, to make up the deficiencies caused by Allied attacks on shipping routes.

(v) *Summary.*—The Germans realized the true efficacy of air transport of supplies in the early days of the war, and have built up the system into an extensive organization. The basic air transport organization is the wing (*Gruppe*) composed of four squadrons (*Staffeln*) each of 12 Ju's 52 and a wing HQ (*Gruppenstab*) of 5 aircraft, though wings equipped with obsolescent Heinkel 111 bombers are also known. The primary function of these wings is the transport of supplies for the army and GAF, and they are usually under the control of air fleets (*Luftflotten*). Air transport wings may be formed into transport groups for large-scale operations. These groups, which vary in size, are normally disbanded as soon as the purpose for which they were formed has been accomplished. Glider-towing units may be subordinated to air fleets.

The shortage of suitable tugs has induced the Germans to equip the Go 242 and Me 321 gliders with aero engines, the powered versions being named Go 244 and Me 323. The Me 323, though extremely vulnerable to air attack, has proved very valuable for transporting MT, guns and other bulky freight, and is organized in wings of 25 aircraft.

(v) *Capacities, ranges, etc, of German aircraft and gliders used for transporting supplies and personnel—*

Aircraft	Max. useful load	Range (miles)	Remarks
Ju 52	4,480 lbs 18–20 men	500	with extra tanks, range 700 miles.
He 111	3,360 lbs 10–15 men	about 500	

Gliders	Max. useful load	Tugs with extra tanks	Range (miles)	Remarks
Assault glider— DFS 230...	2,800 lbs 10 men	Ju 52 He 111 Ju 87 Me 110 Hs 126	630 1,340 760 1,420 430	
Freight carrying gliders— Go 242	5,300 lbs 23 men	Ju 52 He 111 Me 110	620 1,030 1,210	
Powered gliders— Me 323 (Gigant)	26,400 lbs 120 men	...	640	

13. *Ammunition Supply in the field.*

(a) *Introductory Notes.*—Ammunition is handled as far as divisions by the supply services commander (*Nachschubführer*) at Division, Corps or Army HQ.

Supply companies are responsible for the labour in army dumps and parks at railhead, re-loading points, ammunition points and petrol points, repair collecting centres and salvage dumps.

Supply companies are as a rule allotted to tasks in platoons or half platoons. depending on the time available for carrying out the job and the number of transport vehicles and men available for loading and unloading.

Examples of the man-hours necessary to perform various tasks are given below:—

    (i) Assuming that 10 railway trucks can be unloaded, that the lorries can be brought direct up to the railway trucks, and that unloading proceeds uninterruptedly, an ammunition train (450 tons) can be unloaded by one platoon in five hours (a platoon comprising some 40 men).

    (ii) Assuming that 40 railway trucks can be unloaded simultaneously under the same conditions as above an ammunition train (450 tons) can be unloaded by three platoons in two hours.

    (iii) The time necessary for direct loading of a lorry is 20 minutes.

    (iv) The stacking of the contents of a large MT column (60 tons) in an army ammunition dump can be carried out by two platoons in 40 minutes.

    (v) A small MT column (30 tons) can be loaded in an army ammunition dump by one platoon in one hour, if the column can be brought up direct to the ammunition stacks.

    (vi) The stacking of 60 tons of ammunition in an ammunition point can be carried out by one platoon in 1½ hours.

    (vii) 60 tons of ammunition in an ammunition point can be issued by one platoon in two hours.

    (viii) Re-loading of 60 tons of ammunition from a large MT column on to two small MT columns can be carried out by one platoon in one hour, the ammunition being transhipped direct from one lorry to the other.

    (ix) 30 tons of ammunition can be reloaded from light artillery columns on to battle transport vehicles in 1½ hours.

Supply companies are not normally employed on regular guard duty though they must find sentries for their own premises. Local labour may be employed temporarily to assist supply units. Prisoners of war are made use of in assisting supply units in the army L of C area. However, the large dump at SYTSCHEVKA of a capacity of 120,000 tons shown in the sketch at the end of Part II of the Handbook was guarded by the same supply company, 200 strong, which furnished the labour. The staff of the dump comprised a captain assisted by three other officers and 10 NCOs. The supply company was employed at any one time as follows:—

    60 men off duty,
    60 men guards,
    60 men loading and unloading,
    20 men fatigues.

Whilst there is at division a fixed establishment of one supply company under the divisional supply officer, there is no such establishment at Corps or Army, though at Army HQ the Army supply officer normally has an allotment of two supply battalions. Each of these consists of HQ and three companies. Battalion HQ includes an ammunition section which is similar to the *Munitionsverwaltung* of the divisional supply officer's HQ and is responsible for the administration of the army ammunition dump. All this is found to work in practice as it is laid down in theory.

(b) *Transport.*—(i) Generally speaking ammunition is carried from Army dumps in Army supply columns (*Armee-Nachschubkolonnen*) as far as re-loading points (*Umschlagstellen*) in the corps or forward army area, or even as far as the divisional ammunition dump, whence the divisional supply columns take it to the divisional ammunition points (*Ausgabestellen*). For an illustration of such an ammunition point *see* page 204. Here it is collected by light unit columns (unless taken by the latter direct from the divisional ammunition dump).

Again if there is a corps dump, ammunition may be brought to it from the army dump and delivered to the divisional dump by corps supply columns.

Or again ammunition may be brought up direct on GHQ ammunition trains to divisional railhead to avoid unnecessary handling, if rail facilities exist. The Germans certainly use rail whenever they can.

(ii) *Horse-drawn vehicles.*—German HD transport vehicles include heavy and light wooden wagons (*Feldwagen*) for 4- and 2-horse teams with four iron-tyred wheels as well as a steel built 2-horse 4-wheeler (rubber tyred) wagon (*Stahlfeldwagen*) with an overall length of 23 ft (including horses) and a width of 6 ft.

Considerable use is also made of local vehicles in Occupied Territory; in Russia for instance the *Panjewagen* or peasant cart has proved so useful that entire transport columns have been equipped with this vehicle. The *Panjewagen* is normally four-wheeled and may have one or two horses, and is of all wood construction.

(iii) *Motor transport.*—The MT used in divisional supply columns normally consists of 3-3½ ton medium lorries, of such makes as Henschel, Borgward, Opel, etc, with a weight of up to 5 tons loaded. They vary from 19 ft 2 ins to 21 ft in length from 6 ft 11 ins to 7 ft 3 ins in width and from 7 ft 10½ ins to 8 ft 6 ins in height. Various types of medium lorries are illustrated at the end of Part II of the Handbook.

Heavy commercial type lorries of several makes are also employed in non-divisional, *e.g.*, army supply columns. They vary in weight from 4 to 10 tons (unladen) or 6 to 18 tons (loaded).

The Mercedes-Benz vehicle shown in the illustration on page 207 is typical of the 10 ton lorries employed in the German Army. It is equipped with twin or double rear wheels and has a maximum speed of 34-35 mph on the road (hill climbing 1 in 4). It is 9½ ft in height and width, and 34 ft 3 ins in length.

Other makes include the Faun 4-wheel 5-6-ton lorries and 6-wheel 9-tonner; Henshell 4, 4½ and 9-9½-ton lorries, Krupp and Hansa-Lloyd 5-tonners and the Büssing NAG 4-4½ and 9-ton lorries. The load of any of these heavy lorries is increased by the use of trailers, where these can be used.

Trailers vary in weight from the 1·5 tons (4·8 tons laden) single axle trailer to the 5-ton multi-axle trailer (with a weight (laden) of up to 16 tons). This multi-axle trailer is 25 ft 6 in long, 7 ft 9 in wide and 6 ft 6 in high, and has a load space of 24 ft 7 in × 7 ft 3 in × 2 ft. The trailers are extensively used on good roads, but rarely very far forward into, say, divisional areas.

It is to be noted that in addition to German commercial lorries use is also made of requisitioned civilian MT in occupied territories.

(iv) The following rules are laid down for the loading of vehicles carrying ammunition:—

The vehicle must not be loaded beyond three-quarters of its capacity; in no case may the ammunition top the sides of the vehicle. Ammunition in open vehicles must be covered with tarpaulins in rainy weather.

Maximum speed of lorries carrying ammunition: 20 km (12½ mph) inside the dump; 30 km (19 mph) elsewhere.

If the lorry is fitted with a trailer the driver's mate is required to be with the trailer. Smoking or the use of naked lights is forbidden.

The engine must always be shut off when unloading or loading the lorry. Lorries must not refuel when loaded with ammunition or in the vicinity of ammunition dumps (stacks or buildings).

(v) *Trains.*—The size of ammunition and other supply trains will vary in accordance with the line gradient and the prevailing requirements. The capacity of the standard ammunition trains is given as 450 tons; assuming the 15-ton truck to be used the train will therefore consist of 30 trucks. Trains of 45 to 50 15-ton trucks are not uncommon on the Eastern Front.

The following regulations apply to trains carrying ammunition:—

Railway trucks conveying ammunition must be locked and sealed. In the dump the doors and windows of ammunition sheds of buildings must be closed as the engine passes. Steam locomotives must be fitted with spark arresters. The vicinity of the track must be kept clear of easily inflammable material such as baskets, wooden packing cases, etc. Any live coals or glowing ash left behind by the engine after shunting its trucks and leaving the dump, such as might cause a fire, must be stamped out.

The quantity of ammunition which a 15-ton railway truck is capable of taking is included in the table on pages 147-148.

(c) *Storage of ammunition.*—(i) *General.*—Much of the information given in Part I, section 2 (d) is relevant here and should be studied in conjunction with the information below.

Ammunition dumps may be classified, broadly speaking under three headings, *viz*:—

Divisional ammunition dumps (*Divisions-Munitionslager*) on the fringe of the battle zone (*Gefechtsgebiet*);

Forward army ammunition dumps taken over by Corps (*Korps-Munitionslager or KML*) and Army ammunition dumps (*Armee-Munitionslager* or *AML*) in the Army L of C area (*Rückwärtiges Armeegebiet*); and

Ammunition depots (*Heeres-Munitionsanstalten*) administered by the Head of Army Supply in the home area (*Heimatgebiet*), and already dealt with in Part I, section 2.

(ii) Distinction was made by the RAOC in reporting on German dumps in North Africa between forward (operational) dumps and base dumps. In the former instance ammunition was literally " dumped " in the open with little attempt to follow dunnage, camouflage or stacking regulations. Though this was not the case in base dumps, such as at Benghazi the lack of weather protection or fire-fighting equipment was just as marked there also (*see* illustration on page 200).

The practice of " dumping " ammunition (and other supplies) in operational dumps obtains in the European theatre only in a war of rapid movement, since storage facilities (either in the open or in buildings) are infinitely greater there than in North Africa.

In interpreting air photographs the following distinctions are made:— Forward ammunition dumps, on the lines of communication, usually consisting of rows of individual stacks sunk into the ground with earth walls around the stacks often located in woods some distance away from a railhead; permanent or semi-permanent dumps in which the ammunition is stacked in brick or concrete sheds set out in parallel rows with regular intervals between each stack, and all connected by rail sidings; main (base) dumps and depots for ammunition and other supplies and material. Established on sidings at some distance from the main railway line these dumps or depots usually consist of a large number of storage sheds each with its own siding and loading ramp. These depots often cover a large area and may be deliberately dispersed to present a less favourable target to air bombing. Examples of these have already been shown at the end of Part I.

Use may also be made of fortresses and other buildings for storing ammunition, whilst underground constructions are not uncommon.

For the purposes of this Handbook these various categories of dumps have been reduced to two types, firstly dumps in which ammunition is stored in the open and in which the only weather protection consists of waterproof sheeting, tarpaulin and roofing felt thrown over the stacks dealt with in Part II, section 13 (d) (ii) and secondly dumps in which the ammunition is housed under cover, e.g., in buildings already dealt with in Part I, section 2 (d).

(iii) *Storage of ammunition in the open.—Siting and general layout.—* Concealment being a primary requirement in siting ammunition dumps the Germans make the greatest possible use of woods and forests, dumps often being sited in a clearing or just inside the periphery of the wood. Advantage is also taken of any natural cover such as trees and bushes, orchards, thickets, spinneys, olive groves, parks, caves, quarries or depressions in the ground to store ammunition.

The necessity for adequate communcation to the dump by road or rail is stressed, whilst emphasis is also laid on good natural drainage in siting a dump. The following rules apply to the general arrangement of German dumps.

Different types of ammunition and varieties of these types are kept separate from one another as far as this is feasible. Shells are stored separately from charges in order to avoid detonation of the shells on combustion of the charges; the charges are stored in special stacks alongside or behind the shell stacks, the number of charges in a stack corresponding to the number of shells in the corresponding shell stack. Star shells, flares, smoke grenades or candles are stored well away (100 yards) from other ammunition. The spacing of shell stacks from charge stacks or of detonator stacks from HE stacks is 30-40 yards.

Ammunition belonging to different danger categories (*Gefahrenklassen*) is never stored together, whilst fuzes, detonators, etc, are stacked separately from and at the back of HE stacks. Incendiary and gas shells are required to be stored 500 yards down wind from the ammunition dump.

Ammunition of the same type and calibre must according to regulations be distributed in several stacks in order to avoid loss of the entire stock as a result of enemy action, and in order to facilitate simultaneous loading on to several vehicles.

It is the practice to stack the largest calibre ammunition at the entrance to the dump in view of the advantage in loading that this method offers.

Empty shell cases and returned live ammunition should be stored in special dumps 100 yards from the entrance to the main ammunition dump itself.

(iv) *Layout, size and spacing of stacks in ammunition dumps at division or army.—*The size of stack for an army ammunition dump is laid down as 15 tons and up to 30 tons under exceptional conditions.

A spacing of 50 yards is recommended for stacks arranged in chessboard pattern, on either side of the road, the distance to the road from the nearest stacks being 5-10 yards. In the case of smaller stacks of six tons content spacing is reduced to about 30 yards between stacks.

3×2 yards to 8×3 yards is given as a convenient size of a shell stack. The number of shells which can be stored in a stack of this size is as follows :—

Up to 10·5 cm calibre ...	600 shells.
Up to 15 cm ,, ...	300 shells.
Over 15 cm ,, ...	100 shells.

The sizes of stacks may, however, vary very considerably. Thus at the German ammunition and bomb dump at Benghazi, where some 4,000 tons were stored in an area of about three-quarters of a mile square, the quantity of ammunition in each stack generally varied from six to 20 tons, the spacing between stacks being about 10 yards and the stack height 4-6 ft. In some cases indeed stacks of only one ton content were met with, *e.g.*, in the 3·7 cm ammunition area of about 200 yards square where the stacks varied from one to 10 tons. Here it was found that stacks running from east to west contained ammunition and stacks running from north to south boxes of fired cases which had been repacked in their standard packages, and these in turn in the transporting packages.

A notable feature of this dump was the stacking of ammunition contained in cylinders (8·8 and 10·5 cm). These cylinders were stacked along the periphery of the dump adjacent to the road. The length of each stack varied, some extending a distance of 50 yards. The tops of the stacks were very irregular, the shadow thrown being identical with that of a road hedge.

In the tank and A Tk ammunition dump at Benghazi the stacks consisted of approximately 6 tons, the stacks being about 6 feet high and the average spacing between stacks 20 yards.

In the ammunition dump at Gambut which occupied an area of about two square miles and contained approximately 3,000 tons, the stacks consisted of one layer of packages of about 2 tons and were square in shape. Though neither numbered or marked in any way for identification, stacks were set out according to a uniform pattern, and once a stack was located it was a simple matter to locate the remainder. At Gambut distances between stacks varied, the minimum being about 30 yards.

Illustrations of the stacking of various types of ammunition in dumps behind the *Westwall*, in Europe, are shown on page 202.

(v) The following table summarizes the spacings (safety distances) recommended by the Germans in setting out stacks.

Spacings of ammunition stacks.

Type of ammunition	Size of stack in tons	Minimum distance apart of stacks in yards		Distance from road in yards	Remarks
		Without earthern safety wall	With earthern safety wall		
All kinds ... ... except	2·5	20	10	15	...
incendiary or gas shells	7·5	50	10	30	
Incendiary and gas shells	3	50	...	50 (10m for charges)	Shells laid on wooden grids over pits 2 yds long 1 yd wide and 1 yd deep.
Returned live parts	6	50—50	...	50—150	...
Expended ammunition (cases)	10 sq yds	40—40	...	15—25	...

(vi) *Camouflage.*—In the absence of natural cover, use is made of artificial camouflage nets, wire netting, matting, etc, in addition to the natural camouflage offered by twigs, branches, foliage, turf, snow, etc. Equal importance is attached to camouflaging the approaches to the dump.

In laying out dumps and ammunition points, German regulations emphasize the importance of rounding off angles or lines capable of throwing well defined shadows and matching the colour to that of the ground.

To prevent shadows the sides of stacks are sometimes built up with sand or earth thus making them practically invisible from the air, as at the Gambut (N Africa) dump. In many operational dumps in North Africa, however, no attempt was made to camouflage, and the same is undoubtedly true of Russia and Italy to a very great extent.

(vii) *Dunnage.*—Poor natural drainage may be offset by adequate dunnage to which great importance is attached. Dunnage in operational dumps in North Africa was often conspicuous by its absence, though main dumps were well provided for in this respect, ammunition being stacked in many instances on very heavy timber, in the form of wooden floors of 4 in by 4 in timber. In other cases stones were used to good effect as dunnage.

The use of stones or bricks is in any case recommended as a bed for the stack-timbering (blocks and planks), the distance of the bottom-most layer of the stack from the ground being 4-7 in.

To ensure sufficient ventilation also, stacks are placed on planks supported on blocks of timber, pit props or logs so that the ammunition is at least 4-7 in above the ground. When ammunition is stored in recesses or excavations in the ground a 14 in space is left between the ammunition and the wall, shell fuzes being turned away from the wall.

(viii) *Weather protection.*—When ammunition cannot be stored in huts, sheds or other buildings the German regulations emphasize the importance of providing adequate protection against sun, rain, etc, and recommend the use of tent sheeting, roofing felt, corrugated iron and tarpaulins such as are carried on the 15-ton trucks of the *Reichsbahn,* roofing felt being reserved for ammunition points. Little if any attention was, however, paid to these regulations in North Africa where weather protection was nearly always completely neglected. This will also doubtless apply to many operational dumps in Europe of a temporary nature.

(ix) *Fire protection.*—German regulations recommend that stacks be protected from fire by fire-protection belts 3 to 4 yds in width: if this is impossible owing to the nature of the ground, stacks may be protected by earth, stone or brick walls. The site of the dump as a whole is protected from risk of fire by cutting a trench or fire belt round it, emphasis being laid on the importance of removing dead timber and undergrowth and on keeping the ground clear.

Open fires are not permitted within 200 yards of the dump.

(d) *Divisional Ammunition Points.*—(i) *Siting.*—Divisional ammunition points are of a temporary nature and are preferably sited in dry wooded country such as provides natural cover from aerial observation. They may be set up in straggling villages but only in the absence of natural cover; the layout of the point will be the same as if the ammunition were stored in the open. The site chosen should be sufficiently extensive (500-1,000 yards in length) to facilitate the loading or unloading of as large a number as possible of vehicles simultaneously. Positions likely to draw enemy fire, *e.g.,* periphery of woods, road crossings, are avoided in the case of ammunition points, which are often 3-6 miles behind the front line in the case of infantry ammunition points and 8-10 miles for artillery ammunition points.

The size of the ammunition point depends on the quantity of ammunition to be held, and it may be necessary to duplicate points.

Accessibility from the main road by loop roads (or tracks capable of taking MT) allowing of one-way traffic so as to facilitate the loading and unloading of vehicles is an important consideration in siting the point, a duty devolving upon the divisional supply officer or the ammunition section of his HQ. Other considerations in siting an ammunition point are the state of the approach roads or tracks, facilities offered in marshalling vehicles under cover at the form-up and assembly points near the entrance and exit to the ammunition point, proximity of water for fire fighting and drinking purposes, connection to telephone system.

(ii) *Layout.*—Ammunition points may be divided into the following areas:—

Forming-up point.

Unloading area for shell or cartridge cases to be taken back by columns returning empty to the ammunition dump.

Stack area from which the ammunition is issued.

Assembly point (prior to moving-off loaded).

Both the forming-up and assembly points must be sufficiently extensive for the vehicles to be marshalled in their correct order before and after loading.

Ammunition should be stacked so that the heaviest types are loaded first.

The average size of stack is 6 tons (shells and charges together), *i.e.*, equal to the load of two lorries. Different types of ammunition or fuzes are stored in separate stacks in order to avoid confusion particularly at night.

Ammunition must be protected from rain or sun by means of tarpaulins, roofing felt, corrugated iron and the like. Stack timber (planks, boards, etc) will, like the ammunition, be obtained from the divisional ammunition dump.

Ammunition is stored in separate stacks according to type of ammunition. The individual stacks are numbered and named.

(iii) *Administration.*—The officer or NCO in charge of the ammunition point is responsible for setting-up the ammunition point (erection of sign-posts and stacks) and for the allotment of administration and labour duties among his personnel.

A proportion of the divisional supply company ($\frac{1}{2}$ to 1 platoon) is usually allotted to the ammunition point for loading and unloading, traffic control (if necessary) protection and special local jobs. Instructions given by the officer i/c the ammunition point to the platoon commander may be accompanied to advantage by a sketch plan of the point.

Traffic control inside the ammunition point is especially important at night.

The erection of direction signs begins and ends at the turn-off from the main supply route (*Nachschubstrasse*). The divisional supply officer may ask div HQ for the assistance of *Feldgendarmerie* for this purpose or for acting as special traffic points.

The officer or NCO i/c ammunition point indicates from which stacks ammunition is to be taken for loading the column with the quantities given him by the column commander, what quantities are to be issued and when. The issue of simple loading (or unloading) slips to every vehicle (*see* example below) is the most satisfactory method.

Example:

Fahrzeug Nr 1 Stapel 5
................Schuss 1 FH 18

Vehicle No. 1 Stack 5
.... rounds light field howitzer 18.

The local protection, especially AA, of the ammunition point is usually reinforced during loading and unloading by the supply column's weapons. Higher Authority is responsible for special protection such as by A tk units.

The following sign-boards, stack boards and tools are required for a divisional ammunition point.

Signboards and Stack boards.—80 boards numbered 1 to 80 for the individual stacks.

> 10 boards marked " *Munitions-Ausgabestelle* " (ammunition point).
> 6 boards marked " *Bis Munitionsaugebestelle . . .* ". (To ammunition point.)
> 4 boards marked " *Beutemunition* " (captured ammunition).
> 4 boards marked " *Ablaufplatz* " (forming-up point).
> 4 boards marked " *Bis Sammelplatz* " (to assembly point).
> 4 boards marked " *Leermaterial* " (empties).
> 4 boards marked " *Zurückgelieferte scharfe Munitionsteile* " (returned parts).
> 4 boards marked " *Rauchen verboten* " (Smoking Forbidden).
> 4 boards marked " *Abmarschweg zur Front* " (Exit route to front).
> 4 boards marked " *Abmarschweg Div Nachschubkolonnen* " (Exit route for Div Supply Columns).
> and 30 direction arrows.

Tools.—26 long spades, 6 axes, 6 pit saws, 4 hand saws, 6 flat picks, 6 mattocks, 6 hammers, 4 pairs pincers, nails, wire, 3 fire extinguishers, 8 buckets, 20 lamps, 110 lbs. decontaminating material (*Losantin*).

(e) *Army Ammunition Dumps.*—(i) *Siting and layout.*—The siting, layout, stack arrangement of army ammunition dumps are based on the same considerations as for divisional ammunition points.

Advantage is taken of forest, particularly fir woods (for the sake of dryness) in siting army ammunition dumps whether the ammunition is stacked in the open, in huts or in existing buildings.

Army ammunition dumps are usually sited close to the railway (within 100 yards) with a well-developed network of roads in the immediate vicinity.

No specific figure can be given for stocks normally held at army ammunition dumps since dumps varying from 1,500 to 120,000 tons have been identified.

The interval between the various stack areas is, as a rule, at least 300 yards. Chessboard arrangement of stacks is recommended.

(ii) *Administration.*—Approaches to the dump are confined to one-way traffic. Direction boards are set up not higher than the headlamps of MT.

About 100 yards before the entrance to the dump a notice board, often with reflectors, carries the following wording:—

> *Halt*: *Kolonnenführer nach vorn.*
> (Halt: convoy commander forward.)

Warning signs forbidding smoking are erected, convoy commanders being especially warned in this connection. As a rule about five times the number of signboards, stackboards and tools required for divisional ammunition points will be required for an army dump.

Equipment for fire fighting is provided. (This may take the form of fire extinguishers nailed to trees every 200 yards and spades and mattocks (in sets of ten) every 50 yards.)

The administration of an army ammunition dump is normally in the hands of 10 officers (or officials), 3 serjeant-artificers, 6 NCO ammunition specialists and 3 ORs, *i.e.*, a total of 22 all ranks. The work of setting-up the dump, issuing supplies, etc, is performed by the supply unit. Neither the administration personnel nor the supply unit usually furnishes guards. These are supplied from *Wachtruppen* (*see* under Protection and Guarding of Dumps, *see* also the remarks about the army ammunition dump at SYTSCHEVKA in para (*a*) (ii) above).

The administration offices include accommodation for the personnel and reception office. Documents should include a stack plan, ammunition stock book, files, receipts and issue forms.

The illustration on page 209 shows the layout of a typical army ammunition dump.

(*f*) *Destruction of ammunition.*—The following table is given for the quantities of explosive and lengths of fuze necessary for destroying shells and bombs. SAA and cases of mortar bombs are treated according to the size of the case and quantity of ammunition, the demolition charge being normally placed inside the case.

Calibre of shell or bomb (H.E.)	Explosive slabs (*Sprengkorper* 80, 02 or 28)	or	Blasting cartridges (*Bohrpatronen*)	Length of time fuze (*Zeitzünd-schnur* 94)	Safety radius
	No.		No.	Yards	Yards
Shells—					
under 5 cm	1	or	1	3	500
over 5 cm and under 7·5 cm	2	,,	5	3	500
over 7·5 cm and under 10·5 cm	2	,,	5	4	750
over 10·5 cm and under 15 cm	4	,.	10	5	1,000
over 15 cm and under 21 cm	15		...	6	1,250
over 21 cm	15		...	10	2,000
Bombs—					
SC 10	3	or	5	4	500
SC 50	6		...	6	1,000
SC 250 and SC 500 ...	15		...	10	2,000

Army ammunition dumps have a destruction pit at a distance of 1,000 yards from the dump, a special shed being set aside for housing detonating apparatus, fuzes, etc.

In destroying stacks the following method has been adopted by the Germans in their ammunition dumps, in' North Africa, Sicily and Italy:—

On the top of each stack is placed—

1 petrol container filled with petrol,
2 TNT slabs fitted with detonator and safety fuze,
2 Molotov cocktails,
1 tin of motor grease (7 lb estimated weight).

The TNT slabs are placed on the petrol container each slab being independent of the other, the difference being in the length of fuze (one length burning for about one minute and the other for about six minutes).

German ammunition dumps are normally prepared for destruction from the moment they are set up.

(g) *Table for computing quantities of ammunition in stacks of various sizes.*

		Propellent or HE Content		2·5 tons	3 tons	3·5 tons
Patr f Gew u MG	SAA	2·9	g	862,000	1,034,000	1,207,000
Pist Patr aller Art ...	Pistol amn all types	0·36	g	6,950,000	8,340,000	9,725,000
Patr f Pz B	A/Tk rifle amn...	15	g	166,700	200,000	233,350
Patr f s Pz B 41 ...	Amn for A/Tk Gun 41 ...	153	g	16,350	19,600	22,875
2 cm Sprgr Patr L'spur ...	2 cm HE fixed amn tracer ...	53	g	47,170	56,600	66,000
2 cm Pz gr Patr L/sp ...	2 cm AP fixed amn tracer ...	41	g	61,000	73,200	85,400
3·7 cm Gr Patr aller Art ...	3·7 cm fixed amn—all types...	0·228	kg	10,965	13,160	15,350
4·7 u 5 cm Gr Patr aller Art ...	4·7 cm and 5 cm fixed amn—all types.	0·476	kg	5,250	6,300	7,355
5 cm Wgr	5 cm mortar bombs ...	0·125	kg	20,000	24,000	28,000
7·5 cm Gr Patr ...	7·5 cm fixed amn ...	1·096	kg	2,280	2,740	3,195
7·5 cm Pzgr Patr ...	7·5 AP fixed amn ...	0·490	kg	5,100	6,120	7,140
7·5 cm Nb Gr Patr ...	7·5 cm smoke fixed amn ...	0·505	kg	4,950	5,940	6,930
7·5 cm Gr aller Art ...	7·5 cm shell—all types ...	0·680	kg	3,675	4,410	5,150
7·5 cm Nb Gesch ...	7·5 cm smoke shells ...	0·095	kg	26.315	31,580	36,840
7·5 cm Pz Gesch ...	7·5 cm AP shells ...	0·080	kg	31,250	37,500	43,750
8 ch Wgr	8 cm mortar bombs ...	0·602	kg	4,155	4,985	5,815
8 cm Wgr Nb	8 cm smoke mortar bombs ...	0·072	kg	34,700	41,650	48,600
15 cm Gr aller Art (sussors. J. Gr).	15 cm shells all types, except Inf gun.	5·100	kg	490	588	686
10 cm Wgr 35	10 cm mortar bomb 35 ...	0·170	kg	14,705	17,650	20,590
10 cm Wgr 37	10 cm mortar bomb 37 ...	1·833	kg	1,370	1,640	1,910
15 cm K Gr 18	15 cm HE shell 18 ...	5·688	kg	440	527	615
21 cm Geschosse ...	21 cm shells	13·4	kg	186	224	261
Hüls Kart f 1 J G 18 u 1 Geb J G 18	Cartridges for 1 inf ; gun 18 and 1 mtn gun 18.	0·0715	kg	34,965	41,960	48,950
Hüls Kert f 1 F H 18 ...	Cartridges for light fd how 18	0·590	kg	4,235	5,085	5,930
Hüls Kart f 15 cm K 39 ...	Cartridges for 15 cm gun 39 ...	17·725	kg	141	169	197
Hüls Kart f s F H 18 ...	Cartridges for heavy fd how 18	2·23	kg	1,120	1,345	1,570
Hüls Kart f 21 cm Mrs 18 ...	Cartridges for long 21 cm mortar 18.	7·830	kg	319	383	447
Stielhandgr 24 vollst ...	Stick handgrenades 24 complete.	0·167	kg	14,970	17,965	20,960
Eihandgr 39 vollst ...	Egg handgrenades 39 complete	0·130	kg	19,230	23,080	26,925
Sprengm. Kasten Satz a ...	Explosives box—Set a ...	28·8	kg	87	104	122
„ „ „ b ...	„ „ — „ b ...	24	kg	104	125	146
„ „ „ c ...	„ „ — „ c ...	26	kg	96	115	135
„ „ „ d ...	„ „ — „ d ...	25	kg	100	120	140
Knallzündschnur m ...	FID metres	8·00kg in 100 m		312,500	375,000	437,500
T-Minen	Teller Mines	4·00	kg	625	750	875
S-Minen	S Mines	2·74	kg	912	1,094	1,278
S-Jgr	Heavy inf shell ...	8·7	kg	287	345	402

NOTE :—The fifteen ton column is especially important since this is the standard railway wagon load will comprise 2,640 rounds.

Number of rounds in stacks of :—

4 tons	5 tons	6 tons	7·5 tons	8 tons	10 tons	11 tons	15 tons	20 tons
1,379,000	1,725,000	2,068,000	2,586,000	2,758,000	3,450,000	3,793,000	5,175,000	6,900,000
11,112,000	13,900,000	16,680,000	20,850,000	22,224,000	27,800,000	30,580,000	41,700,000	55,600,000
266,750	333,400	200,000	500,100	533,500	666,800	733,400	1,000,000	1,333,200
26,150	32,700	39,200	49,050	52,300	65,400	71,900	98,100	130,800
75,500	94,350	113,200	141,500	151,000	188,700	207,550	283,000	376,800
109,750	122,000	146,400	183,000	219,500	244,000	268,400	366,000	488,000
17,545	21,930	26,315	32,895	35,090	43,860	48,245	65,790	—
8,400	10,500	12,600	15,750	16,800	21,000	23,100	31,500	—
32,000	40,000	48,000	60,000	64,000	80,000	88,000	120,000	—
3,650	4,560	5,480	6,840	7,300	9,120	10,040	13,680	—
8,165	10,200	12,245	15,300	16,325	20,400	22,450	30,610	—
7,920	9,900	11,880	14,850	15,840	19,800	21,780	29,700	—
5,885	7,350	8,820	11,025	11,770	14,700	16,180	22,050	—
42,105	52,630	63,155	78,945	84,210	105,260	115,790	157,890	—
50,000	62,500	75,000	93,750	100,000	125,000	137,500	250,000	—
6,645	8,310	9,970	12,465	13,290	16,620	18,280	24,930	33,240
55,550	69,400	83,300	104,100	111,100	138,800	152,700	208,200	—
785	980	1,176	1,470	1,570	1,960	2,156	2,940	—
23,530	29,410	35,295	44,110	48,050	58,820	64,700	88,230	—
2,185	2,730	3,275	4,095	4,370	5,470	6,000	8,185	—
703	880	1,054	1,320	1,406	1,760	1,934	2,640	—
298	373	448	560	597	746	821	1,120	—
55,945	69,930	83,916	104,895	111,888	139,870	153,845	209,790	—
6,780	8,475	10,170	12,710	13,560	16,950	18,645	25,420	—
226	282	338	423	452	564	620	846	—
1,795	2,240	2,690	3,360	3,590	4,485	4,930	6,725	—
511	638	766	957	1,022	1,276	1,404	1,915	—
23,950	29,940	35,930	44,910	47,900	59,880	65,870	89,820	119,760
30,770	38,460	46,150	57,690	61,540	76,920	84,620	115,380	153,840
139	174	208	261	278	348	382	522	—
167	208	250	313	334	416	458	624	—
154	192	230	289	308	384	424	577	—
160	200	240	300	320	400	440	600	—
500,000	625,000	750,000	937,500	1,000,000	1,250,000	1,375,000	1,875,000	—
1,000	1,250	1,500	1,875	2,000	2,500	2,750	3,750	—
1,460	1,824	2,188	2,738	2,920	3,648	4,012	5,472	—
460	574	690	852	920	1,148	1,264	1,722	—

(*Kalibereinheit*). Thus, for example, a standard wagon load of 15 cm HE shell 18 will weigh 15 tons and

(h) German Weapons which will fire Allied ammunition.

German Weapon	German Ammunition	Allied Ammunition which may be fired	Remarks
7·92-mm rifles and MGs.	7·92-mm ball (sS). AP (SmK) etc.	British 7·92-mm Besa ball.	Occasional stoppages may be experienced.
9-mm Pistols 08 and 38. 9-mm machine carbines. MP 38 and 40, MP 34. (Bergmann), MP 18 (Bergmann) and MP 28. (Schmeisser)	9-mm ball, semi AP.	British and American 9-mm ball (parabellum type).	The German 9-mm. machine carbine MP 34 (ö) Steyr-Solothurn will not function with 9-mm parabellum ammunition.
8-cm mortar ... ... 8-cm mortar (short) ...	8-cm mortar bomb.	British 3-inch mortar bomb. American 81-mm mortar bomb.	The British bomb can only be fired if an adaptor is fitted to German mortar, lengthening the striker stud.
40-mm Flak 28 (Bofors) AA gun.	40-mm HE ammunition.	British Bofors AA gun amn. American Bofors AA gun amn.	British amn. gives a similar ballistic performance when fired from the German gun. There is an increase in tracer filling and a reduction in TNT British and German charges are similar and interchangeable.

German Ammunition which may be fired from Allied weapons.

German ammunition	German weapon from which fired	Allied weapon from which fired	Remarks
7·92-mm ball (sS), AP (SmK) etc.	7·92-mm rifles and MGs.	British 7·92-mm Besa MGs.	Occasional stoppages may be experienced. German amn with *steel cases* is liable to give hard extraction when used in British 7·92-mm Besa MG.
9-mm ball (Pist Patr 08) and semi AP (Pist Patr 08m E).	All 9-mm weapons (except 9-mm machine carbine MP 34 (ö) Steyr-Solothurn.	Sten and Lanchester machine carbines and American machine carbine M 3.	The German MP 34 (ö) Steyr-Solothurn is chambered for the long 9-mm. Mauser cartridge.
5-cm mortar bomb ...	5-cm mortar ...	British 2-inch mortar.	Average loss in range of 162·5 yds. Utility restricted to angles of elevation on either scale giving readings between 525 and 400 yds.
8-cm mortar bomb ...	8-cm mortar ... 8-cm mortar (short).	British 3-inch mortar. American 81-mm mortar. Polish 8-cm mortar 31. Dutch 8·1-cm mortar.	German bomb will only function in British mortars if strikers pipped or striker clips fitted to German primaries.

German ammunition	German weapon from which fired	Allied weapon from which fired	Remarks
40-mm (Bofors) HE amn.	Flak 28 AA gun	British Bofors AA gun. American Bofors AA gun.	May be used in British Mark I or III guns with German or British amn charges. German charges may be used with British amn. Amn is fitted with tracer burning 11 or 12 seconds. No variation of sights or deflection needed for normal engagements. Prematures may occur owing to fuze or tracer failures.

NOTES

British 2-inch mortar bombs may not be loaded in the German 5-cm mortar.

The German 10·5-cm gun-how shell might be fired in the American 105-mm howitzer but the design of the cartridge case precludes the use of the cartridge. The opposite (American amn in German guns,) equally obtains.

French 75-mm amn is interchangeable with German 7·5-cm Pak 97/38 and Polish 75-mm amn.

French 155-mm amn (Schneider How Mod 1917) is interchangeable with American 155-mm Amn (155-mm how M 1917 and 1918).

French 155-mm amn (C 175) is interchangeable with Polish 155-mm how M 17.

14. *POL supply in the field.*

(*a*) *Introductory notes.*—Under this heading is included fuel for petrol and Diesel-engined vehicles, lubricating oil (engine oil), gear oil, lubricants like grease, cotton waste, and anti-freeze compounds.

Petrol is calculated in consumption units (*Verbrauchssätze*), the consumption unit of a unit or formation being the amount required to take each of its vehicles 100 km. Mechanized units are required to keep a reserve of so many consumption units.

GHQ maintains a mobile stock of petrol on trains, and petrol is forwarded from these stocks or from GHQ dumps direct to army. Army in its turn holds stocks either loaded on tanker trains or forward of railhead in containers (*e.g.*, barrels or standard petrol cans) in army petrol dumps (*Armee-Betriebsstofflager*). Transport to those dumps will usually be by army POL columns. The barrels are the 200 litre and the cans the 20 litre containers referred to in Part I, section 3.

Dumps are almost *always* preferred to mobile stocks in trains, which are only held very far back. Army, it appears, very rarely has a mobile stock of this nature.

In the division area petrol points (*Betriebsstoff-Ausgabestellen*) are set up by the divisional supply officer and his POL column as directed by the *Divisions-Ingenieur* (divisional technical officer) at divisional HQ, supplies being brought to these points by the divisional POL column or, if required, by the corps or army POL columns. This is text-book practice and has been found to be the rule in Russia and Italy.

Petrol is transferred at divisional petrol points to unit petrol lorries in the case of armoured or mechanized units, or at special petrol points for individual vehicles (*Tankstellen für Einzelkraftfahrzeuge* or *Einzel Kfz*) in the case of non-mechanized units which send their motor vehicles, such as staff cars, individually to be refuelled there.

In addition to the army petrol dumps (in the corps and army areas) from which the divisional POL columns mainly draw supplies for the divisional petrol points, petrol points or filling stations for individual vehicles will also be found in these areas, for the purpose of refuelling motor vehicles in corps and army HQs, etc. These points are set up by corps and army POL columns under the Corps and Army supply officers as directed by the Corps technical officer and the MT officer at army HQ. Only under exceptional circumstances are single vehicles of a POL column sent to refuel a unit at its billets as a matter of urgency. Any such arrangement is only carried out by the supply officer at the express orders of higher authority.

(*b*) *Handling of POL in the field.*—Regular times for the issue of petrol, etc, to fighting troops, rearward services and individual motor vehicles are laid down in order to prevent such massing of motor vehicles as would present a good target to enemy aircraft.

Petrol points and filling stations are put under the charge of NCOs or ORs, labour being provided by the personnel of the POL columns. When issuing petrol to fighting troops, drivers and drivers' mates of the unit POL lorries assist. In the case of petrol points holding barrels or standard cans in stacks a section from a supply company may be attached to furnish labour.

POL columns take their supplies (barrels or cans) from army fuel dumps. They may also refuel their containers at railhead from railway tanker wagons, though this is exceptional.

It is to be noted that as a rule only army POL columns will include tanker lorries, fuel supplies on corps and divisional POL columns being nearly always carried in barrels or standard petrol cans (Jerricans). Illustrations of these tanker lorries and the 200-litre barrels and the 20-litre jerricans will be found at the end of Part II on pages 210, 211 and 212.

The troops responsible for setting up army dumps and issuing petrol, etc, are MT companies from army MT parks, and not supply units. These MT companies also unload POL trains at army railhead, and load empty barrels or cans received at petrol points in exchange for filled containers into trains returning empty to the home depot. They may also be employed in refuelling POL columns or units direct from POL or tanker trains. This has been found to be especially true in Russia.

(c) *Transport of POL in the field.*—(i) *Road.*—Included in the divisional supply services of most infantry divisions, is one small POL column, whilst armoured divisions have six large POL columns, and motorized divisions two large POL columns. Occasionally, in Italy, divisional columns have been reinforced from Army. The same is almost certainly true of Russia.

There will usually be only one large POL column at Corps and one large POL column in each of the two supply column battalions at Army.

There are in addition such specialized columns as POL tanker columns (*Kesselkraftwagen-Kolonnen für Betriebsstoff*) consisting entirely of tanker vehicles (*see* illustrations at end of Part II).

All these are additional to the large and small MT columns under supply officers at division, corps and army.

(ii) *Rail.*—Petrol on rail comes either in POL trains (*Betriebsstoffzüge*), carrying supplies in containers, *i.e.*, in barrels and standard cans, or in tanker trains. Experience in Italy has provided the following information.

All trains, tanker or otherwise, are provided with escort personnel whose duty it is to hand over the train complete with travelling papers (*Fahrpapiere*) and waybills.

However important it may be not to delay return, the escort personnel are never employed in unloading or guarding the train at railhead. The escort party will retain fire extinguishers, tools, etc, or any other special apparatus belonging to its home depot.

Every truck must be checked when the train is handed over. The seals on goods trucks are always examined. In booking the contents of POL trains (*i.e.*, trains carrying barrels or cans) quantities are not entered in cubic metres as shown on the waybill, but in accordance with the type and number of containers; thus 2,000 barrels equal 400 cubic metres, even if the waybill may mention a total quantity of about 390 cubic metres.

Fuel supplied by tanker trains, however, is taken over as per waybill in cbm, a check being made from the tables marked on the tanks.

In loading barrels into trucks bungholes must be uppermost and lie in the direction in which the train is travelling. Barrels must be secured from rolling about by means of wedges. Cans must be loaded vertically. If the truck is not fully loaded, containers must be secured by wooden distance pieces.

(d) *Siting and layout of petrol points and dumps.*—(i) *Petrol points.*— Since fuel is as a rule pumped or poured directly into vehicles at petrol points, the best sites are at the entrances of villages, offering facilities for pulling in from, and pulling out into the supply route (*Nachschubstrasse*). Adequate parking places must be provided in order not to interfere with through traffic.

A typical layout for a petrol point is shown at the end of Part II. Use may of course also be made of existing civilian filling stations.

Filling stations are only supplied on the written instructions of the supply staffs responsible for their administration and only on receipt of a corresponding number of petrol vouchers (*Tankscheine*) which must be duly cancelled by stamp.

(ii) *Dumps of POL.*—Petrol dumps will as a rule be sited in the vicinity of railhead. (POL columns rarely refill direct from tanker trains.) Petrol dumps should not be set up, according to the Germans, in the vicinity of inhabited buildings, from which they must be distant at least 100 yards. Natural camouflage (trees) is utilized to the full; when little exists, foliage, branches are used (as protection not only from air observation, but from the sun). Petrol stored in barrels or cans may expand as much as 7 per cent under the action of sun, so increasing the risk of fire due to loosening of the seals.

Use is frequently made of caves, factories, garages, etc, for storing petrol, and underground dumps are sometimes employed.

When petrol is held in storage tanks, the latter are as widely dispersed as the layout and size of the dump permit, so that losses due to fire or enemy action are reduced to a minimum.

Different types of fuel are stored separately. Container stacks will likewise be well dispersed. Barrels will be stacked three high at the most and standard cans eight high (*see* illustration at end of Part II). In the latter instance the bottom-most layer rests on a suitable foundation to prevent rust.

The space between stacks amounts to at least 25 yards, stacks being moreover surrounded by fire-protection trenches with the excavated soil thrown on the side furthest removed from the stack as an additional protection from fire. These trenches are about two feet deep and two feet wide.

The trenches must be at least three yards from the stack. In addition fire extinguishers, picks and shovels should be kept ready in sufficient numbers in the vicinity of stacks, as well as close to living quarters and offices. In North Africa fire fighting apparatus was usually completely absent, but in Italy and Russia good provision is made.

Wooden sign-boards about 8 ins square with a black " F " on a white circular background bordered with red are set up at all places where fire-fighting equipment is held, in addition to warning boards bearing the words " *Rauchen verboten* " (smoking forbidden).

Barrels are marked to show the type of fuel they contain, a white " 1 " being painted alongside the bunghole for petrol; diesel oil barrels are similarly marked with a red " D ". In the case of standard fuel cans the letter is painted on to the right of the cap.

The storage of lubricants requires special care. Neither cellulose bottles for engine and gear oil nor cardboard containers for grease are resistant to wet or high air humidity and tend to become soft when stored in damp rooms or kept in the open; in the latter case they are stacked loosely (for ventilation) and covered over with roofing felt. Stacks are no higher than a man's height. Storage in roofed buildings or lean-to sheds is the rule whenever possible.

Storage cards stating the quantities issued and received and the stock in hand are affixed to stacks in covered premises, stack boards being used in the case of outdoor stacks.

The dump office normally has a simple layout plan showing in which rooms or areas the stocks are distributed.

The " Q " personnel at formation HQ order the checking of stocks from time to time. Independently of this the officer in charge of the dump or the administrative personnel must be able to account for the quantities in stock, issued or received at all times.

Examples of siting and layout of petrol dumps are shown at the end of Part II.

In Italy, petrol dumps are usually sited next to main roads or tracks and in all cases vehicles are able to approach very close to the stacks. In Russia, petrol dumps are usually near railhead, but are, at any rate, accessible for vehicles.

Barrels and cans are in nearly every case found to have been stacked round the trunks of trees, as far as halfway up the trunk; barrels being six to eight to a tree, and petrol cans (jerricans) 25-30.

The only alternative methods of storing usually found are small pits dug into the ground at the base of trees about 2 ft 6 in deep, and holding four barrels; and the stacking of barrels on their sides (as many as ten high), or on their backs (four high), with the bungs uppermost.

Except for the cover of the trees under which containers are stacked, there is often no attempt at camouflage.

Drainage systems seldom exist though well-drained ground seems to be chosen for POL dumps as a general rule.

(e) *Security of petrol dumps and points.*—Premises or areas holding fuel may be roped off to prevent unauthorized access at petrol points, *Feldgendarmerie* being employed at the same time if required.

Petrol dumps are guarded day and night from entry by unauthorized persons, from sabotage and theft, the strength of the guard varying according to circumstances.

Slit trenches are normally provided for guard and dump personnel unless shelters exist in the immediate vicinity. Particular emphasis is laid on the importance of vouchers for all fuel, lubricants, equipment, spares, etc, coming into and leaving petrol dumps or points.

Receipt vouchers in June, 1943, were red, and issue vouchers blue, and are probably still the same; they are numbered consecutively and must be torn out one by one.

(f) *Miscellaneous data.*—The following is a list of miscellaneous data which are useful in the assessment of problems of POL supply.

(i) Fuel is normally classed as " white " (petrol, kerosene, etc) or as " black " (gas oil, heavy fuel, etc).

(ii) One cubic metre of white fuel=1,000 litres=220 gallons=$\frac{3}{4}$ metric ton.
One cubic metre of black fuel=1,000 litres=220 gallons=$\frac{5}{6}$ metric ton.

To convert litres to tons.—Multiply the number of thousands of litres by the density of the commodity.

Example.—To convert 600,000 litres of Diesel fuel, petrol, lubricants, etc, to tons:—

$$600,000 \text{ litres} = 600 \times \cdot 85 \text{ Diesel} = 510 \text{ tons.}$$
$$= 600 \times (\text{say}) \cdot 75 \text{ Petrol} = 450 \text{ tons.}$$
$$= 600 \times (\text{say}) \cdot 85 \text{ lubricants} = 510 \text{ tons.}$$

(iii) There are 300 bulk gallons of petrol in one ton.
There are 220 (container) gallons of petrol in one ton.

(iv) A train of 30 tank cars will carry 450 tons, each tanker holding 15 tons or 20,000 litres.

(v) It has been found, as a rough guide, that to empty a 20,000 litre railway petrol tanker into 1,000 of the 20 litre jerricans using 1 filling appliance (of 10 pipes), and the normal detachment of 20 men, takes about two hours.

(vi) Various petrol capacities are as follows:—

Using tins:—
A standard tin (jerrican) holds 20 litres (4¼ gallons) and when full weighs about 20 kg (44 lbs).
A light, open petrol lorry will caryy 75 tins, *i.e.,* 1,500 litres.
A light cross-country petrol lorry carries 35 tins, *i.e.,* 700 litres.
A medium open petrol lorry carries 110 tins, *i.e.,* 2,200 litres.
A heavy open petrol lorry carries 2,500 tins, *i.e.,* 3,000 litres.
A heavy petrol column carries 1,250 tins, *i.e.,* 50 cbm.
A light petrol column carries 1,250 tins, *i.e.,* 25 cbm.
A light MT column (30 tons) carries 1,500 tins, *i.e.,* 30 cbm (one 3-ton lorry can carry 150 tins).

Using barrels:—
A standard barrel, or drum, holds 200 litres (44 gallons) and when full weighs about 200 kg (440 lbs).
A light open petrol lorry will carry 7½ drums, *i.e.,* 1,500 litres.
A light cross-country petrol lorry carries 3½ drums, *i.e.,* 700 litres.
A medium open petrol lorry carries 11 drums, *i.e.,* 2,200 litres.
A heavy open petrol lorry carries 15 drums, *ie,* 3,000 litres.
A heavy petrol column carries 250 drums, *i.e.,* 50 cbm.
A light petrol column carries 125 drums, *i.e.,* 25 cbm.
A light MT column (30 tons) carries 150 drums, *i.e.,* 30 cbm (one 3-ton lorry can carry 15 drums).

Using tanker lorries:—
A petrol tanker lorry carries from 3 to 5 cbm.
A heavy petrol column carries a minimum of 50 cbm.
A light petrol column carries a minimum of 25 cbm.

Using railway wagons:—
Railway petrol tank cars carry from 17 to 22 cbm.
Open wagons (20 tons) carry 80 drums, *i.e.,* 16 cbm or alternatively 800 tins, *i.e.,* 16 cbm.

Using petrol trains:—
A petrol train, load not exceeding 450 tons, may consist of 20 railway petrol tank cars carrying 340 to 440 cbm (or 25 wagons with drums or tins and carrying 400 cbm) with five covered wagons of oil, engine oil, gear oil, paraffin and cotton-waste, and (in winter), anti-freeze mixture.

(vii) *Petrol stocks.*—Army HQ normally has at its disposal three consumption units (300 km) of petrol, for all vehicles in the army, kept in petrol trains, railside filling stations, petrol parks, petrol columns or fixed petrol dumps or filling stations.

The amount of first-line and second-line petrol kept with units is generally as follows, and experience in Italy and Russia lends confirmation to this:—

Armoured units; except recce units: 400 km (300 km in vehicles, unit petrol lorries and light columns, the remaining 100 km in the petrol columns of the formation).
All other units; except recce units: 500 km (350 km in vehicles and in unit transport, and 150 km in the petrol columns of the formation.
Recce units: 650 km in vehicles, unit transport and light columns.

(viii) *Consumption of POL.*—Oil is normally 5 per cent of petrol consumption, gear oil ·5 per cent, grease ·25 per cent (·5 per cent for tanks, ·75 per cent for tracked vehicles other than tanks), and Diesel oil 75 per cent of petrol consumption.

(g) *Use of German fuels in German and British vehicles.*

		Uses in German Forces			Remarks
	Colour	Octane Number (nominal)	Type of vehicle for which used	Special Characteristics	
(i) Fuels for petrol driven vehicles— General name in German Army "OTTO".					German MT petrols vary considerably in chemical composition and physical properties. As a general rule they contain less light fractions than British petrols. The amount of loading is generally less than in British 80 octane petrol. German petrol often contains a considerable percentage of benzol but alcohol blends do not appear to be in general use by the German army though these are likely to be met with in certain areas such as France where they are in general use.
TROPENKRAFTSTOFF	Violet	78	Tanks, MT and MCs.	For use in hot climates, where (ii) or (iii) may cause vapour lock	
FAHRBENZIN	Yellow	74	,, ,,	...	
GEMISCH BI-BO	Red	74	,, ,,	This is a petrol benzol mixture	
(ii) Diesel fuels— DIESEL KRAFTSTOFF	...	...	All types of diesel-engined vehicles	...	
(iii) Others— B4—Aviation petrol... ...	Blue	90	Bombers and transport aircraft	Can be used for MT blended with ordinary MT petrol	

Suitability of the above for use in British vehicles.

(i) The fuels for petrol-driven vehicles, listed in paragraph (i) are all suitable for use in British "B" vehicles, but are not suitable for all "A" vehicles.

(ii) The diesel index number of any captured German diesel fuel requires to be checked to establish its suitability for use in place of W.D. Derv or Gas Oil. The diesel index requires to be 47 or above, and the condition of the fuel clear and bright. if it is to be used.

(iii) B4 can be used in all types of British "A" or "B" vehicles either unblended or mixed with MT petrol provided it is clear and uncontaminated.

15. *Supply of Rations in the field.*

(a) *Introductory Notes.*—Responsibility for the supply of rations in the field lies with the Intendants at division, corps and army (*see* New Notes No. 4, page 9). In occupied countries there is usually a Chief Intendant (*Chefintendant*) at the HQ of the military commander of the area with very wide powers for the exploitation of the country for military purposes. Divisional and Army Intendants are also responsible for making full use of local resources.

(b) *System of Supply.*—The Intendant at Army sets up a number of army rations dumps (*Armee Verpflegungslager* or *AVL*) *see* illustration at end of Part II. The AVLs have, as staff, some 30 officials and 80 NCOs and men. An Army with say, four Corps has been found, particularly on the Russian front, to have four forward and two rear army rations dumps each containing 8 to 10 days' rations for a single corps. The two rear dumps, in effect, constitute, in such a case, an additional Army reserve of food. In general the AVLs should contain about 8 days' rations for the Army plus an iron ration and a specified reserve of bread (not fresh bread). Supply to the AVLs is by rail from Reich territory and it is the function of the EVMs, mentioned in Part I, section 4, to maintain 8 days' supply in the AVLs.

Corps Intendants may set up corps rations dumps (*Korps Verpflegungslager—KVL*) which are, in effect, forward army rations dumps, to which rations are brought in corps or army columns.

The divisional Intendant sets up divisional rations points (*Verpflegungs—Ausgabestellen*) manned by the divisional rations office, and for which rations are brought up from army (or corps) rations dumps (*see* illustration at end of Part II). This may be done, in practice, directly on army, corps or divisional columns under the supply officers at army, corps or divisional HQ. Alternatively army (or corps) Intendant may set up reloading points (*Umschlagstellen*) from which rations are fetched by divisional columns.

The fighting troops collect rations from the divisional rations points with unit rations transport (*Verpflegungstross*).

(c) *Rations supply for Norway.*—The rations supply system for Norway is an interesting example of how the Germans set up an organization in advance, put it into practice and then modify or expand it according to need. Briefly the system evolved as follows:—

(i) Before the invasion, a great number of supply ships were loaded with rations, and a staff (*Heimatstab Nord*) was set up in BERLIN for the purposes of administration. When the invasion began, many of these ships were sunk, but the troops in Southern Norway lived off the land for some weeks, as arrangements had been made in advance to seize the Norwegian army stocks. The small reserve of rations in ships was hastily supplemented by every available means including warships, coasting vessels, U-boats and transport aircraft. Supplies were dropped by parachute to the troops in Northern Norway, particularly at Narvik.

(ii) As soon as it became possible, a full-scale supply system was operated by rail and train ferry through Denmark, Sweden and, to some extent, Finland. By the end of June, 1940, it could be said that the rations supply system was functioning without hindrance.

(iii) In July, 1940, Hitler ordered a reserve of rations sufficient for one year for the troops in Norway to be created. This implied some 150,000 tons of victuals and a similar amount of fodder. Of the 300,000 tons total supplies, it is significant that it was estimated that about 140,000 tons victuals and fodder could be drawn from Norway itself, while the rest would have to come from Germany.

(iv) Norway's contribution was fixed at the following percentages of total German requirements in the country:—

from 70 to 80 per cent of fresh meat.
    100 per cent of potatoes.
    100 per cent of coffee.
    90 per cent of fats.
almost 100 per cent of hay.
and 70 per cent of straw.

(v) Of the year's reserves, 6 months' were to be stored in Army rations depots (AVLs); the rest were to be the responsibility of the individual divisions who had to undertake to store them in the divisional area. This system of reserve was very quickly built up, as it was more a question of transportation than anything else. Four main shipping routes from Germany were used:—

Flensburg—Denmark—Aalsborg—Oslo, etc.
Warnemünde—Gjedser—Copenhagen—Helsingborg—Oslo, etc.
Stettin—Sassnitz/Trelleborg—Oslo or through Sweden to Lulea in Sweden (where a German rations depot was set up)—Narvik, etc.
Stettin—Lulea or to Tornea in Finland—Sodankylæ thence by road to Kirkenes where there is an AVL.

(vi) AVLs have been set up in Oslo, Frederikstad, Stavanger, Bergen, Drontheim, Narvik and Kirkenes, with the German rations depot at Lulea in Sweden.

(d) *The divisional rations office.*—In Sicily, the divisional rations office of 15 PG Div operated as one main and four subsidiary offices. At the main office there were two officers, seven NCOs and 40 to 50 men. It had eight 3-ton lorries, two Opel cars and a motor-cycle; each subsidiary office had one officer and about 20 men. This principle of dividing the rations office into a number of subsidiary offices has been noted in Russia also. It would appear that it is the best practical way of operating, when formations are thin upon the ground, to ensure the efficiency of rations supply arrangements.

(e) *Army refrigerating system.*—A GHQ refrigerating centre (*Heereskühldienststelle*) operated in North Africa and is believed to be in Italy. It was 78 men strong. It controlled a number of railway refrigerating trucks in Tunisia which were the ordinary 15-ton vans with containers for carbon dioxide blocks. They were marked with a large " K ". The unit also had some three-ton static refrigerators which were carried on Mercedes lorries. These were intended for use in the forward hospitals and at divisional HQs.

These refrigerators were 6 ft wide by 10 ft long and 6 ft high, with a sloping roof. At one end was a single-panelled door. The refrigerating plant was installed at the opposite end, halfway up the side. The petrol engine could be reached from the outside through two small doors. The temperature could be kept at $-5°$ C.

(f) *Miscellaneous data.*—The following is a list of miscellaneous data useful in assessing problems of rations supply:—

Time required—

  (i) The time taken to establish a field bakery (*see* illustration on page 215), before first loaves can be put to bake is about 4½ hours.

(ii) The time taken to dismantle a field bakery is about two hours.

(iii) The time taken to load the rations for a division from the AVL is from two to six hours.

(iv) The time taken to set up a divisional rations point is about two hours.

(v) A rations train of 450 tons under the most favourable circumstances can be unloaded in about 12 hours.

Weights of rations (approximate)—

(i) A complete field ration with bread weighs 1,500 gr. (53 oz).

(ii) A bread ration weighs 750 gr (26 oz).

(iii) A fodder ration weighs normally 5,000 gr (11 lbs) oats and 5,000 gr (11 lbs) hay.

(iv) A straw ration weighs about 2,500 gr (5½ lbs).

(v) An iron ration weighs 650 gr (23 oz) (825 gr (27 oz) with packing).

Capacities.

(i) A field bakery can travel 15 to 20 miles per day, and a mechanized field bakery up to 100 miles per day. It can produce daily between 15,000 and 19,200 bread rations of 750 gr (26 oz) each. For this it requires approximately 10 tons flour, 120 kg (250 lbs) salt, 6 to 13 cbm of wood and 8,000 litres (1,760 gallons) water.
    The bread cannot be transported or delivered until it has been kept for 24 hours.

(ii) A mechanized butchery platoon can move 100 miles a day. It slaughters in a day 40 cows, yielding 40,000 meat rations, or 80 pigs yielding 24,000 meat rations or 240 sheep yielding 19,200 meat rations.

Rations trains.—The 450 tons load may be made up as follows:—

(i) Iron rations: 300,000 full and 300,000 half iron rations come to 442 tons.

(ii) Full rations with fodder: 180,000 human and 40,000 animal rations amount to 454 tons.

(iii) Full rations without bread but with baking materials: 300,000 rations amount to 450 tons.

(iv) Flour: 833,000 rations amount to 450 tons.

(v) Fodder: 90,000 rations amount to 450 tons.

(vi) Cattle-train: load up to 450 tons but length not more than 530 yards. A covered 15-ton goods wagon will hold 12 cattle, 40 pigs or 60 sheep.

Rations transport—

(i) 1st echelon unit rations transport (*Verpflegungstross I*) holds a minimum of one day's supply for man and animal, and can move 15 to 20 miles per day.

(ii) 2nd echelon unit rations transport (*Verpflegungstross II*) which is mechanized holds a minimum of one day's supply for man and animal and can move up to 100 miles per day.

For basic field rations *see* Part I section 4 (*c*) (i).

16. *Supply of MT in the field with notes on repair and maintenance of M.T, AFVs and other equipment.*

(*a*) *Repair and maintenance in the field.*—(i) On 15 Oct 42 the MT Park Corps was formed as a separate arm, and it embraced all MT repair services, workshops and supply services, the most important of which are set out in the following list:—

> Army MT parks.
> MT centres.
> Army MT districts.
> Home MT districts.
> Home MT parks.
> Workshop companies (except for ordnance stores MT vehicle workshop platoons).
> MT vehicle workshop platoons.
> MT vehicle repair battalions.
> Mobile MT vehicle repair companies.
> Repair columns.
> Tyre supply, repair and retreading detachments.
> Central spare parts parks.
> Vehicle track stores.
> Towing platoons.
> MT park depot battalions.
> MT park depot companies.

The task of MT parks was laid down as being " mechanization and repairs for the forces and industry in the zone of the interior and occupied territories." The work of the MT districts and MT centres seems to have been planned as a further development of that of the parks and can be considered as that part of the basic organization of the repair system, constituting the link between the factory and the field.

By an amendment issued on 28 Jan 43, workshop units allocated by war establishment to particular units, such as to tank regiments, MT battalions. etc, do not belong to the MT Park Corps but to the same arm of the service as the unit to which they are allocated. The distinguishing colour (*Waffenfarbe*) of the MT Park Corps is pink, and the letter " J " is worn on the shoulder straps.

(ii) Early in 1943 the former General of Motorization in the High Command of the Armed Forces was renamed Chief of Motor Transport in the Armed Forces, and his duties were laid down as being the planning, standardization and steady development of MT, with the important exception of armoured vehicles. The special provisions for armoured fighting vehicles were set out as follows:—

AFVs including assault guns, self-propelled guns, armoured cars and armoured troop-carrying vehicles will be repaired by their own repair services or the workshop company of their own division. In cases where, by reason of extensive damage, this is impracticable, the vehicles will be turned over to the appropriate AFV repair battalions (probably at Army) or to AFV repair centres such as those at RIGA, MINSK or DNJEPRO-PETROVSK (under GHQ). Further special arrangements were made for the repair of AFVs of French origin.

(iii) In the field there are officers responsible for MT in each Army Group. These officers may be either the Army Group MT Officer or Army Group Engineer Officer, among whose special duties are the employment of allotted units of the MT Park Corps, the supply of MT, equipment and spare parts, the equipping of workshops and repair services, the replacement and allocation of MT vehicles, the salvage and re-employment of captured vehicles, including tanks, the exploitation of MT facilities in occupied countries and the training of repair personnel generally.

(iv) In February, 1943, official reasons were given for the setting up of the MT Park Corps. It was stated that the formation of the MT Park Corps became necessary when the strain on equipment and vehicles on the Russian front compelled the overhaul of whole units at a time and in the shortest possible space of time. For this purpose also rest and refitting areas, or recommissioning areas (*Auffrischungsräume*) were set up in Germany and Italy and occupied territories. When a formation was pulled out of the battle area, the Ib officer (DAQMG) of the formation could now contact the MT park unit in the appropriate recommissioning area, submitting a list of all defective vehicles and necessary repairs. Mobile recommissioning staffs were also set up with the function of easing liaison between the " Q " side of active formations and the appropriate MT park units in the recommissioning areas.

(v) The functions of the MT Park Corps link on to the previous system of MT repair in the following way. At the outbreak of war repair of vehicles, and to a less extent, of all ordnance equipment, was organized somewhat sketchily within units, through the setting up of light aid sections called *Hilfstrupps*. By November, 1940, however, a very comprehensive system of repair services was laid down, consisting of three main types of unit : —

Repair sub-sections (*Instandsetzungstrupps*, or *I-Trupps*)—types " a " " b " " c ".

Repair detachments (*Instandsetzungsstaffel*, or *I-Staffel*)—types " a ", " b " " c ".

Repair sections (*Instandsetzungsgruppen*, or *I-Gruppen*)—types " a " and " b ".

This system has proved unsatisfactory, for, with the setting up of the MT Park Corps, the following modifications have taken place. The repair sub-sections are still standardized and substantially unaltered. They are allocated to companies, etc (normally, those with a minimum of 25 vehicles) (type " a "), to companies, etc equipped with special vehicles (type " b ") and to armoured car squadrons (type " c "). Repair detachments, at HQ of regiments and units are no longer standardized. Instead, a detachment to fit the needs of the unit is included in the war establishment of the unit HQ. The average strength of these repair detachments would appear to be about 20 all ranks. The repair sections for tank squadrons and tank battalion HQs are still standardized. Sections " a " are allocated to squadrons of all types, sections " b " to battalion and regiment HQ. In addition, tank regiments have an armoured workshop company (*Panzerwerkstattkompanie*). The tank regiment of three battalions (of three squadrons each) used to have a further workshop platoon, but this has now been incorporated in the company, which simplifies the organization and avoids some duplication. The company now contains three workshop platoons, a recovery platoon, an armoury, a signals workshop and transport. Tank regiments with two battalions have only two workshop platoons in their workshop company. Independent tank battalions have an armoured workshop platoon which includes an armoury. Heavy independent tank battalions have an armoured workshop company consisting of two platoons, recovery platoon, an armoury and a signals workshop. The recovery platoon, in this case, appears to have two possible variants of establishment, and would seem capable of transporting broken-down "Tiger" tanks. The services of a division include a number of mechanized workshop companies (strength of each about 113 in all ranks) possibly grouped together as a workshop unit. There are four mechanized workshop companies in the services of an armoured division, one in a normal infantry division of average mechanization.

(vi) *The working of the repair system.*—All active units include an armoury (*Waffenmeisterei*) at unit HQ or in the HQ company or similar sub-unit. In mechanized units, as seen above, the armoury normally forms part of the repair detachment, and in tank units part of the armoured workshop company. The armoury deals essentially with arms and equipment and its repair equipment is comparatively simple. It usually has no more than one lorry at its disposal. It is controlled by the armourer, who is an official, and who usually has an armourer NCO and two armourer's assistants to help him. Companies or equivalent sub-units frequently have an armourer's assistant for minor repairs and maintenance and usually a shoemaker and tailor. Infantry companies often have a saddler and one or two other skilled tradesmen.

Repair of MT vehicles is done as far forward as possible. It appears that the normal practice is for repair units to carry out repairs which will not take more than four working hours, and workshop units do repairs taking up to 12 working hours. Vehicles requiring repairs which would take up to 24 working hours are sent back to Corps or Army MT park, and vehicles which would need even more extensive repairs are either "cannibalized" on the spot or sent back to Home MT parks. A workshop company, however, can do quite extensive repairs, for it has power tools, its own power and light, apparatus for oxyacetylene and electric welding and a crane. Any existing civilian facilities are invariably used whenever possible. This has been found to be true in Italy and even more so in Russia. In Russia the Army MT parks are reported as being often at least 120 miles behind the front line.

Corps or army may have a number of mechanized workshop companies and usually at least one armoured workshop. The facilities of these workshops are believed to be much the same as those in the division.

In the event of tank casualties during an action, the squadron repair unit reports the location of the casualty and nature of the damage to the squadron commander, who, if his own repair unit cannot execute the repairs, reports to regiment. The regimental workshop commander sends off his recovery section either to do the repairs *in situ* or bring the tank back to a pre-arranged spot, either on a tractor or in tow. The armoured regimental workshop can carry out complete overhaul of a tank, including changing the engine or turret, repairs to wireless sets and repairing or exchanging the armament. Whereas the unit repair section or sub-section is not allowed to do welding in armour of gashes of more than 10 cm (about 4 in) in length, the regimental workshop can repair holes up to about 10 cm by 10 cm and gashes of up to 30 cm in length. Tank repairs taking more than three days to complete are normally a matter for the repair services at Army or at Corps. Armoured regimental workshops do not keep spare tanks, and the number of spare engines, for example, which they hold, rarely exceeds ten in all.

The German policy in regard to the moving forward of tanks would appear to be, as far as possible, to move them under their own power, rather than on transporters, which are intended primarily for recovery purposes. Normal sizes of transporters are of 10, 22 and 60 tons.

(*b*) *The MT Parks in the field.*—(i) The system of delivery of tanks and MT to the field has already been outlined in Part I, Section 5. MT is delivered from the home parks by rail, less often by road to the GHQ MT parks and thence to the Army MT parks. Tanks are held at the depot at Magdeburg—Königsborn or at one of the branch depots and forwarded by rail to the unit's nearest railhead. Tank parks do exist, chiefly in Russia, but are not as a rule large. They would appear to be situated with the main AFV repair centres such as that at MINSK. The reserve of AFVs does not appear to be so large as to warrant the holding of large numbers of them in parks as a reserve pool. During the fighting in the Dnieper Bend in the winter of 1943-44, AFVs were brought right up to the Army railheads direct from the home depots and were immediately taken over by the units.

(ii) The GHQ MT Parks (*He KP*) and the Army MT Parks (*AKP*) are directly under the QMG at GHQ and are similar in constitution and function to the home MT parks, save that they normally do *all* repairs themselves. Each Army normally has one AKP, and each army group may have two or three He KPs. Further He KPs are at the disposal of GHQ. The area in which an He KP works is considerable. Those in France cover several *departements*. Like AKPs the He KPs are numbered.

He KPs may also be grouped together to form a single GHQ MT district or *Heeres Kraftfahrbezirk*—abbreviated *HKB*. HKB 32 for example, controls Holland.

(iii) All damaged vehicles between advanced railheads and the front which cannot be repaired by unit or formation workshops are collected by the AKPs or He KPs. If the AKPs are unable to deal with the repair, the vehicles come back to He KPs. These parks contain workshops of one or both of two different types, one type being highly mobile, the other being more or less static. The mobile workshops work as far forward as the Army area, the static workshops are a long way back in the L of C area and customarily take over existing repair facilities in occupied towns. Both types are well stocked with spare parts and, in addition may control the central spare parts depots (*Zentral Ersatzteillager or ZEL*). He KPs also control tyre depots (*Reifenlager*), tank spare parts depots (*Panzer Ersatzteillager*), track depots (*Gleiskettenlager*) and various types of retreading shops. A great proportion of the personnel for this system consists of foreigners and prisoners of war. The spare parts depot organization is widespread. In the West the chief centre is Paris, in the East it is Warsaw, for the South and the Balkans it is Stuttgart. Berlin is the centre for spare parts for foreign motor vehicles and Cologne for German motor vehicles.

(iv) Experience in Russia has shown that the MT parks were normally at least 120 miles (200 km) behind the front, and that damaged vehicles had a long journey from the front. It was usual for such parks to hold a steady reserve of about 200 new vehicles. An interesting feature of the parks in Russia was that they held huge numbers of the Russian-type distributors (made by Bosch of Stuttgart), together with other small spare parts, since a very large number of the Russian vehicles captured on the Eastern Front were found to have been immobilized merely by the removal of the distributor. The commonest types of Russian lorry thus re-mobilized were the " Stalin " 6-cylinder 3-ton lorry and the " Molotov " 4-cylinder 2-3-ton lorry. All German MT on the Russian front must be equipped with a hand starter and spare distributor.

Most German parks are equipped with certain spare parts of foreign vehicles. Allied MT which has to be abandoned in the face of capture, should have carburettor, starter dynamo and radiator wrecked as a minimum, because such spare parts are normally *not* held by the German parks.

As bogged vehicles are very common on most battle fronts, almost every German lorry is fitted with a special draw bar and hooks at the front and rear, and most lorries are provided with mats for putting under the wheels in loose ground. These mats are about 2 ft wide by 6 to 12 ft in length, and are made of wood slats connected by 5 mm wire to form a ladder-like structure which can be rolled up. These mats are usually made by the lorry crews, but prisoners of war have often been employed on their making.

(v) The Speer and NSKK and Todt systems have their own transport organizations, the actual MT consisting largely of commercial lorries fitted with tipping bodies. It would appear that about half of these lorries are Opel or Daimler-Benz, and the rest chiefly French, including Renaults, Peugeots and Berliets. Up to the end of 1941 the Todt organization was responsible for its own repairs. No proper organization for this work existed, however, and the orders were given to any civilian shop which could accept them, and very high prices were undoubtedly paid to ensure a reasonable date of delivery. Since the beginning of 1942, however, all these para-military organizations depend upon the MT parks for repair in the same way as does the Army. Most of these para-military organizations work very far back in the L of C area and are rarely seen as far forward as Army; their work includes the transport of shells from the munitions works to the filling depots (*Munas*), the supply of raw materials from ports or railheads to the factories and so on.

In occupied territory there is no doubt but that the NSKK and the Organization Todt do control their own parks, but most of these would appear to be essentially training areas for drivers. The He KPs do sometimes train drivers but this would appear to be rare and not among their normal duties. They are, however, responsible, in the occupied territories, for the requisitioning of civilian vehicles and the registration of captured vehicles. When, recently, the order was made for all German Armed Forces vehicles to be repainted in a flat beige colour this work was carried out by the MT parks. The conversion of vehicles to run on producer gas and the painting out of formation emblems on vehicles are others of the tasks performed by the MT parks. For the whole subject of substitute fuels *see* Part I, section 3 (*c*).

MAINTENANCE, REPAIR AND SUPPLY OF TANKS,

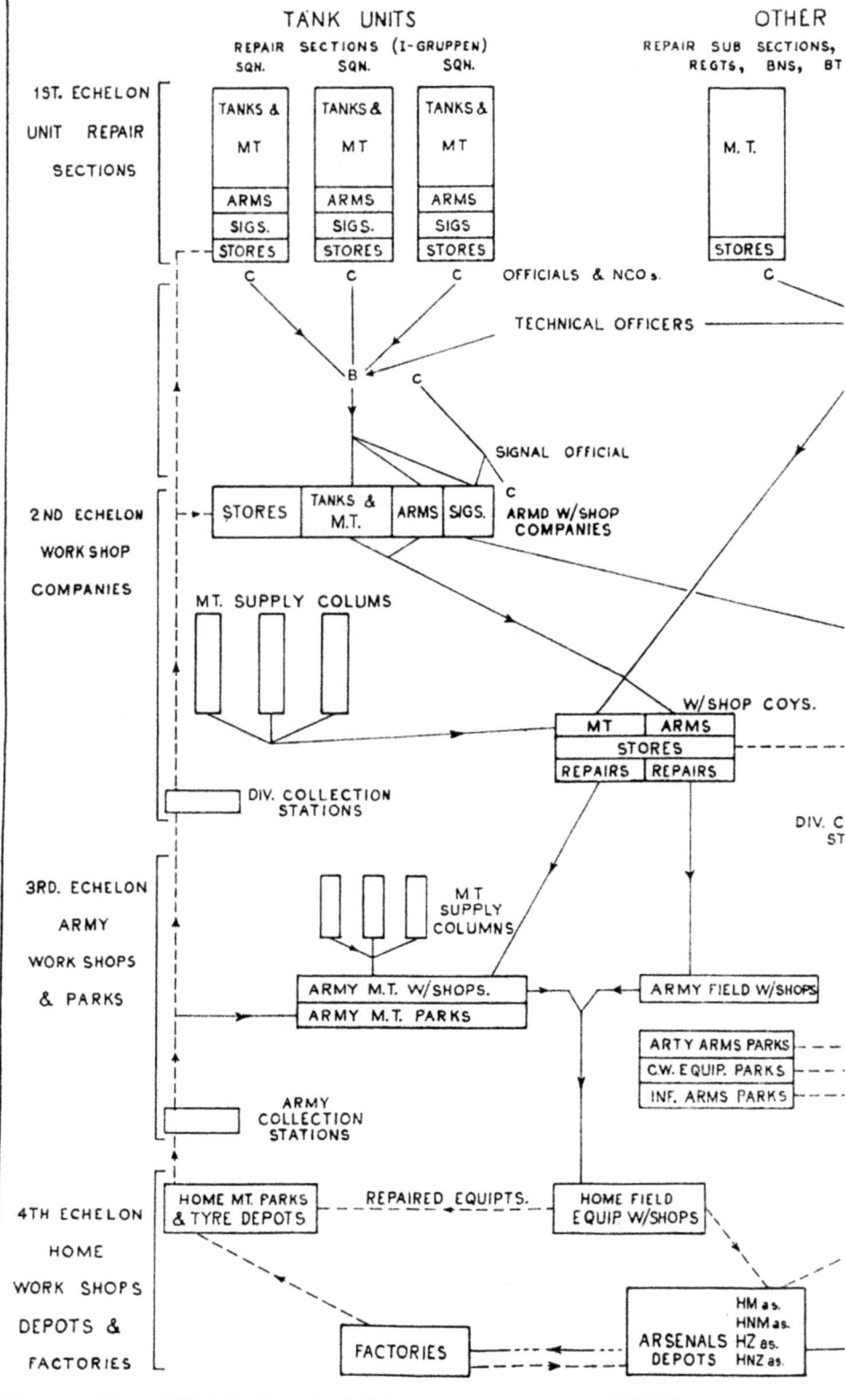

Diagram labels

TANK UNITS

REPAIR SECTIONS (I-GRUPPEN)

OTHER

REPAIR SUB SECTIONS, REGTS, BNS, BT

1ST. ECHELON UNIT REPAIR SECTIONS

SQN. — TANKS & MT / ARMS / SIGS. / STORES — C

SQN. — TANKS & MT / ARMS / SIGS. / STORES — C

SQN. — TANKS & MT / ARMS / SIGS / STORES — C

M.T. / STORES — C

OFFICIALS & NCO s.

TECHNICAL OFFICERS

B

C

SIGNAL OFFICIAL

C

2ND ECHELON WORKSHOP COMPANIES

STORES | TANKS & M.T. | ARMS | SIGS | ARMD W/SHOP COMPANIES

MT. SUPPLY COLUMS

W/SHOP COYS.

MT | ARMS

STORES

REPAIRS | REPAIRS

DIV. COLLECTION STATIONS

DIV. C ST

3RD. ECHELON ARMY WORK SHOPS & PARKS

MT SUPPLY COLUMNS

ARMY M.T. W/SHOPS. / ARMY M.T. PARKS

ARMY FIELD W/SHOPS

ARTY ARMS PARKS

C.W. EQUIP. PARKS

INF. ARMS PARKS

ARMY COLLECTION STATIONS

4TH ECHELON HOME WORK SHOPS DEPOTS & FACTORIES

HOME MT. PARKS & TYRE DEPOTS

REPAIRED EQUIPTS.

HOME FIELD EQUIP W/SHOPS

FACTORIES

ARSENALS DEPOTS

HM as.
HNM as.
HZ as.
HNZ as.

A = "Q" OFFICER WITH OFFICIALS AT H.Q's.

B = TECHNICAL OFFICERS SUPERVISING REPAIR SECTIONS ETC.

C = TECHNICAL OFFICIALS & N.C O's WITH REPAIR SECTIONS ETC.

M.T., ARMS, EQUIPMENT AND SPARE PARTS

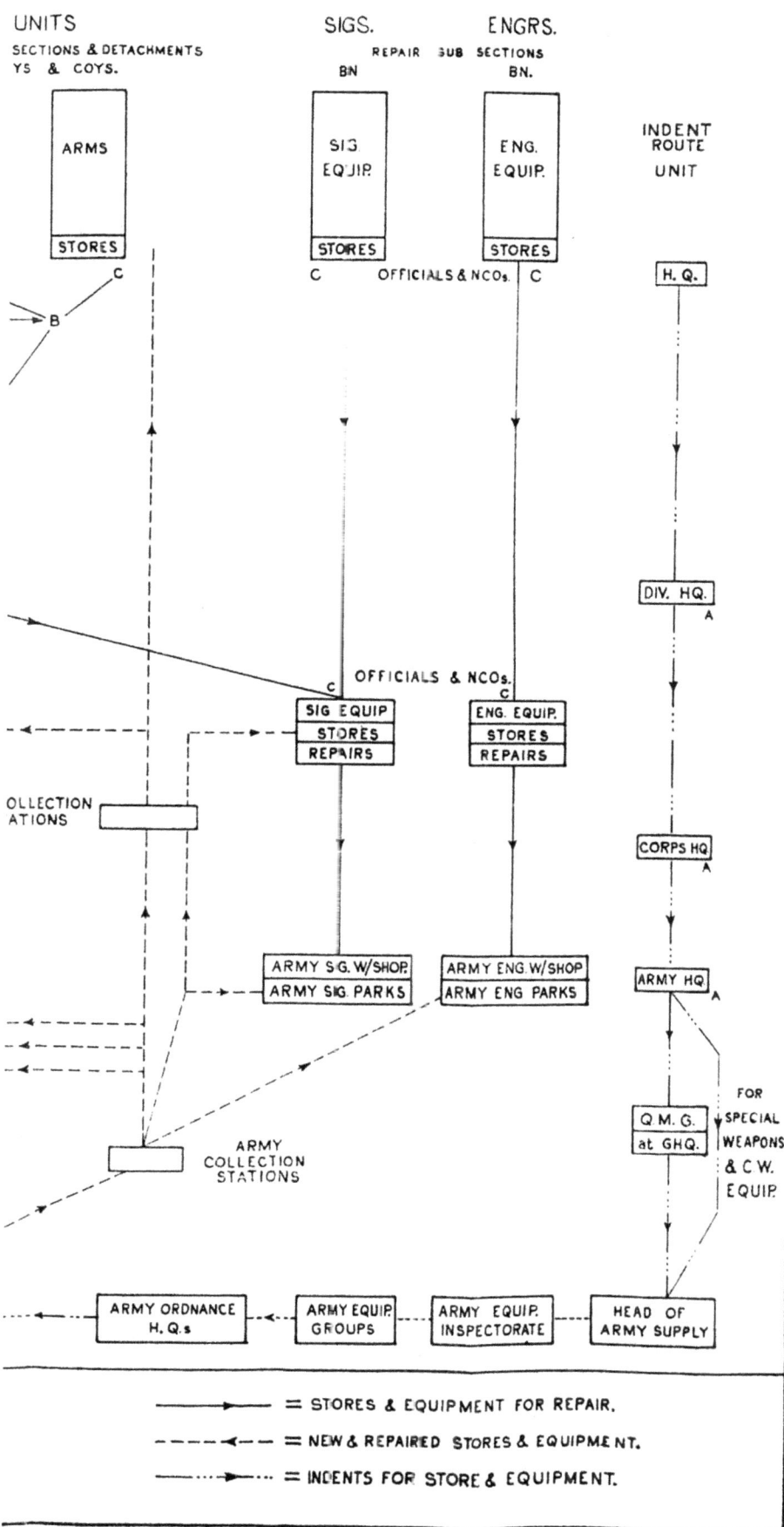

UNITS

SECTIONS & DETACHMENTS
YS & COYS.

SIGS.

REPAIR SUB SECTIONS
BN

ENGRS.

BN.

INDENT
ROUTE
UNIT

ARMS

STORES
C

→ B

SIG
EQUIP.

STORES
C

ENG.
EQUIP.

STORES
C

OFFICIALS & NCOs.

H. Q.

DIV. HQ.
A

C
OFFICIALS & NCOs.
C

SIG EQUIP
STORES
REPAIRS

ENG. EQUIP.
STORES
REPAIRS

COLLECTION
ATIONS

CORPS HQ
A

ARMY SIG. W/SHOP.
ARMY SIG. PARKS

ARMY ENG. W/SHOP.
ARMY ENG PARKS

ARMY HQ
A

ARMY
COLLECTION
STATIONS

Q. M. G.
at GHQ.

FOR
SPECIAL
WEAPONS
& C.W.
EQUIP.

ARMY ORDNANCE
H. Q.s

ARMY EQUIP.
GROUPS

ARMY EQUIP.
INSPECTORATE

HEAD OF
ARMY SUPPLY

———————→ = STORES & EQUIPMENT FOR REPAIR.

– – – –◄– – = NEW & REPAIRED STORES & EQUIPMENT.

———·——·—►·—·· = INDENTS FOR STORE & EQUIPMENT.

17. *Medical system in the field.*

(a) *General Notes.*—At the disposal of GHQ for the reinforcement and relief of corresponding army units are ambulance units (*Krankentransport-abteilungen*), base hospital units (*Kriegslazarettabteilungen*) and GHQ medical units (*Heeressanitätsabteilungen*). Hospital trains and ships are used for the evacuation of sick and wounded from the theatre of operations. They are provided with all necessary equipment and have permanent personnel. Light hospital trains and ships are used for the evacuation of sitting-up cases. Hospital trains and ships of both types are placed at the disposal of Armies by GHQ according to the requests or proposals of the Army MO, and controlled by the Director-General of Transportation.

Below this level, allotment of medical units is determined by the principles of flexibility, mobility and speed. Thus:—

(i) *Flexibility.*—Each unarmoured division normally has two medical companies and a field hospital. If the division is fighting on a wide front both companies may be in action at once, and the field hospital is set up at some central convenient point, some four miles behind the fighting line. If the divisional front is narrow only one company may be in action, with the second in reserve. If casualties are heavy, the two may be combined under the orders of the senior company commander. In an advance or retreat they may leapfrog each other which has been particularly noticed in Russia of late. Behind the divisional area, the MO Army has a number of units in reserve which may move up to reinforce or relieve the divisional units. Normally, before an action, the MO Army will place certain of these units at the disposal of MO Corps; it is only when this is done that MO Corps has any medical units at his disposal, as none are included in the establishment of corps.

(ii) *Mobility.*—Medical companies may be horsedrawn, partially mechanized or wholly mechanized, and usually the last-named is employed, though in Russia the emphasis is upon the horse-drawn type. One report from Russia said that a front-line infantry division should normally have 25 motor-ambulance cars, but that most divisions had none, or an average of less than three per division. This is mentioned because it was confirmed by several independent sources in 1943. It was stated, for example that any horsed wagon, without springs was eagerly requisitioned for ambulance work during periods of heavy fighting and that wounded had to walk or be carried from three to eight miles before transport was available. However, special vehicles are not much used and the loads of equipment are simple, compact and in easily handled cases. Hence the loss of a vehicle does not imply that it is impossible to transfer the load to any other standard vehicle. For example, the stretcher-support in ambulances is so constructed that it is easily adapted to fit any standard lorry. Such ambulances as have been seen in Russia and Italy have been very good, with stout rubber suspensory straps for the stretchers.

(iii) *Speed.*—The battalion aid post is as close to the fighting line as possible and may or may not be under cover. The divisional field hospital has been brought as far forward as is feasible. In armoured divisions the MO travels with the fighting vehicles in a specially adapted armoured car or a tank, and has special armoured ambulances to remove casualties. A very recent report spoke of this MO's tank as being fitted with a MG which the doctor must be able to use. Other reports have said that these tanks are unarmed. Parachute units have MOs who drop by parachute, and, as such units are likely to have heavy casualties the establishment of MOs is increased to one per company, and there are three medical companies and one field hospital, and the evacuation of wounded is carried out by aircraft in the initial stages of operations (*see* para. (v) below).

(b) *Organization.*—(i) The Inspector-General of the Army Medical Services (*Heeressanitäts-Inspektor*) is at the head of the Army Medical Services and has his HQ with that of the Director-General of Training and Equipment in the OKH He is the supreme authority over all medical personnel in matters of training, discipline and technical concerns. (By " medical personnel " is meant:—Medical officers, medical officers' assistants (these may be *Unterarzt,* an NCO, or *Hilfsarzt,* usually a junior assistant MO), medical NCOs, orderlies, stretcher bearers, special ambulance drivers and officials of the medical services (including dentists, pharmacists and administrative officials) and members of the voluntary nursing services with the army). He is assisted in his duties by his staff, the Inspectorate-General of Medical Services.

In addition, the MO (*Heeresarzt*) at GHQ controls the employment of members of the voluntary nursing services in the zone of operations and is responsible for laying down the general lines for protection from, and the fighting of disease among, the armies and civilians. To a lesser extent the regimental MO (*Truppenarzt*) carries out similar duties. He is responsible for supervising the employment of the battalion medical services and the evacuation of sick and wounded.

(ii) The medical units under control of GHQ include the following:—

GHQ Medical Units (*Heeressanitätsabteilungen*).
Base Hospital Units (*Kriegslazarettabteilungen*).
Ambulance Units (*Krankentransportabteilungen*).
Hospital Trains.
Hospital Ships.

These reinforce or relieve the corresponding units in the armies and provide the medical units required for the care of sick and wounded in GHQ area, *i.e.,* general and base hospitals.

Hospital trains and ships are obtained as required through the GHQ staff from the Director-General of Transportation. Their return to hospitals at home or elsewhere outside the zone of operations is arranged by the QMG in consultation with the Director-General of Transportation and the Director-General of Training.

(iii) *Army Units.*—The army medical unit is composed of medical companies, field hospital detachments and MT ambulance sections.

Army hospital units establish two types of army field hospitals—one for serious cases, which has 500 beds, the other of 1,000 beds for lightly wounded cases (fit to return to duty in 3-4 weeks). All the normal specialist departments (maxillo-facial, mental, ophthalmic, physio-therapy, radiology, neuro-surgery and laboratory), are included, and surgical and other equipment is in all respects adequate.

(iv) *Corps.*—No medical units are allotted to a corps in the German army. It is customary, however, for the MO army to place various medical units at the disposal of the MO corps before an action. Consequently reports are received from time to time which speak of the corps medical organization.

(v) *Division.*—The medical units within the division are as follows:—

The divisional field hospital (not in armoured division).
The medical company or companies.
The MT ambulance platoons.

The divisional field hospital is primarily intended for the reception and retention of casualties requiring urgent operation or whose condition will not permit of further evacuation without a period for rest and resuscitation. In theory, therefore, only the severest casualties should pass through the divisional field hospital. It is completely mechanized and fully equipped, its medical stores being packed in 14 cases. The radiology equipment of this hospital is packed in cases, is simple, easy to erect and very efficient. Dental equipment is also carried: Its capacity is 200 casualties and it can be set up in three hours. Most sources agree that the equipment of the majority of divisional field hospitals is adequate in most respects.

, There are usually two medical companies in a division though in some instances there is only one, and usually one at least of the medical companies is fully mechanized. The functions of the medical companies are as has already been fully described in " New Notes on the German Army, No. 4 ".

There are two MT ambulance platoons attached to the divisional field hospital in the infantry and mountain divisions. In the motorized and armoured divisions there are three of these ambulance platoons. They are employed in evacuating casualties from the dressing station to the field hospital, or from either of those and the lightly wounded collecting post to the casualty collecting post. They would appear almost always to be under strength.

The battalion medical services include the battalion MO assisted by an assistant or auxiliary MO (*Assistenzarzt* or *Hilfsarzt*). In an infantry battalion there is a medical NCO and a stretcher bearer at each rifle company HQ.

Parachute Divisions.—In these divisions there are not only battalion MOs but it is believed that there are, in addition, MOs with each company, while each platoon has a trained medical orderly attached. Latterly it is reported that these numbers have tended to be reduced, possibly because these troops are being used as infantry. Medical officers in parachute units act as combatants and do not claim the protection of the Geneva Convention. There is older evidence of this in Crete in 1941 and Holland in 1940. There are three medical companies, and all the above drop by parachute with their units. In addition, there is a field hospital which is probably air landing only.

(c) *Evacuation of Casualties.*—(i) *Channels of Evacuation.*—Speed of evacuation is of the greatest importance. To this end, the stretcher bearer section of the medical company assists the battalion stretcher bearers in the collection of wounded from the battlefield and sometimes specially trained dogs are used to help find casualties. The theoretical stages of evacuation have often been described and it has sometimes been the case that reports have confirmed that these channels are used in practice. However, a very great concensus of opinion and experience, originating chiefly from the Russian front gives the following as the stages of the evacuation as carried out in practice.

Unit stretcher-bearers, usually trained in first aid, bring the wounded to the unit aid post, manned by the company medical NCO—in a tent, dug-out or other shelter. Parachute troops would have a MO at this level.

Battalion (Battery, etc.) Dressing Station (Truppenverbandplatz). This is from 2½ to 5 miles behind the fighting line. At this level parachutists have what amounts to a mobile surgical unit, with operating table and anæsthetics, transfusion equipment, etc. Other units regard this as the advanced dressing station where cases are sorted and the most urgent measures carried out. Lightly wounded men are nowadays mostly dressed here by the MO and returned to duty, whereas formerly they would have been sent home.

Regimental (or Main) Dressing Station (Hauptverbandplatz).—It has to be borne in mind that a German regiment approximates in size and organization to a British brigade. The MDS is equipped as a surgical unit, and is the terminus for the less severe casualties who can be operated and treated to return to duty, if their case does not require more than a few days, and if accommodation is not overtaxed. It has two sections—one for those to be treated here to recovery, and those to be sent on. Amputations, for example, are often carried out at this point, before the cases are sent on.

The Divisional Hospital (Feldlazarett).—This may be located beside the MDS, or a little further back. Cases may be admitted here who require longer or more elaborate treatment, but for the more severe cases this stage may be eliminated, and they may be sent direct from the MDS to army field hospitals, or even to a rear hospital—*e.g.,* in a large town in Germany or an occupied country. The divisional hospital, though mobile, is in more permanent buildings, and can deal with a limited number of conditions of all degrees of seriousness.

Large permanent hospitals in the rear.—These are located in big towns in occupied territories and in the Reich. In addition to normal hospital accommodation, blocks of flats, schools and hotels have been converted for their use. Casualties are frequently sent direct from the MDS to these hospitals, at the discretion of the medical staffs of the MDS.

Casualty Collecting Posts.—These have not been mentioned by any source as actually operating in the field, and no light can be thrown on their position in the chain of evacuation in actual practice.

German sick and wounded are given an " accompanying label " (*Begleitzettel*).

There are three types of " *Begleitzettel* "; the appropriate one is tied to the clothing of the casualty (or to a button on the clothing) at the *Truppenverbandplatz*, which is conducted by the *Truppenarzt*, and is from 500-2,000 yards behind the fighting line. The labels are of the following types :—

Red, wound label—for wounded and surgical cases.
Two red stripes—not able to be moved by transport.
One red stripe—capable of being moved by transport.
No red stripes—capable of walking.
(The stripes are perforated edgestrips which can be torn off.)
Yellow-green, sick label—for sick only.
Yellow stripe—capable of being moved, infectious.
Green stripe—capable of being moved, not infectious.
No stripes—capable of walking, not infectious.
Violet, gas-casualty—for gas casualties.
Two violet stripes—not able to be moved by transport.
One violet stripe—capable of being moved by transport.
No stripes—capable of walking.

(ii) *Transport.*—Ambulance trains, hospital ships and transport aircraft are used in the evacuation of casualties, where such special means are necessary. The use of specially marked and fitted air ambulances has been almost completely abandoned by the German army medical services and instead of the ordinary transport aircraft, such as the Ju 52 is used, or more frequently the *Fieseler Storch*. No special fittings are employed, the stretchers merely being placed on the floor of the cabin. The Ju 52 will take eight stretchers. The casualties are accompanied by a medical orderly who has a small outfit of medical equipment. This form of transport has been found most suitable for fracture cases, for example, fractured femur. Head injury cases also benefit, but hæmorrhage cases do not appear to have taken kindly to such transport. Air ambulances were freely used in Poland, and are being used most extensively in Russia. The *Fieseler Storch* usually takes three or four sitting cases. Aircraft are used for the evacuation of the sick from GAF units in Greece and the neighbouring islands to Germany.

The pattern of MT ambulance in service at the beginning of the war proved to be unsatisfactory for cross-country work and has been replaced by a vehicle with four driving wheels, instead of two, and double differentials. This type takes four lying or 10 sitting cases and has a very good cross-country performance. There does not appear to be an adequate number available.

Stretcher carriages.—There are two patterns of stretcher carriages. The first is single-wheeled and is not much used. The second is two-wheeled and is said to be extremely efficient. An improved pattern of the latter is probably now being used fairly extensively.

Hospital Trains.—These vary according to the type of rolling stock used, and also according to whether the train is intended for lying or sitting cases.

For slightly wounded cases ... Capacity 920
For lying cases:—
  Two or three axled coaches with heating car ... Capacity 358
  Two or three axled coaches without heating car ... Capacity 386
  Four axled corridor coaches with or without heating car ... ... Capacity 364

The composition of one hospital train has been given as follows, the coaches being listed in successive order behind the engine:—

  1 baggage waggon.
  1 stores waggon.
  1 ambulance coach for officers.
  14 ambulance coaches for men.
  1 coach for personnel.
  1 coach for the MO and his assistants.
  1 coach for nurses and administrative staff.
  1 coach for operating theatre and dispensary.
  1 field kitchen waggon.
  1 waggon for kitchen utensils and provisions.
  1 hot water boiler waggon.
  1 coach for personnel.
  13 ambulance coaches for men.

i.e., a total of 38 coaches and wagons of which 28 coaches are ambulances and will accommodate 359 lying cases.

Railway Transport.—Trains are used for long-distance evacuation of casualties. Some trains are reported to be comfortable, with well-sprung bunks. One report speaks of a case who made the journey from VYASMA to a point west of WARSAW with a convoy of other sick and wounded. The train took three days and four nights to reach its destination, and it consisted entirely of box goods waggons. The floor was covered with hemp-tow as the only bedding for all types of patients. The only sanitary facility was the sliding door of the truck. Rations were cold issue and chocolate and at longer stops the wounded received a hot drink. There was no MO on the train, and the sick and wounded were inspected by a MO at the larger stopping places on the railway route. A senior NCO was in command and complete clinical charge of this train. Conditions were very bad, wounds were smelling, and the medical NCOs used morphia. Such conditions were said to be routine at the Russian front. Further reports say that near the Polish-German border, the convoy was transferred to a luxurious ambulance train " to impress the German people ", and it was implied that in Russia and out of sight of critics anything was good enough, and that proper ambulance trains never went far beyond the Reich. Many sources confirm this statement. One case was transported, lying on straw, in a goods truck from the DON as far as LEMBERG. Here, after a stay in a good hospital, he was transported in a luxurious hospital train to Germany.

The emergency use of horse transport waggons, peasant carts and sleighs is most extensive.

(iii) *Conditions of treatment.*—A tendency to decentralization of treatment of all possible cases, by giving fuller equipment and more authority to forward members and units of the medical service to do responsible work, has been authoritatively described by many reliable sources.

Combatant units and forward medical companies sometimes carry more stores than their establishment allows, if they can obtain them, and even *Unterärzte* (not yet commissioned junior assistant MOs) carry out work at battery or battalion aid posts—*e.g.*, for extensive burns. This policy may be an attempt to reduce the strain on transport.

Divisional field hospitals during periods of active operations in RUSSIA, seem to have been unable to cope adequately with the numbers of casualties. The staffs have been described as competent but overworked. Treatment is described as rough and hurried, and reports speak of cases who had foreign bodies extracted and debriment of wounds carried out *without anæsthesia* of any kind. It is known that the period of convalescence is drastically cut down.

It would appear that the majority of cases who experienced hospital treatment in rear zones (*e.g.*, at LEMBERG and SHIRARDOV in POLAND; at NASSAU, WIESBADEN and INSTERBURG in GERMANY) were satisfied with the medical competence and kindliness of staffs, the diet and general amenities. Sources speak of the encouraging results of plastic surgery. One man with a septic abdominal wound was back graded fit for front-line duty, within three months, at the STALINGRAD front, whence he had come.

Convalescence.—Any officer or man is encouraged to leave hospital and live at home while undergoing private after-treatment at his local hospital or doctor's for which the State reimburses the agency concerned. Complaint of the monotonous and unimaginative routine prevailing at convalescent homes is heard. The " Strength through Joy " organization assists in entertaining men here.

The concensus of judgment based on all available information is that there has been a great lowering of category standards. Many sources speak of virtual abrogation of mental and physical standards of selection. Men are not only posted unfit to combatant units, but are prematurely discharged as fit for re-posting without adequate examination, owing to overcrowding of hospitals and man-power shortage. Men with flat feet and missing fingers go to infantry as MG loaders, etc. Many unfit men are categorized and posted in the most perfunctory manner.

(d) The Blood Transfusion Service.—(i) The blood group of every German soldier is stamped on his identity disc and is also recorded on page 1 of the *Soldbuch* (Paybook). The method in which the various bloodgroups are determined and the way in which they can be used is shown in the table following. Blood is taken from the lobe of the ear for these tests. Three drops are treated with blood test sera A, B and O respectively. After a wait of from five to ten minutes the drops of blood are observed for agglutination, and thereby the blood group is determined. In the back areas, blood of all groups is employed for transfusions, but in the forward areas only Universal Donor blood (bloodgroup O) is used. Soldiers not actually in the fighting line are encouraged to become donors and after blood has been taken from a man he used to be given a special allowance of 0·5 Reichmarks daily for 20 days to buy additional food, or if this was impossible, additional rations were issued. Now, however, it would appear unusual for the blood-donors to receive either money or extra rations.

(ii) In the field the Schilling Portable Blood Transfusion outfit is used. This apparatus consists of a cylindrical glass blood container, which narrows off at either end to fit the rubber tubing, a small rubber bulb, two short lengths of rubber tubing joined by a glass inspection connection with a bulb in the centre presumably for filtration of the blood, a screw clamp and an intravenous needle. The whole apparatus is packed in a cylindrical cardboard carton approximately 16 in. long.

For use, the rubber bulb is attached to the outlet at the upper end of the blood container and the rubber tubing with glass connection and filtration chamber screw clamp and intravenous needle to the outlet at the lower end. The blood is slightly warmed by holding the container under the armpit and the container is then suspended by a short length of string from one of the MO's tunic buttons. The needle is inserted into a vein and fixed in position by a piece of strapping. The injection of blood is carried out by means of pumping air slowly into the upper end of the blood container and regulating the flow by means of the screw clamp which is placed on the lower length of rubber tubing close to the needle.

The blood reservoir is filled with universal donor blood to which has been added grape sugar and citrate solution.

This apparatus can be used on the battlefield away from any dressing station and the transfusion can be given by one man without assistance.

(iii) Determination of Bloodgroups.

Blood treated with test sera, O, A and B $\left\{ \begin{array}{l} - = \text{no agglutination.} \\ + = \text{agglutination.} \end{array} \right.$

			A agglutination	—	} Bloodgroup A.
			B ,,	+	
			O ,,	+	

			A agglutination	+	} Bloodgroup B.
			B ,,	—	
			O ,,	+	

			A agglutination	—	} Bloodgroup O.
			B ,,	—	
			O ,,	—	

			A agglutination	+	} Bloodgroup AB.
			B ,,	+	
			O ,,	+	

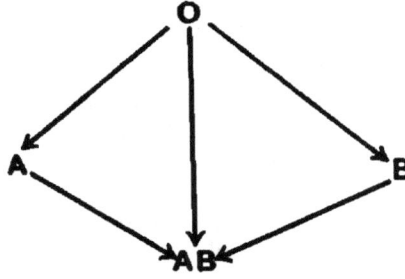

Bloodgroup O can receive from Bloodgroup O only.
     ,,   A ,,   ,,   ,,   ,,   O and A.
     ,,   B ,,   ,,   ,,   ,,   O and B.
     ,,   AB ,,   ,,   ,,   ,,   OA, B and AB.

Therefore bloodgroup O can give blood to any other group and is a universal blood donor; bloodgroup AB can receive blood from any other group and is a universal blood recipient.

(e) *Anti-Gas Equipment.*—(i) Personal anti-gas equipment consists of the following:—

Respirator anti-gas.
Sheet anti-gas.
A small bakelite container for *Losantin* (chloride of lime) tablets.

The respirator, which is carried in a cylindrical metal canister, consists of a facepiece and a container which screws into a special fitting on the facepiece. There is no corrugated rubber connecting tube and so the container can easily be changed without removing the facepiece.

The A/G sheet consists of a rectangular sheet of rubberized fabric, crepe paper, waxed paper, or non-rubberized material probably of plastic origin. The paper types are expendible and are discarded after use. To obtain protection against spray attack with blister-gas the German soldier lies down, crouches or kneels, with his sheet A/G spread over him and is thus completely immobilized while taking shelter. For personal decontamination he carries losantin tablets. Free blister gas is " picked off ", not rubbed off, with swabs which are then destroyed. Losantin tablets are then rubbed to a powder in the hand and then mixed to a paste with a little water. The paste is spread on the gas affected parts and allowed to stay on for from ten to fifteen minutes, after, which it is washed off. No eyeshields are provided for personal protection.

For casualties with head injuries who are unable to wear the normal respirator a special anti-gas helmet has been issued. This helmet is made of thin sheet rubber with an over window of cellulose acetate and provided with inlet and outlet valves. Over the inlet valve is a screw fitting into which is fastened the standard respirator container. When in use the window is bent to conform to the shape of the casualty's face, and the helmet is then drawn over the bandaged head and fastened round the neck by means of a tape. A second tape passing over the vertex and crossing under the chin is used to cut down dead space within the helmet. Finally the container belonging to the casualty's own respirator is screwed into the fitting on the helmet.

(ii) The Decontamination Company, Medical (*Entgiftigungs Kompanie*). This unit may be attached to an Army or divisional field hospital or can function independently. It is equipped with a tent with metal supports, a tent heating apparatus, an apparatus for decontaminating clothing, a shower bath outfit and a hot air blower. The blower is used for drying the men after they have been under the shower. Thus only rough paper towels are needed. Transport consists of a lorry on which the hot air blower plant is installed and a trailer carrying the shower bath outfit.

(f) *German Medical treatment of Gas Casualties.*—(i) *Cases of Asphyxia*—(*choking gases*).—These are transported lying, with head and shoulders supported. No narcotics are allowed, but morphia up to 0·01 may be used. Analeptics are allowed. Any wounds of the thorax or lungs are treated at once, unless there is cyanosis, in which case only lung wounds receive priority. If the '' grey '' stage has been reached wounds receive no priority, thoracic wounds being covered with a wet sterile cloth. Only local anæsthetics may be used. Intravenous injection of strophantine may be used; blood letting of from 500 to 800 ccs may be resorted to, and the inhalation of oxygen is general.

(ii) *Cases of Blistering*—(*vesicant gases*).—First personal decontamination as in paragraph (f) (i) above. Vaseline or cream may be rubbed into the skin after the washing off of the Losantin paste. As Losantin is dangerous to the eyes, it is not put on the face, but the skin of the face is washed repeatedly with hot soapy water, but this is only efficacious if done in the first ten minutes. Blisters are pierced several times over a period and thoroughly evacuated. They are then protected with wet bandages impregnated with potassium permanganate. When granulation has commenced treatment reverts to the application of ointment and dry bandages.

The eyes are washed with a 3 per cent saline solution or 5 per cent bicarbonate of soda solution. If the mouth or throat are affected a gargle with a saline or potassium permanganate solution is given.

Open wounds affected by blister gas must be rinsed copiously with potassium permanganate solution. A certain degree of bleeding is not undesirable in this instance, and hæmorrhage need not be stopped immediately unless dangerous or excessive. During treatment of the wound, both gloves and instruments must be kept wet.

(g) *Capacity and time of erecting or dismantling of various medical units.*

Unit	Capacity	Time to set up or dismantle or to load	Remarks
Army field hospital ...	500 beds	24 hours	Set up by Army field hospital detachments
Army field hospitals for slightly wounded cases	1,000 beds... ...	24 hours	Set up by Army field hospital detachments
Field hospital	200 beds	3 hours	Set up by divisional field hospital detachments
Casualty collecting station medical railhead	Limited only by accommodation available	3 hours	Set up by MT ambulance coy
Field dressing station ...	Unlimited	½—1 hour	Set up by divisional medical coy
Slightly wounded collecting post	Unlimited	A few minutes	Set up by divisional medical coy

Unit	Capacity	Time to set up or dismantle or to load	Remarks
Motor ambulance ...	4 lying 10 sitting ...	...	Four driving wheels and double differential for cross-country performance
Hospital train 2 or 3 axled coaches with heating coach; without heating coach 4 axled corridor each with or without heating coach	358 lying ... ... 386 ,, 364 ,,	2—6 hours	Depends on personnel available and layout of lines and loading platforms
Hospital train for slightly wounded	920 sitting... ...	1—2 hours	...

(h) *Individual Medical Equipment.*—(i) *The combatant*:—

1 large packet of dressing material (field dressing).
1 small packet of dressing material.

Losantin tablets for use against blister gas.

(ii) *The stretcher-bearer*—in the unit:—

2 stretcher-bearers' haversacks, containing—

    1 pair of scissors,
    1 pair or dissecting forceps,
    6 packets of dressing material,
    3 triangular bandages (*Dreiecktücher*),
    3 strips of gauze (5 yds × 2¾ in),
    6 squares of gauze,
    1 roll of adhesive plaster,
    1 waterproof bandage (about 19 × 21 in),
    1 improvized tourniquet (*Abschnürbinde*),
    20 safety pins.

In the medical units.—In medical units, the stretcher-bearers are not all equipped with the haversack, as above, but each group of four is given a haversack of dressing materials (*Verbandtasche*) containing—

    1 pair of cloth cutting scissors (*Kleiderschere*),
    1 improvized tourniquet (*Abschnürbinde*),
    12 strips of gauze,
    10 *Mullstreifen* (gauze squares) of absorbent cotton (*entfettete Watte*),
    6 triangular handkerchiefs,
    2 *Brandbinden* (absorbent gauze, treated with bismuth, for burns),
    1 waterproof bandage (about 35 × 40 in),
    4 rolls of rubberized adhesive plaster (*Zinkkautschukheftplaster*),
    35 safety pins,
    4 small detachable splints, with cradle,
    2 slings (11 × 5 in).

In addition, each stretcher-bearer carries a mug, and a bottle containing about a pint of cordial.

(iii) *The medical service NCOs and the medical orderlies.*—Each carries a bottle of cordial, a case of dressing material, and two medical haversacks (dressings haversack and medicines haversack).

Dressing material, etc—

1 pair of straight scissors,
1 pair of dissecting forceps,
1 nail-file,
1 thermometer.

Medical haversack No. 1—

2 bottles of tincture of iodine (4 ccs), made of artificial resin,
2 tubes of 2 per cent salicylic acid, each 10 ccs,
2 tubes of formaldehyde, each 10 ccs,
1 aluminium tube containing 20 compressed tablets of 0·1 cardiazol,
1 aluminium tube containing 20 compressed tablets of acid, acetyl salicyl, 0·5,
1 aluminium tube containing 20 compressed tablets of opium, 0·03,
1 aluminium tube containing 15 compressed tablets of rhubarb,
1 empty aluminium tube,
1 case, containing a roll of adhesive plaster,
5 first-aid dressings (3 × 4 in), done up in paper envelopes.

Medical haversack No. 2 (dressings haversack)—

1 compressed packet containing $\begin{cases} 3 \text{ strips of gauze,} \\ 3 \text{ squares of gauze,} \end{cases}$
3 small packets of dressings,
1 waterproof bandage (a quarter of a yard square),
20 safety pins, in a leather case,
1 rubber improvized tourniquet.

(iv) *Officers of the medical service* carry the MOs haversack, containing—

1 pair of straight scissors,
1 pointed lancet,
1 convex lancet ("*bauchig*"),
1 pair of dissecting forceps,
1 ligature forceps, 3·5 mm broad,
1 ligature forceps, 4·5 mm broad ("*Unterbindungspinzette*"),
1 hollowed steel probe, 6-in long,
1 probe with olive-shaped ends ("*Knopfsonde*"),
1 detachable needle-holder (5 in),
6 round needles, of different sizes,
3 single-pointed crochets, in metal cases,
12 mm cannula, for bloodletting on gauze,
17 metal catheter (*Metallkatheter*),
1 re-entrant platinum-iridium vaccinostyle,
1 thermometer,
1 glass tube, with silk thread,
1 detachable stethoscope,
1 metal tongue-depressor,
1 small percussion hammer,
1 150-yard measure,
3 small packets of dressings,
1 roll of adhesive plaster,
several packets of first aid dressings.
cotton wool,

1 tin-plate case for tablets, containing—

> 10 tablets of acetylosalicyl acid, 0·5,
> 15 tablets of pyramidone, 0·2,
> 10 tablets of cardiazol, 0·1,
> 5 tablets of quinine hydrochloride, 0·3,
> 5 tablets of veronal, 0·3,
> 5 tablets of solventes, 0·4 (against colds—liquorice and ammonium chloride),
> 10 tablets of phosphate of codein, 0·3,
> 5 tablets of boric acid, 1·0,
> 5 tablets of bicarbonate of soda, 1·0,
> 10 tablets of opium, 0·03,
> 5 tablets of tannalbin, 0·5,
> 5 tablets of rhubarb, 0·5.
> 5 tablets of calomel, 0·2,
> 10 tablets of atropine-mannite, 0·0003, in glass tubes,
> 10 tablets of cocain chloride, 0·003, in glass tubes,
> 10 tablets of sublimate.

1 tin-plate case for ampoules, containing—

> 3 ampoules of caffein salicylate of soda, 0·2,
> 1 ampoule of 1 cc of a 1/1,000 solution of suprarenine chloride (adrenaline),
> 2 ampoules of morphin hydrochloride, 0·02,
> 4 ampoules of 7 per cent tincture of iodine, with brushes.

1 tube of white vaseline (1 cc),
1 glass rod,
1 file for ampoules,
1 case containing 2 ampoules of lobelin, 0·01.
> 1 empty cardboard case, for optional articles (lobelin, sympatol, strophantin, scopolamine and morphine are recommended).
1 syringe (1 cc) with two needles,
1 brass flask, containing 50 ccs alcohol, at 70°,
1 improvized tourniquet,
1 douche in a case of parachute silk,
1 nickel case, containing soap.

(i) *Unit equipment.*—(i) The medical equipment of battalions, regiments and similar units is normally identical. It is carried far forward and is rarely destroyed when capture is imminent. Almost all of it can be put to immediate use. It comprises:—

Box No. 1—Miscellaneous contents (Fighting box—" *Gefechtskasten* " marked by two white strokes, in the form of a cross).
Box No. II.—Medicaments.
Box No. III—Dressings.
Box No. IV—Supplementary to II and III.
Box No. V—Anti-tetanus serum.

and also—

> 2 medical haversacks, filled with equipment,
> 2 empty rucksacks,
> 1 set of equipment for fractures with a pair of splints,
> 1 unit medical outfit or troop haversack plus a medical pannier,

1 set of oxygen apparatus (each apparatus is packed in a case, with steel mouthpiece and flask; this flask has a volume of about 2 litres, and contains 300 litres of oxygen, at normal pressure). For the two apparatus, there is also a box of spare parts, containing two identical steel flasks.

4 pliable stretchers, each with 2 straps,
12 woollen blankets,
1 box of tools,
1 portable filter apparatus (*Tornisterfiltergerät*),
Gas protection caps for those with head wounds (number unknown),
Losantin for protection against blister gas.

(ii) Contents of medical haversack (*Sanitätstornister*)—

10 ampoules of strophantin, 0·00025,
10 ampoules of caffein salicylate of soda 0·2,
 3 ampoules of cardiazol, 0·1,
 4 ampoules of lobelin, 0·01,
20 ampoules of morphin hydro chloride, 0·20,
 3 ampoules of eucodol, 0·01,
25 gr of simple tincture of opium,
30 tablets of cardiazol, 0·1,
15 tablets of boric acid, 0·1,
 6 tubes (10 ccs) of boric acid vaseline,
 3 tubes (10 ccs) of alkaline ointment, for the eyes,
20 gr of alcohol,
10 ampoules strong camphor oil.

Dressings—

9 packets of compressed gauze,
1 packet of 100 gr absorbent cotton wool,
1 packet of 100 gr of ordinary wadding,
5 packets, each containing 6 strips of gauze, 2¼ in × 5 yds,
15 small packets (or 5 large and 5 small) of dressings,
2 rolls of adhesive plaster,
4 detachable splints,
6 slings 11¾ in × 5 in,
5 triangular bandages,
35 safety pins,
1 improvized tourniquet (strip),
1 improvized tourniquet (tube),
1 1 cc syringe, in metal case,
1 metal bowl, for dressing,
1 pair of cloth cutting scissors,
1 block of labels for wounded,
1 block of labels for sick.

(iii) Contents of medical satchel (*Sanitätspacktasche*)—

Medicaments—

6 ampoules of cardiazol, 0·1,
10 ampoules of camphorated oil, 2·0,
10 ampoules of caffein salicylate of soda, 0·2,
10 ampoules of digipuratum, 0·1,
10 ampoules of strophantin, 0·00025,
10 ampoules of suprarenin 1 : 1000, 1·0,
2 ampoules of lobelin, 0·003,
3 ampoules of eucodal, 0·01,

30 ampoules of morphin hydrochloride, 0·02,
30 tablets of cardiazol, 0·1,
60 tablets of bicarbonate of soda,
60 tablets of carbonate of soda, 1·0,
1 flask (50 ccs) of compound tincture of quinine,
10 flasks (made of artificial resin, each of capacity 4 ccs) containing tincture of iodine,
10 ampoules of capacity 2·0 ccs, novocain, 0·04, suprarenin, 0·0001,
1 flask of chloroform, 50·0,
20 flasks (5 ccs) of anti-tetanus serum, 3000AE,
3 tubes (10 ccs) of alkaline ointment for the eyes,
3 tubes (10 ccs) of zinc ointment,
3 tubes (10 ccs) of salicylic acid vaseline, 2 per cent,
2 tubes (10 ccs) of sulphichthyolic ammonium vaseline, 10 per cent,
10 tubes (10 ccs) of formaldehyde vaseline, 8 per cent,
10 tubes (10 ccs) of boric acid vaseline,
1 box containing zinc oxide and talc, 100·00,
1 flask with 100 ccs aluminium acetate,
20 tablets of sublimate, 0·5.

Dressings—

2 compressed packets of ordinary wadding, 100 gr,
1 compressed packet of ordinary wadding, 1,000 gr,
2 compressed packets of absorbent wadding, 100 gr,
1 compressed packet of absorbent wadding, 1,000 gr,
3 compressed packets each containing 16 strips of gauze 4 in × 10 yards,
15 compressed packets each containing 6 strips of gauze 2¾ in × 5 yards,
1 compressed packet containing 20 strips of gauze, 4 in × 5 yards,
20 compressed packets each containing 4 yard-squares of gauze,
1 compressed packet containing 40 gauze pads a yard square,
1 compressed packet containing 40 gauze cloths a yard square,
60 small (or 20 small and 20 large packets of dressing),
2 cases, each containing 1 yard of first aid dressing,
3 yards of waterproof bandage,
2 strips of absorbent gauze, treated with bismuth, for burns (4¼ in × 4 yds),
6 rolls of adhesive plaster,
10 slings (18 in × 8 in),
10 triangular dressing bandages,
30 safety pins,
1 improved tourniquet (strip),
1 improvized tourniquet (tube),
2 suspensory bandages,
1 syringe, 1·0 ccs,
1 syringe, 5·0 ccs,
1 dressing bowl (kidney shaped),
1 case of iodized catgut (medium),
1 case of linen thread (fine, medium and thick),
1 small spirit lamp for the medical instruments (300 ccs of spirit for burning),
1 pliable douche,
1 œsophageal probe, 27½ in in length, and ½-in in diameter,
1 pair of cloth-cutting scissors,
1 razor, with accessories,
1 artificial resin case, for soap.
1 nail brush,

2 hand towels,
1 block of labels for sick,
1 block of labels for wounded,
2 improvized stretchers,

(iv) *Medical panniers* (*Sanitätskasten*):—
Medicaments—

12 ampoules of cardiazol, 0·1,
20 ampoules of strong camphorated oil, 2·0,
30 ampoules of caffein salicylate of soda, 0·2,
10 ampoules of strophantine, 0·00025,
10 ampoules of digipuratum solution, 0·1,
10 ampoules of suprarenine, 1:1000, 1·0,
30 tablets of cardiazol, 0·1,
 4 ampoules of lobelin, 0·01,
 4 ampoules of lobelin, 0·003,
 9 ampoules of eucodal, 0·01,
40 ampoules of morphin hydrochloride, 0·2,
60 tablets of carbonate of soda, 1·0,
60 tablets of bicarbonate of soda, 1·0,
60 gr spirits of turpentine,
100 gr tincture of valerian ether,
100 gr tincture of opium,
100 gr castor oil,
10 (4 ccs) artificial resin flasks containing tincture of iodine,
10 (2 ccs) ampoules novocain, 0·04, suprarenine, 0·0001,
 4 50-ccs flasks of chloroform,
 5 15-ccs atomizers of ethyl chloride,
25 5-ccs flasks of anti-tetanus serum, at 3,000 AE,
90 tablets of sublimate, 0·5,
100 tablets of hydrogen peroxide,
75 gr of crude chloramin, in powder form,
150 gr of liquor (alum, acetic acid, tartaric acid),
10 10-ccs tubes of alkaline ointment, for the eyes,
10 10-ccs tubes of zinc ointment,
20 10-ccs tubes of boric vaseline,
20 10-ccs tubes sulphichthyolic ammonium vaseline, 10 per cent,
50 10-ccs tubes of salicylic acid vaseline, 2 per cent,
20 10-ccs tubes of formaldehyde vaseline, 8 per cent,
60 gr of balsam of Peru,
 1 powder box containing zinc oxide and talc, 100·0,
120 gr of glycerine,
100 gr of a solution of mastic,
100 gr of alcohol at 90°,
200 tablets of *Losantin*.

Dressing equipment—

 1 compressed packet containing 10 strips of gauze, 4¾ in × 8 yds,
 6 compressed packets each containing 6 strips of gauze, 2½ in × 5 yds,
 5 compressed packets containing squares of gauze,
 1 compressed packet containing gauze pads,
 2 compressed packets each containing 100 gr absorbent wadding,
 3 compressed packets each containing 100 gr ordinary wadding,
25 small, or 12 large packets of dressings,
 6 bismuth-treated strips, 4¾ in × 4 yds,
 2 boxes of first aid dressings,

12 rolls of adhesive plaster,
 4 metal wire splints (32 in × 3 in),
 2 slings (24 in × 6 in),
 4 triangular dressing bandages,
35 safety pins,
 1 improvized tourniquet (strip),
 1 improvized tourniquet (tube),
 2 suspensory bandages,
 1 œsophageal probe of soft rubber, with rounded end,
 1 rubber tube, 150 cm long,
 1 rubber tube, 100 cm long,
 1 medium drainage tube, 50 cm long,
 1 nickelled injection douche, with two cannulæ of glass, and two of
     hardened rubber,
 1 graduated measuring apparatus, of pewter,
 1 small spirit lamp,
 1 small sterilizer, for surgical instruments,
 1 1·0 cc syringe,
 1 5·0 cc syringe,
24 hollow needles,
 1 case containing fine, medium and coarse linen thread,
 2 cases of medium iodized catgut,
 6 droppers, with rubber bulb,
 3 thermometers,
 1 pair of cloth cutting scissors,
 1 razor with accessories,
 1 nickel soap-box, containing 50 gr of soap,
 1 nail brush,
 1 hand towel,
 2 overalls,
 2 blocks of labels for wounded,
 2 blocks of labels for sick.

(v) *Pannier No.* 1 (*T.S.A. Kasten I—Gefechtskasten—Battle Pannier*): —
Medicaments—

 6 ampoules of cardiazol, 0·1,
10 ampoules of caffein, solium salicylate, 0·2,
10 ampoules of strong camphorated oil, 2·0,
10 ampoules of digipuratum, 0·1,
10 ampoules of strophantine, 0·00025,
 4 ampoules of lobelin, 0·01,
 4 ampoules of lobelin, 0·003,
20 ampoules of morphin hydrochloride, 0·02,
10 ampoules of eucodal, 0·01,
20 flasks, each 5 ccs of anti-tetanus serum, at 3,000AE,
10 2-ccs ampoules, novacain, suprarenine, 0·0001,
 2 15-ccs atomizers containing ethyl chloride,
10 artificial resin flasks, 4 ccs of tincture of iodine,
20 pastilles of sublimate,
 1 flask of solution of mastic (*Mastixlösung*).

Dressing materials—

 1 compressed packet containing 72 strips of gauze, 2¾ in × 5 yds,
 1 compressed packet containing 16 strips of gauze, 4 in × 10 yds,
 1 compressed packet containing 40 sq yds of gauze cloth,
 1 compressed packet containing 4 sq yds of gauze pads,

10 compressed packets each containing 4 sq yds of gauze squares,
1 compressed packet containing 1,000 gr of ordinary wadding,
1 compressed packet containing 1,000 gr of absorbent wadding,
1 box containing 2 ccs of iodoform,
10 small packets of dressings,
10 strips treated with bismuth, $1\frac{3}{4}$ in × $4\frac{3}{4}$ ins,
36 slings 24 in × 6 in,
30 triangular dressing bandages,
70 safety pins,
1 compressed packet containing 20 strips of gauze, 4 in × 5 yds,
1 Esmarch improvized rubber tourniquet,
3 improvized tourniquets (strip),
1 improvized tourniquet (tube),
1 œsophageal probe,
1 large draining tube. 1 m,
2 boxes of thick iodized catgut,
4 boxes of medium iodized catgut,
2 boxes of fine iodized catgut,
2 boxes of thick linen thread,
2 boxes of medium linen thread,
1 box of fine linen thread,
5 pairs of rubber gloves,
2 operating overalls,
3 linen table cloths,
2 pairs of goggles,
4 eye-flaps,
6 droppers,
10 wooden spatulas,
1 spirit lamp,
1 300-ccs spirit lamp,
1 dressing basin,
1 folding bidet,
1 iron basin,
1 artificial resin soap-box with 50 gr of soap,
2 nail brushes,
1 sponge,
2 hand towels,
1 razor, with accessories,
1 pair of clippers,
5 thermometers,
2 pairs of scissors,
2 blocks of labels, for sick and wounded.

(iv) *Pannier No. 2 TSA Kasten 2 (Arzneimeitelkasten)*: —

Medicaments—

16 ampoules of lobelin, 0·01,
16 ampoules of lobelin, 0·003,
60 ampoules of cardiazol, 0·1,
40 ampoules of strong camphorated oil, 2·0,
10 ampoules of digipuratum,
10 ampoules of suprarenine, 1:1,000, 1·0,
10 ampoules of calcium glusoniate, 10 per cent, 5·0,
10 ampoules of scopolamin hydrobromide, 0·0003,
40 ampoules of eucodal, 0·01,
5 ampoules of diluted hydrochloride acid, 10°,

10 ampoules of 10-ccs iodine, 7·0, potassium iodide, 3·0,
5 ampoules of Di-Serum No. III, 1500 AE,
90 gr of compound tincture of quinine,
80 gr tincture of valerian ether,
100 gr tincture of opium,
275 gr castor oil,
100 gr turpentine spirit,
30 gr potassium permanganate,
150 gr crude chloramine,
120 tablets of bicarbonate of soda, 1·0,
150 tablets of carbonate of soda, 1·0,
50 gr caustic soda,
500 gr alcohol,
10 2-ccs ampoules: novocain, 0·04, suprarenine, 0·0001,
2 flasks each containing 50 gr ether,
4 flasks each containing 50 gr chloroform,
3 atomizers each containing 15 gr ethyl chloride,
100 pastilles of sublimate, 0·5,
50 pastilles of mercury oxycyanate, 0·5,
100 tablets of Perhydrite, 1·0,
10 tablets of Rivanol, 1·0,
60 tablets of chlorina, 0·5 (Chloramine),
100 tablets of zinc sulphate, 0·25,
40 tablets of potassium iodide, 1·0,
40 tablets of potassium bromide, 1·0,
2 flasks, each containing 100 gr of solution of mastic,
40 10-ccs tubes of boric vaseline,
120 10-ccs tubes of salicylic acid vaseline, 2 per cent,
10 10-ccs tubes of alkaline ointment, for the eyes,
15 10-ccs tubes of zinc ointment,
15 10-ccs tubes of mercury ointment (grey ointment),
90 gr of arachide oil,
250 gr of balsam of Peru,
800 gr of tartaric acid alum liquor,
120 gr of glycerine,
100 gr of talc,
15 gr of silver nitrate (bars),
1 pewter probe, with 25 ccs of patent substance for facilitating its
   entry into the urethra,
1 syringe, 1·0 ccs,
1 syringe, 5·0 ccs,
24 hollow needles,
1 metal spirit lamp,
1 spoon for medicines,
1 pewter measure, 250 ccs,
500 gr of soap.

(vii) *Pannier No. 3—TSA Kasten 3 (Verbandmittel)*:—
Dressing Equipment—

115 small, or 58 large packets of dressing,
61 compressed packets, each containing 100 gr of ordinary wadding,
2 compressed packets, each containing 1,000 gr of ordinary wadding,
4 compressed packets, each containing 100 gr of absorbent wadding,
2 compressed packets, each containing 40 sq yds of gauze cloths,
3 compressed packets, each containing 40 sq yds of gauze pads,
1 compressed packet containing 40 sq yds of gauze rolls,

12 compressed packets, each containing 4 sq yds of gauze,
16 compressed packets, each containing 6 strips of gauze, 2¾ in × 5 yds; and 6 squares of gauze,
5 compressed packets, each containing 16 strips of gauze, 4 in × 10 yds,
16 compressed packets, each containing 3 strips of gauze, 2¾ in × 5 yds, and 6 squares of gauze,
10 boxes of first aid dressing, each 1 yd,
30 plaster strips 4 yds × 4¾ in,
5 pairs of rubber gloves,

(viii) *Pannier No. 4—TSA Kasten* 4 (Supplement to 2 and 3):—

Medicaments—

90 ampoules of caffein, sodium salicylate, 0·2,
80 ampoules of morphin hydrochloride, 0·02,
20 ampoules of strophantin 0·00025,
10 flasks 4-ccs of tincture of iodine,
1920 *Losantin* tablets.

Dressings—

2 boxes each containing 2 sq yds of iodoformal gauze,
2 compressed packets, each containing 40 sq yds of gauze pads,
1 compressed packet containing 40 sq yds gauze cloths,
1 compressed packet containing 40 sq yds gauze strips,
1 compressed packet containing 72 strips of gauze, 2¾ in × 5 yds,
1 compressed packet containing 16 strips of gauze, 4 in × 10 yds,
2 compressed packets containing 20 strips of gauze, 4 in × 5 yds,
1 compressed packet containing 1,000 gr absorbent wadding,
1 compressed packet containing 1,000 gr ordinary wadding,
5 suspensory bandages,
1 injection douche, with 6 canulæ of glass, and 2 of hardened rubber,
1 rubber tube, 150-cm long,
1 rubber tube, 100-cm long,
2 dressing basins, kidney-shaped,
1 funnel,
1 glass funnel,
1 reel of thread (three strands),
5 pairs of thread gloves,
4 hand towels,
1 cylindrical lamp, with 4 candles,
5 cases for transmission of throat swabs,
2 boxes for transmission of samples of excrement.

(ix) *Pannier No. 5—TSA Kasten* 5 (Anti-tetanus serum):—
280 flasks (5ccs) containing anti-tetanus serum 3,000 AE.

Einrollvorrichtung (Fracture equipment)—

16 slings 24 in × 6 in,
10 cardboard splints 40 in × 4 in,
10 cardboard splints 27½ in × 4 in,
6 yards of waterproof bandage,
10 metal wire splints, 40 in × 4 in (*Kramerschiene*),
20 metal wire splints, 32 in × 2¼ in,
2 aluminium splints, 40 in × ½-in,
2 aluminium splints, 40 in × ⅓-in,

(x) *Troop haversack or unit medical outfit:* —

1 syringe, 2 ccs,
1 syringe, 5 ccs,
1 syringe, 10 ccs,
12 hollow needles,
1 needle for bleeding, 1·8 mm in diameter,
1 needle for bleeding, 2 mm in diameter,
2 pairs of straight scissors,
2 pairs of curved scissors,
3 convex lancets,
1 pointed lancet,
1 straight lancet,
1 scraper, spoon-shaped,
1 hollow probe, with a needle for ligature (*Unterbindungsnadel*),
1 probe with olivary ends, 14·5 cm long,
1 myrtle-leaf probe (*Myrtenblattsonde*) of silver, 18 cm long,
1 dentist's probe,
1 hooked probe,
1 Volsella (*Kornzange*) curved, and 20 cm long,
1 pair of pincers (for removal of splinters) 11·5 cm long,
2 pairs of dissecting forceps,
4 pairs of surgical forceps,
1 pair of dentist's forceps,
1 pair of aural forceps,
1 wadding holder,
4 pairs of hæmostatic pincers, 12 cm long, 1·5 mm wide,
4 pairs of hæmostatic pincers, 12 cm long, and 5 mm wide,
3 pairs of hæmostatic pincers, 16 cm long,
2 flat retractors, with obtuse grips, 1·5 mm wide,
2 flat retractors, with 4 grips, 19 mm wide,
2 single " sharp " retractors for trachea,
1 " blunt " retractor for trachea,
2 double retractors, for trachea,
2 silver cannulæ, for arterial trachea,
3 soft rubber probes,
1 needle holder,
1 case of needles,
3 tubes of linen thread,
1 gag,
1 pair of forceps,
1 anæsthetics mask,
1 dropper for anæsthetics,
1 nail-file,
1 razor,
5 teeth-extractors,
100 vaccinostyles in 6 metal cases,
1 mirror,
1 nasal mirror,
1 laryngoscope,
3 ear-cloths,
1 eye-mirror, with handle,
2 lenses, diopters 13 and 20,
1 wash leather,
1 spirit lamp,
1 sterilizer for surgical instruments,

(vi) *Case of dressings carried on every motor vehicle:* —

 10 small, or 5 large packets of dressings,
 2 compressed packets, each containing 3 strips of gauze, 5 yds × 2¾ in and 6 gauze squares,
 1 compressed packet of gauze squares,
 2 compressed packets of ordinary wadding, each weighing 100 gr.
 1 triangular dressing bandage,
 20 safety pins,
 1 roll of adhesive plaster,
 2 rolls of bismuth absorbent gauze,
 1 improvized tourniquet,
 1 pair of dissecting pincers,
 1 pair of straight scissors,
 1 pair of cloth cutting scissors,
 2 flasks (4ccs) of tincture of iodine, made of artificial resin.

18. *Postal System in the Field.*

(*a*) As outlined in Section 7, " The Postal System ", the Army Postmaster-General (*Heeres Feldpostmeister—HPM*), under the QMG, maintains a register of field post locations (*Feldpostübersicht*) which gives the field post number of every unit or separate detachment of the German Armed Forces outside the Reich and the appropriate field post offices (*Feldpostämter*) to which mail is to be sent.

(*b*) On the staff of each army HQ is an army field postmaster (*Armee Feldpostmeister—APM*). There is also an APM at each army group HQ. The APM is responsible for the setting up of an army postal station (*Armee Briefstelle*) which keeps extracts from the register of field post locations and which is responsible for re-addressing mail to new locations as well as for receiving mail and forwarding it to units directly subordinated to Army HQ. The APM also looks after the field post office in the army L of C area. He sets up field post despatch offices (*Feldpostleitellen*), and field post offices (*Feldpostämter*). At Munich, which is the main sorting centre for Italy there is an army postal station, as well as a field post despatch office.

(*c*) Each division in the field has a field post office, and some independent formations also have one, bearing the same number as the ancillary services of the formation. In addition to these field post offices, and those set up in the army area and on the L of C by the APMs, there are special field post offices (*Feldpostämter · zbV*) directly under the Army Postmaster-General bearing their own particular numbers. The Army Postmaster-General allocates these at need to various sectors of the various fronts, for example, where formations are being transferred from one theatre of operations to another.

(*d*) Mail is passed from the field post despatch office, on or near the Reich frontier (at Munich) to the field post office of an army, thence to that of corps and thence to that of the division, or if it is possible, direct from despatch office to the divisional post office. Units collect mail from and send mail to the field post office of the formation. In the case of small independent units, or units of the GAF, the mail has to be collected from the field post office to the nearest division or other formation.

(*e*) Experience on the Russian front showed that these arrangements worked very well. The Germans lay great stress on the importance of the system as a predominant factor in the maintenance of morale. As long as the front was stable in Russia, trains frequently ran to within 12 miles of the front, and under these conditions, a letter from Germany took about five days to reach Army and two to three days longer to reach units. When the front was in a fluid state letters sometimes took as long as six weeks, but rarely longer. There were no special mail trains. Normally two or three wagons were attached to the end of the supply trains. There is a system of registration for important and valuable parcels and letters.

19. *Military Administration of L of C Areas.*

The military administration of Occupied Territory is closely linked with the civil and police administrations. Consideration of the German civil administration of Occupied Territory will be limited to the statement that it is subordinate to the military (and police) administrative authorities, whom it is required to assist at all times, particularly in requisitioning supplies and labour.

(a) *Duties of the Commandant of the army L of C area.*—The officer responsible for the military administration of an army L of C area is the *Kommandant des Rückwärtigen Armeegebiets**. He is responsible for military security throughout his area including the safeguarding of all buildings, premises, dumps, etc, occupied by the army's rearward services; counter espionage measures in accordance with the instructions of Army HQ (Ic/AO)†; billeting of troops and accommodation of staffs, technical and administrative units; disposal of the provost services (*Feldgendarmerie*) under his command; utilization of civilian labour (through the medium of the civil administrative authorities); care and evacuation of Ps/W and their employment as labour.

The *Kommandant des Rückwärtigen Armeegebiets* controls his area through the various *Feldkommandanturen* subordinate to him. These include *Ortskommandanturen* (Town HQ), *Stadt-Kommandanturen* (City HQ), equivalent respectively to town major's commands in small and large towns, and *Kreiskommandanturen* (Rural HQ), *i.e.*, town major's commands in rural districts.

A particularly important type of *Kommandantur* in back areas is the *Feldnachrichtenkommandantur (Field Signals Command)*.

(b) *Security and L of C troops.*—Just as the police authorities in the persons of the Senior SS and Police Commanders (*i.e.*, the opposite numbers in police administration of the Commanders of Army Group L of C areas) have at their disposal SS and police troops (*Waffen SS* units, barrack police (regiments and battalions), SS security personnel (*Sicherheitsdienst*)), so also do the Commandants of L of C areas dispose of troops for maintaining order on the army's lines of communication. They collaborate closely at all times with the police authorities. The forces under the commandant of the Army L of C area include *Feldgendarmerie;* Secret Field Police (*Geheime Feldpolizei*—the military counterpart of the *Sicherheitsdienst*), detachments of the *Heeresstreifendienst* (Army Patrol Service); the L of C troops proper, *i.e.*, the *Sicherungstruppen*. L of C troops may also include GAF field divisions and *Landeschützen* and *Wach* units attached to the GAF for guard duties.

(i) *Security troops.*—Secret Field Police (*Geheime Feldpolizei*) and *Feldgendarmerie;* their duties and responsibilities are fully described in " New Notes No. 4 " and very little further information is available.

Army Patrol Service (*Heeresstreifendienst*).—The Army Patrol Service was created in November, 1939, as an additional means for the maintenance

---

* The several army L. of C. areas are controlled by the *Befehlshaber des Rückwärtigen Heeresgebiets* (Commander of the Army Group L of C area).

† Ic=Intelligence ; AO=*Abwehroffizier* (counter-espionage officer). He is the security officer of the formation.

of discipline in the German army (including officials) but not in the SS. It does not form part of the Provost Service. Originally the army patrol service group was appointed by the Chief of Staff at Army HQ, recently however, Commandants of Army L of C Area have the same power. Appointments to the army patrol service are not permanent, officers and NCOs being relieved every 4-6 months.

Every army HQ has an army patrol service group commanded by a field officer, the *Kdeur, dGrHStrD,* who has under him six officer patrols, each consisting of commander (major or captain) and one NCO, and six NCO patrols (*Feldwebelstreifen*), each consisting of commander—a serjeant and one corporal or other NCO—a total strength for the group of 7 officers and 18 NCOs. The group also has 13 motor-cars and drivers, a senior NCO (*Hauptfeldwebel*), clerk (OR) and three orderlies. All ranks carry pistols and the patrol commander a machine carbine as well; these they are entitled to use as a last resort in enforcing orders.

The activities of army patrols extend to behaviour of troops in the streets, in taverns, places of entertainment, the scrutiny of passes and pay-books (particularly at railway stations).

Their tour of evening duty extends from 2000 to 0100 hours and from 1600 to 0100 hours on Sundays. An important part of their duties is the checking of maintenance and road-worthiness of *Wehrmacht* vehicles, supervision of traffic discipline, *i.e.*, speeding, careless driving, work tickets, etc.

Particular attention is paid to the camouflage and dispersal of parked vehicles. They also maintain a constant check on the security of the large dumps of war material.

Army patrol personnel carry a special identity card issued by the authority responsible for their appointment and when on duty wear a distinguishing lanyard similar to the old *Adjutantsabzeichen.*

Army Patrol Service personnel are also distinguished by white arm bands with one of the following inscriptions : —

Armee-Streife (Army Patrol); *Mil Befh-Streife* (Patrol of Military C-in-C). They wear drill order (*Dienstanzug*) with steel helmets.

The commander of an army patrol group has the disciplinary powers of a regimental commander, and field officers and captains i/c patrols those of a battalion commander over all ORs. Officer patrols may deal summarily with the offending OR if the CO of the unit cannot be immediately contacted by taking the offender before the *Ortskommandant*, senior garrison officer or legal official at a formation.

(ii) *Lines of communication troops.*—L of C troops are called *Sicherungstruppen. Sicherungstruppen,* in the earlier stages of the Russian campaign consisted of low category infantry divisions (*Sicherungsdivisionen*) or regiments; they were largely employed in mopping up conquered territory in the wake of the German advance. L of C troops in the occupied territories of Western Europe have hitherto been employed mainly on guard duties and have consisted of *Wach* (guard) or *Landeschützen* (local defence) units drawn from the " *Landsturm* " category, *i.e.*, composed chiefly of men over 40 years of age.

These units, it would appear, have been reorganized in France and the Low Countries into *Sicherungsregimenter* and *Sicherungsbataillone, Wachregimenter* being changed to *Sicherungsregimenter* and *Landesschützenbataillone* to *Sicherungsbataillone.*

Wach and *Landesschützen* units have hitherto worn the letters W and L (in white) on their shoulder straps, but they may now wear the S normal to *Sicherungs* units in view of this reorganization.

The peacetime establishment of a *Wachbataillon* composed of HQ and 3 companies was 15 officers, 2 officials and 470 ORs. This strength has now probably been increased (the nominal strength of the *Wachkompanie* at Tunis airfield in February, 1943 was 235 all ranks).

Landesschützenbataillone vary in strength from two to six companies. With the *Wach* units they provide the main support of the military administration on lines of communication, where they may be used to guard bridges, tunnels, dumps, parks, etc.

The German Air Force also disposes of *Landesschützen* units; these may be distinguished from army units of this type by the double numeral (Roman for the *Luftgau*, *i.e.*, Air Force Command, and Arabic for the unit) on the shoulder straps which, like the army's *Wach* and *Landesschützen* units, have white backings. These are additional to certain of the GAF field divisions employed in airfield defence and on other L of C duties.

Other German troops found on lines of communication are constructional units (*Baubataillone*); employed occasionally on guard duties, they may be distinguished from *Wach or Landesschützen* units by their brown pipings.

Lines of communication troops also include foreign (*fremdvölkische*) units raised in Russia, *e.g.*, Cossack, Georgian and Tartar levies. Georgian and Tartar units have for some time been serving in France, whilst Cossack troops have recently appeared in Yugoslavia. They wear the normal German field grey uniforms with the addition of badges or shields (in the national colours) on the sleeves. (The *Waffen SS* also include elements from all parts of Europe, and it is not unlikely that Dutch, French, Belgian and Norwegian units of the *Waffen SS* will be specially employed on lines of communication in their own countries in the event of invasion for the sake of their local knowledge. These units wear the normal *Waffen SS* uniform with the addition of national badges).

German para-military organizations to be met with on lines of communication also with a considerable proportion of foreign personnel, are the OT (Organization Todt) and (to a lesser extent) the NSKK which, organization in brigade, assists GAF transport.

(c) *Protection of roads, railways, convoys and dumps.*—The troops responsible for escorting transport trains, guarding bridges, dumps, MT parks and general guard duties on lines of communication are mainly drawn from *Landesschützen* units, whether organized as *Wachregimenter, Landesschützenbataillone* or *Transportbegleitregimenter* (railway convoy escort regiments).

(i) *Protection of Roads and Road Convoys.*—Supply columns are responsible at all times for their own safety. As a rule unescorted, the convoy is in fact expected to fight its way out of an ambush and to adopt a defensive role only when attacked by an enemy greatly superior in numbers and firepower; in such cases L of C troops may be called on to extricate the column.

Especially vulnerable points, *e.g.*, bridges, defiles on the supply route will usually be guarded by *Landesschützen* and/or AA detachments.

Examples of bridge defences which may be quoted are the important bridge over the DORDOGNE, NE of BORDEAUX which is blocked by heavy chains at night, with MG posts at either end of the bridge, and the bridges in the vicinity of BORDEAUX and OSTENDE which are defended by weapon pits manned by 10-20 men.

(ii) *Protection of railway and rail convoys.—Convoys.—*Rail convoys to the eastern front are taken care of by *Transport-Begleitregimenter* with HQ at Königsberg, Posen, Breslau and Vienna. They consist of *Landes-schützen* personnel from whom the escort parties are detailed. Their duty is to protect military equipment and rations transports by rail (and water) from attack, theft and fire.

Inside Germany escort detachments, usually consisting of an officer or NCO in charge and 3 ORs are detailed by the particular *Wehrkreis* (Military District) authorities concerned.

Outside Germany, *i.e.*, in Occupied Territory, the escort parties are detailed by the appropriate branch of the *Wehrmacht* (Army, Navy and Air Force) or provided by the Transport Escort Regiments (*Transport-Begleitregimenter*). It is to be noted that the *Organization Todt* and *Reichs-arbeitsdienst* have their own special escort detachments.

Trains out of Germany requiring escorts are*:—

Wehrmacht supply and equipment trains; POL and tanker trains, mail trains and coal trains.

Trains into Germany provided with escorts are†:—

Tanker trains; P/W convoys; trains carrying equipment for repair or expended ammunition (shell cases).

*Strength of Escort.—*This varies according to the type of trains as follows:—

	Officers or NCOs	ORs
Rations train	1	6
Coal, POL or MT trains ...	1	4
All other trains	1	3

In the case of trains of 30 or more trucks the commander will be an officer or senior NCO, and an experienced NCO (serjeant or corporal) when the train consists of less than 30 trucks.

*Documents.—*The escort commander carries on him the following documents:—identity papers, job order, log book, movement order, way bill, receipt and acceptance forms, travelling warrants for the return journey.

*Armament of escort parties.—*Officer or NCO in charge: pistol and 60 cartridges or machine carbines.

ORs: rifles and 40 cartridges apiece.
In notoriously dangerous areas: MGs machine carbines and hand grenades.

(iii) *Duties of Escort Detachments.—*According to instructions for transport escort detachments of 1.9.42, the duties and rights of escort detachments are as follows:—

*Duties during transportation.—*The train must be continually guarded directly the escort takes over. The transport commander will immediately draw up the guard duty roster and enter it in the transport log books. A look-out will be kept on both sides of the train. Seals, locks, labels must

---

* Also craft carrying *Wehrmacht* equipment on inland waterways.
† Also tanker barges on inland waterways.

be checked frequently, as well as freight in open trucks. Irregularities are to be reported to the transport officer who will decide on the measures to be taken.

The transport escort detachment must not leave the train and should not be given any duties other than guard duties.

If the train stops in the day time in the open country the sentries may only descend from the train on the transport commander's orders and when so agreed to by the train guard. They must not relax their watchfulness. Should the train stop on a bend they should take up positions on the outer arc.

At night, particularly in localities where thefts have been found to occur, the necessary safeguards—especially at stops—should be taken by distributing the men throughout the length of the train. Lights should be put out.

AA defence measures on railways are the responsibility of the competent railway units. Escort detachments should, however, take part in the AA defence of material entrusted to their charge in accordance with the directions of the competent AA officer.

To this effect the escort commanders should on the occasion of a prolonged halt report to the senior AA officer and designate trucks carrying goods especially dangerous in the event of aircraft attack (ammunition, fuel, fodder, etc), so that the senior AA officer may take the necessary steps, *e.g.*, shunt into sidings or space out trucks with dangerous freights.

Soldiers or civilians are categorically forbidden to board the train. Requests on the part of civilians (risk of espionage) or verbal demands emanating from military authorities are to be refused. If, however, the detachment is forced to accept such demands it will insist on a written order and the necessary particulars (rank, name, Field Post No) of the authority giving the order; these will be entered in the transport log book. This instruction does not apply to personnel of transport units.

Rules for keeping the transport log book.—The escort commander will enter in the log book:—

the number of the journey.
the number and type of trucks,
contents,
place and date of taking over,
condition of transport escort vehicle on taking over,
hour of departure,
all transport units met at intermediate stations,
occurrences *en route* such as delays (reasons), thefts (including precise description), measures taken, attacks, acts of sabotage.

Inspection of escort detachments.—Transport inspection officers provided with identity cards bearing their photographs will be appointed by units responsible for escorting transports for the purpose of inspecting escort detachments. On duty they will wear a white arm-band bearing the inscription "*Transport-Kontrolloffizier*" and the stamp of their unit.

(iv) *Railway Troops.*—*Railway Construction Units.*—There are special troops available for the construction and maintenance of railways and are subordinate ultimately to the Director-General of Transportation and comprise:—

Befehlshaber der Eisenbahneinheiten (GOC railway units).
Gruppen-Kdr der Eisenbahneinheiten (Sector commander of railway units).
Kdr der Eisenbahneinheiten (Commander of railway units).
Eisenbahntruppen (Railway troops).

Eisenbahntruppen comprise:—

Engineers—

Eisb Pi Oberbaustab (Railway Engineer Higher Construction Staff).
Eisb Pi Park (Railway Engineer Park).
Eisb Pi Stab zbV (Railway Engineer Special Staff).
Eisb Pi Rgt (Railway Engineer Rgt).
Eisb Pi Btl. (Railway Engineer Bn).
Eisb Pi Kp (Railway Engineer Coy).
Eisb Pi Werkstatt Abt (Railway Engineer Workshop Bn).

Operating Units—

Eisb Fernsprech Kp (Railway Telephone Coy).
Eisb Funk Kp (Railway Wireless Coy).
Eisb Stellwerks Kp (Railway Signals Coy).
Eisb Betriebs Kp (Railway Operating Coy).
Eisb Peilerbau Kp (Railway Pier Construction Coy).
Eisb Wasserstrassen Kp (Railway Canal Coy).

Construction Units—

Eisb Brückenbau Btl (Railway Bridge Building Bn).
Eisb Bau Btl (Railway Construction Bn).
Eisb Bau Kp (Railway Construction Coy).
Feldbahn Kp (Field Rlwy Construction Coy).

Railway Signal Units.—Though the railways have their own systems of communications (*Bahneigene Nachrichtenmittel*) it is emphasized that these telephone and telegraph facilities are to be used by the *Wehrmacht* only in cases of necessity. The *Wehrmacht* has at its disposal special signals troops, of which the following have been identified:—

Eisb Nachrichten Rgt zbV (Special Railway Signals Rgt).
Eisb Nachrichten Abt zbV (Special Railway Signals Bn).

(v) *Organization in the Field.*—The Eastern Front and the Balkans present special problems in railway organization. Here, where railways have to be repaired or constructed, there is naturally a considerable concentration of railway engineer and construction units.

To administer field railways repaired or constructed by railway troops, the *OKW* sets up *Feldeisenbahn Kommandos*, organizations which may be roughly equated to the Transport *Kommandanturen* of Germany and the occupied countries of Europe. (*See* Part I Section 10 (*a*).)

For the maintenance of the services of field railways there exist *Feldeisenbahnbetriebs-Abteilungen,* which provide personnel to run a local railway system. They may be roughly equated to the Area Operating Offices of Germany and the occupied countries. These have sub-divisions for mechanical repair and maintenance (*Feldeisenbahnmaschinen-Abteilungen* and *FE Werkstattabteilungen*) and for the maintenance of railway canals (*Feldwasserstrassenabteilungen*).

The whole of the local administration of a field railway system is under the command of a Transport Commissioner (*Bevollmächtigter Transport Offizier*) at Army Group or Army HQ.

(vi) *Protection of track, bridges and tunnels.*—These notes apply principally to Russia. In regard to the protection of the track itself the number and strength of guards and sentry posts will depend on the number of bridges, tunnels, etc, to be guarded and on the nature of the terrain. Under average conditions a battalion is necessary per 100 kilometres of track, of which two men are required per kilometre for local protection, with the remainder on patrol duty or acting as reserves.

Each company takes over a given section, piquets of two N.C.Os. and 10 men being entrusted with the protection of specified points (the N.C.Os. relieving one another, with nine men for sentry duty and reliefs and one man in reserve for special duties).

Heavy weapons are distributed among the various sub-units.

Battalion and company commanders' headquarters are usually located with the reserves in the centre of each section. Piquets and reserves occupy strong points with a good field of fire and protected by barbed wire. In guarding railways a locomotive coupled to a truck is held ready at the strong-points garrisoned by the reserves.

Vital points such as bridges are guarded by a single sentry by day and by double sentries at night. In the case of long bridges or tunnels, sentries are posted at either end, while covering parties may be employed too, where dead ground conceals the approaches. Extra sentries may be posted below the bridges at night time (at the bridge piers).

Energetic patrolling is carried out by day on both sides of the railway— sometimes with cyclist patrols. Foot patrols make contact with one another during the night by moving along the permanent way or keeping to the roadway.

Special attention is given to testing fishplates, bolts and rail joints and a good look-out is kept for explosives secured to the inner flanges of rails and for any disturbances of the ballast such as would indicate the laying of mines.

Powered trolleys are at times employed for purpose of inspection or for supply posts. An armoured trolley is sometimes sent ahead of transport trains instead of a pilot engine.

If sufficient troops are available, patrols are sent off deep into the country on either side of the railway to search villages and question their inhabitants. (This practice appears to have arisen as a result of the order given to partisans not to withdraw more than 20 kms from the main lines of communication). Crops or woods adjacent to railways and capable of affording cover to guerillas are often burnt or cut down to a width of 200 yards or so on either side of the line. Farms adjacent to the railway may for the same reason be evacuated or burnt down. The inhabitants of villages adjacent to the railways are made responsible for safeguarding the line of their neighbour-hood.

The same practice is followed in France. Thus at the Chenevieres tunnel on the Champigny-Chenevieres-Suey line two armed Frenchmen are employed day and night in addition to a German sentry at the southern exit to the tunnel (doubled at night), the bridge at Champigny-la-Varenne being guarded by two sentries day and night.

(vii) *Protection of dumps.*—The strength laid down for the guard of an army ammunition dump is 20 all ranks, but reports vary widely as to the strengths used in practice. *See* under Part II, section 13, paragraphs (*d*) and (*e*) for details of the protection of ammunition dumps.

(*d*) *Transport Columns.*—(i) *March orders.*—March orders will usually include the information concerning:—

the enemy (*e.g.* possibility of air attack or attack by parachute or airlanding troops, tanks or attacks from the flank);

time and place of departure, route, telephone points, halts, maximum speed of leading vehicle (MT columns) and possibly the interval between vehicles;

places at which the column can obtain supplies (rations, ammunition) and medical attention, collect mail, and in the case of MT columns fill up with petrol and have break-down repaired.

Special orders are issued regarding protection on the march and the position of the commander of the supply column battalion and of the unit (column) commander. Duties in the column will be divided into march, and battle duties and every man must know what to do without special orders being given in the event of surprise attack.

Orders on the march are usually given by signals passed from vehicle to vehicle—otherwise by orderly (motor-cyclist or mounted man).

(ii) *Traffic control and march discipline.*—Move-off is preceded by the command "*Stillgesessen*" ("Still!") and the men may not smoke, talk, sing or eat before the signal "*Rührt Euch*" is given (the driver in any case may not smoke while at the wheel). Steel helmets will only be removed when so ordered.

The speed of MT columns varies according to the road conditions (gradients, curves), weather, time (day or night) and conditions of the vehicles. The leading vehicle is given a maximum speed which it must not exceed. The column is never told to maintain average speed. In working out an average speed, the formula—interval in metres=speed in hour/km is the best guide. The important thing is to keep the column moving as a coherent unit. As a rule every driver goes as fast as his brakes permit. Every driver must keep the vehicle in front and behind in sight. Risk of going astray at road forks and crossings, especially in woods and villages, is prevented by posting road points (motor-cyclists). Drivers unable to keep up drop back to the rear and join a succeeding column on completing repairs, rejoining their column at the next halt. In Russia the speed of the convoy was always the maximum possible. Averages were low, however, usually about 15 mph being maintained.

The speed of HT columns will also depend on the loading of the vehicles. For HT columns it is important to maintain a uniform rate of march and to retain the intervals between columns in order to avoid blocks.

The only vehicles which are permitted to use the road in the opposite direction in the case of one-way roads are motor-cycles and staff cars.

On other roads columns are required to keep well into the right side of the road to enable traffic in the opposite direction to proceed unhindered and to facilitate overtaking. An MT column may only overtake a HT column after obtaining the HT column commander's consent, when room must be made at once for the overtaking column. Traffic moving to the front always takes precedence especially on narrow roads.

Passage through built-up areas or level crossings is taken care of by motor-cyclists or mounted men detailed for point duties, unless traffic control is taken over by the Provost Service.

Vehicles are inspected before and on completion of the march, particular attention being given to topping up with fuel, oil and water, tyre pressure, steering and brakes in the case of MT and to wheels, axles, brakes, steering, saddlery, traces and harness for horse drawn transport.

Night marches are made by MT columns either with head lamps full on or dimmed; with the head lamps of the leading vehicles on but dimmed (the head lamps of the other vehicles being switched off) and with dimmed tail lights; or without lights. This ruling applies to all vehicles including

(16779)   M the column commander and orderlies' motor-cycles. The speed of the column and the intervals between vehicles are correspondingly reduced, road points being stationed ahead at dangerous places on the road at road crossings. Front and rear vehicles in Russia used their lights. Vehicles in between had a tail light or an axle light.

In fog the leading vehicles use their fog lamps; scouts are sent ahead in thick fog.

(iii) *Reconnaissance and protection on the march.*—The strength and armament of supply troops permit only of the simplest measures of protection, the guarding of the actual supply routes and installations being the responsibility of higher authority.

Before moving, the column commander appoints a second-in-command, details his vehicle sections (platoons in the case of HT columns), the defence detachments (*Schützentrupp*), aircraft spotter (with relief), gas sentry.

In MT columns motor-cyclists ride ahead (keeping in sight of the column) or the leading lorry may act as a point (advanced guard). HT supply columns employ mounted men or cyclists for this purpose; two or three mounted men usually constituting a point; its distance from the unit depends on road visibility. Connecting files (mounted men or cyclists) maintain touch with the point. A rear point (rear guard) of two or three mounted men may also be employed. The column commander retains a few mounted men for close reconnaissance. In Russia depending upon the area in which the column operated, protection often consisted of MG's mounted on the leading and rear vehicles.

When the local population is hostile or flanking attacks are to be expected, several columns may be made up into march units (*Marschstaffeln*) under the control of a joint commander.

Particular attention is given to aircraft spotting and warning of air attack, one or more spotters (in pairs) on open vehicles being allotted.

The vehicle leading the column as well as the vehicle bringing up the rear are the two vehicles usually to be equipped with AA MG's.

Ground attack.—Supply units are frequently involved in fighting (as in Russia) as a result of surprise attacks combined with obstacle-laying. If a MT column cannot escape by taking advantage of the speed of its vehicles or in the case of a HT column, the cross country abilities of the horse-drawn vehicle cannot be utilized, the enemy must be attacked without delay. Any orders which may be necessary are given by signal, though the reaction of the column to attack should be automatic and as follows:—

Vehicles take cover without loss of time in folds in the ground, among trees on either side of the road (MT being careful to keep to firm ground whilst HT can take to the surrounding country). MT drivers remain seated in their lorries. Horses are protected as far as possible by the body of the wagon.

The section leaders quickly assemble the men detailed for defence.

The remainder take cover and open independent fire on the enemy after making contact with the column commander.

The defence detachment (*Schützentrupp*) then attacks, provided the enemy is not vastly superior in strength or armament in which case its role is purely defensive and limited to protecting the column till help arrives or the column can escape.

If impending attack by AFVs is reported in time, use is made of natural obstacles to block the road, otherwise the road may be blocked by slewing vehicles across it. Drivers and mates take cover off the road in defence of the lorries. HT can take to the country on either side of the road and fight back from widely dispersed points. Fire is concentrated on the vision slits of the AFVs.

Parts of road under artillery fire are taken at increased speed by small groups under the personal supervision of the column commander during intervals in shelling.

Air attack.—MT columns continue to move whether attacked by day or by night. If forced to halt vehicles must be placed under cover and be well dispersed, drivers, etc, taking cover near by. If the column is equipped with MGs mounted on vehicles the latter must be kept ready for action throughout the march, fire being opened automatically as soon as the aircraft comes within effective range (extreme range 1,000 yards).

HT columns halt on being attacked by aircraft; the drivers apply their brakes and remain seated (drivers' mates take cover); fire is opened by MGs automatically against low-level attacks. Rifle fire (in groups of 20 rifles) is effective against aircraft at any range below 500 yards. At night HT columns halt only if parachute flares are dropped and when ordered to do so by their commanders. If horse transport cannot leave the road the effects of air attack can be reduced by dispersal in depth, *i.e.*, by doubling the interval between vehicles and sections of vehicles. In other cases HT units may deploy on either side of the road; on the order or signal " Deploy " (*Entfaltung*) being given the unit disperses by section at minimum intervals of 50 yards under the section commanders. High level attacks are to be expected at defiles for whose defence AA batteries will be provided.

Gas Attack.—MT can pass through stretches contaminated by gas if duly warned and if respirators are worn. It will be necessary for H.T. to by-pass such stretches; if small, however, they can be decontaminated or bridged. Otherwise respirators must be worn and leg bindings and gas masks fitted to animals.

(iv) *Protection when halted.*—Simple road blocks may be employed to protect transport columns at halts, in billets or at supply points against surprise attack by AFVs. The main supply (through) route may only be blocked if ordered by higher authority.

Road blocks may take the form of concertina wire; strong wire cable drawn obliquely across the road at radiator height; felled trees; local or army vehicles drawn across the road. HT vehicles should be joined together by their shafts, wheels removed and body or wagon filled with sand, stones, etc.

The advantage of concertina wire is that it can be quickly put in place and removed to allow passage of traffic as can vehicles also. The latter have, however, the disadvantage of being visible at some distance and of being easily thrust aside by AFVs. In Russia convoys, when halted, were responsible for all round local protection and one out of every three of the drivers were usually responsible for staying with the vehicles at all times.

(v) *Halts.*—Long halts are only given if the convoy's arrival at its destination in time will not be affected and then only when the greater part of the march has been accomplished.

MT vehicles do not close up on halting unless specially ordered. Vehicles will be halted under cover with an interval of 20 yards between vehicles. Rifles are either left in the vehicle or taken out and piled, depending on the circumstances.

Short halts are made every two hours.

Halting places are guarded by sentries and aircraft spotters equipped with MGs against ground or air attack.

(vi) *Billets.*—Supply units may be accommodated in billets, close billets (*Ortsbiwak*) or bivouacs, the senior supply officer acting as *Ortskommandant,* if the place has not already been allotted a town-major (*Ortskommandant*). Billets are prepared by the billeting NCO (*Quartiermacher*), the duties of the *Ortskommandant* being restricted to measures connected with the safety of the locality (guards, inlying and outlying picquets, traffic control, security (counter-espionage and supervision of local population), street patrols, fire-fighting, water supply, and the issue of regulations regarding alerts, stand-to and camp duties.

Billets are preferably located in houses or buildings close to one another or in large farms, as this enables the duties of inlying and outlying picquets to be combined and reduces the chances of attack by hostile elements in the civil population.

Infected houses are provided with warning signs.

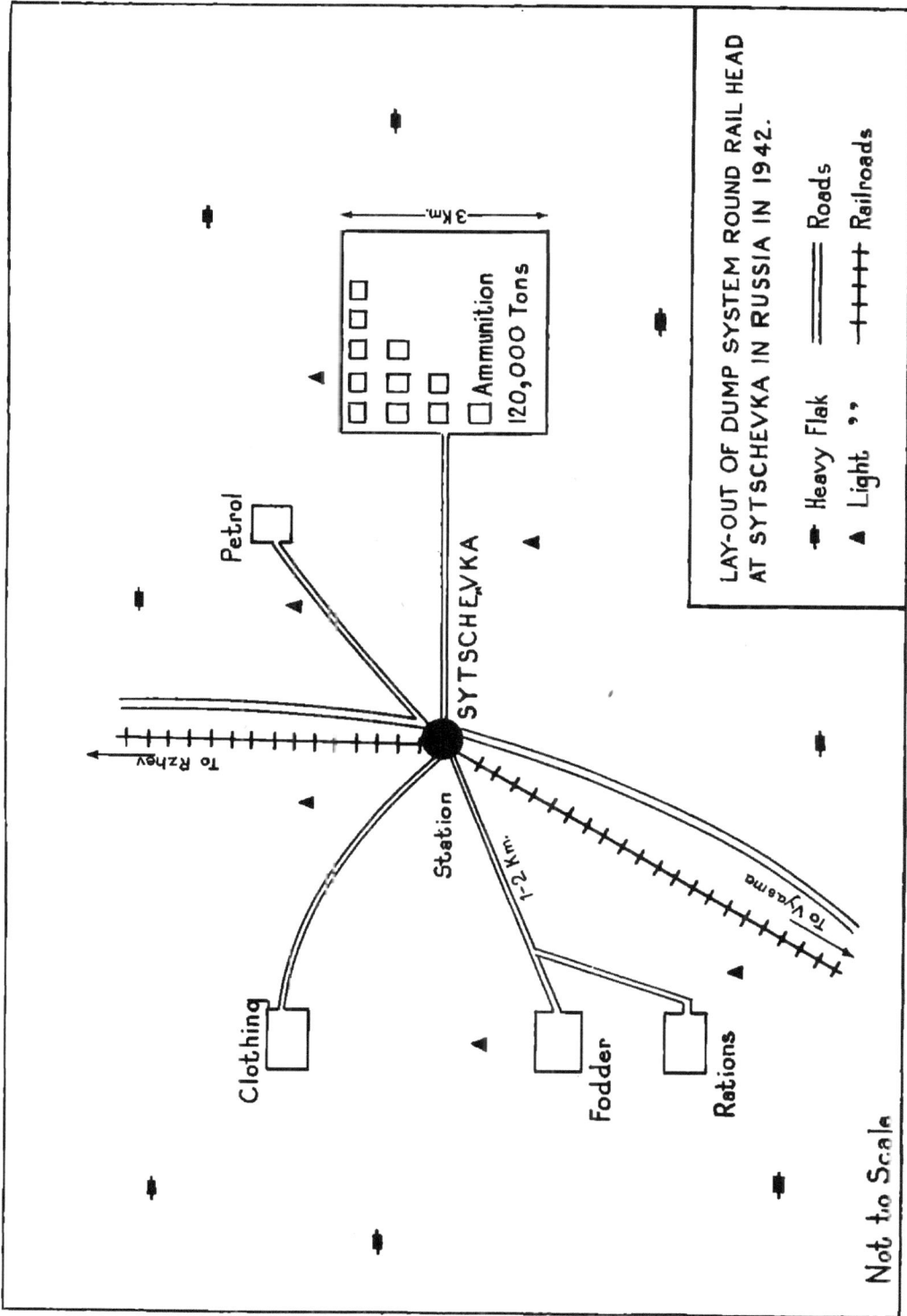

LAY-OUT OF DUMP SYSTEM ROUND RAIL HEAD
AT SYTSCHEVKA IN RUSSIA IN 1942.

Heavy Flak
Light "
Roads
Railroads

Ammunition
120,000 Tons

3 Km.

Petrol

SYTSCHEVKA

To Rzhev

Station

1-2 Km.

To Vyasma

Clothing

Fodder

Rations

Not to Scale

AMMUNITION DUMP AT BENGHAZI

Ammunition and explosives laid out in plantations, in some cases covered with nets.
An example of camouflage by following the pattern.

The boxes of munitions are placed close to the walls, as well as being dispersed around.

Bomb Dump at Benghazi

Brick
Concrete.

ENTRANCE AND UNLOADING PLATFORM

Blast Wall.

SLOPING REVET WALLS AND LIGHT RAILWAY LINE

AMMUNITION STACKS IN WOODS BEHIND WESTWALL

Mercedes-Benz heavy 10-ton lorry.

Hansa-Lloyd heavy 4·5—5-ton lorry.

Example of layout of ammunition issue point (*Munitions Ausgabestelle*)

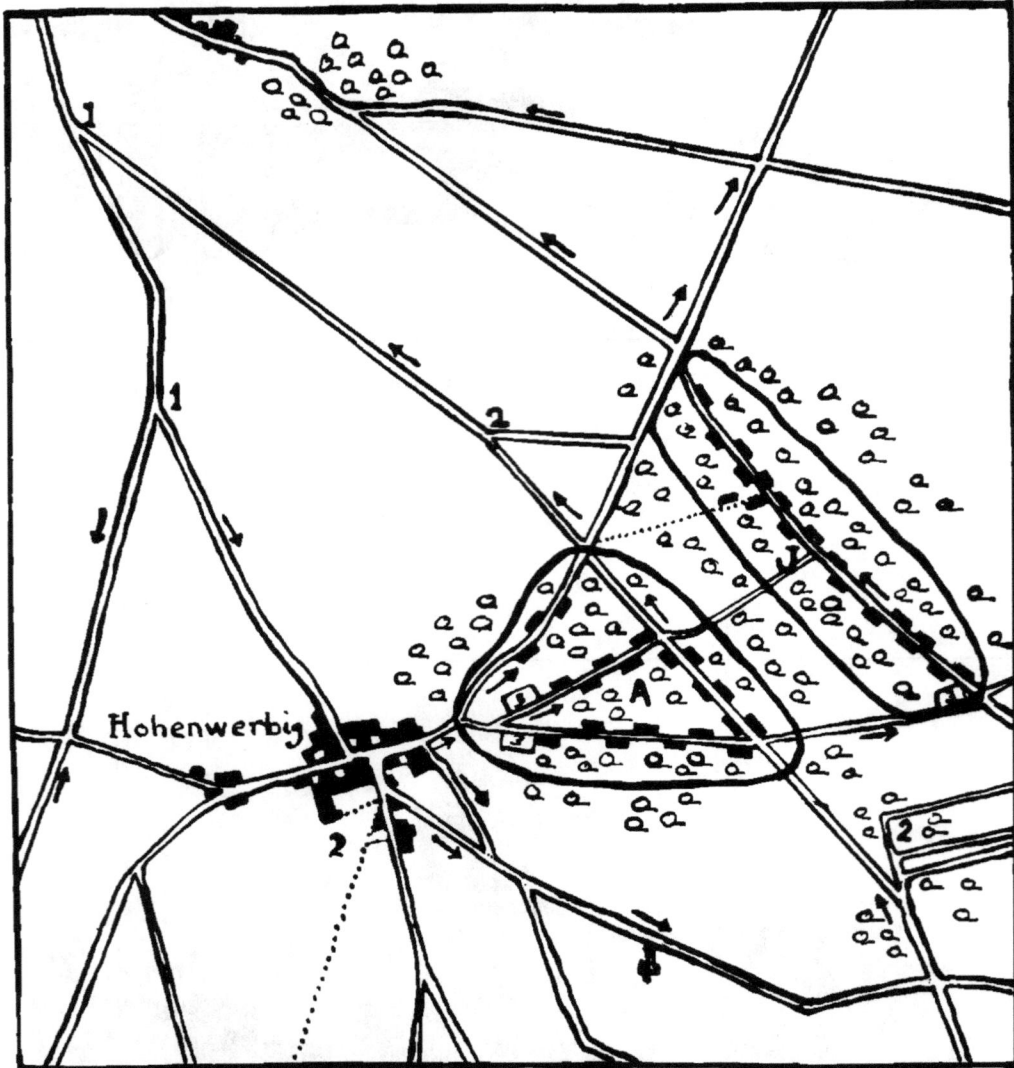

Hohenwerbig

KEY TO EXAMPLE OF AMMUNITION ISSUE POINT

1. T.C. Posts.
2. A.A. Warning Posts (A.A.M.G.).
3. Delivery point for empties and unserviceable ammunition.
A. Artillery ammunition.
J. Infantry ammunition.

Stacking of 15 cm Shells in Baskets

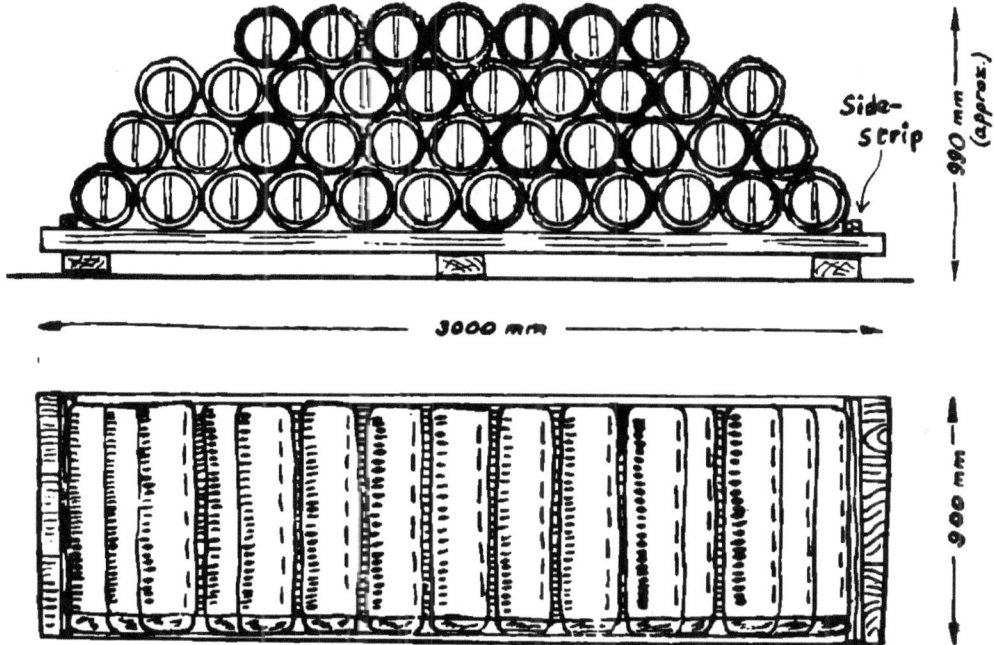

KEY TO DIAGRAM OF STACKING OF 15 CM SHELLS IN BASKETS

Shells of **up** to 10·5 cm. calibre in baskets may be stacked in 6–7 layers.

,,	,,	15 cm	,,	,,	,,	,,	4–5 ,,
,,	over 15 cm		,,	,,	,,	,,	2–3 ,,

If necessary the stacks may be 1–2 **layers** higher.
The wooden side strips must not be omitted.

Example of Layout of a Rations Supply Point (*Verpflegungs Ausgabestelle*)

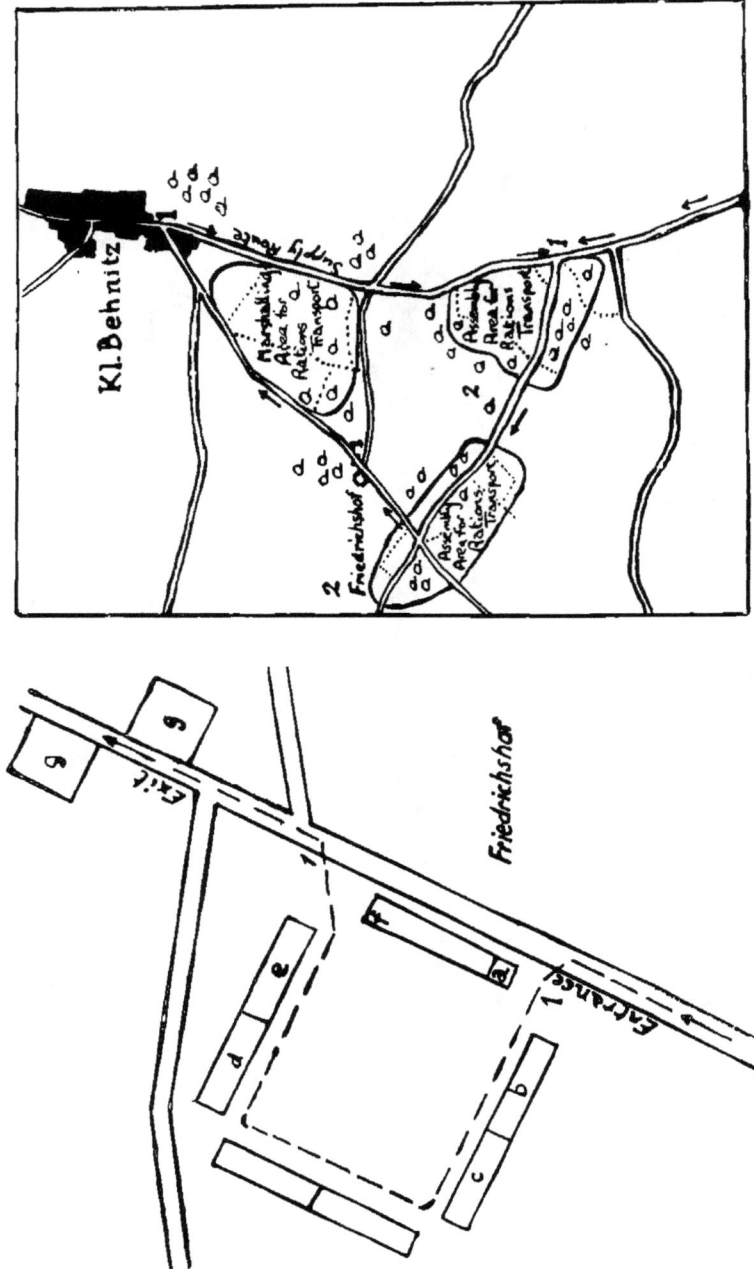

Kl.Behnitz

Friedrichshof

KEY TO EXAMPLE OF LAYOUT OF A SUPPLY POINT

a. Indent office.
b. Issue of oats.
c. Issue of bread.
d. Issue of vegetables and groceries.

e. Issue of meat.
f. Field post, receipts and deliveries.
g. Issue of forage.

1. T.C. posts.
2. A.A. warning posts (A.A.M.G.).

207

Example of Layout of a Depot for P.O.L. and M.T. Supplies, only for standard containers.
(*Betriebsstofflager, nur bei Einheitsbehältern*)

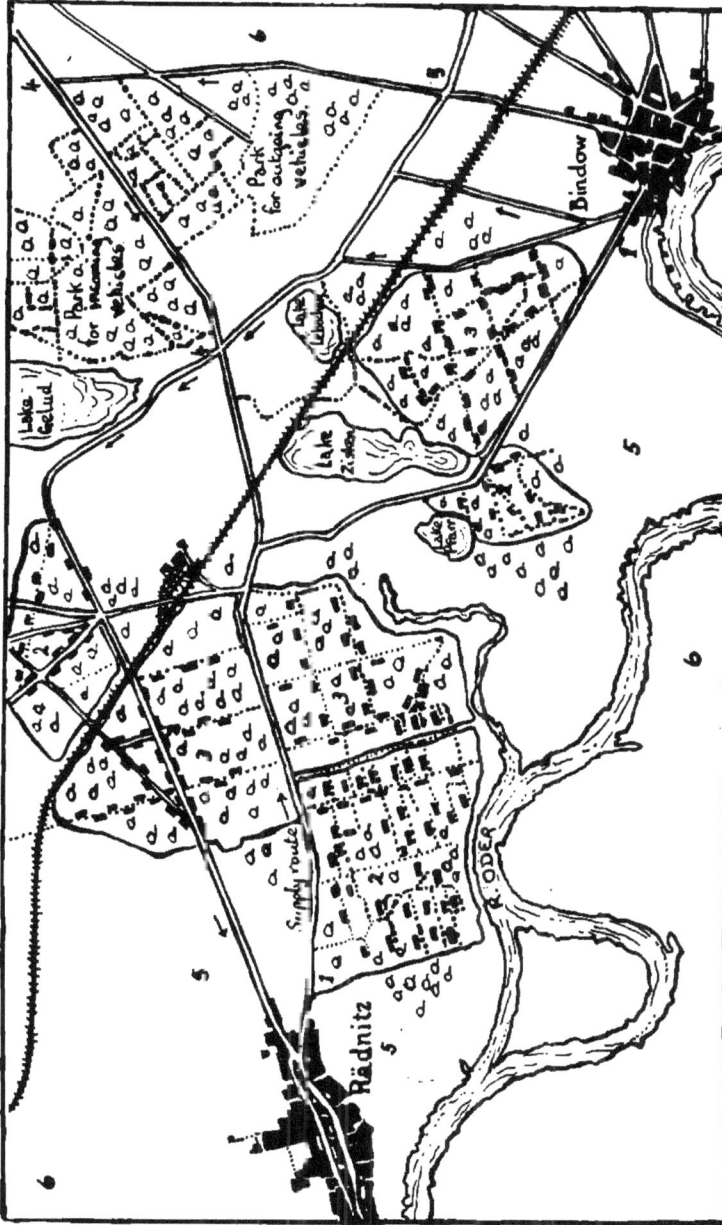

KEY TO EXAMPLE OF LAYOUT OF A DEPOT FOR P.O.L. AND M.T. SUPPLIES

1. Reception office and dump for oil, cotton waste, tyres, spare parts, etc.
2. Dump for petrol.
3. Dump for Diesel fuel.
4. T.C. posts.
5. A.A. warning posts.
6. A.A.M.G. posts.

Specimen Layout of a Field Dressing Station. (*Hauptverbandplatz*)

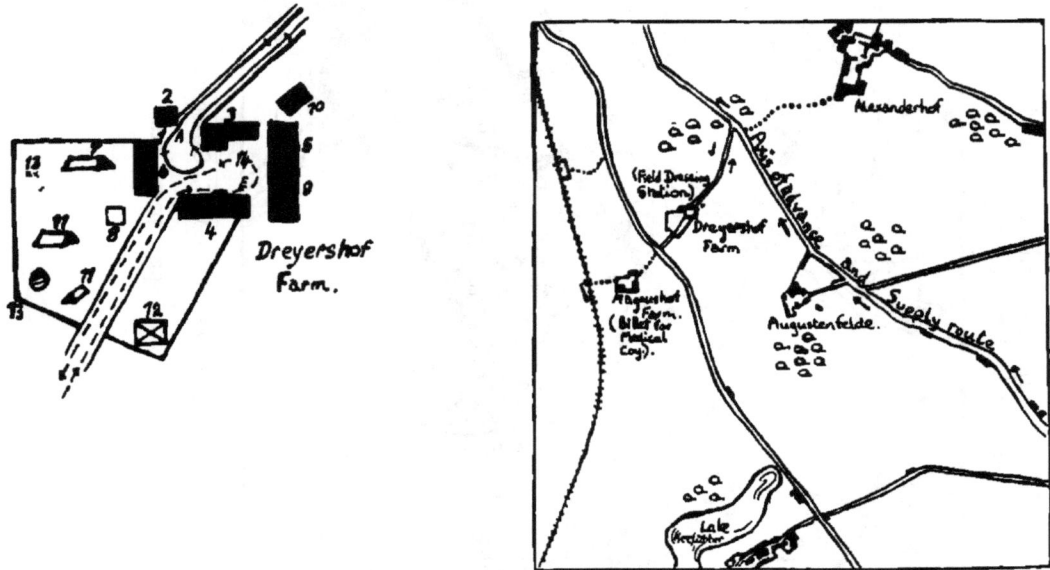

KEY TO DIAGRAM OF FIELD DRESSING STATION

1. Unloading place A.
2. Administrative building, reception and dressing station.
3. Farmhouse; furnished as an operating theatre, dispensary, office—(telephone) also some of the personnel are billeted here.
4. Barn furnished as ward, for looking after wounded capable of being moved.
5. Machine outhouse; laid out as 4.
6. Barn; section for those severely wounded not able to be transported.
7. Tent; for personnel of medical coy.
8. Cookhouse.
9. Animal stall; stall for horses.
10. Open shed; shelter for vehicles.
11. Tent for gas cases (as many tents as required).
12. Tent for dead.
13. Lavatories.
14. Route; to and from field hospital or C.C.S. Loading place E.

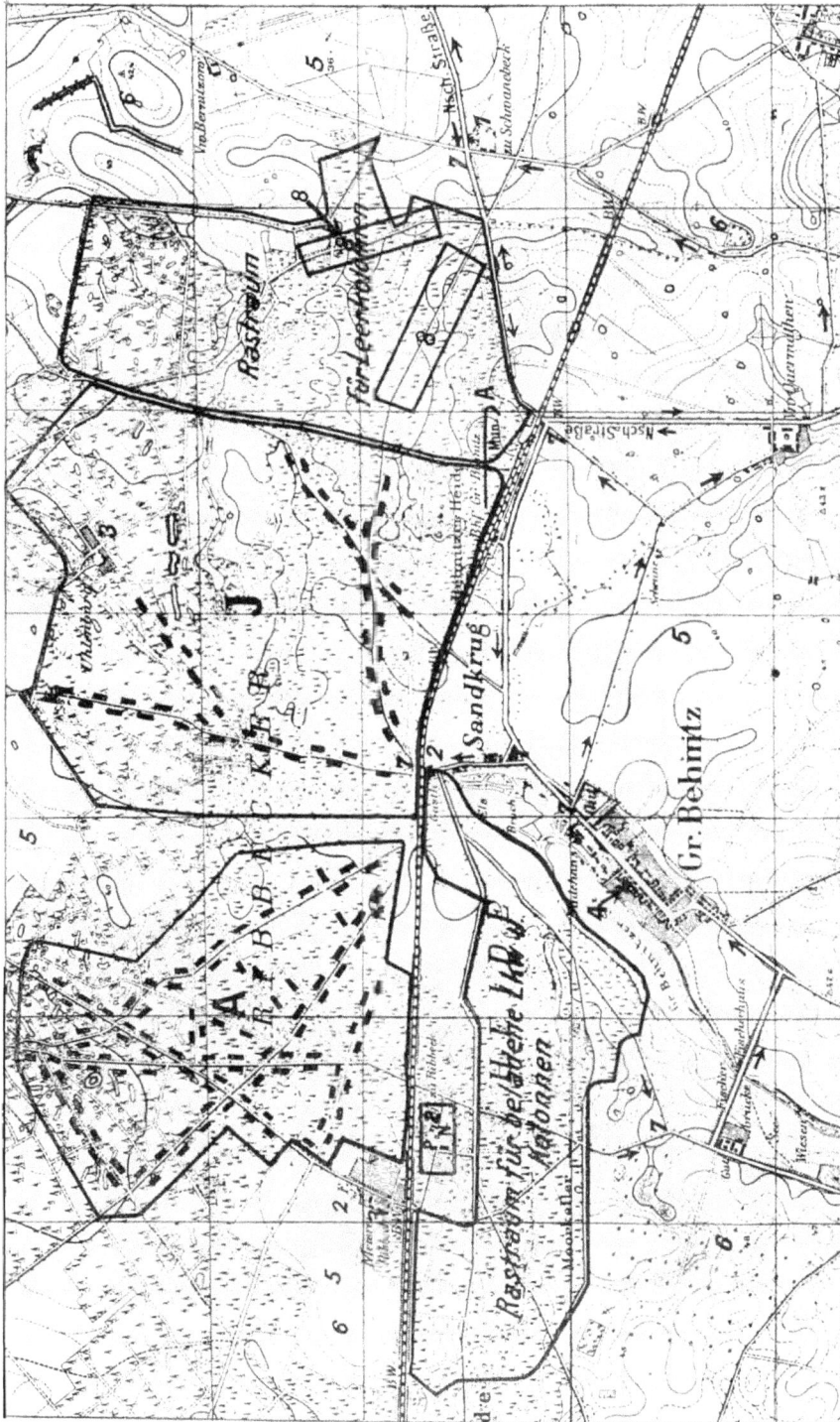

209

Example of Layout of Army Amn Dump
Beispiel für Anlage eines Armee Munitionslagers

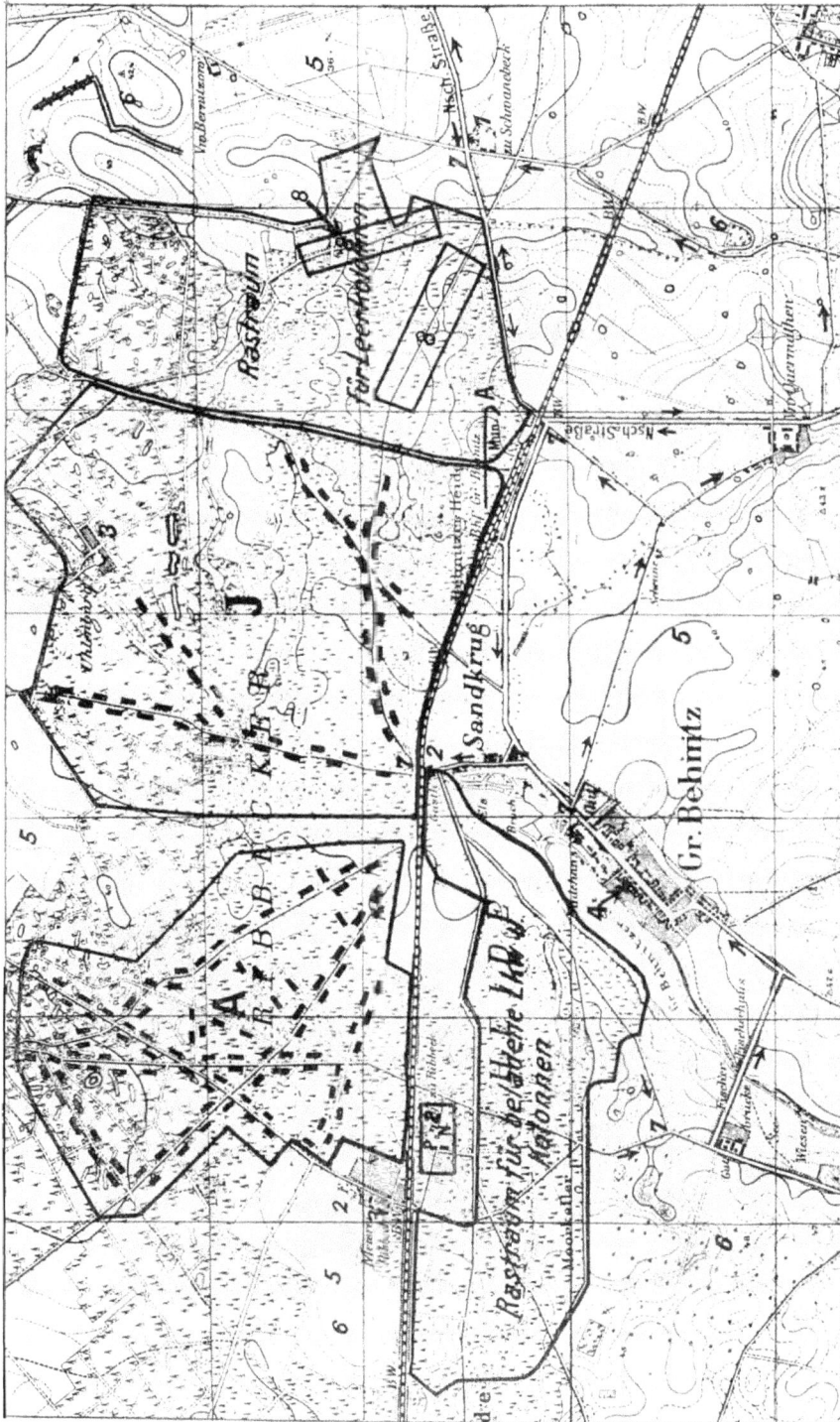

Anlage 13

Anmerkung :

1 = Anmeldung zum Mun. Empfang
2 = Verwaltung der einzelnen Lager
3 = Unterkunft der Lagerwachen
4 = Unterkunft der Nachsch. Kp
5 = Luftschutzwarndienst
6 = Flak (Flieger M.G.)
7 = Verkehrsregelungsposten

8 = Abgabestelle für beschossene
   Mun. Teile, Leermaterial
   u. unbrauchb. Mun.
J = Inf. Mun. Lager.
A = Art.
P = Lager f. Nahk," Spreng. u. Zmtl.

N = „   „   L.u.S. Mun.

Reception office for incoming amn.
Dump offices.
Billets for camp guard.
Billets for sup coy.
A.A. warning posts.
A.A.M.G. warning posts.
T.C. posts.

Delivery point for empties
5 u/s amn.

Inf amn dump.
Arty amn dump.
Dump for charges, explosives
  and igniters.
Dump for pyrotechnic amn.

(16770)

Filling standard petrol cans at a Petrol Point.

PETROL DUMP AT BENGHAZI

Stacked barrels (2–3 high).

Trenched barrels.

MEDIUM PETROL TANKER

Wheel base	...	14 ft. 9 ins.	Weight (laden)	...	8 tons 6 cwts.
Length	...	22 ft. 1 in.	Clearance	...	8 ins.
Width	...	7 ft. 4 ins.	Water f rding	...	19½ ins.
Height	...	8 ft. 6 ins.	Turning radius	...	20 yards.
			Petrol engine.		

HEAVY PETROL TANKER

Wheel base	...	17 ft.	Capacity	...	1820 gallons
Length	...	27 ft. 10 ins.	Hill climbing	...	15°
Width	...	8 ft. 2 ins.	Water fording	...	17½ ins.
Height	...	8 ft. 6 ins.	Turning radius	...	23 yards

Front wheel steering.   Petrol engine.

Beispiel für Anlage einer Betr. Stoff Ausgabe-Stelle

(*für Einheitsbehälter*)

Example of Layout for P.O.L. and M.T. Sups. Issue Point (only for standard containers)

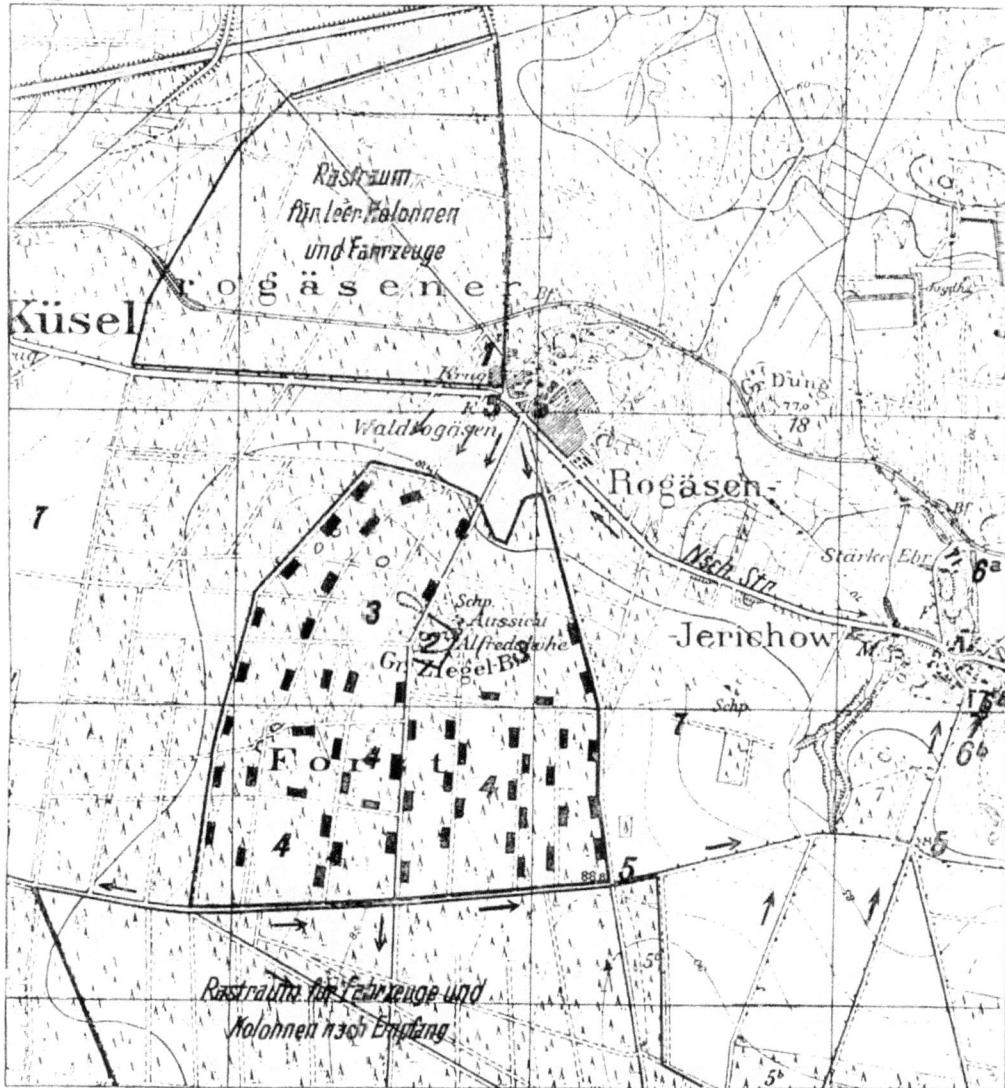

Anmerkung :

1	*Leiter der Ausgabestelle-Anmeldung zum Empfang.*	O.C. Issue Pt. and Reception.
2	*Lager für Öl, Putzwolle, Werg, Bereifung, Ersatzteile usw.*	Dumps for oil, cotton waste, oakum, tyres, spare parts, etc.
3	*Lager für Vergaserkraftstoffe.*	Petrol Dump.
4	*Lage für Dieselkraftstoffe.*	Diesel Oil Dump.
5	*Verkehrsregelungsposten.*	T.C. Posts.
6a	*Werkstattkompanie-Kw. Werkstattzüge (-zug.).*	Wksp Coy—M.T. Repair Pts. (or Pt).
6b	*Werkstattkompanie-Waffenmeisterei.*	Wksp Coy—Artificer.
7	*Luftschutzwarndienst (oder Fl. Abw. MG).*	A.A. Warning Posts (or A.A.M.G. Posts).

Beispiel für Einrichtung eines Armee-Verpflegungslagers
Example of Layout of an Army Supply Depot

Erläuterung :
Legend

1 = 4 Lagerhallen mit Gleisanschluss :
  1. *Halle : Brot und Mehl.*
  2.   ,,   *Hafer.*
  3.   ,,   *Rauchfutter.*
  4.   ,,   *Kolonialwaren, Gemüse und Fleisch (Dauerwaren).*
2 = Schlachthof : Lagerraum für Frisch-und Gefrierfleisch.
3 = Lagerhallen mit Gleisanschluss : Verteilung wie zu 1.
4 = Zivile Grossbäckerei.
5 = Mühle.
6 = Gutshof : Verpfl. Ausg. Stelle für Armeetruppen usw.
a = Verkehrsregelungsposten.
Luftschutzwarndienst und Fl. Abwehr nicht eingezeichnet.

Warehouses with rail facilities.
  1. Shed : Bread and Flour.
  2.   ,,   Hay.
  3.   ,,   Fodder.
  4. Provisions : Vegetables and meat (durable goods).
Slaughter yard ; place for fresh and frozen meat.
Warehouses with rail facilities, divided as 1.

Civilian Bakery.
Mill.
Storehouse supply point for Army troops, etc.
T.C. posts.
P.A.D. system and A.A. layout not shown.

BAKERY COMPANY (MOTORISED) - FIELD INSTALLATION.

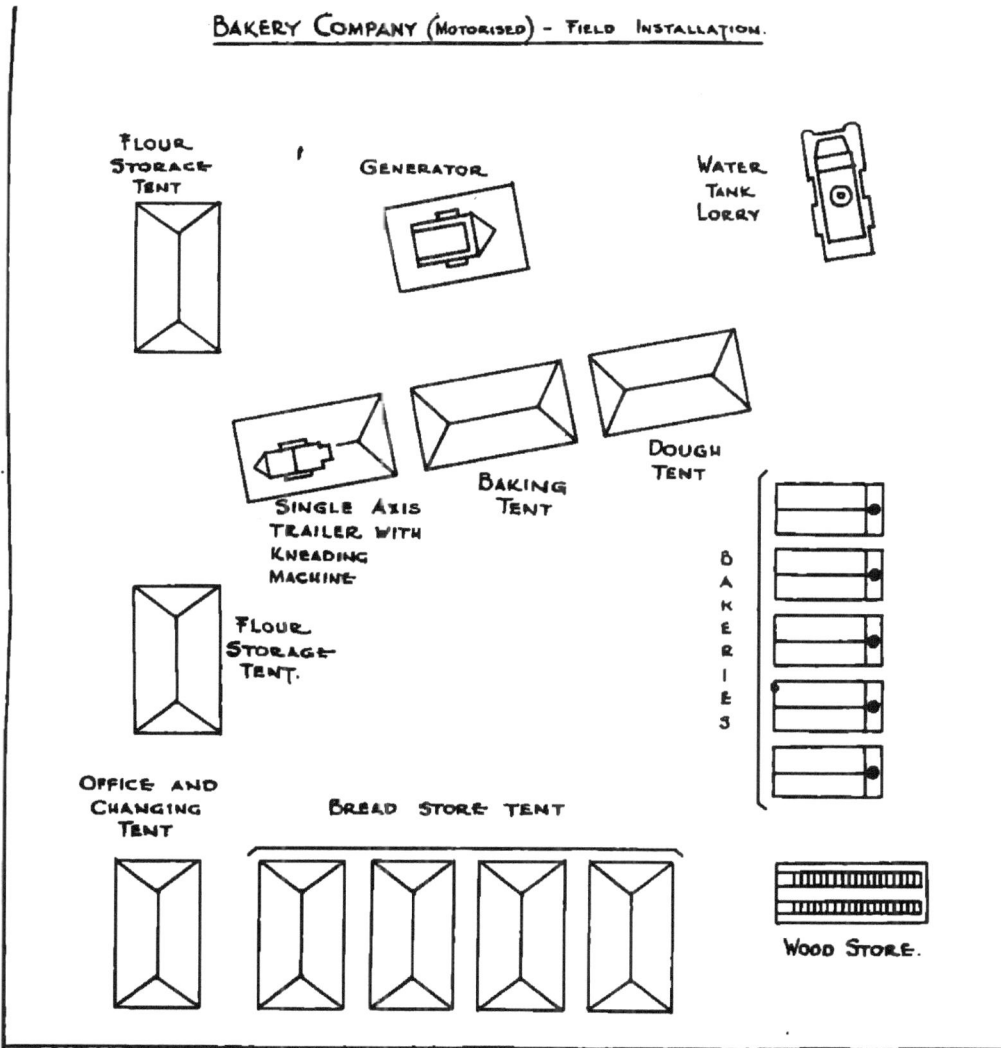

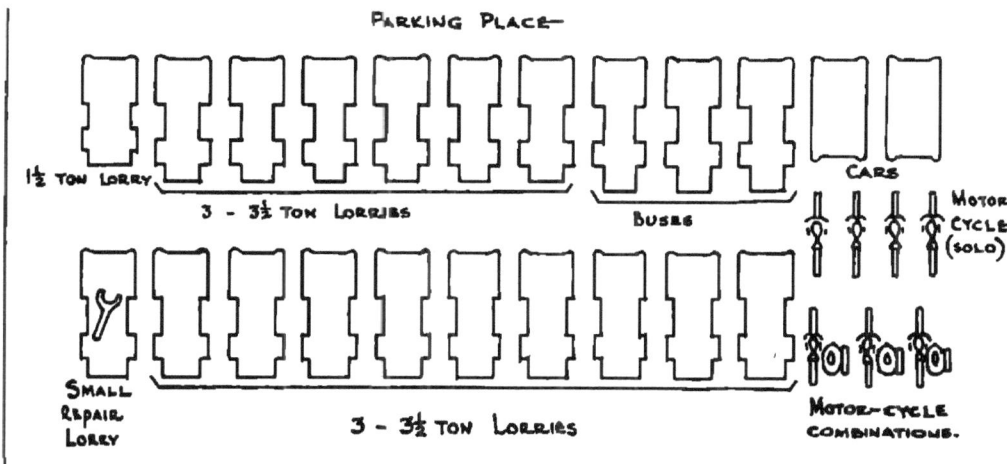

FLOUR STORAGE TENT

GENERATOR

WATER TANK LORRY

SINGLE AXIS TRAILER WITH KNEADING MACHINE

BAKING TENT

DOUGH TENT

B A K E R I E S

FLOUR STORAGE TENT.

OFFICE AND CHANGING TENT

BREAD STORE TENT

WOOD STORE.

PARKING PLACE

1½ TON LORRY

3 - 3½ TON LORRIES

BUSES

CARS

MOTOR CYCLE (SOLO)

SMALL REPAIR LORRY

3 - 3½ TON LORRIES

MOTOR-CYCLE COMBINATIONS.

(B44/70) 5000 4/44 W.O.P. 16770

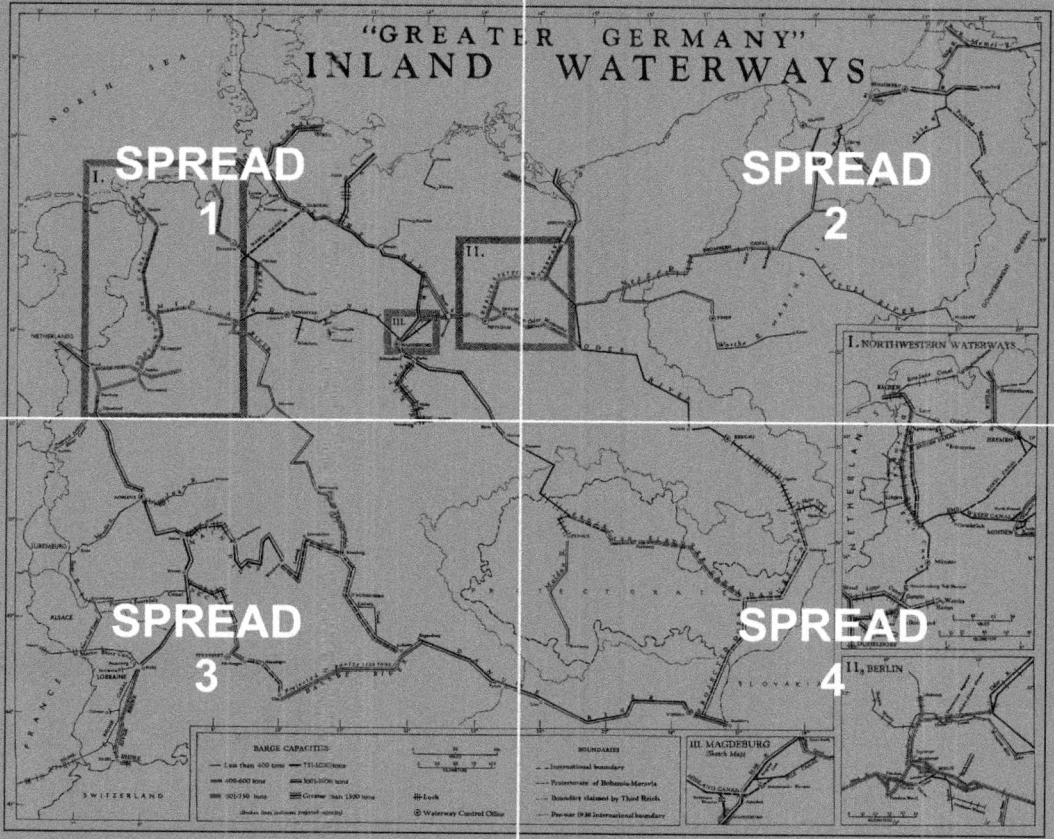

"GREATER GERMANY"
INLAND WATERWAYS

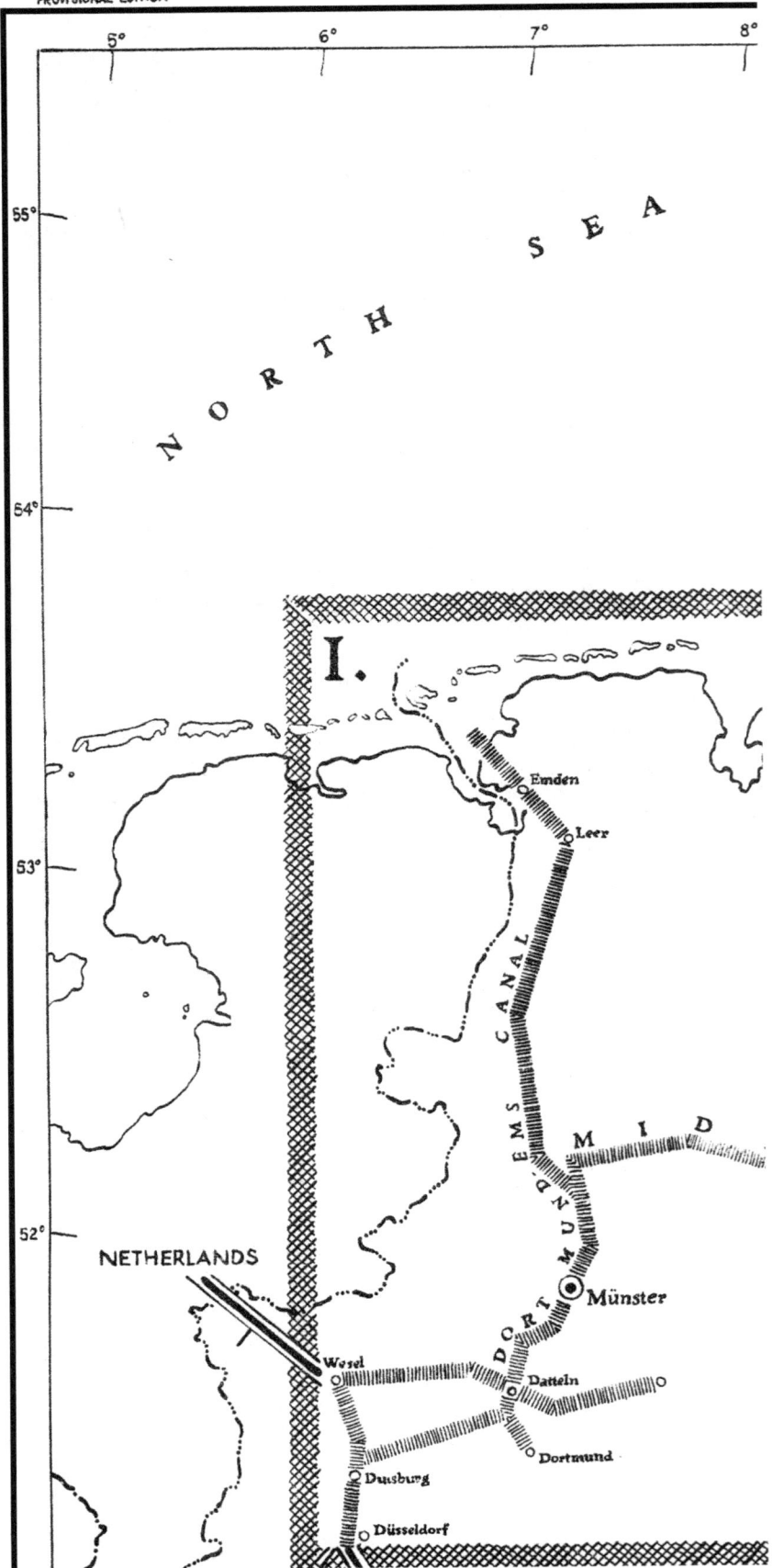

5° 6° 7° 8°

55°

N O R T H   S E A

54°

I.

Emden

Leer

53°

E M S   C A N A L

M I D

52°

NETHERLANDS

Münster

Wesel

Datteln

Dortmund

Duisburg

Düsseldorf

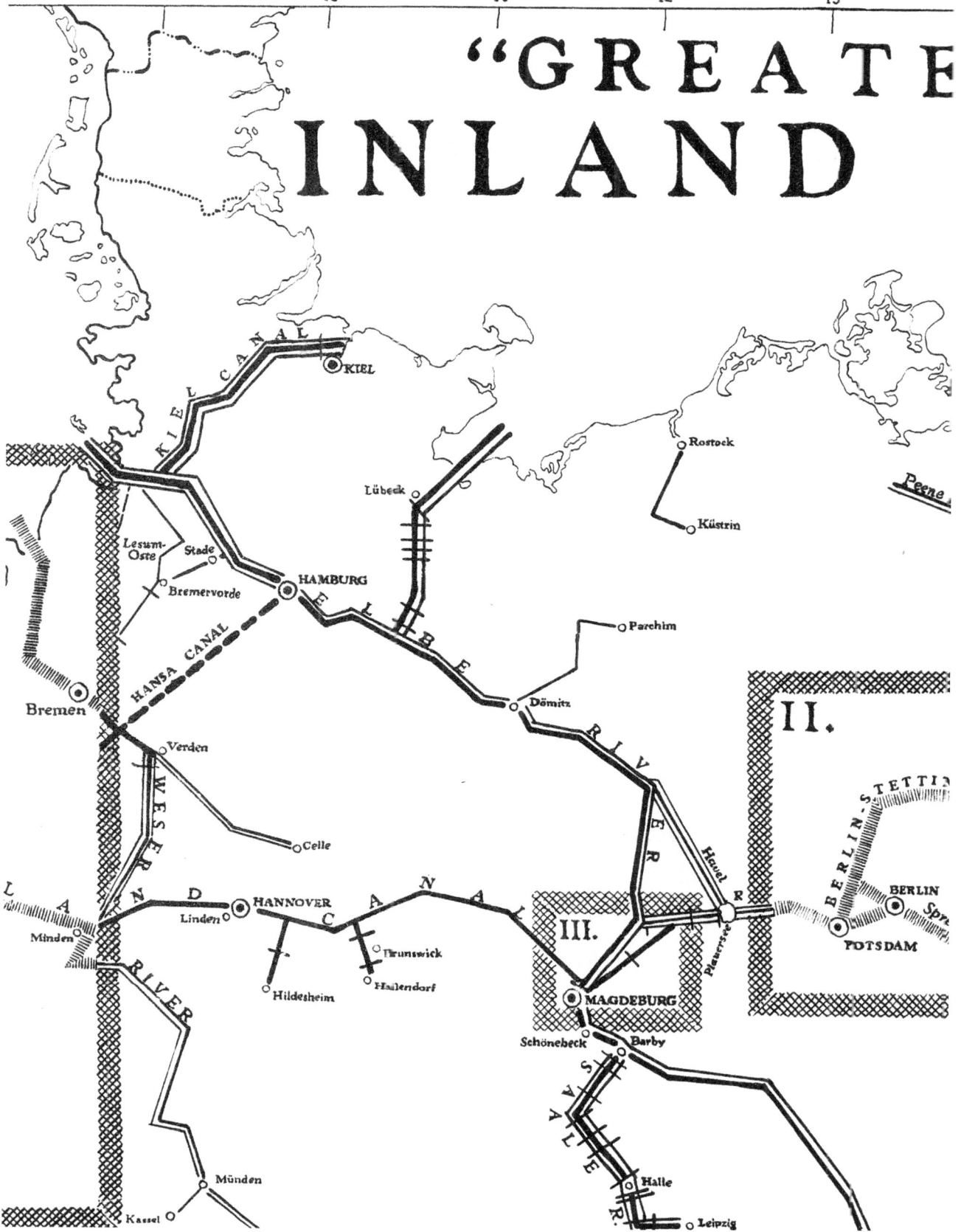

9° 10° 11° 12° 13°

KIEL CANAL

KIEL

Rostock

Lübeck

Küstrin

Peene

Lesum-Oste

Stade

Bremervorde

HAMBURG

ELBE

Parchim

HANSA CANAL

Dömitz

II.

Bremen

Verden

RIVER

BERLIN-STETTIN

WESER

Celle

Havel

BERLIN

Spre

L A N D

C A N A L

R

HANNOVER

III.

Linden

POTSDAM

Minden

Brunswick

Plauersee

RIVER

Hildesheim

Hallendorf

MAGDEBURG

Schönebeck

Barby

S A A L E

Münden

Halle

R.

Kassel

Leipzig

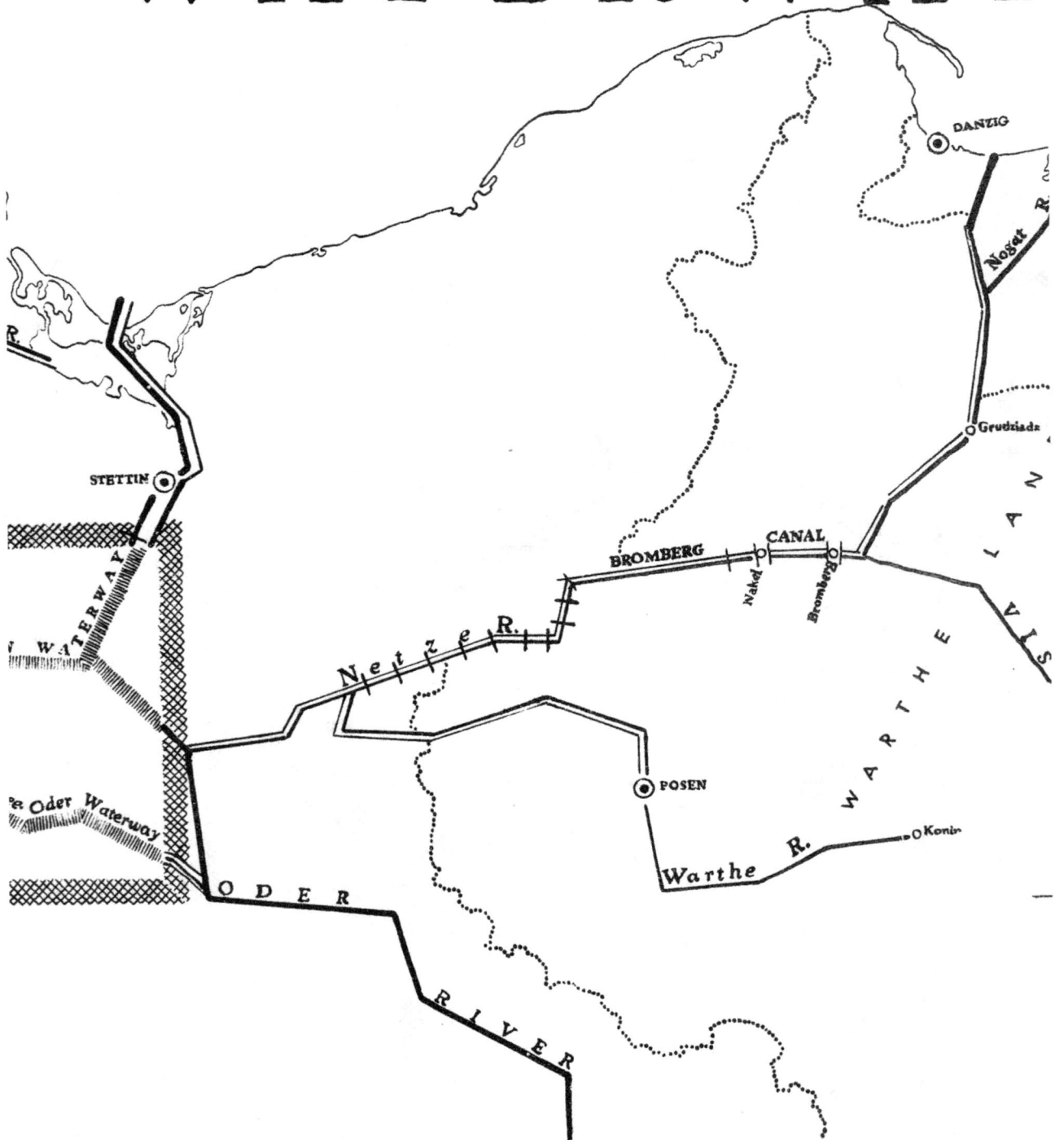

14°   15°   16°   17°   18°   19°

DANZIG

Nogat R.

Grudziadz

STETTIN

WATERWAY

BROMBERG   CANAL

Nakel

Bromberg

Netze R.

WATER

e Oder Waterway

POSEN

WARTHE   VIS

ODER

Warthe R.

O Konin

RIVER

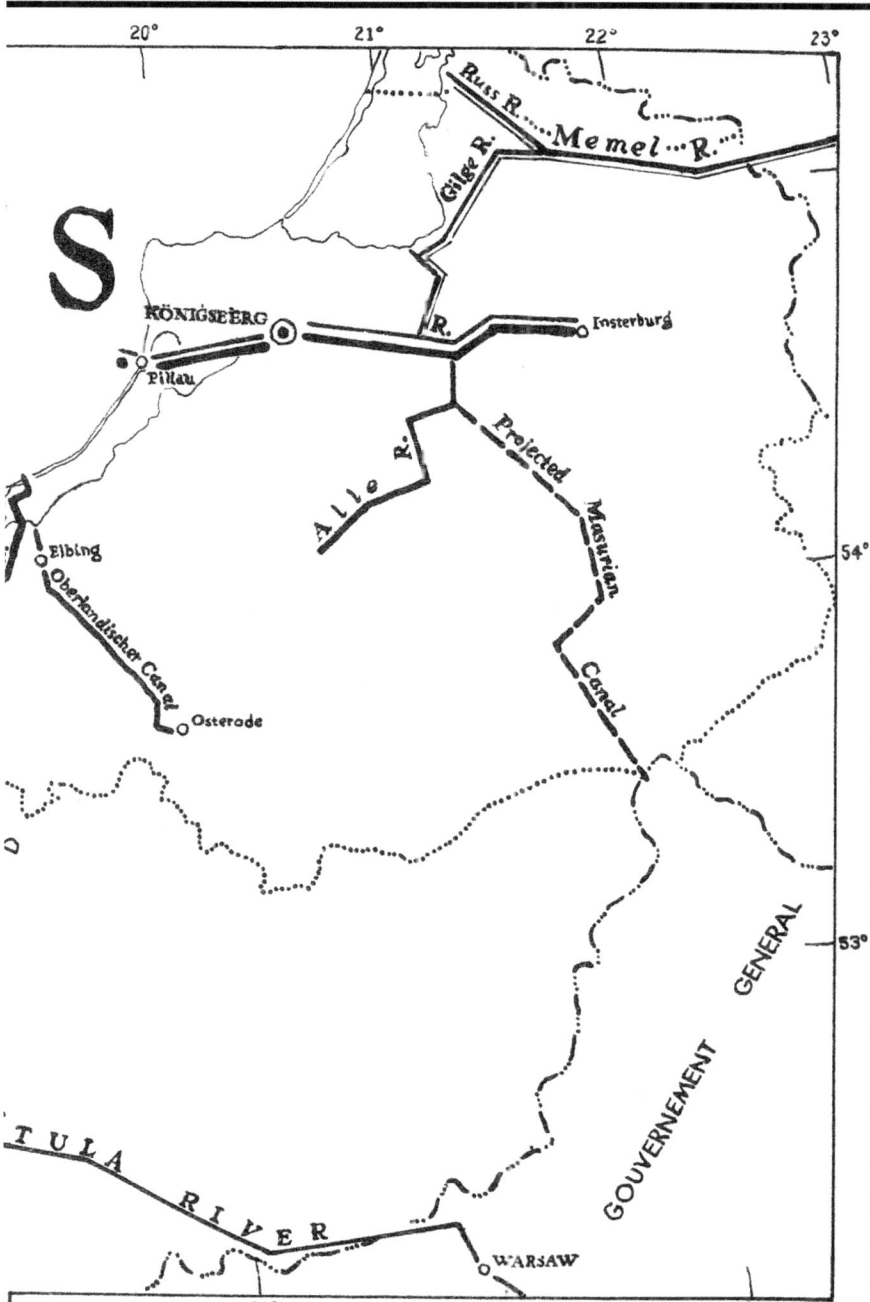

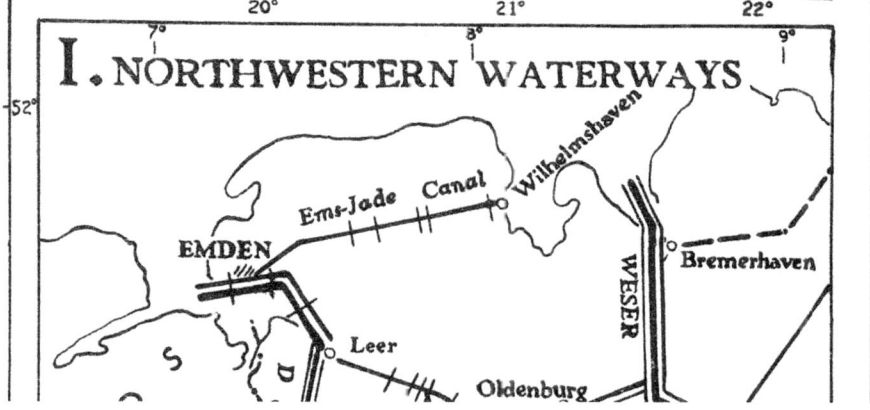

I. NORTHWESTERN WATERWAYS

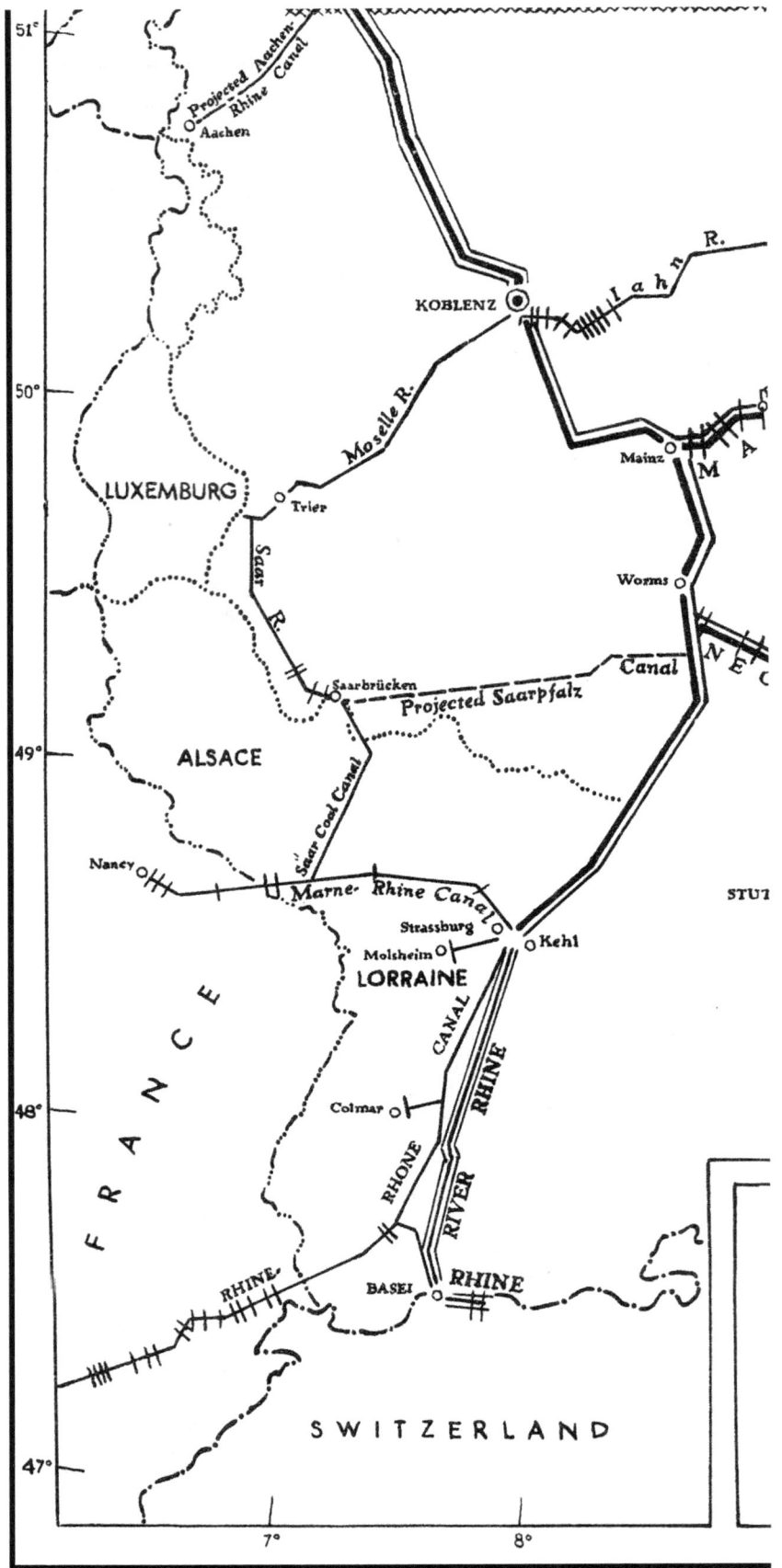

51°

Projected Aachen
Rhine Canal
Aachen

KOBLENZ

Lahn R.

50°

LUXEMBURG

Moselle R.

Trier

Mainz

M

A

Saar R.

Worms

Saarbrücken

Projected Saarpfalz

Canal

NE

49°

ALSACE

Saar Coal Canal

Nancy

Marne-Rhine Canal

Strassburg

Molsheim

Kehl

STUT

LORRAINE

F R A N C E

Colmar

RHONE

RHINE

48°

CANAL

RIVER

RHINE

RHINE

BASEI

RHINE

47°

S W I T Z E R L A N D

7°

8°

MAP NO. 1994
2S AUGUST 1943
8357WT53716/Y1639.504.0444

Merseburg ○╫╫   Riesa &
○ Meissen

○ Giessen

Frankfurt ╫╫╫
I   Aschaffenburg
N ○
Meiningen ○
Projected Werra-Weser-Main
Canal

R   Würzburg   Ludwig   Schweinfurt ○
I   ○   Canal
V   Bromberg
E   ○ Bromberg
R

K   ○ NUREMBERG
A   R.   Ludwig
Heilbronn ○   Canal
R.
ΓTGART ◉   Regensburg
Plöchingen ○   Göppingen ○   Kelheim ○
             Projected Capacity 1200 tons   D   A   N   U
                  D A N U B E   R I V E R
Ulm   Passau ○

P   R   C

9°   10°   11°   12°   13°

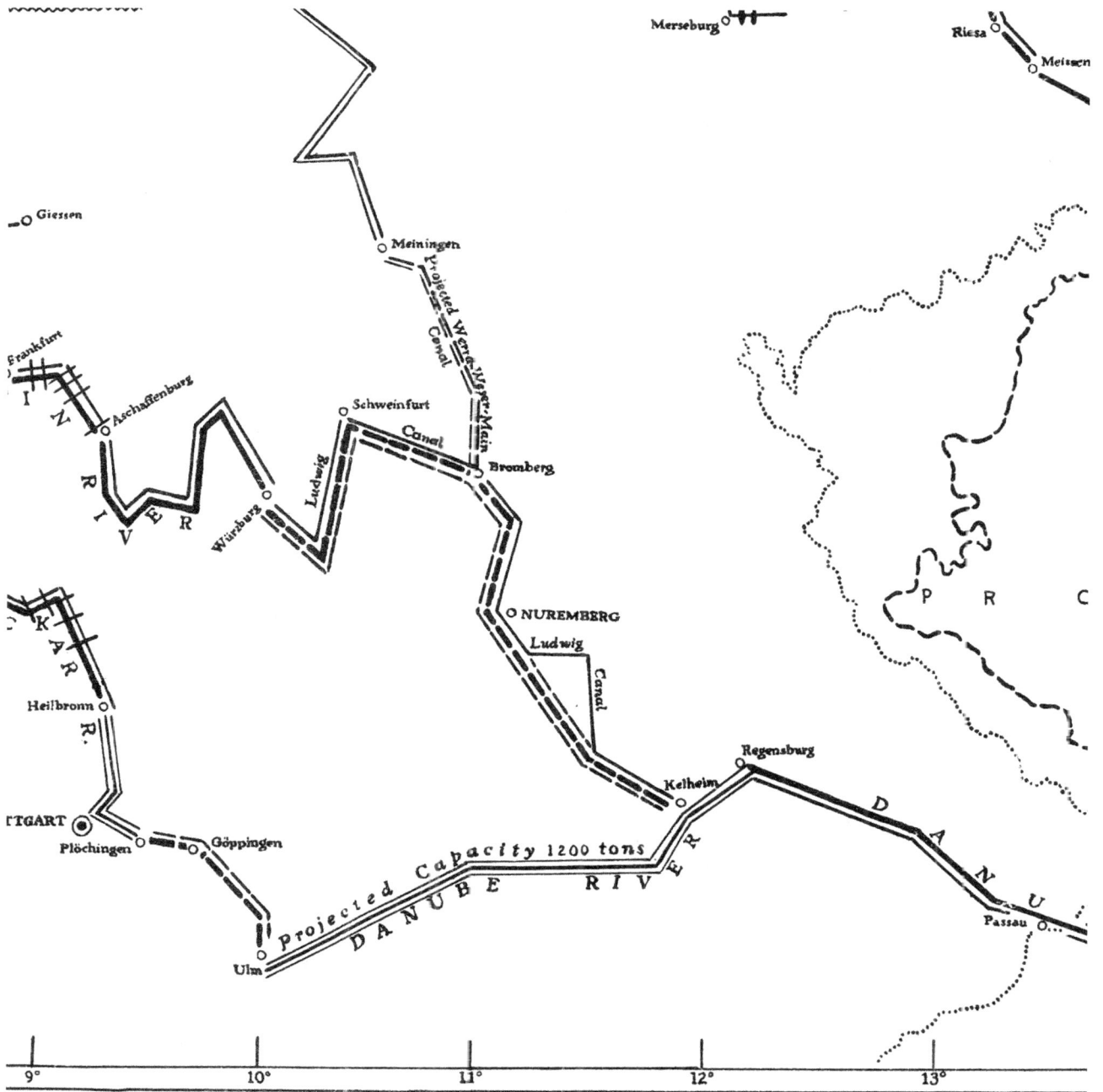

BARGE CAPACITIES

—— Less than 400 tons   ⟨══ 751-1000 tons

══ 400-600 tons   ≡ 1001-1500 tons

≡ 601-750 tons   ≣ Greater than 1500 tons

(Broken lines indicates projected capacity)

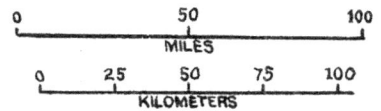

0	50	100
MILES

0	25	50	75	100
KILOMETERS

╫ Lock

◉ Waterway Control Office

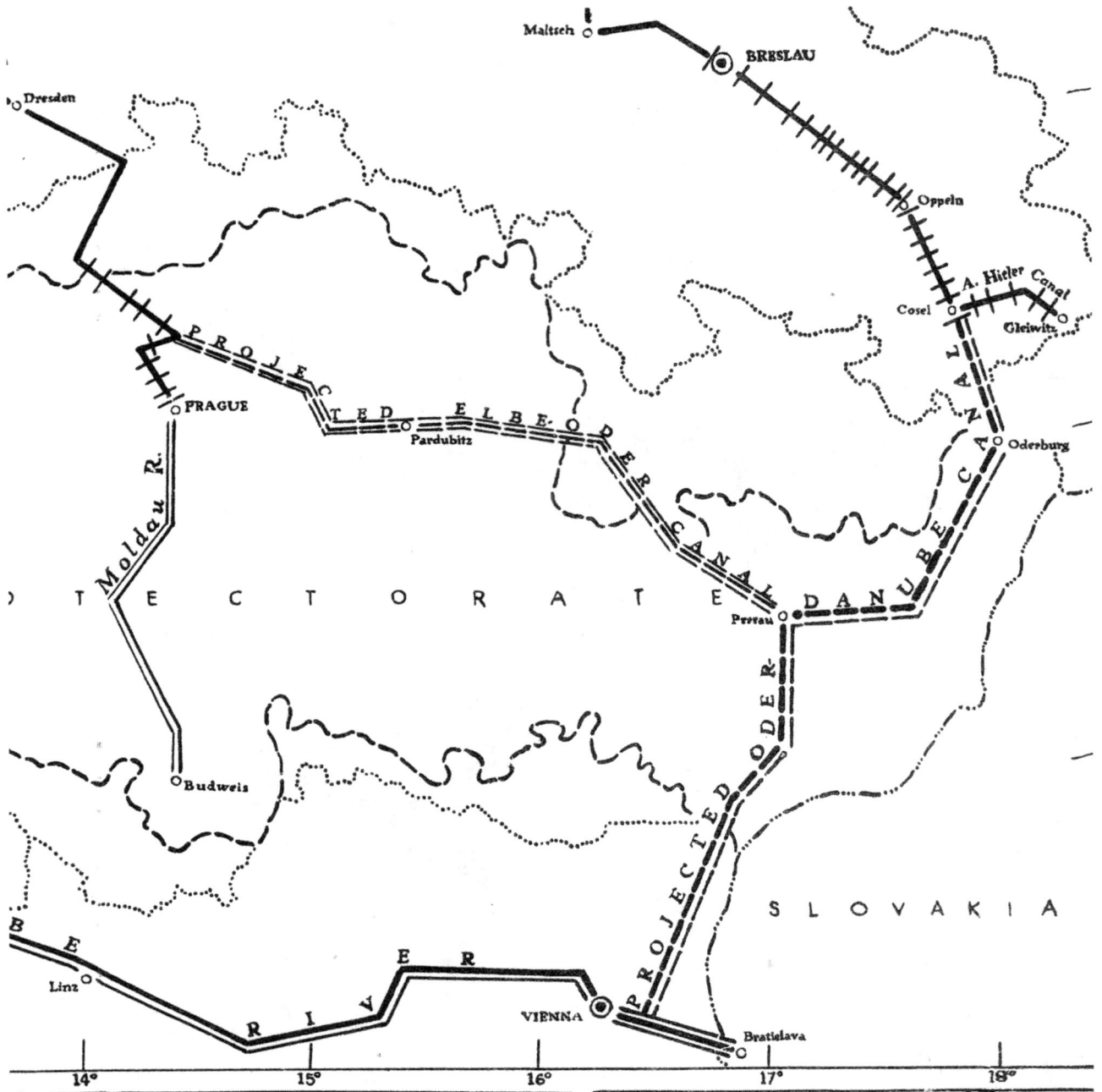

Maltsch
BRESLAU
Dresden
Oppeln
A. Hitler Canal
Cosel
Gleiwitz
PRAGUE
PROJECTED ELBE-ODER CANAL
Pardubitz
Oderburg
Moldau R.
CANAL
DANUBE
TECTORATE
Prerau
PROJECTED ODER-
Budweis
SLOVAKIA
ELBE RIVER
Linz
VIENNA
Bratislava
14°
15°
16°
17°
18°
BOUNDARIES
International boundary
Protectorate of Bohemia-Moravia
Boundary claimed by Third Reich
Pre-war 1938 International boundary
III. MAGDEBURG
(Sketch Map)
Parey Lock
Plaue Canal
ELBE R.
Niegripp Lock
IHLE CANAL
MIDLAND CANAL
Hohenwarthe Elevator
Rothensee Elevator
Aqueduct
MAGDEBURG

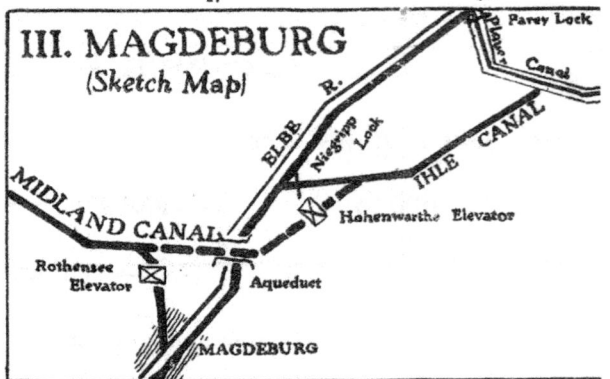

Papenburg

KÜSTEN CANAL

Friesoythe

BREMEN

R

53°

53°

NETHERLAND

HANSA CANAL

Lingen

Ems

North Descent

EMS-WESER CANAL

Aqueduct

Osnabrück

South Descent

MINDEN

50°

52°

52°

Canal

Münster

Wesel   Lippe   Canal

Henrichenburg Ship Elevator

Datteln

Werries

Hamm

10   20   30

MILES

Herne   Dortmund

Mülheim

0   10   20   40   60   80

KILOMETERS

49°

DÜSSELDORF

8°

9°

13°   14°

II. BERLIN

Oder R.

53°

53°-

Ruppin

Zehdenick

Eberswalde Aqueduct

Nieder-Finow Elevator

Waters

Finow   Canal

Wriezener Alte

Oder

Hohenzollern

Tegelersee

Spandauer

Wilmersdorfer

BERLIN

Havel R.   Potsdam

Landwehr

Telow   Teltow   Canal

Dahme

Potsdam Havel

Storkower Waters

Upper Spree

0   10   20   30   40   50

KILOMETERS   13°

14°

13°

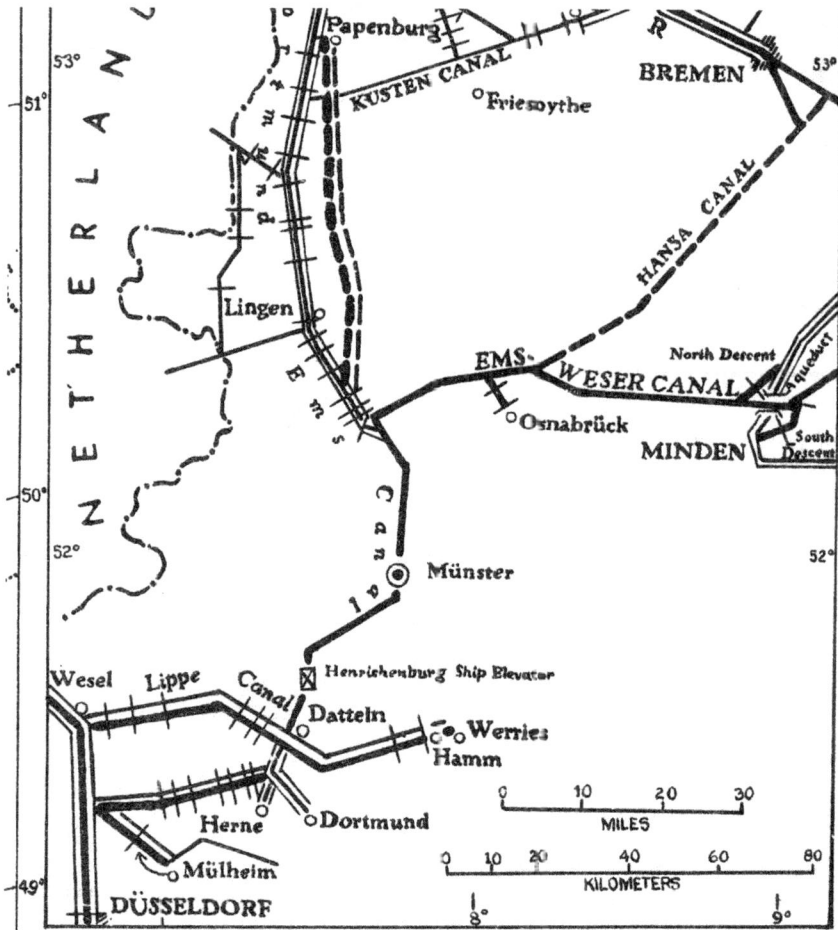

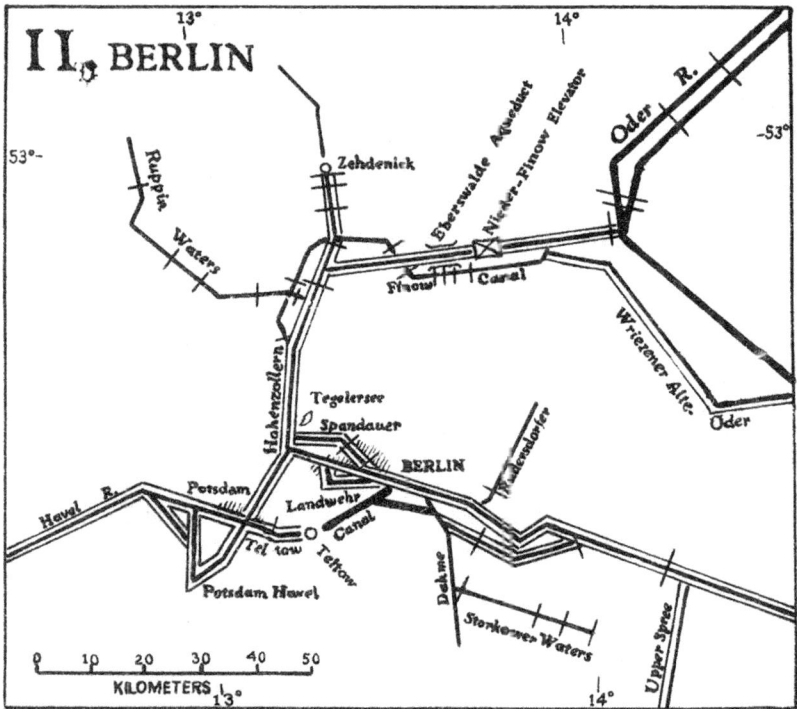

COMPILED AND DRAWN IN THE BRANCH OF RESEARCH AND ANALYSIS, OSS
LITHOGRAPHED IN THE REPRODUCTION BRANCH, OSS

TRAINING MANUALS, TEXT BOOKS AND INSTRUCTIONS

The backbone of all successful armies is its training and tactics. The Naval and Military Press publishes many such manuals of instruction – all perviously long out of print . So, whether your interest lies in the infantry and cavalry tactics of the earliest regiments of the British army in the 18th century, or the weapons manuals and firing instructions of 20th century warfare, the Naval and Military Press has the right book for you.

www.naval-military-press.com

MINES AND BOOBY TRAPS 1943

This is a War Office pamphlet, issued mid-war, in 1943. Its purpose is to introduce sappers to mines commonly used by the British Army – and how to deal with similar devices set by the Germans. The devices described and illustrated cover British anti-tank; grenade; shrapnel and assorted booby trap switches. Enemy mines are covered in chapter 2 with anti-tank, Teller mine types; French anti-tank; Hungarian; anti-personnel German and Italian; and igniters.This is a concise but comprehensive guide for British Army sappers in the art of demining or mine clearance.

9781474539395

THE .303 LEWIS GUN

Illustrated with good clear line drawings this 1941 weapon guide tells the Home Guard Volunteer how to use the 303 Lewis Gun effectively against the invading enemy.A reprint of an original handbook for the .303 Lewis Gun, that was first published in 1941. This book is a practical guide to the handling and maintenance of this iconic weapon.In the crisis following the Fall of France, where a large part of the British Army's equipment had been lost up to and at Dunkirk, stocks of Lewis guns in both .303 and .30-06 were hurriedly pressed back into service, primarily for Home Guard use. Full of fascinating information, this book taught the user the guns capabilities and all he needed to know about maintenance and combat use. Number 2 in the wartime Nicholson & Watson "Know Your Weapons" series, that offer all the important information in a more vivid style than an official publication. Illustrated with good clear line drawings.

9781474539456

ANTI-TANK WEAPONS
Smash The Tank

An insight into the amateur side of World War 2. Diagrams illustrate the main points and the devices, such as the Thermos Bomb;Phosrhorus Bomb;Sticky Bombs; that could be cobbled together from household items are described.This pamphlet was available to the Home Guard and describes the German tank and how to destroy it. It is an early War publication c1940, dealing with the light tanks used by the Germans, also the author gives examples of anti-tank actions in the Spanish Civil War, in which he took part. I'ts is a fascinating look at the "enthusiastic" approach to killing tanks.

9781474539449

TANK HUNTING AND DESTRUCTION 1940

The stated object for the distributing of this War Office manual was as "A guide and help to troops who have the determination and nerve to destroy tanks at close quarters". Intended for fighting on home soil after the very real possibility of a full German invasion, "Operation Sea Lion", this is a remarkable if somewhat naive snap shot of Britain state of preparedness,in her most dangerous hour.

The contents details Tank hunting, Tank characteristics,Tactical action,Road blocks,ambushes Ect,also includes an interesting appendix on Molotov Cocktails, and materials on other ways to destroy tanks.

9781474539401

TROOP TRAINING FOR LIGHT TANK TROOPS NOVEMBER 1939

Very early War tactics pertaining to various aspects of training with and employing armour in the British Army. Covering in concise detail that which a Light tank crew needed to know to be effective in action.

In the early years of the war, Germany held the initiative. German forces used Blitzkrieg tactics in France in 1940, making full use of the speed and armour of tanks to break through enemy defences. It was clear that German tank tactics had evolved during the inter-war period. By contrast, Britain and the Allies were playing catch-up.

9781474539302

JAPANESE WEAPONS ILLUSTRATED
September 1944

This period 'Restricted' laced binding manual was intended to be an aid to the identification of Japanese Army equipment, with sections covering: Tanks, both two-man, Tankette, light and medium; Armoured Cars; Self-Propelled Guns; Anti-Tank Guns; Artillery; Anti-Aircraft Guns; Mortars & Grenade Dischargers; Small Arms; Flamethrowers etc. Produced one year before the surrender of Japan, this work gives a good overview of the weapons the allies would find, fighting an army that despite being on the back foot, was still capable of stiff resistance in an almost entirely defensive role..

9781474539432

NOTES ON THE GERMAN ARMY-WAR
December 1940

An early war 393-page 'Notes' periodical manual from December 1940. It is a detailed review, for use in the field. The manual looks at every aspect of the "Blitzkrieg" German Army (and, to some extent, the Air Force) and gives details as known at the time.

It covers the fighting arms and the services behind them – tactics, organisation, weapons and equipment. It usefully also includes a colour section on uniforms and insignia, a black-and-white plate section of small arms, infantry support and anti-tank weapons, artillery and AFVs. A series of pull-outs related to the text covering tanks etc. are also reproduced.

This is an important first-class picture of the complex fighting machine that was the German Army at the end of the campaigns of 1940, only six months before the invasion of Russia.

9781474539203

NOTES ON ENEMY ARMY IDENTIFICATIONS ITALY
October 1941

This period handbook was published to give British military personnel a better understanding of the principal characteristics of both the Italian army and the Black Shirt Militia under active service conditions , it is dated October 1941. It begins with a description of distinctive branches, or specialities, the most characteristic of which was the arm of the Royal Carabinieri, a semi-military body occupying, historically, the senior position in the Army. Other specialities included the Grenadiers of Sardinia, the Bersaglieri, the Alpini and the San Marco Marine Regiment
The handbook then goes on to show, in order, the organisation of Command and Staff, of formations (corps and divisions) and of the arms and services; services, supply and transportation; ranks, plates (many in colour) cover uniforms, insignia, medals and decorations; armament and equipment and a chapter on the Air Force, There are chapters on tactical doctrine and principles of employment, on permanent fortifications, camouflage and abbreviations. Finally there is a brief index.
9781474539746

THE OFFENSIVE OF SMALL UNITS
September 1916

This is a periodical tactical manual from 1916, it focuses on the manner in which the French organised and executed their attacks and counterattacks . Summarised from the French, it lays out the process by which to operate in attacks on the German trenches. Focused purely on the operation of infantry, the purpose of this British translation is to give small infantry units the benefit of the French experience in regard to the best methods of combat, in offensive operations.
9781474537971

TRENCH WARFARE
Notes on attack and defence, February 1915

This important period manual was published in early 1915 when hope of a quick ending to the war disappeared, and trench warfare had begun to dominate the Western Front.
The manual strives to instil an offensive spirit and gives practical examples on: Close quarter, local, methods of successful warfare, and German attacks. The salient points to gather were preparation and co-operation between artillery and infantry, and that the capture of trenches is easier than their retention. Two plates illustrating tactics complete this official publication.
9781474539807

Ministry Of Home Security
OBJECTS DROPPED FROM THE AIR 1941

An illustrated Official and confidential publication, covering the many and varied types of objects that were falling from principally German aircraft during the Second phase of the blitz, including high explosives,incendiary bombs and small arms ammunition. Complete with 8 page addendum.
9781783319541

THE MUSKETRY INSTRUCTIONS FOR THE GERMAN INFANTRY 1887
(Schiessvorshrift fur die Infanterie) Translated for the intelligence Division War Office

Translated for the War Office by Colonel C W Bowdler Bell

A facsimile that includes the supplement for the German Infantry for 1887. Musketry exercises were intended to give the infantry instruction in shooting, to make effective use of their firearm in battle. As such the manual shows important details designed to make the infantry soldier battle-ready by the end of his first year of service. Instruction is subdivided into Preparatory exercises; Target practice; Field firing; Instructional firing; Inspection in musketry; Proving the rifle M/61.84 and revolver M/83. Many black powder weapons were still used, mainly for training purposes, up to end of the First World War.

9781783313631

MANUAL OF GUERILLA TACTICS

Specially Prepared And Based On Lessons From The Spanish And Russian Campaigns One of the excellent, concise Bernards Pocket Books, intended to show members of the Home Guard and the regular forces that war is not conducted in a gentlemanly way – it is kill or be killed.

9781474539463

GERMAN MINES AND TRAPS

Mid-1940 War Office manual with details of German mines, both the Teller and S-mine (Bouncing Betty) are covered, with techniques for disarming. Good clear full-page line drawings give both practical and technical information. Highly recommended because of the illustrations, which show how these devices worked and the components.

9781474535809

www.ingramcontent.com/pod-product-compliance
Lightning Source LLC
Chambersburg PA
CBHW062039090426

42740CB00016B/2959